A GAP IN THE MARK
Seven More years
1974 - 1981

C000124931

The author asserts the moral right under the Cop
Act 1988 to be identified as the auth

Arts Council England

(feederead.com/Lightning Source)

First published 2019 – This edition 2023

Also by J F Macdonogh

A GAP YEAR OR TWO
Adventures in Europe between 1970 -1974
2007, Athena Press
Reedited 2012 and Published by Arts Council England

(feedaread.com/Lightning Source)

MIND THE GAP
Adventures in Europe between 1982 -1993
2007, Published by Arts Council England

(feedaread.com/Lightning Source)

*

THE HOUSE OF DUHALLOW

- a trilogy of historical novels –

THE LAST IRISHMEN – ANNIHILATION – THE GREAT COUNCILLOR

3

Descartes spent far too much time in bed subject to the persistent hallucination that he was thinking. You are not free from a similar disorder.

Flann O'Brien

Acknowledgements

The author is indebted to Paul Hrynaszkiewicz, Caraline Clarke and Anne Swift for their invaluable proof reading. Michael Proom helped him with his rusty Spanish. He would like to thank all those mentioned in the narrative, mostly for not taking him to court. Above all, he would like to thank his long-suffering wife, Helen Kelsey, for her patience in reading and rereading this memoire, noting many errors of fact and style, and suggesting refinements in the narrative which have all been enthusiastically adopted. Not only that; she has been both a vademecum and an inspiration for the last forty years of his life.

Dedication

This book is for my handsome grandson Raphael. One day, it may help him realise how lucky he is to have avoided the 1970s.

Contents

The Future Starts Here
1968

In which our naïf author doesn't quite meet the Prince of Wales. He replaces his military jacket with a suit and tie. When Samuel Montagu & Co retains him he discovers that a job in the City means long weeks addressing envelopes, running errands and being baffled by documentary credits. He does, however, manage a trip in a private jet.

*

Like every other drunk, stoned or simply deranged teenager in Kensington, that summer of 1968, I was a Carnabetian dandy. To celebrate turning nineteen I went to *I Was Lord Kitchener's Valet* and bought myself a military jacket: pillar-box red and adorned with bright brass buttons. It was the sort of thing the Boers liked to take a pot shot at in 1901. I wore it home, pleased as punch, every inch of my frame dedicated to the latest fashion.

I was trying to break free from the well-intended husbandry of my family. Lodged in Canning Place, just off London's Gloucester Road, I found myself in a boxroom in a run-down late-Georgian house with three likely lads. Lancelot Sharpus-Jones, a great big Scotsman with a taste for golf, Anthony Watts-Russell, who liked to liven up his daily tedium with membership of the Dangerous Sports Club and James Henderson, scion of the huge fund-management company which bore his family's name. He did very little. I, the last and very temporary member of the team, was merely an undergraduate with an uncertain future.

Things in London seemed quiet, too much so, perhaps. Harold Wilson, Prime Minister, had tried, so far unsuccessfully, to lever us into the Common Market – a free-trade association, signed in Rome by France,

Italy, Germany, Holland, Luxembourg and Belgium. I let most of the associated debate pass over my head.

The European thing was largely academic, anyway, as we were not allowed to work on the Continent without a work permit and had to ask the Bank of England for permission to take more than £5, later generously increased to £50, with us on holiday.

Even our application annoyed Charles de Gaulle. Many of our parents' generation thought that France and Spain were about to burst into flames. They had long taken exception to Johnny Foreigner. They disliked or distrusted Catholic Europe but, when Germany had descended to savagery, they didn't care much for Protestant Europe either.

I spoke to a mate.

'The *Café Tournon* in the *boulevard St Germain* reeks of tear gas while the *bourse* lies smouldering. Italy's streets are menaced by the *Red Brigades*. In Germany, *Baader Meinhof* are scaring the Huns witless, while in Spain *Eta* is busy killing subjects of the Spanish *caudillo* by the busload.'

I was in London, down from Cambridge for what we called the 'long vac'. Life for my contemporaries in the capital was mostly untroubled by these international issues. The *IRA* was not yet 'provisional' and we had heard little from them since their pre-war attempt to blow up Hammersmith Bridge.[1] In 1968, June had little better to do than flame away. Wilson, bless him, had

---

[1] The IRA's attempt to destroy Hammersmith Bridge was on Wednesday 29 March. 1939. Maurice Childs, a women's hairdresser from Chiswick, was walking home across the bridge at one o'clock in the morning when he noticed smoke and sparks coming from a suitcase that was lying on the pavement. He opened it to find a bomb and threw the bag into the river. The resulting explosion sent up a 60-foot (18 m) column of water. Moments later, a second device exploded causing some girders on the west side of the bridge to collapse and windows in nearby houses to shatter. Childs was awarded the MBE for his courage and quick-thinking. Eddie Connell and William Browne were subsequently jailed for 20 and 10 years respectively for their involvement in the attack.

steered us away from the Vietnam War and had also abolished capital punishment, a marginally less arbitrary version of the same thing, as the Americans were to discover.

One insouciant day I had walked the mile or so from Canning Place as far as *Finch's* in the Fulham Road, looking for the world like an escapee from the cover of *Sergeant Pepper*. My pointy shoes may have been gleaming like an eel's back but they tortured my feet. To make matters worse, the weather had turned tropical. By the time a foaming beaker was safely in my right hand I was in a muck sweat. The satirical banter of the regulars did little to mitigate the sauna.

'Which outfit have you been cashiered from?'

'The Artist's Rifles,' I answered, underlining my drollery with an affected yawn.

They had a point. What had possessed me to don such an intemperate outfit? I was not alone in wearing that cretinous costume. Half a dozen young men at the bar were similarly clad.

Women were far too sensible to fall into the same trap. They were wearing pelmets (as we renamed their miniskirts) and see-through blouses. Looking deeply into the matter, I was happy to lend them my personal support. One thing was certain; in the prevailing heat they had the better half of the deal.

*

Undergraduates in the late '60s were asked by dons, family, friends, and especially mothers, all the time, where they would fetch up once real life began. All our replies were optimistic but, in my case at least, I had no idea. I would murmur astrophysicist. Or brain surgeon. I had certainly never thought of the City.

Few of my contemporaries were impressed by the blandishments of England's financial hub on the north bank of the Thames, 'E.C. Street' they called it, a heavily forced pun characterised (as puns always are) by unsophisticated humour.

Stockbroking? Our privileged band thought the challenge of coupon clipping had all the daring of picking strawberries, in a friendly neighbour's garden, and with permission.

Most of us had distinguished ourselves at school and if to a lesser extent, at Cambridge. Now we were all too aware that our future in what grown-ups laughingly called the 'real world' would be akin to climbing the north face of the Eiger. When my friend Michael Hutchinson forced me to consider the options, he placed my feet firmly on the ground.

'I was thinking of becoming a painter. Or maybe a filmmaker?' I volunteered.

'I've seen one of your drawings. A set-dresser is your best hope, a cinema usher your worst.'

'I see. Well then, I could be a politician?'

'Do you know what is true and what is not?'

'Yes. I think I do.'

'Then you should rule out politics and the Bar.'

'OK. An architect, then.'

'A long time ago that was worth the trouble. The Egyptians made Imhotep a god, after all. Today you would be lucky to earn a knighthood.'

That said, in the '60s, Frank Lloyd Wright and Le Corbusier looked more likely to revert to the earlier model.

'Those who can, do. I could always teach.'

'It's a career fit only for egomaniacs. You truly want to strut about in a classroom stacked with besotted youth?'

'I could always beat the ungrateful brats. Maybe I could teach them cricket?'

'You would soon discover the best place to deal with cricket is on your sofa with a party-four of Watney's finest.'

'Well then, what about a soldier? Girls love a uniform.'

'Do you actually enjoy the sight of blood? You won't see much of that in the army. Britain is hardly at war with anyone.'

'Blood doesn't worry me. I have pints of it.'

'Then you should be a doctor. Or a dentist. Or, should you want to be rich, be a vet. A sick animal has paid many a vet to extend his villa in the Caribbean.'

'Holy orders?'

'Yes, that's good. One day's work a week. Of course, if you really want to counsel your fellows, become a barman. Their patients come to them and they're better paid than priests. Every so often they even get a free drink.'

'Well, perhaps I could write?'

'Every idiot believes they have a great book in them. Try a memoire. It's the perfect outlet for delusions of grandeur, self-righteousness, lightly seasoned with fantasy. It's the highest level of fiction - and you would excel.'

'Your talk,' I said, 'is surely the handiwork of wisdom because not one word of it I understand.' I had been reading Flann O'Brien.

My interlocutor, Michael Hutchinson, was destined for Aldermaston. His own dream was to build the biggest, shiniest atomic bomb known to Man. His was a truly unique ambition but, as far as I know (and hope) it is still unrealised.

*

Everyone for the last sixty thousand years or so has thought that theirs was a seriously talented generation. For the last thousand, Cambridge has installed in its victims a smug sense of superiority. I am fully aware that you and I are barely into this opus, but I hope you will allow me to mention somewhere in these dispatches my best undergraduate mates; Robert Booth, Gervas Douglas, Andrew Clement, Michael Hashemian, Gavin Stamp, John Molony and the Prince of Wales. I had ten thousand contemporaries, but these are among those I remember best. Hold on! Did I hear you say the Prince of Wales?

You'll be making this up! Well, I confess we were not exactly bosom buddies in my first year at Cambridge, but I had at least seen him around. That's when I met him, if vicariously, in *The Red Lion* in Petty Cury.

Cambridge's *Red Lion* was a pub for which the word 'grotty' would have been a compliment. I had passed it many times but had resisted its blandishments. It was not irresistible. Even from the pavement outside it smelled of urine. In a window a large and badly written sign declared 'No Women Welcome'. One day, I plucked up the courage to penetrate its *cordon insanitaire* to find it unpretentious. It ran to a few stools and a greater number of fruit machines. Its barman eyed me up and down suspiciously.

'What d'you want?' he asked. No point here in wasting time on courtly etiquette. I glanced at the pumps and their clipped on labels. Watneys, Lacons, Tolly, Tetley's... None of them exactly my cup of tea. On the top shelf were a number of bottles. Rum, whisky, gin, but then I saw, to my surprise, an interloping bottle of cherry brandy. I had never even attempted cherry brandy. It had to be disgusting. Nevertheless, make it a rule, even the most spurious of whims should always be surrendered to.

'I'll have a cherry brandy, please,' I said. I was rewarded for my sense of adventure with a suite of raised eyebrows, suspicion and a quizzical study, admiring and appalled, both from the barman and from the other imbiber, perched on the stool at the far end of the bar.

To my astonishment, the barman opened the door into the pub's inner depths and shouted out, 'Oi, Betty, we've got another!' The barman's wife or mother emerged and looked me up and down, while her husband or son poured the precious red liquor into a wine glass. 'It's on the house, son. You're the second young man to ask for one of those this week.'

I raised the glass to him and his wife or mother, taking a sip. Cherry brandy is actually rather good.

'The other one was His Highness,' the female persisted. 'Charlie Boy.'

I seemed to be was treading in royal footsteps. Had the gods revealed the first rung of the ladder? Inadvertently. Did my future hinge on Cherry Brandy?

*

Though only in my first year at Cambridge, I was already thinking about what would happen next. I was not in line for any inheritance and, in the dark wood where I found myself, the true path to a comfortable future was obscure. Had it already occurred to me to try for the City of London?

No, is my final answer.

For most of our Cantabridgiensian élite the Square Mile held few attractions. John Cleese and his pals' blistering satire, *Monty Python's Flying Circus*, defined what faced filing clerks, brokers or book-keepers - a career at the end of a forked path that either led to (1) celibacy and morose introspection, or (2) 2.4 children, a Ford Cortina and a semi in Suburbiton. The City's chief weapons fear, surprise, and ruthless efficiency. An interview with the Spanish Inquisition was more appealing, no matter how unexpected.

Of course, if you were wise enough to come from a well-upholstered family, there were two very different packs of hunting dogs on campus out to get you; MI5 and the Counting Houses. The Secret Service believed that such good fortune - or 'accidents of birth' as Marxists prefer - underwrote loyalty to Crown and Country. Philby *et al* had not yet gained general currency.

The City was equally enthusiastic. Personal capital and social connections were the top two not-so-very-secret ingredients of a stellar city future. Running a poor third was a good head for figures.

Of course, those fortunate enough to have those qualifications were also in a good position to run an art gallery. There the perks would include flexible hours with a ravishing Girl Friday thrown in. There were few real prospects of making a mint in Cork Street but, since you had one already, that mattered little. It all sounded a lot more gratifying than managing someone else's money.

Unfortunately no one cared to ask me if I wanted or needed a licence to kill, nor did anyone suggest that I might enter the recondite worlds of the Acceptance House or Lloyd's of London. In no way did I qualify for such favoured treatment. In the circumstances I decided to put a brave face on it. I was a little like Algernon in *The Importance of Being Earnest*. He had nothing but looked everything. At least I had a dinner jacket. That was a start.

*

My indefatigable mother got me going. She had befriended a prosperous denizen of the Chelsea Arts Club, Christiane Françoise, the other half of the hon. David Montagu, not quite yet Lord Swaythling. Montagu was the top dog at the blue chip *Samuel Montagu & Co*. He had also been educated at Cambridge and my mother thought that was enough of a link. His degree was in English Literature, while I was muddling through a strange mixture of history and philosophy.

'He can tell you all about Shakespeare,' she suggested, somewhat pointedly, making an appointment for me to meet him. This was five or six days after the start of the long vacation that ended my year as a freshman.

*

Regrettably, I had terminally damaged my only suit when trying to smuggle a girlfriend into my college after curfew. Despite a leg up from a friendly policeman, I had torn an embarrassing hole in my trousers. The girl on my arm had sensibly shed her evening frock to scale the wall and enjoyed the same constabulary aid. She had come off far worse, having had to sacrifice her dignity, but she had rewarded that gallant officer with a glimpse of paradise.

Before I dared cross the threshold of a gent's outfitter, I had some research to do. Clad in the garb of my generation, I took the tube to Bank and arrived at a quarter to nine. I found myself on the steps of the Royal Exchange, under the imposing statue of Arthur Wellesley, 1st Duke of Wellington.

The Iron Duke, whose effigy had been cast from the cannons captured during his Iberian Campaign, was also wearing a military jacket. I sat at his feet like a squaddy.

At last I was in pole position to review the sartorial customs of my future colleagues, just as the duke had once reviewed his troops. Was I in foreign and hostile territory?

This was the superior ventricle of the beating mercantile heart of The City. The Bank was a few yards away, the Stock Exchange perhaps a hundred. Lloyd's maybe three. Various commodity exchanges - base metals, gold and silver, hogs' bristle,[2] mink hulls, whole ships and cargos - were littered around as if at random. Conspicuous by their absence were shops, theatres and hotels.[3] Oliver Cromwell, long ago, had exiled all such

---

[2] At the time used in toothbrushes and shaving brushes.
[3] Excepting the Great Eastern Hotel, where rooms could be hired by the hour.

17

trivia from the square mile. For recreation there was only alcohol. A million pubs (and restaurants) punctuated every street.[4] Aside from a peppering of architectural historians, lending a splash of corduroy to a sea of worsted, what I saw was as far removed from the Royal Borough of Kensington and Chelsea as I imagined Frankfurt, Shanghai or the moon.

If you want to get ahead, get a hat. In 1968, real men wore hats. Some of those scurrying by sported bowlers, pinstripe trousers and black jackets, wing collars atop their starched 'English' shirts,[5] and watch chains strung across their waistcoats. Some swung a furled umbrella over their mirror-bright brogues while the other hand held a briefcase. Only Brian Rix could describe this surreal regiment as realism.

Slightly less formal financiers wore three-piece grey suits topped with trilbies. If their shirts had soft collars they still had regulation umbrellas and neatly folded copies of The Times under the starboard arm. I was encouraged. Like them, I thought, I would soon be dealing in millions, buying controlling interests in SE30 companies for playboy princes who might one day grant me an hour or so on the poop-deck of a baronial yacht.

The gentler sex, in regulation twin-sets, pearls and high heels, were also rushing to wherever they were needed. The uniform they had adopted made them look both older and grander than they could ever have been in real life. Was it a dream? Or was it just a chimera that was I buying into? Even then I suspected that these were not the millionaires for whom the lanes and streets of the city were paved in gold. They were all in too much of a hurry. The greatest luxury, after all, is leisure.

---

[4] These stern impositions have been substantially relaxed since the time of the Puritans but were still in force in the1960s.

[5] These days we all wear 'American' shirts. 'English' shirts went over your head. The part that would be visible above your waistcoat was in two-ply cotton. Collars were attached with studs.

By five past nine, the street had rid itself of everyday, commonplace pedestrians. Two gentlemen in full morning dress, resplendent in their toppers, were strolling towards the Bank of England. Their plutocratic swagger was such that the pavements freed themselves to accommodate these fine fellows.

These grandees didn't even see the messengers in their scruffy, heavy suiting, presumably supplied by the War Office when they had left the army twenty or so years before. Such men scurried in every direction, their heavy document cases clasped to their chests.

On the metalled roads, taxis, motorbikes, cars, vans, lorries and double-decker buses sped smokily along, noisily backfiring as they went. I descended the steps to take the tube to Oxford Street.

*

By the close of day, I was the proud owner of a new Burton suit, a number of 'American' white shirts and a pair of black shoes, so shiny I could have shaved in them. I had also bought a striped strip of polyester, a tie that vaguely resembled my school one.

A college prankster had cut the original in two. This replacement would suffice, at least until I got paid. If, that is, I got the job.

*

A school friend, Peter Cooper, had remained in contact while our prospective ambitions diverged. He already had a plan. He was going to be a general.

He called on me in Canning Place. I thought he looked and sounded like Michael Caine in *Zulu*, Cy Endfield's excellent 1964 film depicting the Battle of Rorke's Drift. Second-Lieutenant Cooper had joined the Royal Corps of Signals, where he would soon shoot up to the rank of captain. Peter was a hero to me and my sister - perhaps even more to her. His blend of

19

derring-do and athleticism worked wonders on the fair sex. Throw in a love of music and an alchemical reaction can be guaranteed. To up the ante he had brought two young ladies with him to Canning Place. When I asked their provenance he explained that they had fallen onto his arms just a few minutes before. That was one of the early evenings that goes down in every red-blooded boy's memories.

*

I had an interview the next day. It would have been silly to have been self-indulgent. I was in bed by 2 am. My own single bed was not good enough for two, but I put my back into it.

Sadly, I was not to be interviewed by the aristocratic chief. Instead, I benefitted from the scrutiny of an office manager, whose forebears had certainly never worn either purple or ermine.

Samuel Montagu, I was about to learn, was the occupier of a post-war *Bauhaus* building around the corner from the Dutch Reformed Church.

The office manager wasted no time in recounting that the eponymous Samuel Montagu had founded it in 1853. It had had its moments. It had swept up a pile of money during the Australian gold rush, brokering deals and, in the process, the Swaythlings had assembled a spectacular collection of Georgian silver. The manager added that the company had just been bought by Midland. It was the first ever merchant bank to be owned by a joint-stock bank.

'How's your handwriting?' this colossus of international finance asked me. I was a little taken aback. I had been expecting some impenetrable question on compound interest.

'Adequate,' I replied, though 'barely adequate' would have been more truthful.

'Good. While we are not a retail bank, we have a 'white label' arrangement with Midland Bank and we offer a few of our high net worth customers a current account. We return their cheques in batches every month and we need someone with a neat hand to address the envelopes.'

'Excellent! I'll do my very best.'

'Good. You start tomorrow. Our hours are nine to five, five days a week, plus alternate Saturday mornings. Being late three times in a month is a sackable offence.'

A strange tectonic rumble could be heard throughout EC4. It was the irrevocable sound of my translation from scruffy student into City Slicker.

*

I reported to an affable cove called Eric. He asked me if I were the 'sort of fellow who might occasionally partake of a spot of luncheon'. When I admitted to this vice, after much deliberation, he settled on the tap room at the *George and Vulture*. He required I should keep him company. If I didn't like it there, he had an alternative, the *Old Doctor Butler's Head*. Apparently he had wrestled with the issue for a while, as my mentor he would take me to both.

Our mission would be to taste and compare and we would pay with our three shilling Luncheon Vouchers, enough for an alcohol-free lunch, but where else to begin our adventure? 'The horns of a dilemma,' as Charles Dickens, a regular in both, had written.

Eric's taste in conversation was little short of hair-raising. He was a veteran of the Forgotten Army,[6] and over our simple lunches, he liked to share with me his memories of the Japanese prisoner-of-war camp where, twenty-four years before, he had been confined for eighteen ghastly months.

---

[6] Our WW2 army in Burma was known as the Forgotten Army, sadly for obvious reasons.

'A young man has needs,' he informed me, his tone sombre and grave. Not anticipating what might come next, I smiled agreeably over my Barnsley chop and roasted onion.

'A floozy and a bike shed?' I suggested. 'Not too many of those in Burma.'

'Some of the younger soldiers were yet to start shaving.'

This was not a line of conversation I was keen to pursue. I was already regretting that I had become a receptacle for his memories. At least his terrifying tales of Japanese soldiers practising their skills with Samurai swords on the prisoners in the camp caused the tedium of addressing envelopes in my finest copperplate to vanish like morning dew.

There came a day when the Great Man himself passed through the vast office where Eric habitually entertained me with torrid tales. The boss was wearing a fabulously cut charcoal grey suit, clearly made for him by the same tailor who fitted out James Bond. I saw a good-looking and sociable man who would be well at ease with a shaken martini in one hand and a gently stirred chorus girl in the other. He was not even forty years old. That's a little more like it.

'What's he like in real life?' I asked Eric, after the boss had quit our rabble-infested quarters.

'He's a keen racehorse owner. He's on the British Horse Racing Board. He plays bridge, collects paintings and supports the National Theatre. All sorts of Jewish societies, curiously including the Anti-Zionist League.'

'Has he any children?'

'Three. His eldest, a girl, is a little younger than you.'

'Is her father accessible?'

'Accessible? Do you mean, does he speak to grunts like us? Yes he does. He knows us all by name.'

22

This 'accessibility' was soon to be put to the test. The London Opera House was putting on its last opera before it closed for the summer and an old friend David Levy rang me to declare that Paisiello's *Barber of Seville* (not Rossini's) was to have a matinée. 'Still black tie, I'm afraid. Can you get away?'

There were two chances I could go. One was fat, the other slim. I slipped into David Montagu's gilded cage to ask his permission, knowing that he would say no.

'Come in,' he said without looking up. I moved a foot or so further into his impressive office.

Only then did he raise his gaze. He was obviously baffled. Just who was this teenager in that badly fitting suit? After a moment, however, he remembered.

'Geoffrey, isn't it? Lisa's son?'

'Jeremy,' I said.

'Yes, of course. You're at Cambridge. I trust you're profiting from your time here. Well, what can I do for you?'

'Er, I'd like to take Friday afternoon off.'

'Then you should be negotiating with your manager, and he should be saying no. Why, as if it matters?'

'I've been invited to see a rare opera in Covent Garden. Paisiello's *Barber*. It's a matinée.'

'Yes, of course you should go. Foolish not to. Take the afternoon off. I'll tell Eric.'

*

On that very Friday, Eric had determined to introduce me to the joys of *Simpson's* in Cornhill. I brought my hold-all with me, a crumpled dinner jacket rammed inside. Over a chump chop and a baked potato Eric told me a tale of rice bowls and rats. Lunch was an endurance test but soon I was in a taxi, stopping only at *The Nag's Head* in Covent Garden to pick up David

Levy. He was an unusual sociologist. He had rejected what he liked to call 'the shallow protest culture of the Left'.

'Erich Voegelin and Hans Jonas,' he listed. 'These are the philosophers I most respect.

'Their conservative ideas are far more revolutionary than the post-Marxist orthodoxies that hold sway in most universities.'

His contemporaries were marching on Aldermaston. They were led by a donkey-jacketed Michael Foot and supported by Lord Soper and Terry Waite.

Levy, meanwhile, was quietly helping dissidents in Eastern Europe. He rarely talked about these missions. They were often undertaken at short notice, and always at considerable risk.

With Roger Scruton and Jessica Douglas-Home, David was among those who brought relief to the victims of persecution and censorship in Czechoslovakia, Poland and Romania. With a handful of others, he maintained a flow of forbidden books and essays in both directions. He and his friends helped keep intellectual life possible under Stalin's Communism. Despite being an active counter-revolutionary he had real friends to either side of the barricade.

Even at Stowe, David had been a colourful character, brilliant at everything from fencing to debate. He sailed effortlessly into Oxford, back in 1965, to read History at Christ Church. I met him through his friend and fellow church-goer Jonathan Sumption,[7] the Catholic historian and barrister. At Oxford, David joined the *Monday Club* to serve as literary editor of *Monday World*. He championed such unfashionable figures as Charles Maurras, leader of *Action Française*. David, a romantic and

---

[7] Lord Sumption, OBE, PC, FSA, FRHistS, is today (2019) a British judge, author and medieval historian. He was sworn in as a Justice of the Supreme Court on 11 January 2012, succeeding The Lord Collins of Mapesbury.

a conservative, then took his 1st class BA to the heart of student radicalism, the *London School of Economics*, to be taught by the Marxist Ralph Milliband. He steered a courageous course, especially as he was immune to his spurious philosophy.

His confidence, never sabotaged by his unhip views, was hugely reinforced when Lord Salisbury invited him and others of a like mind to wild if slightly mad gatherings at Hatfield House. In the taxi he was telling me a thrilling story about clambering over its Elizabethan roof. I, meanwhile, was putting on my dinner jacket, no easy task as the driver violently swerved his car through London's twisted and narrow streets. David seemed to enjoy the cabaret of my attempting to get my trousers on, so did many a pedestrian at a traffic light.

I am now the only person who does not laugh when Elke Sommer travels in her taxi, in the nude, to the amused delight of the Parisians.[8]

'Rossini was a crook,' said David while I stuffed my Burton's suit into the hold-all. 'He stole swathes of Paisiello's libretto and his music. Prepare for the real thing.'

Levy had a taste for waylaid or wayward operas. The opera was magic, of course, and afterwards we had a smashing supper at Bertorelli's.

*

August was at last around the corner. My handwriting was causing blind panic among the postmen who served the larger houses of the shires, so I was moved to Documentary Credits.[9] Eric's role in my initiation had been replaced by another old soldier, Albert.

---

[8] *A Shot in the Dark*, the 1964 comedy film directed by Blake Edwards.
[9] A letter of credit, or documentary credit, is a payment mechanism used to serve international trade as an economic guarantee.

Clearly he lacked any vestige of level-headed discernment as he held me in abject contempt.

'They should never have abolished National Service,' he would frequently opine if he saw me with an untied shoelace or a spot of gravy on my synthetic tie.

'The label said 'machine washable', I unwisely told him on one occasion.

'Those who make such claims need to be put to the test. Those who believe them are simply idiots,' he told me.

I will admit I was struggling with what my better-dressed colleagues seemed to dismiss as 'paper'. Why did the value of these bills or bonds go down when interest rates went up? And, frankly, did I really care?

*

An old friend, Richard Turner, had invited me to Scotland for the 'glorious twelfth' of August, the first day of the grouse season. His mother, my prospective hostess, was Lady Turner, consort of Sir Mark, chairman of *Kleinwort Benson Lonsdale*, the illustrious merchant bank. If I knew him, I did not know his family.

It had all begun when Caroline Smythe, a friend of my former flatmate, Sian Rhys, had introduced me to her friend Adrian Stroude, one of Richard's best mates. As easy as that. Aware that his father was a City legend, a merchant prince with a brain like a greased planet, huge and slippery, the newspapers focussed on his two private jets, one for Europe and the other for the Atlantic. As I saw it, there was no way I could possibly accept the invitation without resigning my choice position. I was therefore in a quandary.

The only thing to do was to take a deep breath and knock at Mr Montagu's famously open door a second time. The boss would surely not agree, but he had already surprised me with the opera.

26

'I want to do two things that may be impossible to combine,' I told him baldly.

'Impossible?' He smiled. 'Few things are. What's on your mind?'

'The first is that I want to continue working here over the summer. I'm learning a lot.'

'All right. So what's getting in the way?'

'I've been invited to stay in Perthshire for the second half of August.'

'Perthshire? That's practically the Arctic! Two weeks? That may indeed be problematic. What will you be doing up there?'

'I have been asked if I want to shoot a grouse.'

'Really!' He looked me up and down, reassessing his first impression. Had he somehow hired an opera-loving field sportsman?

'Have you ever done that before?'

'No. This will be my first time.'

'Well, you will certainly want to go. Who's your hostess?'

'Lady Turner. Sir Mark's other half.'

'Turner? The head of Kleinwort's?'

'Yes. That's him.'

'Then it's imperative that you go. Far more important than being here. Who's your manager? Ask him to have a word with me. We'll keep your place open for you while you're away. You'll need a little money. Do we pay you every month?'

'Every week, Sir.'

'Then we'll pay you in advance for your holiday. Can't have one of my young staff pleading poverty with the Turners.'

*

That Saturday, flush with cash, I went to that excellent second hand clothes shop off Ladbroke Grove.

I bought a worn tweed jacket and a pair of slightly ragged 'previously owned' cavalry twills. In my judgement such rags might suggest that I frequently journeyed to Scotland to help suppress the local wildlife.

And that is why, on August 10, 1968, Richard, his twin brother Roger and I were sitting in the back of Sir Mark's eight-seater Learjet 23 on our way to the fair city of Perth.

I was an undergraduate, struggling with book-keeping. On board the little jet, I had to rub my eyes to confirm I was not dreaming. When I had accepted the invitation I had thought I would have to get to Perthshire's Kinross in the back of a clapped out Morris Minor, having to endure three or four days of acute discomfort including breaking down in Grimsby. As it was, on arriving at the lodge, I was greeted and treated to flattering indifference by the party. I was not included in any of the driven shoots, of course. The 'shooting box' would fill with experienced guns who will have paid a small fortune, I accurately concluded, for the privilege.

There was also to be some deer stalking, but I was not included in that, either. Deer stalking was not for beginners. Paradoxically, no one was ever allowed to do it if they had never done it before. Richard came to my rescue. He suggested that he and I should take a gun each, find a ghillie to look after us and go coarse shooting over the moors. If we put up a grouse, so much the better. If we only bagged a rabbit, the retrievers would be internally grateful and lick our faces.

After a sizable breakfast - porridge and breaded trout - Richard and I set out with two gundogs, one ghillie and a pair of lethal weapons.

'Ye'll perceive nary a grouse,' the ghillie warned us after ordering me to 'break' my gun. 'They're no deaf. They'll hear you a-coming half-a-league away.'

He was right, of course. We walked, walked some more, and then we walked. Mile upon mile, over yielding and crunching heather, uphill, down dale, our twelve bores broken over our arms. If beautiful, it was certainly exhausting.

We had tramped for around ten miles when a plump black grouse confidently if idiotically fluttered into the air.

To my amazement, Richard brought up and levelly aimed his Purdey.

The grouse fell clumsily to earth. I can't speak for Tom the ghillie, but I was rather impressed.

We celebrated with the delicious sandwiches those two pretty girls, the sort more typically deployed in Swiss chalets, had made for us. We washed them down with a tinny or two, though if the pause in our route march was thoroughly welcome, the sun had caused the midges to come out in search of blood. We hunters were now the hunted and, if we were not to be devoured alive, it was time to plod on.

*

Five hours later we reached a country pub. I fell into one of its threadbare wing chairs, feeling incapable of returning to my feet. Over a long summer's day we will have walked a good twenty miles. While Richard and Tom the Ghillie were untousled, I needed traction.

It had been a grand day, rounded off with a pint o' heavy in *The Drovers' Arms*. If the ale was average, our circumstances made it the tastiest I have ever downed. It somehow reached my legs where it began to work its restorative magic.

Richard found a telephone and called in. A minute or so later he could happily report that a shooting brake had been dispatched to find us. Its cargo was to be two young men, an elderly ghillie, two retrievers called Dindins and Walkies, one nameless grouse (or sick parrot, as my fellow huntsman called it) and two rabbits, all shot by Richard.

*

Sir Mark spent his day in profound chinwag with the Labour peer Lord Shackleton, the former Paymaster General and now the Leader of the Labour Party in the Lords. Confined in Sir Mark's study, there was no doubt that they were plotting something.

Richard filled me in on Edward Shackleton's story. He was more than a mere Labour grandee. He was the son of the justly garlanded Antarctic explorer, Ernest. Edward's career, Richard now told me, had begun before the war, when he had become a close friend of Herbert Morrison.

I should have known much more. Caius library, after all, was filled with spectacular photographs of his father Ernest's heroic mission to rescue the crew of the *Endurance*. The explorer's ship had been trapped in pack ice and was being slowly crushed. The crew had to resort to camping on the sea ice - until it disintegrated - and then attempt a stormy voyage of more than seven hundred nautical miles in the *Endurance's* lifeboats until they reached South Georgia, the most southerly island of the Falklands.

'Edward Shackleton became Morrison's Parliamentary Private Secretary, his PPS. His boss was awarded charge of Labour's nationalisation programme, while Shackleton was asked to drum up support.'

'Nationalisation? You must mean the railways? Steel? Coal-mining? The National Health Service?'

'All of the above. Even Morrison was only partially convinced. He actually opposed Aneurin Bevan's proposals to nationalise the hospitals.'

'Did they believe they could accommodate the hordes of returning servicemen by over-staffing our larger industries?'

'That's a slightly Tory way of looking at it, if to an extent you are right. During the war, to the dismay of the unions, it had become clear that the country could cope with reduced manpower and increased womanpower. That did not suit the brothers. To put this trend into reverse, to put men back in control, they would first have to take over the boardrooms. That meant nationalisation. Attlee's ministers saw the need for public works to make a land fit for heroes but also knew the dwindling beacons of socialist enthusiasm had to be relit. If there were risks associated with over-manning they were prepared to overlook them.'

'What harm could it do?'

'Some think a lot. The Right believes a certain level of disquiet, of unemployment, is actually productive. People need to strive and the greater the number of applicants for any position enables employers to select the most able.'

'So what did our post-war socialists think?'

'The greatest happiness for the greatest number was their goal. 'Lord Festival' - as everyone called Morrison after the Festival of Britain - was also determined to raise the educational levels of the working class. New grammar schools were built up and down the country. His 'educational' events on the South Bank were meant to sell curiosity itself to the millions. 'Curiosity is learning's *agent provocateur*' he once said. He meant children to work hard in school and think it fun.'

'But didn't Labour run out of steam in the '50s? Didn't the country feel guilty about rejecting Churchill?'

'There's something in that, for sure. Attlee saw it too. Sadly, he was defeated in a snap election in 1951. The people wanted Winston back.'

'What happened?'

'Attlee remained Labour leader but, in 1955, in another general election, it was clear his magic was spent.'

Richard was only a few months older than me. In 1955 he can only have been seven years old. Even so, he was (I felt) remarkably well-informed.

'The voters thought that Attlee and Morrison had passed their sell-by dates. Labour lost, Attlee retired, taking his earldom and a well-earned place in the House of Lords. Elderly socialists began to fade from history, while an even more elderly Winston Churchill put on his worn but fitting short coat and pinstripe trousers.'

When I asked him about Lord Shackleton he admitted he did not really know why the man had been ennobled. It seemed an oddly great award for a 'humble' PPS.

*

We heard doors open and close and realised the grandees had finished their meeting.

'Come on, I'll introduce you. If you can't manage banking or politics, Dad loves poetry. He conflates all knowledge, arts and sciences alike. He is always willing to discuss these things. This may be a propitious moment for us.'

Richard was right. His father was surprisingly happy to indulge us and sent down for coffee.

'We were discussing those most important if ultimately indecisive years for the country, 1951-1953. They were exciting for Herbert Morrison if not the more so for his PPS, Edward Shackleton,' he said, sweeping an arm towards the peer. 'This old boy you see before you was a participant in an adventure that could have been written by John Buchan. You may have guessed I'm talking of Mohammad Mosaddeq, the prime minister of Iran. At that time he was a serious threat to her Britannic majesty's interests.'

Lord Shackleton and graciously took the story on.

'At first, we did not see Mosaddeq in a dark light. He passed our little tests - educated, charming, happy to champion secular democracy - all mood music that chimed well in our liberal ears,' Lord Shackleton began. 'Unfortunately, he fiercely resisted what he referred to as 'corporate imperialism'. When he threatened to nationalise the *British Anglo-Iranian Oil Company*, the giant we know today as *BP,* we knew we could no longer contain the crisis. Without US support we had no hope. The whole country would stall at the first traffic lights.'

'The US?' I asked, mostly because I thought I should say something.

'MI6 and Sir Anthony Eden's Foreign Office needed to send an emissary to Langley - vital - and Congress - tactful – and had to find one who could travel under the radar. They told me I was young, fit and soldierly, and that was why they gave me the mission.'

Sir Mark agreeably indulged his lordly companion's modesty.

'You were trusted at the very highest levels,' he said. 'You had already visited many corners of the globe where Britain had an interest. The embassy arranged for you to speak at a gala dinner in DC, giving you the cover you needed. You were then and are still a brilliant public speaker and a celebrity in your own right.'

Sir Mark turned to me, indicating his old friend.

'My son tells me you too have a taste for adventure. At your age, Shackleton had already seen places you won't find on a map. In the late thirties, for example, while the world toyed with some of the most dangerous political ideas in history, Shackleton here joined an Oxford University expedition to Sarawak in Borneo, becoming the first climber to reach the summit of Mount Mulu.'

Was it that throwaway line about John Buchan that let me infer that he may even have been in the secret service?

'Let me tell you,' said Sir Mark, 'that this easy-going raconteur found the Eisenhower administration in Washington amenable to classic British polish. His, anyway.'

33

'Well,' Shackleton shrugged, 'when I came home, a military coup d'état, codenamed *TPAJAX* by the CIA and *Operation Boot* by MI6, overthrew Mosaddeq and his National Front.'

Sir Mark chuckled. 'The coup was carried out under CIA direction as an act of US foreign policy...'

'...conceived and approved at the highest levels of both governments,' Lord Shackleton added.

My mind raced. Though these events had happened fifteen years before, surely they would still be secret? It might even have been the first time the United States had wilfully overthrown a foreign government? Was the CIA brighter than its military? And why were they telling me all this?

'There was a cost, however,' Lord Shackleton soberly continued. 'Since the coup, the Shah of Persia has become less of a constitutional head of state. He drifted progressively to being a satrap, a latter-day sultan. He still continues to modernise Iran and means to keep it secular. In so-doing, he and his country have become almost irrevocably allied to and dependent on the US.'

'I imagine that Iran has no room for an opposition, no matter how loyal?' I said, very conscious that I might be saying something impressively idiotic.

'That's right. Any disagreement, rational or emotional, is instantly crushed by the SAVAK, the Shah's secret police. They deploy a formidable armoury of naked violence, arbitrary arrest and torture. The Shah's dictatorship has left Iranians resentful of the US-led intervention and, in the long run, vulnerable to the overtures of the ayatollahs. As for us, we have lost our base in Aden[10] and daily our relations with Iran are more strained.'[11]

---

[10] Aden was a British Protectorate until 1967.
[11] The Shah did not flee from Iran until 1979.

I thought of Michael Hashemian, a Persian at my college. He and his family had left Iran in something of a hurry and nor did they ever go home.

'Jeremy,' said Sir Mark, 'you should be aware that we owe our great *BP* to Edward Shackleton. Barely into his thirties he secured the UK's largest company and it's no exaggeration to say he saved his country's bacon. A grateful Labour Party promised him the presidency of the Board of Trade but, since the conservatives were in power, they couldn't deliver. He was compensated with a seat in the House of Lords, which today he leads.'

Not a trivial outcome. It showed a talented man there could be an exciting present and a brilliant future. Were Documentary Credits really my bag? Perhaps I too could be a PPS to some lucky and prominent member of the House of Lords? How did one apply for such a post?

*

If Shackleton's grand position was owed to the subtle way he had outmanoeuvred a potential enemy there were very few dangerous foreigners in Kensington and none in this corner of Clackmannan.

There was, however, a ferocious and xenophobic cook, lurking and scheming in her kitchen, and whose principal duty was to make sure that nothing foreign invaded our digestive tracks.

Such undesirables formed a very long list, including all fish other than herring, trout and salmon. Vegetables needed to be boiled alive until safely dead. Breakfast cereal, other than oats, was an illegal immigrant, as was any meat other than Aberdeen Angus. She even embargoed pepper.

The blandness of her cooking was compensated by the Gaelic girls, however, who appeared not to notice or care that most of the house party had Saxon origins. The guests, Roger, Richard and I excepted, were all distinguished people. Even when my age they had set the bar far higher than I ever had. Yet again I was made to think long and hard about my future.

*

It took a few days before I had the chance to offer my services as a PPS to the distinguished parliamentarian himself. Well, his lordship listened to me patiently enough but was clearly unimpressed.

He gently informed me that such a post only covered expenses. Bright young men were always of interest, but did I have sufficient means of my own?

Sadly not, but if you don't ask you don't get. Life must go on.

That evening, while the shooting party was already dressing for dinner, the deer-stalkers came back in and made their way upstairs. They were strangely quiet.

The party that night would include Lady Wake (Richard and Roger's great aunt), two investment bankers, a peer of the realm, a sportswoman (an American of Scottish ancestry for whom the adventure was the culmination of a lifetime's ambition), the twins, an undergraduate (me), my host and hostess and the minister of the local kirk, who was kind enough to offer grace.

The meal was a muted affair, characterised by good manners and the briefest of exchanges. I put the mood down to exhaustion - deer stalking must be the most demanding of sports ever conceived, other than rowing. Mind you, Margaret Wake, sitting next to me, made up for it. She was still, I had been told, a competent cello player. She certainly had a musical voice.

'How old are you?' she demanded.

'Nineteen,' I answered. As I heard my reply I thought it sounded a little too young. 'And a bit,' I added.

She smiled.

'Born in '49, then. What is your oldest memory?' she asked.

'Meeting my great-grandmother,' I replied.

'Tell me about that. I like these stories. They are akin to time travel.'

'Well, I must have been three or four years old. I had been taken to meet, or be presented to Gangey, as we called her. She had been born in 1873, I learned much later, though her devotedly Catholic husband had died in 1914, he had already sired six children. Her eyesight had deteriorated in her latter years and she was now quite blind. When she was ready for me, she sent a maid into her library to bring me to her. I sat on a footstool at her feet, while my father and mother stood some way behind. I had been dressed in a sailor suit and had been warned to be on my best behaviour. As a result I was nervous but, as I sat there, she gently took my head in her hands and explored its shape, running her fingers through my hair, as might a phrenologist. I remember a very slight lady, entirely clothed in black, while the little I could see of her hair beneath her head scarf was quite white. Her breast was adorned with an enormous crucifix. It was the only time I ever met her, as she died soon afterwards, but that meeting has since let me boast that I once met someone who was born before the first performance of Bizet's *Carmen*, before anyone had heard Tchaikovsky's first Piano Concerto, and before Mistinguett, the French singer, was even a glint in her father's eye.'

Music was obviously on my mind. Had I been better informed, I might have related that she was born before the Battle of the Little Bighorn, well before Captain Matthew Webb became the first to swim the English Channel and even before Benjamin Disraeli had secured the deal in which Isma'il Pasha sold Egypt's share in the Suez Canal to Britain, without the prior sanction of the British Parliament. For that epoch-changing deal Disraeli, the original 'rain-maker', had

37

borrowed the necessary wherewithal from Messrs N M Rothschild.

Of course, all this was as yesterday to Margaret Wake. Her tradition was that her family descended from Hereward the Wake,[12] the Saxon chieftain who led a resistance movement in the fens against the hirelings of William the Conqueror.

'Thank you for that delightful memoire,' she graciously offered. 'By way of thanks, let me give you one of my own. I am a little older than you. I am ninety next birthday so, as far as years are concerned, you will have to forgive my pulling a little rank.'

The whole table grew attentive. She had everyone's ear.

'When I was a little girl, we sometimes had important men come to my very small school and talk about character forming topics, supposedly to improve us. This was in Northamptonshire, not far from our country house at Courteenhall. Well, this time they had found an old soldier, a Chelsea Pensioner, so old it seemed almost bizarre that he was still alive. He gave a dazzling speech about his time as a drummer boy and he demonstrated the marshal rhythm he had had to play all those years ago on his snare drum. It fair made our hair stand on end, we girls, but when he said he had caught sight of the Emperor Napoleon on the battlefield we shivered, realising we now were experiencing a direct insight into history.'

This is how I can faithfully report that I have met someone who met a soldier who had been on the blood-drenched fields of Waterloo.

*

We were around a week into the shooting party when a force nine squabble descended over the dining table. The deer stalkers had the American lady in their sights,

---

[12] The sobriquet Hereward is derived from the old English 'here' meaning 'army' and 'ward' meaning 'guard', while 'the Wake' implies 'watchful'.

almost literally, even though her rifle was the only one equipped with a telescopic rangefinder. Standard practice in Massachusetts, no doubt, but utterly *outré* in Scotland.

'Shooting is a serious sport, not a gentleman's hobby,' she declared, offended and baffled by the unwarranted *froideur*. 'Why are you all being so beastly?'

'You took your shot at two hundred and fifty yards. That's not how we do things. You could have wounded the beast.'

'But I didn't. My gun will kill at four hundred yards or more.'

'But you might have.'

'I would not. I learned to shoot at Boston's *Mystic Valley Gun Club*, summa cum laude, 1958.'

Silence descended on that end of the table until, that is, Lord Shackleton tactfully chose this moment to ask Lady Turner how her plans were going to help the less fortunate of Highgate, where the Turners had their town house.

'Mark has agreed to put a little money in trust to help students in need.'

Sir Mark looked embarrassed. 'You should know, Edward, that the sums are small. The circumstances will vary, of course, but they will normally be between £100 and £500 apiece. We see medical students as the principal beneficiaries; they so often need help with university expenses and the high cost of text books and equipment.'

I had flown to Scotland in a private jet. Its running costs will have been astronomical. Perhaps £1000 in fuel alone, just to get to the middle of Scotland? Who knows what the pilot and the stewardess charged? I found myself agreeing with my host. Sir Mark's charitable donations were relatively small.

All too soon the Scottish idyll was over. I felt I had learned a lot, not expressly about either field sports or banking, but about the power and nature of such rarified people.

*

On my return to reality, David Montagu called me in.

'How was your break?'

'You were right,' I told him. 'It was educational. Refreshing, even. I feel a new man.'

'I knew you would. Now, tell me, have you ever been to a board meeting?'

'No.'

'Then we'll put that right. I will face the shareholders on Friday in the Bakers' courtroom in Hart Lane. You already know that Midland Bank owns most of our stock and can overrule me if they so choose. My task is to keep them and the other shareholders off my back and keep the inevitable cat-fight out of the papers.

'There is usually a good turn-out. Come along. You'll have to sit quietly at the back but you'll benefit from it. You may even enjoy it.'

'Thank you, Sir. I'll be there.' A few days passed and I was n the edge of my canvas chair.

There were very few serious issues aired at that vaguely feudal meeting. David and his board sat at a high table while the rest of us made do with stackable chairs.

The chairman acknowledged, very discreetly, that the Remuneration Committee had been asked to calculate a suitable increment in his 'compensation'. Its conclusion would be reported by letter to the honourable shareholders. This declaration did make me ponder, though Midland Bank's representative nodded in a sphinx-like way. Of course, he already knew the result. The next question, a technical one on the redemption date of the preference shares, went over my head.

The 'free' picnic hampers for the shareholders who had attended looked very attractive. Not being a shareholder I didn't get one, of course. I will admit to looking for a spare or unallocated freebie, but the provision had been precise.

*

On August 24, 1968, a Saturday, there was a free concert in Hyde Park. *Fleetwood Mac* headed the bill, supported by *Rory Harper*, *Fairport Convention*, *Family* and others. My little sister and I were keen to go.

Little sister? She was sixteen. Our attendance needed some preparation and the dressing up box came to the rescue. I wore a fez and a kaftan, she wore something she called a baby-doll nightie. This was the '60s after all. Under those balmy skies the blessed had dressed as gods and goddesses to waft in the breeze-free air. The music hung around us in motionless stasis.

Blackhill Entertainments had organised the whole shebang. The event would be in the Cockpit, a curious shrine near Hyde Park Corner sometimes called a 'saucer without a rim'. It was more accustomed to military bands playing to colonels in deck chairs. The Ministry of Works had given *Blackhill* the thumbs up - a helpful if unlikely ally.

Some way behind us lay the Serpentine, its boats impatiently awaiting hire. My sister and I took one and rowed out over the water, into the middle to hear Peter Sarstedt and *Ten Years After*.

What of the bands? I had heard most of them on the radio but I never heard them play better than they did that day in the park. Their music suited the event, seeming to fill the heavens. It was 'cosmic', a word we used a lot back then. We were confident that nothing was wrong in the world.

We were, however brought down to earth by the boat-hire people. Our money had only secured a short excursion and our time was up. 'Come in Number 9', they shouted at us though their loudhailers.

'We don't have a number 9,' my sister improvised, affecting a passable imitation of the warden. 'Come in Number 6, you're in trouble.'

On reclaiming *terra firma*, we took our sandwiches and wine into the morass. Vast though it was, we found a space. Most of the audience were dressed as hippies - it was *de rigueur*, after all, but a threesome on our left was rather more formally attired. The male among them was actually wearing a suit.

'Let me guess,' I ventured. 'You're here from the ministry of parks, monitoring the raucous and deciding whether a few new laws should be enacted.'

'No. I'm just not a hippy', said the suited one. 'I'm a student, just as you most probably are. Name's Molony. Current address: Trinity College, Cambridge.'

We shook hands rather stiffly and were introduced to his companions, the Pringle sisters. In an attempt to make light conversation, we agreed on the uncontroversial matter that those who were not there had missed the best afternoon of the year.

Ralph Mctell was unscheduled but came on anyway to play *The Streets of London* as some sort of finale. When the event was declared over, people laughed, talked, finished their drinks and played the guitars they had brought with them to the park. The Ministry of Works would later report that all the litter had been picked up. Those were the days.

I really don't believe that John Molony, whose career would culminate in a gallery in Cork Street, realised at the time that my outfit was just for that evening. To be fair to him, it was rather convincing. Next term, clad in my Burton's suit, I would introduce myself more formally and, fourteen years after that, he would become a godfather to my son.

*

'So', said Eric, over lunch at *Simpsons* in Cornhill, 'what do you make of that arsehole Albert?'

It occurred to me that this was some sort of test.

'I have an inkling you're not best pals?'

'We managers are all stick and carrot. He likes sticks, I like carrots.'

'At least his tales are easier-going than yours.'

'That's because he doesn't have any. I want one from you. You told me you didn't quite meet Prince Charles in some dreary pub but, you did say you had had a second near miss.'

'All right, Eric, I'll trade you. No more tales of your time on the River Kwai for one last story about the prince?'

'Your terms are acceptable to your former manager,' said Eric, bless him. He called for a bottle of Spanish wine.[13] 'It's on me,' he said, settling back in his chair.

'Well,' I began, 'I was walking back to my digs from Magdalene College where I had had lunch with a friend. Passing Trinity, I saw there was some sort of commotion in front of the Great Gate. Twenty spectators, three police cars and a fire engine had arrived in the forecourt and their crews were remonstrating with some unfortunate student. The scallywag had climbed a ladder up to the statue of Henry VIII that sits in a niche in the arch that admits the world to the college and was trying to attach a drain plunger under the king's skirt.

"Come down, Sir,' they shouted.

"He's my ancestor,' the unmistakably reedy tone of the Heir to the Throne came in reply. 'I can do what I want with him'.'

Eric had the grace to laugh.

*

---

13 It will have been a bottle of Rioja, or possibly German. At this time The wines we ordinarily drank were French.

43

An invitation to Sunday lunch had arrived at home. It was from Frances Hogg. 'Nothing formal, just my family and me,' it read.

Frances was at Cambridge. Her father Quintin was in the shadow cabinet. On his father's death he had taken his seat in the House of Lords but, when Macmillan stepped down in 1963, the Conservative Party needed a new leader and Quintin Hogg thought he could do the job at least as well as anyone else.

No peer had been prime minister since Lord Salisbury, I think, so Lord Hailsham announced that he would use the recent Peerage Act to disclaim his title, fight a by-election and return to the House of Commons.

He was already one of a handful of truly great speakers. It didn't quite go according to plan, even if it was as plain Mr Hogg that he fought and won his father's old constituency of St Marylebone.

The problem was that some thought his antics at the Party Conference were vulgar. Macmillan privately 'suggested' that senior party members should not select him and Hogg failed to win the leadership. Even so, there was some compensation. During the Wilson government, the reduction in his workload had let Hogg build up his practice at the Bar. Ironically, one of his more important clients was his principal political opponent, Prime Minister Harold Wilson.

I had never met him, of course, but Sunday lunch certainly sounded promising indeed.

*

At Frances's house in Putney I was soon introduced to her siblings Douglas and Sarah, and to her father and mother. Ordinary conversation proved impossible, for Quintin Hogg's love of English turned his most ordinary sentences into works of art.

'So you're at Cambridge with Frances? Do you ever speak at the Union?' he asked me by way of opening gambit.

I was not shy but I was nervous. I answered candidly.

'Only once, and that was from the floor.'

'Perfectly good place to start. We were all backbenchers once. What was the motion?'

'Whether civilisation is a by-product of religion or vice versa.'

'Interesting. Which side were you on?'

I tried to remember my summary.

'I argued that the fervour involved in religion should enliven all other spheres of argument.'

'Hmm. I hope you let politics off your hook. The introduction of religious passion into politics is the end of honest politics while the introduction of politics into religion is the prostitution of true religion. What did the chamber make of your argument?'

'I enjoyed some mild abuse.'

'Did you indeed? Excellent. Abuse is the very hallmark of liberty.'

'How would you have approached the debate, Sir?'

'Since you ask, the best way I know of to win an argument is to start by being in the right.'

I felt the other members of the household were also assessing me. Perhaps all Frances's friends were regularly interviewed in the same daunting manner?

'I have been thinking of going into politics, Sir, perhaps as a PPS.'

'A PPS? A back door, true, but a good one. What could you offer the House?'

'Not much, if I'm realistic. I suppose I might promote the needs of my constituents and try not to bore too many people in the process.'

'Never mind the blasted constituents. MPs need to promote the needs of their Party.'

'I understand. So a 'surgery' should serve to evangelise the party's polity?'

'Good. We're getting somewhere but you still are missing the vital issue. The prime duty of a politician is never to be dull. The moment politics is dull, democracy itself is in danger. Speak up, even shout out, but play the game. A politician who enters public life may as well face the fact that the best way of not being found out is not to do anything, but if in turn this is found out, it will cause his ruin.'

His deceptively easy banter clean took my breath away. I was wholly out of my depth.

We moved into his drawing room for coffee after a suite of serious platefuls, of roast beef, of trifle. There had been wine with lunch, but it had been served in Georgian glasses, scarcely bigger than thimbles.

As we sat I noticed his shoes - they were brogues but the perforations in the toecaps, customarily drilled in a symmetrical pattern, spelled QH.

'Is Cambridge's supposed scholarship still discernible?' he asked with an Oxonian smile.

'You will have already heard Frances on the subject,' I answered, 'and of course I cannot add to that, but I will admit with a little pride that my college alone has more Nobel Prizes to its name than the whole of the USSR.'

'The enemy is not the East, it is the West. We are suffering from a recruiting drive that is systematically and deliberately undertaken by American business, by American universities, and to a lesser extent, the American government. They send talent scouts here expressly to buy British brains and pre-empt them for service in the US.

'I earnestly look forward to the day when some reform of the American system of education will enable them to produce their own scientists. With an amiable free trade of talent, there could be an adequate interchange between our country and theirs, not a one-way traffic.'

'Well, Sir, have you any advice for this poor student?'

'Play the piano, ride a horse and speak French.'

'I'm afraid my French is little short of execrable'

'*Tant pis*.'[14]

If this made me laugh, it also made me thoughtful. Somehow I would have to deal with my triple *lacuna* in the near future.

*

David Montagu let my manager know that he wanted to see me before the long vacation drew to its close. I wondered what he wanted to say. Indeed, what should I say to him?

In the end, the valedictory was simple enough.

'Have you enjoyed your time here?'

'Yes, Sir, I have. Your people have quite convinced me I should work in the City when I graduate. Here, if you'll have me.'

'Will you come back at Christmas?'

'With great pleasure, Sir.'

'Excellent. I'll make the arrangements. I think we'll put you in stocks. Come now, don't be alarmed! I mean stocks and shares. Equities. You'll see how it all works. Well, that's that.' He stood up, his hand outstretched. 'My best regards to your mother.'

*

What was true was that I was sincerely grateful for the experience, even though some of it had been more lifeless than a stagnant puddle, but this was banking, not lion taming.

---

[14] That's too bad.

What I had seen was a path ahead, while Fiona Montagu, whom I had at last met at a weekend in Gloucestershire, was rather lovely in an intellectually arrogant but physically generous way.

Sadly, that was not the way the wind would blow.

*

Back in Canning Place, I was surprised to see an open landau, driven by a well-groomed blondish, younger man in a shiny black topper, pulled by a fine grey mare, turning into the mews across the road.

I had to know more. As he stabled his horse the softly spoken American driver was happy to talk.

His name was Dennis Severs. It turned out that he had inherited the carriage from the adoptive family that had sheltered him after he had run away from Escondito, California. Fondly believing that Hampshire had been the model for New Hampshire, that made it the nearest terrestrial place to heaven. His parents, Earl and Hellen Severs, had four sons between them by as many marriages. They moved their trailer many times and our Dennis constantly changed schools. A disorientated youngster had been described in his school reports in words that ranged from 'exceptional' to 'mentally retarded'; classic aspects of a dreamy and imaginative child. He was, I soon discovered, humorous, generous, passionate, altogether unpretentious and, it will be admitted, slightly camp.

He had just started to run horse-drawn tours around Hyde Park and the West End, advertising them in the Park Lane hotels. 'I want to show American tourists something different, and graciously', said the committed anglophile.

We were roughly the same age but he had the collector's gene. When I had a coffee in his little flat above the horse box, he showed me a competent drawing he had bought from some stall on the Portobello road.

'It's by Queen Victoria', he told me.

It might have been, too, though if it were true the queen was a far better watercolourist than commonly thought.

Naturally, I wanted to keep in touch with this gifted and talented man. Time to round up the usual suspects.

Gavin Stamp and my sister agreed to come to lunch. Heather Hartley-Davies thought she might accept.

She lived nearby, as did Anthony Watts-Russell and his girlfriend Flavia Merton.[15]

There we are, quorate. Should be a damned good lunch and, I'm pleased to relate, it was.

*

All of a sudden, my second year at Cambridge was upon me. I was to be in Caius's Harvey Court, an angular modernist residence whose Spartan gardens celebrated Cambridge's only bomb crater. The architect, who obviously felt sympathy for the Hun, had left that relic of the Conflict unruffled.

While I waited, my princely friend (whom I had not actually met) had been sent off to Aberystwyth to become a little more Welsh. Our status as bosom buddies would have to wait until he was safely repatriated.

I had a new princely friend, an overseas student with a certain level of veneration in religious circles. The young nobleman descended from Demetrius Gallitzin, 'Servant of God and Apostle of the Alleghenies' and a campaign for his ancestor's canonisation in the orthodox

---

[15] They were to marry in 1977 and are now both deceased. They left two daughters, Elisabeth Caroline Watts-Russell, b. 30 Dec 1978 and Henrietta Rose Watts-Russell, b. 15 Oct 1981.

community had just been initiated. He stabled a villainous mare at a nearby riding school, the *White Horse Stables*. I cannot now recall how many times I fell off Gallitzin's tamest of nags.

None of his saintliness, however, had protected my friend when he had ridden his nag across King's Lawn to dine with me at the Pitt Club. The porters fined him a mark - six shillings and eight pence - for every hoof print his charger had left on the sacred turf. The prince was deeply aggrieved. The aggregated fine was enormous. He had had to pay the proctors the equivalent of an entire term's fees.

*

I was back to learning about the Vienna Circle's logical positivism, Christiaan Huygens's system of hypothetico-deductive analysis, digesting an exegesis on Kierkegaard's Teleological Suspension of the Ethical and the normative refutation of the Hegelian/Kantian dichotomy. My supervisor regularly liked to tick me off for depending on a catalogue of recondite conceptualisations, wrapped in a cloak of obscurantist jargon.

'Your talk,' he told me, 'is surely the handiwork of wisdom because not one word of it do I understand.'[16]

*

My father and Lord Hailsham concurred on education. 'Any man of breeding can speak French, ride a horse and play the piano. Oh yes, and play bridge.'

Unfortunately, I failed on every count. Even though I resolved to put this right, this ever-longer list of *desiderata* was proving a bridge too far.

I had scarcely a word of French and could barely manage the national anthem on the Joannah. I was clearly not a gentleman. Despite that, for some reason I

---

[16] He was quoting Flann O'Brien, and was telling me in his round-about way that I was not nearly as clever as I thought I was.

was getting onto some very gentrified lists. Mind you, back then, anyone who owned his own DJ and was at Oxford or Cambridge was *ipso facto* eligible. Despite manifold good reasons for my blackballing, my social life actually blossomed.

The Michaelmas Term turned my attention back to the groves of academe, but all too soon we were preparing for the Christmas break.

A telephone call. True to Montagu's word, I was back at the bank. The chairman did not lack style. This time I was apprenticed to a messenger.

Dick, my new master, was a joy, if sartorially challenged. He dressed in flannel suit and bowler, both of which had seen better days. He knew the City like the back of his hand; hairs, liver spots and dirty fingernails included.

On my very first morning, he had to deliver a 'Certificate of Deposit' to the National Provincial Bank in Bishopsgate. It was raining lightly and, when we left Austin Friars, I opened my umbrella to keep us dry.

'No need for that' he said. Passing a wholly anonymous doorway, Dick pulled it open. 'Fire exit', he added with a conspiratorial wink. We walked along a bland and featureless corridor, took the third door on the left and were in the busy kitchen of a branch of *J. Lyons and Co.*

No one took any notice of us. We passed the 'nippies', arrived at the street door, crossed the road ahead and were at our destination. Sum total, fifteen yards in the rain, if that. Dampened, yes a bit, but far from soggy. Dick was wholly at home in the postroom and with its occupants. The lads there made a big fuss of him. I felt I had stumbled into a secret world. He put his case down where he could and the both of us were rewarded with an enamelled tankard of sweet tea.

'Ever seen one of these?' he asked me. I was looking at a Certificate of Deposit. No, it looked like a banknote and, no, I had never seen one before.

Where it might have said 'The Bank of England promises to pay the Bearer on Demand the Sum of Five Pounds', it actually said 'Samuel Montagu & Co promises to pay the Bearer on Demand the Sum of One Million Pounds'. It was an *objet d'art*, a wonderfully engraved hand-scutched antique interwoven demidevilled superfine piece of 'scrip'.

What arrested me, however, was the word 'bearer'. Dick was looking at me oddly.

'Think you could pocket it and make your way to Monte Carlo? Think again, chum. No one would cash it for you.'

'What's it for, Dick?'

'It's a money transfer. There will have been some trade between us and this place and this will settle the account. That's my best guess anyway. Now, finish your tea. We have to get to Martins in Lombard Street.' Martins Bank was a private concern, tracing its origins to the heyday of the London goldsmiths. It had been doing business with Samuel Montagu for more than a century.

Mercifully it had stopped raining. Almost. The weather was what the Irish refer to as sunshine. Walking along Bishopsgate, we ducked into St Helen's Priory church and its former Benedictine nunnery, to emerge via its south door into Leadenhall Street. We weaved our way through its covered market into Gracechurch Street. Thence we ducked down an alley, passing a strange terracotta pub called *The Jamaica*, taking a left to reappear in Lombard Street exactly under the sign of the grasshopper.

'Here we are,' said Dick proudly, in another postroom, over another cuppa. 'You'll never get lost with me, Son.'

This time Dick unearthed bundles of Gold Certificates from his capacious bag. Again, they promised to pay various sums 'as authorised by law', some for as little as $10, some for as much as $1000. These handsome bits of paper meant that Dick did not have to carry bullion in his bag - that would have been illegal, heavy, and an invitation to lurking blackguards.

'Denominated in American dollars?'

'That is the currency that gold is traded in', Dick explained to an idiot.

*

Christmas was almost upon us, and I was back with my family in Ashburn Place and, when Christiane Montagu rang to invite me to her town house in Holland Park for drinks on Christmas Eve, my mother was thrilled.

'You must be doing very well at her husband's bank,' she divined, quite inaccurately.

I think she thought I was dealing in millions, rather than providing the messengers with company. Our own Christmas at home was always taken very seriously. Masses of presents formed a small mountain under the tree which the cat vainly tried to open, even moistening them to loosen the glue.

Our mother had a knack for choosing those little things that suited us well and, of course, we repaid the compliment. Our feast owed quite a lot to France and, perhaps, a little to Austro-Hungary. We would typically begin with some sort of *amuse bouche*. Smoked sturgeon or olives stuffed with anchovies nicely fitted the bill. The *hors d'oeuvres* would be meat, often *bresaola* or *jamon iberico*. The first course was fish; typically a stuffed and baked carp. We would stuff ourselves to a standstill on a main course of roast goose or beef. Turkey, considering it came from Norfolk, Virginia, was

American and Protestant, inappropriate for European Catholics.[17]

Cheese and, finally, pineapple in kirschwasser, signalled that all that was left were Brazil nuts and a snooze in front of Stanley Baxter on ATV.

*

Months passed. Now that we were approaching the Easter break I decided my twentieth birthday needed to be celebrated in style. My 'set' in Harvey Court was not large but if I moved the modest furniture to the wall it could accommodate a dozen people so long as they remained standing. If the weather stayed fine we could always decamp to the garden crater. In Spring, however, English weather is notoriously unpredictable.

I had a number of data-entry punch cards, those postcard-sized pieces of cardboard used at the time to put numbers into the machines. I spent a tedious day carefully clipping the cards so that the recipients could read their names and see the time and place.

Then came the question of money and the non-negotiable fact that I didn't have any. I was moaning about this in the college bar when a chum came up with an interesting suggestion.

'People are suggestible,' he explained. 'They will see what they are told they can see. If you pour cider from a champagne bottle, they will believe they are drinking Epernay's finest.'

'Really?' I said as The Idea materialised above my head. Empty Champagne bottles were easy to locate - there was always a plentiful supply just outside the dons' Senior Combination Room. Presumably Champagne helped them kill time.

Now was the time to test the theory. I liberated one and carefully decanted a bottle of Bulmers' very

---

[17] Americans like to abbreviate 'White Anglo-Saxon Protestant' to 'WASP'. I'm glad they never abbreviate 'White Anglo-Norman Catholics'.

driest into it. When Andrew Clement came over a little later I tried it out on him. Two champagne glasses and the bottle that had once held Pol Roger was removed from its cooler with a carefully rehearsed flourish.

'Bit early for me,' he said. It was not quite midday. He then drank his glass without further comment. Twenty minutes later the bottle was empty. Of course, even if Andrew had sussed my secret he still might not have said anything. His manners were perfect. The experiment needed to be repeated with someone who said what he thought. Jocelyn Crocker, however, managed to wrong foot me, but in the nicest if oddest way.

'This champagne is rubbish,' he ruefully observed after a single sip. 'Wait there. I have something rather better in my set.'

Three minutes later he was back with an unopened bottle of *Dom Perignon*. 'I always buy this one. I find that girls like the shape of the bottle better.'

*

In London, my great aunt Christine had told me how my great-grandfather John Henry Frederick Bacon, a highly successful portraitist in the Edwardian era, had invited the king and queen to his studio in Queensgate. On one occasion George V and Queen Mary had accepted but brought a clutch of royal princelings with them.

Princes Henry, George and John were intrigued by the paints and brushes and were a right royal nuisance, Aunt Christine told me. To make matters worse, they were determined to discover how the pianola worked.

They were amazed by the portrait studio lighting, which they playfully rearranged. Finally the king authorised the artist to confine the boys to the library.

'They don't read so they should be safe there, unless you keep a train set on the shelves. They want to be engine drivers when they grow up.' Do engine drivers, for their part, wish to be small boys? Their doting father continued with his assessment. 'No need to worry about the boys' aversion to them,' said their doting father, before adding that in royal circles at least, 'aversions are both hereditary, compulsory and irreparable.'

It was time to make amends for such lèse-majesté and I sent the Prince of Wales a punchcard invitation to my party, enclosed in a letter of apology for the brief captivity of his forebears. I had the prince's reply by return.

He declined, of course, but had the courtesy to explain or pretend that he had a prior commitment. He had to catch a train, he wrote. He also took the trouble to apologise 'for the paint-throwing inclination of my forebears'.

When his letter was shown to my great aunt, she was very satisfactorily moved.

*

I have since learned that in fact he had a date with a certain Camilla Rosemary Shand. To entertain this singularly beautiful young lady he had commandeered the royal train, which would steam out of Cambridge in its stately way. Once dinner had been served to the happy couple, a sated prince and blond paramour could retreat to the royal sleeping car for a night cap after their meal. The train would not reappear in Cambridge until the following morning.

*

I decided that I might take the chance with the cider, but what about the smoked salmon?

As it turned out, my guests would happily tuck into carefully boned thinly sliced raw kipper, laid on buttered brown bread and liberally seasoned with salt, pepper and lemon juice.

*

Easter was upon the world but your author chose not to spend his University holidays in the City.

Peter Cooper and I had decided to hitch-hike to Paris. Peter needed to celebrate his recent commission in the Royal Signals and had to celebrate before the army began to control his every move.

Of course, and like me, he had 'O' Level French, which served no purpose whatsoever, save a passing acquaintance with a few irregular verbs. Our French master had said the point of a language was to read its literature. I had carefully opened a work of Racine and closed it rapidly. I already knew that the point of a foreign language was to order a brew.

Peter was based in Sandhurst, while I was in South Kensington. We compromised on Croydon, our Millets backpacks over our shoulders. Our wallets held £5 apiece. The Bank of England would only allow us £50, but neither of us could raise anything like that. Mind you, £5 was still quite a lot in those days. After all, lunch cost three bob.[18]

As I remember, it had been my silly idea. I had been challenged by horses and the piano, but was more determined to learn French than ever. But just how was this going to happen? I had spent ten minutes in front of the mirror mouthing phrases like *la plume de ma tante est plus longue que le pène de mon oncle*. Nearly cracked it, I decided.

Standing by a roundabout, it started to rain. The 'humorous' words, *Dover and Out*, on our cardboard sign began to run. Even worse, the card itself was beginning to dissolve.

No cars stopped for us. Their drivers had no need of two dripping, badly dressed young men on board. We were about to call it a day when a lorry pulled into the

---

[18] 15p. Exchange controls in the UK were not abolished by Prime Minister Margaret Thatcher's Conservative Government in October 1979.

lay-by and a hairy haulier beckoned us in. Unfortunately, he was not going as far as Dover.

It was dark before we reached those greyish cliffs. If there had been bluebirds, we did not see any. Peter was not going to give up (though I would have done at the drop of a hat) so we trudged on, still waving our futile thumbs over an empty sea of tarmac. Finally, at midnight, we were at the ferry terminal.

'Sorry, Gents, the next crossing is at 5 am tomorrow.'

Peter looked at me as if this were all my doing.

'There are some benches over there,' I weakly suggested.

'Sod that,' said Peter. 'Some holiday. To make it worse, we will have missed the last train home.'

We moved to the benches.

'Don't even think of it, lads,' said the official, not unkindly but firmly.

'We're locking down the terminal. You'll find a B & B in Dover somewhere. If, that is, they haven't already shut.'

We smooched around Dover for two sodden, irritable, argumentative, disillusioned hours. Dover had dozens of cheap hotels, but most had signs in their windows saying 'No Vacancies'. We rang the bell of half a dozen of ever less exclusive guest houses. Their signs said 'No Irish'. I began to wonder if some Hibernian horror had once occurred in Dover.

At last, one let us in.

*

When at last we woke it was too late for breakfast. As the bathroom was locked, and from within came the tuneless aria of a contented bather, it was time to check out. Our ten bob had earned us a few hours sleep and honorary membership of the Great Unwashed. To make matters worse, it was now raining heavily.

'I know you'll think me a damp squib and you're half right. I may even be the whole thing, if I actually knew what a squib was,' said Peter.

'What are you trying to say?'

'If hitch-hiking is this hard, where we can speak the language, it will be worse in France. Let's call it a day.'

Thus ended my first lesson - as an adult, anyway. How not to cross the sea to France.

*

When I spoke to David Montagu about the long summer vacation, he hesitated.

'Our problem is that we have arranged for another student to join us. You may know him - you and he are, I think, at the same college. His name's Philip Afia.'

'I do know him. Like me, a Highgate man but not, I think, one of Sir Mark's poor scholars.'

'Well, if you get on, we could put you through the ropes together. Fancy that?'

I did.

'He'll be a credit to your generosity, Sir.'

'Yes. On that matter, it seems, you and his father agree.'

Philip was the quiet type, dead set on a career in banking. I felt that long before his gold watch was delivered he would be on the board of half a dozen public companies. We were both assigned to Bill Discounting and were seated across a pair of metal desks, facing one another. Our team leader was in charge of issuing trade bills, the preferred means by which the bank lent a company capital. Instead of lending it, say, £1000, it lent them £950. That was a discount of £50, but the company would still have to pay £1000 on the redemption date. The size of the discount represented the customer's credit rating, the cost of money in the money

59

market (i.e., what would the merchant bank have to pay for it – it was never its own money after all), the chances of repeat business and the general desirability of the deal. A large number of variables.

I thought it a trifle dull but Philip took to it like a duck does to a puddle. I was still reflecting on my inability to master the tamest of nags or to make an impression on the ivories of the Chelsea Arts Club's piano. I had relegated French, for the time being, to the nice-to-have.

I was also aware that I had less than a year before my finals and had done so little work that I was in danger of qualifying out of any career anywhere.

*

My Supervisor - the title the university gives to whom everyone else would call a 'tutor' - had been asking me some very testing questions on such geniuses as Galen or Galileo.[19]

When he asked me about Dr Frankenstein, I thought he might be teasing me but I did my best to argue that, while fictional, in some way he summed up the spirit of his age.

'Mary Shelley,' I ventured, 'was asking the world if the creation of life might not be confined forever to God. Perhaps someday Mankind might also be able to do it? Would that make God redundant? And if so, what would be the result?'

My Supervisor leant back.

'Fiction often anticipates discovery. Read more. Begin with Paradise Lost - especially Book Seven. Milton saw more clearly than most how the wholly mutable concept of 'common sense' shifts every decade

---

[19] To make matters even more complicated, a 'tutor' in Cambridge is a don 'in loco parentis' to a small number of students. This today is for the most part a nice matter only, since the age of majority was reduced from 21 to 18 in 1970 in the UK (and 1971 in the USA).

or so. The tragedy of Man is that hardly anyone notices.'

He looked at his class rather levelly.

'Is the world flat? "Of course it is" was once the answer. Today, everyone would say, "of course it's not". Common sense is as fickle as a girl.'

I don't think he liked girls that much. No question, nevertheless; I should buckle down. Holiday work and holiday pay were all very well, but course work would be vital to whatever came next.

*

In 1969, the 'pocket Venus' Ana Bianchi was 'doing the season', while her elder brother Carlos was a fellow student me at Cambridge.

Carlos J Bianchi and I had become chums. He was Chilean. Having a keen sense of justice he was all too aware that a diabolical coupling of ruthless politics and desperate poverty had deprived many of his countrymen of equable governance and a fair future. Their father had been ambassador to the Court of St James until his untimely death. That was when his widow had married Jack Sangster, then chairman of BSA. Philanthropist versus arms dealer? A strange raft in a troubled sea.

The family lived in London's Belgravia and would make an occasional retreat to their country house in Bembridge, a sailing resort on the Isle of Wight. This will be why the odd idea came to me that I might advance my cause with the adorable Ana if we 'accidentally' met in Bembridge.

A huge pop concert was going to happen down there that very summer, which gave me an 'innocent' motive to further my acquaintance. Money was again the fly in the ointment. I hardly needed to check my pockets to know I couldn't possibly afford to go to the Isle of Wight. Travel, a four-day festival and an hotel, together they would break me.

Yet the more I thought about it the more I was hooked. This was the 1960s, the greatest decade since the 1920s when Cole Porter had sung *Let's Do It*, George Gershwin had written *The Man I Love* and Irving Berlin was delivering *What'll I Do*.

The line-up this time was equally dazzling. The Foulk brothers had assembled an incredible roll call of artistes - the heroes of our generation - to line up on the Festival Program. I had stumbled upon the apogee of popular music, in which every band in the land was at the peak of its career.

The Who had released their rock opera *Tommy*. Everyone else was humming or whistling *Summertime Blues, I Can't Explain* and, indeed, *My Generation*. Joe Cocker had just released *With a Little Help From My Friends*. The *Moody Blues* had just cut *Knights in White Satin* and *The Pretty Things* had brought out *Don't Bring Me Down*. The *Bonzo Dog Doo-Dah Band* would surely play *The Intro And The Outro*.

The year's surprise was Bob Dylan. No one had heard much from Dylan since his near-fatal motorcycle accident three years before. Having shunned Woodstock, even though it was near his home in upstate New York, he had been reluctant to stage a comeback on the Isle of Wight. The Foulk brothers showed him a short film of the island's literary heritage. It was a shrewd move, as Dylan would prove enthusiastic about combining a family holiday with a live performance in 'Tennyson country'.

His latest album, *John Wesley Harding*, had already soared to the top of the charts. There was hardly a soul between the ages of 15 and 30 who didn't want to hear him sing *Mr Tambourine Man, I Pity The Poor Immigrant, I'll be Your Baby Tonight* and, of course, *Maggie's Farm*.

The Dylan family was scheduled to come to Britain on the QE2 but, when their fleet-footed son Jesse collided with a cabin door and had to be rushed to hospital, Dylan looked likely to miss the gig. Only at the last minute did he decide to come by plane.

*

I withdrew what I could from my meagre bank account, packed my hold-all and set off on the road to Southampton, driven by hope and thumb. My hope was good and so was my thumb.

At least this time it didn't rain. I had allowed myself all day to get to the coast, and a good thing too. An affable lorry driver took me most of the way. A bus would provide the last leg, but it was mid-afternoon when I bought my ferry ticket.

As I stepped onto the Hard at East Cowes the sun was about to set. My mind was focussed on the issue of how to get to The Royal Spithead Hotel in Bembridge, fifteen miles away, far too far to walk.

*

The artistes had planned things rather better. Dylan and *The Band* were already at Maggie's Farm, to be joined at rehearsal by George Harrison.

It was Saturday, August 30, the day before Dylan would take to the stage. John Lennon and Ringo Starr had already arrived on the island, along with Keith Richard and Eric Clapton. Bringing up the rear, so to speak, were the 'wags', Pattie Harrison, Yoko Ono and Maureen Starkey. So too were Jane Fonda, Françoise Hardy, Georges Moustaki and Elton John.

If I had known any of this I would not have bothered going. Rooms in the Spithead were going to be rarer than hens' teeth, but I didn't and soon I was in the passenger seat of an elderly motorcar. It was ten o'clock at night when the driver put me down at Westridge. I had travelled six or seven miles and it was growing dark.

I was twenty years old, brimming with unbridled and inappropriate optimism, but now what was I to do? It occurred to me that if I slept in a barn somewhere I

63

would save the cost of a night in what sounded like a Grand Hotel.

I was in farming country. Not much happens on farms before the harvest and after the plough. It was in August and I shinned a five-bar gate, headed towards a large barn and went inside. The place was filled with bales. There was a Land Rover parked by the entrance and a gallery stacked with straw. The latter would do nicely. I climbed the ladder, lay down on a bale and was almost immediately in the Land of Nod.

I was troubled by the most graphic of horror dreams. Giant rats had found their way into my subconscious. They were wearing bibs, white gloves and were carrying knives and forks. They had settled onto my naked feet and were preparing to devour them.

A short sear of pain brought me to my senses. Looking at my feet I saw two huge rats, not dressed for dinner but hungry, nevertheless. With surprising agility I propelled the plague-bearing enemy into the barn below. I was not prepared to be a midnight feast to a pair of peckish rodents.

The Land Rover looked a better bet. I glanced at my watch as I climbed down from my eyrie. Even as early as four o'clock there was a hint of light in the sky. It would soon be dawn. Moments later I was stretched out on the bench seat in the rear, comfortably pushing up the Zs.

I might have slept there much longer had it not been for the beam of a flashlight in my face.

'What the hell are you doing in my car?' asked an annoyed farmer, not unreasonably. A difficult question to answer when it's six o'clock in the morning and you're still half asleep.

'I'm on my way to Bembridge,' I replied. 'Sorry. I ran out of light.'

To my amazed relief he smiled.

'Then you won't have had breakfast. Put your shoes on and come into the farmhouse. My wife will cook up some bacon and eggs for us and I'll drive you to Bembridge myself.'

*

The Royal Spithead Hotel, a large, ramshackle purpose-built hotel, dating back to (I suspect) the 1890s when the Isle of Wight had been considered 'abroad', or as close as dammit, found me at reception. I asked if by any chance there was a room of any kind to be had.

'During the Festival? Have you been too long in Parkhurst? Are you actually mad?'

Perhaps I was. It rather seemed as though I was destined to spend another night in a million-star hotel. The open air, in other words. The concierge looked me up and down and made a fast assessment of my means.

'You may use the public rooms,' he volunteered, his tone surprisingly emollient.

'Thank you,' I sleepily replied. 'I'll find a coffee somewhere.'

'The dining room is over there. Charge your coffee. When you're asked which room you're in, say 'Peter's spare'. It's a redundant maid's room. That's code - you won't have to pay.'

What did this mean? Did I look so down and out I needed charity? That's not to say I was unhappy, and nor was I in the mood to look this gift horse in his mouth. After ten minutes in a bathroom somewhere, I looked a good deal better. Not prosperous, perhaps, but tidier at least.

Wandering into a deserted if aforementioned dining room - a large Victorian saloon that had seen better days - I saw the coffee urns, poured myself a cup and took a seat near the great expanse of window, overlooking the sailing club and its harbour.

'Good heavens!', I heard a voice say. 'It's Jeremy Macdonogh!'

Turning around I found myself rising to say hallo to Vanessa Gent, one of that year's debutantes.

'Are you here for the Festival or the sailing. Or both?'

'The festival. My aim is to see Bob Dylan strut his stuff.'

'Too good a gig to miss?' Vanessa suggested.

*

But what exactly *was* I doing there? The Festival was both free and enticing, but that was not the entire reason why I had made the trip. Nor did I even know for certain if Ana was actually on the Isle of Wight.

Time for another coffee and some deliberation. People always say coffee is good for the brain. I'm not convinced but, since the bar was not yet open, real brain fuel was unavailable.

'I'll be going to the farm after breakfast,' Vanessa was saying. 'Julie Felix will be on at eleven. Her, or Gary Farr.'

Two others had blearily emerged from their slumbers to join Vanessa.

'Come on, Gent!' one of them coaxed. 'We mustn't miss *Marsupilami*, must we?'

He turned to me.

'You coming?'

'Thanks but I'll wait till after lunch. I may catch Marsha Hunt before the big guy comes on.'

'Suit yourself. See you later.'

*

Oilskins and cable-knit pullovers were now filled with all shapes and sizes of sailors, and the dining room was doing the same. They were treating themselves to a hearty breakfast before putting out to sea, not intending to be back until the time came for a sundowner.

I had another coffee, courtesy of Peter's Spare, and took it onto the terrace. From the general direction

66

of Maggie's Farm I heard the sound of a guitar testing a sound system and a voice announcing what sounded like *Marsupilami*, who turned out to be an English prog rock band who had borrowed their name from a Japanese cartoon character. One thing was certain; we could easily hear the music from the hotel.

The Spithead staff were clearing the dining room and the shutters over the bar were being cranked open. Beer o'clock. I checked my wallet. Would I be pushing my luck if my potion were charged to Peter's Spare?

It was around midday when the less intrepid sailors began to return from Neptune's kingdom for lunch. Anything but fish. That was when I saw Carlos, heading for the loos to peel himself out of his oilskins.

'Hullo!' I said, rather obviously.

'Jeremy! Good God! What are you doing here? You're not a sailor, are you?'

'I came to see Bob Dylan.'

'Well, you can't possibly stay here. Go and pack your things. You're staying with us. No, I insist.'

'That's more than kind. Give me ten minutes to check out, and then I'm yours.'

'You'll join Raymond and me for lunch first?'

This was awkward indeed. A hotel lunch would clean me out. But how could I duck it and keep face?

'Don't worry about lunch. I only finished a late breakfast an hour or so ago. You and Raymond should have yours. I'll read the paper in the bar.'

'That's fine. We'll be sticking to something light in any case. Give us half an hour and we will head home.'

The Sangster house in Church Road, Bembridge, looked as if it had been parachuted in from Santiago. A single story ranged around a pool, a vast lawn and a tennis court. Mrs Sangster, Jack's wife, welcomed me as if she had been expecting me all along.

'You've already met Raymond. You did know he's who's doing something admirable for the D of E people?[20] Jack's rather busy in his office at the moment but he'll join us for an early dinner. I am guessing you will all be going to the Festival and catching Dylan's set. He's not expected to play much before ten this evening.'

She glanced at my hold-all. 'You are travelling light. Most commendable. I'll tell Jack not to dress for dinner tonight.'

I knew of Sangster but, obviously, had never met him. I knew he was or had been chairman of BSA, the bicycle maker. He had famously ousted Sir Bernard Docker to become its chairman, ten or so years before, and had done exceptionally well. Millionaires in the '60s were still quite rare. Of course, I didn't know the half if it.

*

We played croquet on the Sangsters' immaculate lawn all afternoon, accompanied in the distance by the clear sounds of Aynsley Dunbar filling the ears of ten thousand happy young pop pickers.

'Jack will join us a little later. He's busy with his charities,' his wife informed us.

The man in question duly made his appearance at a little after six, pre-loaded with a gin and tonic in his hand. He cut an elegant figure, a trim man of 73, fit and athletic. He was blessed with an intelligent brow and a penetrating eye.

'Raymond, good to see you. How's my princely Greek friend treating you?'

'Very well, Sir.'

'And you will be…'

'Jeremy Macdonogh, Sir.'

'How d'you do. Friend of Carlos, I presume?'

'Yes, Sir. We're both at Cambridge.'

'Really? A fellow lawyer?'

'Not in my case. History and philosophy.'

---

[20] Duke of Edinburgh award scheme.

'Indeed? Latterly I've taken an interest in philosophy. Do you know what I do?'

'Don't you manufacture bicycles?'

Jack Sangster laughed.

'Good shot! I used to, yes,' he laughed, 'and I'm proud of it. My father's company produced bicycles for both the police and military. He built a folding bicycle for the Army during the Great War and the folding 'Paratroopers Bicycle' during the Second. He also supplied the Irish Army with bicycles after their civil war. I was destined to step on his pedals. A little later I produced the first Sunbeam bicycles. You've heard of them? We produced our own *derailleur* gears. We also built motorbikes. We bought the New Hudson motorcycle and bicycle business and followed it up with Triumph Motorcycles. All worked well until 1956, when I sold Triumph to BSA.'

'Sounds as though you did well?'

'Some would say so, yes. I made £2½ million. Not a bad return on the £50,000 I had invested before the war. I was then invited to join the board of BSA and I hope you will indulge me when I tell you we became the largest producer of motorcycles in the world.'

It was time to go inside. There was no trace of Ana. Carlos thought she would still be at the Festival. She and her friends had put up a tent at the farm two days before. Unlikely that they would come back home under any circumstances, even to sleep.

We moved into the dining room where Jack pulled a chair back the better for his wife to sit while the rest of us did that for ourselves. Rather disconcertingly, my place was next to the great man.

The family employed a cook and we were waited on by a male and uniformed servant. Someone, somehow, had managed to put printed menus on the table. Very impressive with so few people either expected or invited. I found out, over the smoked salmon, that Jack - for some reason - expected well-bred conversation from me. I had no choice but to push my luck.

'Your fabulous career started with pushbikes, you said?' I was trying to appear bright and curious. In truth I was overwhelmed and well out of my depth. 'How did you set about making them glamorous? When you started weren't they the transport of last resort for district nurses and postmen?'

Sangster laughed.

'Good question. That was down to the young Bob Maitland. Have you heard of him? No, you won't have - you're far too young. In 1952, BSA launched its professional cycling team. Bob was a successful amateur cyclist. He had been the highest placed British finisher in the 1948 Olympic road race. He joined our team as an independent while working in our design office as a draughtsman. He deserves the credit for our post-war range of lightweight sports bicycles. They were all based on his knowledge of the sport.'

The waiter replaced our empty plates with a *cassoulet de poussin*. There followed some light conversation about sailing and the Festival, but when silence fell I felt the others wanted me to press on with my host. I was encouraged when Mrs Sangster rewarded me with a smile and her husband continued.

'So you owe this spectacular house to bicycles?' I persevered, ignoring my worry that I sounded like David Frost.

'Sadly, the good times were coming to an end. With the end of petrol rationing, fourteen years ago, the demand for bicycles fell. Even so, every cloud has a silver lining. It was the bicycle factory that let us create BSA Motorcycles Ltd.'

'Where you became chairman?'

'Only in '56, after a troubling dispute in the media with my predecessor, Sir Bernard Docker. The shareholders at the Annual General Meeting replaced him as Chairman of the BSA Board with your humble servant.'

'Did Docker have to return his wife's golden 1955 Sebra Daimler coupé?'

'Ha ha! You are very well informed. No. Of course not.'

I was indeed proud of myself. My mother had teasingly spoken about Lady Docker's vast and ostentatious limousine and somehow I had remembered the details.

'Was Raleigh your principle competitor?'

'We sold BSA Cycles Ltd, dealer network included, to Raleigh in 1957. Raleigh produced bicycles in Birmingham, using our parts, up to a few years ago but, as the minutes ticked by, so did they.'

'So that's how BSA bikes succumbed to history?'

'The story is not quite over. BSA bicycles are still manufactured and distributed in India. Alas, there is no direct connection to our Birmingham company.'

'And any spare golden Daimlers?'

'We sold Daimler to Jaguar in '60. Should never have owned it in the first place, in my view.'

The main course had been delicious, the table could now be cleared. As Jack seemed interested in my opinions I pushed on.

'BSA stands for Birmingham Small Arms, doesn't it? Do you still make firearms?'

'A few. We have something of a pedigree. The company supplied the War Office with Patent Rifles as early as 1906. A little too late for the Boer War, sadly, but since then we have been a civilian business.

'Saying that, we still produce the *Sportsman* .22 long range bolt-action rifles, various *Martini* action target .22s, the *Ralock & Armatic* semi-automatic .22 long range weapons, not forgetting various bolt action hunting pieces.'

71

There was a choice of puddings on the menu and, when the waiter reappeared, Jack told him he wanted both. 'Really, Jack,' said Mrs Sangster, affecting a shocked expression. 'You're supposed to choose.'

'I don't see why! Why should I submit to house rules. Especially when they're set by the staff. The fact that I pay for everything gives me certain rights.'

Mrs Sangster sighed. 'Jack, I feel sure you are boring Jeremy, reliving your boardroom battles. These days you're a compassionate humanitarian. You have long shed your arms dealer vestments. Jeremy, know that during the war Jack took under his own roof a couple of bombed out Londoners.'

'Ah yes', said Jack, relieved I thought. 'Gordon and Jean Rookledge. That was in 1944. Gordon went on to become an expert on typefaces.'

'And now there's the Minors' Benevolent Association, the Flying Doctor, the Firefighters' Charity and the RNLI. Earth, air, fire and water. You're in your element, Jack, or should it be elements?'

*

It was time for the Festival's big event.

Ana's tent was easy to find, given that it flew the Chilean flag, and we joined the girls on their groundsheet. I presented them with the bottle of wine that I had been given leave to liberate from the Sangster cellar.

Blodwyn Pig's roadies were clearing their stuff away from the enormous stage. That contagious excitement in the atmosphere infected everyone, and in the audience everyone was smoking - not always cigarettes. We were in excited anticipation of the Big Man (who was quite small) and his band was already checking levels, saying 'one-two-three-testing', as they do, and performing other unfathomable rituals.

There were rumours[21] that one or all of the Beatles would be joining him on stage, and that his comeback show would be the 'gig of the decade', but then the crowd fell silent. Dylan had arrived on earth, dressed in a cream suit.

The Beatles were in the VIP box - not on stage - as keen as the rest of us to see the return of the maestro, whose set opened with *She Belongs To Me*. He followed with *Like a Rolling Stone* and *Highway 41 Revisited*, all in countrified versions. Songs from *Nashville Skyline* and *John Wesley Harding*, included such classics as *It Ain't Me Babe* and *The Mighty Quinn*. I had witnessed a phenomenon.

We weren't home until 2 am, maybe later, exhausted but happy. We had shared an experience, always the bedrock of great friendships. Sadly, I left their house the next day. I had a road to put on the show.

*

The academic year 1969-70 was to be my last at university. My finals would soon be on my shoulders so I had no choice but to apply myself to my studies.

Following my last exam a suite of festivities would ensue. Conspicuous among the balls and parties of my last May Week was the *Pitt Club Ball* and the delicious Angie Kirby had consented to take my arm. Now Dr Kirby and a retired GP, Angie was then a medical student, sharing her rooms in Newnham College with Patricia Hewitt, who would go on to become Minister of Health under Tony Blair. Not merely as bright as a new penny, Angie was also ravishing.

The Ball was a 'white tie' event, while the *Pitt Club*, whose purpose was to give its members a chance to practise being a member of a London club, seemed quite as grand as the *Reform* or the *Garrick*. Dinner had barely

---

[21] John Harris in NME.

been cleared before Brian Ferry and his band - not yet called *Roxy Music* - struck up. Angie and I were immediately making shapes on the floor.

It turned out that we had been noticed. Alexander Fermor-Hesketh came up to me. He was not a student - I had no idea who he was - but he lost no time in putting put me in the picture.

'Sorry to interrupt you, but my host in Cambridge,' and here he nodded in the direction of Prince Charles, 'has noticed your companion and wondered if she might grant him the privilege of a turn around the floor.'

I have to say Angie was not in the least put out by the suggestion.

'You'll come back to me, I hope,' I said to her sorrowfully.

Lord Hesketh spoke directly to the object of princely desire. And mine, I frankly admit.

'Have you already been presented to His Royal Highness?'

'No,' she owned rather ruefully.

'Then, I hope you will allow me to explain one or two little matters of protocol. May we step into the corridor for a moment where we can hear ourselves think?'

I rejoined my table alone, feeling like the proverbial sore thumb. Five long minutes later, Hesketh and Angie reappeared and crossed the floor to the prince. From a distance we watched his courtly nod to the prince and her rather graceful curtsey.

The guests cleared the floor for HRH and Miss Kirby. All were keen to see what they were capable of. Nor was the general delight confined to the two paparazzi who had somehow got tickets. When the number was over, the prince nodded a bow to Ferry, who bent from the waist, and to Angie who bobbed a courtly acknowledgement. Normal service could now be resumed, but fun and games were not quite over.

Less than ten minutes later the prince himself was by our table.

'May I present myself,' he said, wholly unnecessarily. 'Charles Wales.'

I stood, imitating the nodded bow I had seen Hesketh make, and said my how-d'you-do.

'Miss Kirby told me who you were. Your name seemed vaguely familiar but I'm afraid at first I couldn't place it. Then I remembered a most novel invitation to a party. You sent it to me around a year ago.'

'Your delightful reply I still keep, Sir. I showed it to my great aunt, who remembered your grandfather the king from when she was a girl herself. She asked me to pay you her compliments, if our paths should ever cross.'

'Excellent, excellent, and please return my compliments to her. Now, Miss Kirby, a foxtrot?'

A GAP IN THE MARKET

CHAPTER ONE

A Career Begins...
1974

Four years of 'gap year' have passed. The author has somehow acquired French and Italian. Coming home to the 'winter of discontent' and the '3-day week' he is nevertheless offered a position in a major Reinsurance brokerage. He manages a deal to give a scion of the Lemos dynasty his own fleet, and dines well as a result. Now has to buy a flat and face the unhelpful challenge of having no money.

It was now 1974. To some small degree I had grown up, figuratively or literally; be my guest and choose for yourself. I and my country had seen a lot of water flow under the Bridge of Sighs since my days as an undergraduate and my ungainly floundering in a merchant bank. Our ruling parties had foolishly allowed populism to drive the nation into one of the most giddying, vertiginous depressions since the 'thirties.

In 1970 I had been ejected from my ivory-plated tower into an England that was showing the inherent flaws in democracy. Even so, I had been lucky. On a whim I had left for Europe where, as it turned out, I would enjoy a sort of extended 'gap year' in Switzerland, Italy, Germany and France. All the time I had hoped to be back in Blighty, but I was dissuaded by what I read in every newspaper - at every turn, matters at home were growing worse. I did try, once or twice, to get back home, to resume my natural place in the order of things - as a City grandee or captain of industry - but my overtures went unappreciated. Everyone agreed I was better off going back to Europe.

'Don't bother with a return ticket', they quipped and they were right. Without gainful employment in London, I could not even buy a cup of tea, let alone a flat. As things stood my noblest prospect was as a filing clerk at the *Gas Board*. I had thought I might return to the City, clad in that crappy Burton suit, but it would not be to *Samuel Montagu & Co*, alas, not this time. I applied but they wouldn't have me. The financial community was now in free fall: enmired by an oil crisis, stagflation, a property crash, the demise of the secondary banks and a morbid fear of 'automation' – ineluctably associated in the collective mind with wholesale sackings.

Nor was it getting any better. Rubbish was not collected and great unhealthy piles of waste were growing on every pavement. In the Royal Borough of Kensington and Chelsea, my father was losing his patience.

TO THE EDITOR OF THE TIMES

Sir,

I write concerning the affair of the Vanishing Dustmen.

I am glad to hear that Sir Malby Crofton,[22] whom I vaguely remember as having something to do with the rates, has intrepidly journeyed as far as Nevern Square (or did the square go to him?) in his efforts to keep Kensington tidy. May I direct his explorations further? May I be his guide and friend?

It is a pleasing demesne, the Royal Borough, especially when viewed from my end. Until the dustmen departed all we had to entertain us were the matutinal visits from the lower classes in the Boltons with their upper class dogs, trained to defecate on sight of Ifield Road's pavements. Since those dull days, the prospect now includes rats playing merrily, mice morris dancing, cats plastic-bag splitting, and curs bone-hunting among the playgrounds of beautifully disarrayed garbage adorning the kerbs. Bluebottles multiply, smells rise sweetly, and soon, I doubt not, we will

---

[22] Later to become mayor of the R B K & C

welcome a vulture or two. Some may even be on order.

I appeal to Sir Malby and his fellow travellers in the Cleansing Department of this rancid, reeking, rotten borough to journey – pomanders may be worn – to the darker areas of the Fulham Road, and there to take a deep breath. I pray it be not their last.

I have the honour to be, Sir, your obedient servant,

Redmond J Macdonogh

Over-mighty trades unions supported inefficient, over-lengthy production lines, always in the deceptively sweet-sounding name of full employment.

Their motives were not entirely altruistic. The more members they had, the richer their union, the happier they were. The government had allowed our larger industries to automatically deduct 'dues' from their workers' pay-packets.

This was of course a stealth tax. To be fair, it had little choice. The TUC was far more powerful than Wilson's minority government or Heath's opposition. It had terrifying weaponry: non-stop industrial disputes, either over pay or 'manning'. The consequences were predictably stratospheric inflation, a redistribution of profits into wages at the expense of innovation and investment, and bromide in the tea of those who actually wanted rationalisation and new technologies. Europe was calling us the 'sick man', while the US simply laughed at the terminal decline of a former rival and once-imperial power.

Over-employment, in both the private and nationalised sectors, had brought the country to a semicolon, if not quite a full stop. Our cut-back railway system had almost ceased to function - there was too little money to give the drivers and guards the pay rises their unions felt they deserved. The State was forced to rob

Peter to pay Paul - the shortfall in money for wages meant that track maintenance and rolling stock renewal had gone on hold. The standard of comfort in what were still pre-war carriages continued to fall. Glue-on patches appeared on every other seat, not always successfully preventing the springs from coming though. Yes, the costly romance of steam was slowly being replaced by lack-lustre diesel, but the much vaunted wholesale electrification of the network was very far from complete.

Every month, or so it seemed, wages would rise and a train would come off the tracks. The railways, once famed for its Pullman carriages, small passenger compartments, station buffets, restaurant cars with table service, a Flying Scotsman, a Brighton Belle, porters, stationmasters in top hats and prize-winning platform gardens, had exchanged such splendours for the sempiternal gloom of industrial incompetence.

Pretty provincial towns, such as Framlingham, saw their train sets taken away. The Carlisle Viaduct, another monument to a golden age, had fallen into threadbare gloom. Provinces, best accessed by trains, watched their properties fall in value.

Nor was the problem confined to the railways. Fleet Street (for example) was if possible even more overmanned than British Railways. Printers - not editors, journalists or even proprietors - controlled the copy. *Notsober* and *Soddit* (as *Private Eye* memorably renamed *Natsopa* and *Sigat*, the two print unions) were of course hailed by the BBC's lefty druids as the saviours of the working class.

A panglossian promotion of society's also-rans - every fanfare for the common man - guaranteed that the future was hostage to convulsive introversion. Contrarian views were noisily shouted down.

'No one should aspire to civilisation's heights', cried some working class hero.[23] 'The grasping irons of

---

[23] Tarik Ali

ambition, excellence and achievement are merely the driving force behind inequality'.

It was widely agreed that sports should no longer be competitive. These political commentators used the word that contaminates everything it comes into contact with: 'élitist'. It would get worse. Eventually they would coin that dreadful phrase; 'dead white men', suggesting to a receptive and gullible youth that there was nothing to be learned from the works of Shakespeare, the sculpture of Michelangelo, the geometry of Euclid, the music of Mozart or the paintings of Raphael.

Children were encouraged to know so much less than their parents that it drove a sharp and irreversible wedge between father and son. Sadly, after all these years, it still does. Even 'grammar schools', which Attlee, the post-war Labour prime minister, had seen as an escape hatch for the brighter children of the working class, was progressively coming under fire; ironically, from 'the left'. It had dawned on the authors of populism that the best way to subvert inequality - élitism again - is to ensure that everybody is equally held back.

Despite mountains of incontrovertible evidence, the BBC still flinches at the accusation that it was and is a fellow traveller with those who wish to 'dumb down' the nation. They prefer to describe their ethos as one that promotes 'even-handedness', 'fair play', or even 'levelling up'. Being doggedly 'neutral', even when one side of an argument is clearly idiotic, their fanatical desire to drive down the middle of the road suppresses debate and promotes indifference. These quixotic utopians are addicted to their panglossian cause, but in the process they fail to see that their beloved 'equality' has made eunuchs of us all.

Both the 'left' and the 'right', then and now, were becoming progressively frustrated by the BBC. It was becoming outspoken and, on occasion, reckless.

Even as late as 1974, Enoch Powell's 1968 'Rivers of Blood' speech was still reverberating in saloon bars and golf clubs. It had divided the nation. Christopher Hitchens had been arrested and briefly imprisoned for heckling the orator. This legal disruption of the Englishman's right to protest provoked my old friend David Levy to send a bottle of *Bollinger* to Hitchens' cell.

That Powell had been misinterpreted is not surprising. The fault lay with the school curriculum itself. Progressively edited, made more 'accessible'. Sounds good? It involved the removal of ancient Greek in the mid '50s, the deletion of Latin in the late '60s and, finally, culminated in a cull of Grammar Schools up and down the land. In particular, the severing of the hawser that tethered the modern world to the ancient one conspired to ensure that few younger commentators realised that the honourable member for Wolverhampton had lifted his ringing prose from the greatest writer of classical civilisation.[24] Powell sought to remind us of antique concerns over an invasion of Etruscans into Rome across the Milvian Bridge. He conflated it with the migration of ever greater numbers of huddled masses from the former Empire to Britain as nurses, bus conductors and street cleaners, suggesting two millennia later that it would presage disputes at home.

The progressives on the 'left' had ignorantly and absently conspired to change the historical racial mix of the British Isles without regard to Parliament,

---

[24] The expression 'rivers of blood' did not appear in the Birmingham speech except as an English rendition of Virgil's *Aeneid*: 'As I look ahead, I am filled with foreboding; like the Roman, I seem to see the River Tiber foaming with much blood', is what he actually said.

referendum or to history.[25] Powell repeated that history always repeats itself, the first time as tragedy, the second time as farce.[26]

That said, these 'new Britons', immigrants from the British Empire, were built of durable stuff. They were adventurous, intelligent, hard-working and ambitious, and almost always too well educated for the lowly but key roles they were allotted in our forward-facing modern nation.

They ought to have been seen as heroes for rescuing a collapsing UK but instead they provoked envy and hostility from the people, especially the indigenous nurses, bus conductors and street cleaners whose numbers they simultaneously supplemented and supplanted. A higher vantage point might have promoted a more realistic assessment of the way the tide was turning but our politicians and journalists were ever-distracted by salient detail. The debate raged over such banal trivialities as to whether a Sikh should wear his turban while riding his motorbike.

Britain, before and during the Second World War, had not known 'racialism' (as it was called in sociological circles) but now the newspapers adopted the American neologism 'racism' to describe this spring tide of prejudice.[27] It perfectly summed up the new narrow-mindedness. While everyone knew in their hearts that in the Christian way of things it was wrong to be racist, the Press thought 'what of it'? Neither the newspapers nor the House of Commons made the slightest effort to oppose it, yet it had been public policy to import so many West

---

[25] Ironically, Brexiteers at the time of writing (Summer 2019) want to replace our immigrant Europeans by raiding the Commonwealth's limited pool of talent.

[26] This anglicised version of Marx's famous aphorism, which drew on Hegel, originally referred to Napoleon Bonaparte, Louis-Napoleon and Napoleon III. Marx added that 'hope always triumphs over experience' and that 'laughter is the only cure for grief.'

[27] Many of today's schoolchildren think that some sort of institutional prejudice against coloured people existed in England until quite recently. The exact opposite is the case. Racism is an American war-time import.

Indians and Pakistanis of higher than average IQ that it was they who had been, to their own surprise, the wet-nurse of racism.

Had Macmillan's 'wind of change' irreversibly reshaped our green and pleasant land? Too right it had. It had blown down our oaks.

This was by no means the only reason why politicians, in their various assemblies, were in the doldrums. Careerist MPs, mayors, town and parish councillors, all these collective cacophonies could not simply sack their supernumerary miners, steel workers, car makers,[28] or railwaymen and retain their own privileges, seats and stipends, even though they knew in the unsentimental parts of their brains that Progress needs Motive. Full employment is an opiate; it makes innovation unnecessary. All it does is get the ruling party re-elected, which is not necessarily desirable.

'Need' as a classic motive for 'change' is desirable, but 'change' should not be desirable in some abstract way, in its own right. Need is the 'mother of invention', and without need there is no investment and, as a consequence, no growth, no profit, just 'stagflation', the ultimate jargon word of the '70s. Despite grandiose talk of a 'new Britain' needing to be 'forged in the white heat of scientific revolution', alternating governments were all too aware that if they reduced chronic over-manning they would incite riots (of which there were many anyway) or even a civil war.

A silly rumour was circulating that a madman called Colonel Sterling was promoting a *coup d'état* and that Lord Mountbatten had consented to be its figurehead! Democracy was considered (by some) as a silly fancy of Pericles and his Athenian fellow-travellers. In the absence

---

[28] The British Leyland Motor Corporation Ltd (BLMC) was formed in 1968. In 1975 it was partly nationalised. The UK government created a holding company called British Leyland, later BL. By 1978 BL had incorporated most of the British motor vehicle industry.

of bright ideas in high places, the country voted every few months to swap Labour for Tory administrations, or vice versa. Minority governments took turns to pretend to govern. To no avail, neither was better than the last. The whole business was as worrying as hell, but what to do?

Electricity was rationed. The dead went unburied. Restaurants struggled to serve their customers by candlelight, and how they actually cooked their offerings no one seemed to know.[29] Dismissing the level-headed view of experienced personnel managers, I saw myself in a positive light. I had bought my talents in a fantastical European hypermarket, so to speak.[30] I could speak French and Italian, passably well though I say it myself. I fell off horses less frequently than before and could just about manage, after passing through a pain barrier, one of Frederick Chopin's easier nocturnes. I would play it when asked and even when not. While the lunatics were busy ruining UK plc I had even learned Bridge.[31]

In the City, there was just one dim ray of sunlight. The world of international insurance. All over the world, everyone still had to insure their ships, aeroplanes, cars, houses, industries, even lives and, in April 1974, preparing to celebrate my twenty-fifth birthday, I secured an interview.

Togged up in my not-very-smart suit, I made my way to the Non-Marine Policy Wordings and Technical Accounts Department of my new employers, *C T Bowring*, where I hoped I might catch on fairly quickly and be of some limited use ere too long.

I had found a lifeboat in a global storm. £2,800 a year, only slightly less than the new unemployment-busting industry of the traffic warden.

---

[29] We should have done. Commercial ovens are gas powered.

[30] The 'shopping list'? A gentleman can 'ride a horse, speak French and play the piano', my father used to say. There are others who argue that a gentleman is a man who can play the bagpipes and doesn't.

[31] For the story of these years, read *A Gap Year or Two*, by the same author.

Charles Forte's 'Leo' - the restaurateur's primitive mainframe computer - had spawned siblings. In CTB a vast whirring machine, with cogs for a heart, held sample paragraphs in its memory for all its policies. Denis Bentley, my line manager, was kind enough to let me arrange in the right order for the benefit of the company's customers.

I should explain. These 'customers' were not mortals like you and me. They were insurance companies. They insured themselves against some catastrophe that might otherwise turn a year's profit into a loss. This was 'reinsurance' and the policy documents were called 'treaties'. Like bookies, reinsurance brokers laid off risk.

The business itself was hardly taxing. With a fellow conspirator from Cambridge, Roger Huggins, late of Sydney Sussex College, we learned our trade and kept ourselves amused by shooting rubber bands at unsuspecting victims many yards away in our immense office. Our victims never knew who or what had hit them and glared at their immediate neighbours, much to Roger's and my satisfaction. He was a damn good shot.

Our production line was not short of characters. James Cole, our Old Etonian, struggled valiantly to appear the democrat that in his heart he could never be. Francis Green, an autodidact expert on atonal and serial music, could hear the melody in a car backfiring. Harry Chambers, the team dipso, brought a thermos flask of chilled vodka and tonic to the office every morning and would take it to *The Lion* to recharge it at 11.01 am and again at 2.29 pm. He probably recharged it at 5.01 pm when the pub reopened after its manager's siesta. He must have been slowly developing an extreme version of that melancholy condition as he began to turn up in the office wearing the top and bottom halves of different suits.

One member of our team was a former policeman. He had been obliged to seek alternative employment after some goody-two-shoes in the precinct had reported him for selling cannabis to his fellow constables. CTB had sheltered him from the storm.

The office tyrant, Bob Bostock, unwittingly modelled himself on Dionysius of Syracuse. Fastidious, yes, but if you were ten minutes late you were dead. He had a book in which he would note the time of your arrival. James Couldrey unerringly arrived at 9.09 am. Cleverly, his name was always just before Mr Bostock's thin red line declared you officially late. Bostock was a little non-plussed by this strategy. He would eventually demand an explanation.

'So why is it, Couldrey, that you are always precisely nine minutes late?'

'Because the 8.41 from Croydon arrives at Fenchurch Street Station at 9.04 and it takes me five minutes to walk the last leg,'

'Could you not catch an earlier train?'

'Of course I could, but that would deliver me to the office at 8.46. Rather less close to my contractual time of commencement. By taking the later train I am, therefore, more punctual, not less.'

A classic example of broker's logic. Mind you, Couldrey was habitually in the wrong place at the wrong time. One morning, sauntering in, he had paused at a news stand outside the tube station to buy his copy of *The Sporting Life*, as was his wont. Noticing a copy of *Penthouse*, whose front cover pretended to offer the reader intimacy with a pneumatic young lady, how could he resist? He bought a copy for reference purposes and tucked it inside the broadsheet. When he came into the office, nine minutes late as always, he collided with one of our directors, Anthony Robertson. His purchases fell to the floor, *Penthouse* opening at its centrefold.

'How curious,' said Anthony, glancing at the fallen papers. 'I had never realised that *The Sporting Life* had a colour supplement.'

I was to spend a year in this holiday camp.

*

So far, slickerdom was slowly turning me from romantic idiot into automaton, occupying a seat in a huge room next door to *Bowring's* vast *Wang* computer, one of those machines that needed half an acre of air conditioned warehouse to house it. A decade later, it would be replaced by a network of computers, each only slightly larger than a TV set, but back then its dozen operators wore lab coats and surgical gloves, to peer with ill-disguised fear into its Winchester or Memorex drives.

These machines failed from time to time. When they did, no one seemed to know what to do. 'Who do you wing when your *Wang* goes wong?' asked a nervous technician.

At least the computer room had a fail-safe mechanism. If something caught fire, hidden cylinders would discharge a blend of Argon, Nitrogen and CO_2, starving Gargantua of oxygen. Such a download of inert gas was supposed to respect the safety of the staff, supposedly reducing oxygen levels to around 6%, low but high enough to sustain life.

The technicians were not convinced. They thought that in such an event, their only chance of survival would lie in a stampede for the automated self-bolting door, abandoning any unlucky stragglers to asphyxiation within.

*

One day, heading into the basement for lunch in *CTB's* rather good staff canteen, I stopped to look at the corporate notice board, just outside.

There were three items pinned to it that made me smile. The first revealed that the Nation had been invited to vote in a referendum to confirm or reject our membership of the *European Economic Community*. The chairman, Peter Bowring, had attached a personal codicil to a carefully unbiased notice.

> If anyone agrees with the board of their company that the UK needs to ratify the Dublin Accord, they may visit their Polling Stations on their way to these offices and cast a favourable vote.

I decided on the spot that I would do this exactly. It meant a lie in and a little longer in the pub the previous night. It was also my duty. I was a European, after all, raised in England and Ireland, and educated at the *University of Life* in Switzerland, Italy, Germany and France.

The second notice reminded Old Etonians that they should not wear their old school ties the forthcoming 4th of June. The reason for this discretion was not given but Dick Cazenove would later explain to me that the chairman did not want to advertise just how many Old Etonians there were in the company.

The third was simpler. It merely announced a meeting of the *CTB* Mountaineering Society, and that it would take place in the basement. Some wag had written below 'why the basement?' and, naturally, another had written 'because it's there'.

*

Elsewhere, all was change. *Mutatis mutandis*. My mother had moved from Ashburn Place, off the Gloucester Road, to a mansion flat in Earl's Court.

My younger brother was about to begin his first year at Balliol, my sister would shortly come down from Somerville and I had found somewhat rundown digs, improbably located in Eaton Terrace, near Sloane Square.

I would share them with some highly-charged lads. Our house resembled the wonderful TV sit-com, *The Young Ones*, but *avant la lettre*. One of my new house-mates was the hon. Nicholas Monson, heir to sprawling acres in Lincolnshire, a plantation in Jamaica and a town house just off High Street Kensington.

Another was the playful Jeremy Browne. Both these young men had gorgeous ladies on their arm - Paula Yates in Nick's case and Pru Murdoch in Jeremy's. Jeremy's relationship with Pru was, I believe, platonic. She was very young but so very well-developed that he may have been deceived. She was certainly wilful enough to know her own mind.

Nicholas was a talented poet, deservedly encouraged by John Betjeman, while Hughie Green's illegitimate daughter Paula's talents lay elsewhere. All too aware of her lissom figure, once in the discreet surroundings of Nick's room, she would change into something more comfortable. Nothing.

Nick had yet to begin a career as a journalist in the Murdoch empire, while Paula also had to begin hers as a music journalist - let alone marry Bob Geldorf - but she had made a start by posing for the occasional centrefold. Whenever I popped into Nick's room for a glass of wine, I would find her in her birthday suit, lying like a siren on Nick's bed.

No doubt she was waiting for his muse to abandon him and let him pay her the attention she deserved. If I might have found it a distraction, Nick seemed merely to dismiss it as a fitting tribute.

Jeremy Browne, for his part, was already a Lloyd's broker, at least he was on weekdays between 9 and 5. The rest of the time he was a semi-professional hellraiser. His partner in crime, Gervase Williams, liked little better than to rattle the cage of any complacent young gentleman enjoying a quiet drink.

Gervase was the brighter of the two but Jeremy was quick and extremely agile. If push came to shove, Jeremy would always pull through. It didn't take much to set him off and he was easily able to bear a grudge for a calendar year. Or decade.

One evening, sipping a pint in *The Antelope*, almost next door to my stately residence, I saw for myself the man in action. Jeremy had recognised someone who had once annoyed him; most likely, some considerable time before.

The poor fellow in Jeremy's sights was quietly enjoying a glass in the company of his intended. Excusing himself, Jeremy left my side to go to the ill-fated man's table, reach over it and take hold of the poor chap's shoulders. He lifted him *at arm's length* into the air.

'I've never liked you,' he said quietly, while the poor man's girlfriend began to panic. 'I recommend you leave and take your strumpet with you.'

If I have failed to render his words in their original Anglo-Saxon, that is their sense. The young couple made for the door, *post haste*. I still wonder if their engagement survived the ordeal?

Jeremy's occasional companion, Pru, was the eldest daughter of the illustrious newspaper magnate, Rupert Murdoch. She had moved to London shortly after her father had bought the *News of the World*. She was now at some state school in London, about to retake her 'O' levels. Jeremy said she was a poor scholar and even I saw she was capricious.[32] I liked her but she was certainly wilful. In due course her father would rehouse her in

---

[32] She is now an executive board member of ***Times Newspapers Ltd*** (2011—present) and a non-executive board member of ***News Corporation*** (2011—present).

New York. Her transgressions in London were soon forgotten.

It isn't easy for a girl to become a woman while her playground contemporaries are playing hopscotch. Her venal sin lay in growing up too early.

Nicholas, a born organiser, had been roped into resurrecting the recently defunct *Queen Charlotte's Ball*. He recruited a committee to set about the challenge with almost-religious devotion. While he had my utmost support, many thought that to curtsey to a cake was simply too silly. Since the monarch was no longer interested in accepting the homage of the nation's debutantes, was the whole concept terminally outdated? Except, said Nicholas (and I agreed), it had never been the concern of the nation. He asked me to write something in the ball's programme.

'What would you like? A eulogy to a fading era?'

'Anything you like, old boy. Never mind the quality; the programme needs people to feel the width.'

Anything to oblige. I wrote a humoresque, a satire perhaps - a short story very vaguely in the inimitable style of P G Wodehouse - about my new friends. I set it in the shade of Dracula's Transylvanian castle. The publishers insisted on a few minor changes but printed it anyway. Most of the families that would normally have attended bought tickets to the Grosvenor House event and, as it turned out, Nick's *The Last Ball* was a wonderful celebration.

It was a triumph for me as well. It marked the moment when I became a published author.

*

My friend, David Chaldecott, known as Tev, decided that we needed somewhere to live and that we should share a flat.

David was working for Dmitri Lemos in London's *World Trade Centre*, very close to my offices,

94

and we would meet for lunch from time to time. Lemos's ship-owning family had been involved in the Hellenic merchant marine since the 18th century. In the twentieth, the family had truly stepped up to the plate when, in 1905, Christos Lemos co-owned and captained the *Marietta Ralli*, Greece's first steamship. During the German blockade of the Atlantic trade routes, the family played a major role in shipping grain and other foodstuffs to Britain.

In recognition of their contribution to the war effort the family was among those rewarded with 'Liberty Ships'.[33] They restored the fortunes of every Greek ship-owner after the Second World War. The rather less camera-shy Niarchos and Onassis were also beneficiaries.

In 1969 Dmitri's grandfather was the wealthiest ship-owner in Greece, even richer than the more famous ones. Costas, his father, was already worth $750m and his fleet numbered sixty vessels. With his principal offices in London and New York, he kept a permanent suite in *Claridge's* and *The Lausanne Palace* respectively.

The family hailed from Οινούσσες, or Oinousses, a cluster of islands a mile off the northeast coast of Chios, five miles west of Turkey, historically disputed by the Venetians and the Ottomans. They must have had some military purpose as without water the islands could not be settled, and Tev made sure I knew a little of the archipelago's story.

'In February 1695, Antonio Seno's Venetian fleet had engaged the Ottoman admiral Hüseyin.' I put my glass down to hear better.

"*Mezzo Morto Hüseyin*' the Venetians called him.[34] There were two sea battles. The first saw the Venetians defeated, losing more than a hundred hands with

---

[33] 'Liberty Ships' were transatlantic vessels made in a hurry out of precast concrete.
[34] 'Half dead Hüseyin'.

another three hundred wounded. Three of their ships were lost to Turkish cannon. While the second engagement ended in a score draw, the Venetians lost another three ships and hundreds more lives in the process. The *Fama Volante*, their flagship, was damaged, as were two princely Ottoman vessels, and the colony in Chios became untenable, yet again.

'Seno was forced to abandon the islands, but the Turks would only garrison them for a century or two. Today they are Greek again and now they have desalination plants. Water has made them habitable.'

Every local ship-owning family, like the Lemos, Pateras, Hadjipateras, Kollakis and the Lyras, treats their ancestral turf with great respect and, every summer, the Oinoussian ship-owners return home to relax. Once home, they attend services led by bearded priests at village churches, swim from rocky beaches, and take to their yachts at sundown if not retreating to shaded villas behind the tidy little port.

The islands are secluded and private, rather like their ship-owners. Nor are they the sole domain of millionaires; there are sea captains and nautical mechanics there too. These will spend their evenings on balconies overlooking the coast, strumming their bouzoukis. They like to drink iced coffee on the marble deck of the *Nauftikos Omilos* Sailing Club to watch their children and grandchildren surf, play beach volleyball as might the possessed and paraglide, this time like autumn leaves.

Barely eight hundred people spend the entire year on the islands, but the population swells to three thousand in the summer. There is plenty to do. Oinousses has a merchant marine academy (a boys-only day-and-boarding school), a stadium so lavish it would look smart in Athens itself, a creditable Nautical Museum and a rather large branch of the *National Bank of Greece*.

'If not for the ship-owners, there would be nothing here,' the mayor had liked to sigh. 'Just a handful of shepherds.'

Back in the mid-'60s, however, Dmitri was yet not ready to follow in his father's footsteps. Instead, he took $1000 to London and set himself up as a *boulevadier*. $1000 may not seem a great deal, but he made it work. He moved into the newly built Hilton hotel and, in the late afternoon, he would saunter to the equally new *Playboy Club*, also in Park Lane. He would play craps, I believe, until he had made a clear, tax-free profit of $100. Then he would go home. That was enough, in the day, to pay his hotel bill of $25 a day, to feed him and to provide him with a high-maintenance companion across the dining table.

For several years this formula had worked well but, one day, the dice decided not to favour him. In 1971, his $1000 now belonged to Hugh Hefner.

It was time for Dmitri to get a job. Mercifully, his father was ready to start the prodigal up with a company of his own.

*

Just three years later, in 1974, Dmitri had his own fleet. Since it had been acquired piecemeal, each vessel was separately financed and insured. Tev asked me if I had any bright ideas.

C T Bowring owned a merchant bank, *Singer and Friedlander*. *CTB* also had a powerful marine division, its oldest division, in fact. It dated from when the company had been a waterfront operation in Merseyside, looking after goods and chattels as they made their way to and from the New World.

I was surprised to discover in our internal telephone directory that the company had a business development director. I made an appointment to see him. He was as surprised to see me as I was him. I knew little about banking, and even less about insuring a fleet.

My presentation must have verged on the preposterous but I will say I was listened to politely.

Within a month, *Singer's* had packaged Dmitri's complex portfolio of large and small financing and CTB had insured his every ship. After such rationalisation, Dmitri was sufficiently flush to celebrate with the purchase of another LPG tanker.

*

Tev called to invite me to his office to meet his grateful boss.

Dmitri was gratitude incarnate.

'I asked Tev to bring you into the office so that I can thank you in the Greek way.'

The Greek way? What was that? Was he offering a fat reward?

'I'd like you and Tev to have supper, on me. Anywhere you like. *Mme Prunier* is very good. Or you might enjoy *Claridge's*?'

'The two of us?' Tev queried.

'No, no, bring a couple of young ladies, by all means. I mean you to enjoy yourselves.'

'When should we go?'

'Ah, yes, it has to be soon. I'm off to Oinousses on Friday. Let me know before you dine so that I can make sure the restaurant is happy with your expenses.'

It was Tuesday. Tev and I began our telethon, trying to find London's finest restaurant. That was our first problem - all such restaurants had been booked well in advance. We crossed *Prunier's* and *Claridge's* off our list. The next to be erased was *The Mirabelle* and the *Ritz* was closed for restoration. It took us 'til Wednesday before we secured the Royal Suite at the *Dorchester*.

'You obviously expect to get lucky,' said Dmitri with a sly chuckle, when Tev told him where we had finished up.

The suite was stunning, vast and the epitome of *grand luxe*. Gilded wood, carved to look like branches, grew over the interior walls. A great and classic Champagne, with a note from Dmitri, was on an occasional table welcoming us into our overnight residence.

We had a drawing room, two bedrooms, a balcony overlooking the park and our own dining room, in which a *Dorchester* footman would serve dinner. Two bathrooms, apparently hewn from single pieces of marble, were ready for us as was a wonderful dressing room to enable our ladies to repair their faces in the morning.

There was just one problem in this little corner of paradise. There were no ladies.

Tev and I, inexplicably, had lost the magic wand we were convinced we owned. Our hypothetical companions had never believed a word we said.

'Come now, you're making this up.'

'I wasn't born yesterday.'

'You're suggesting a one night stand?'

'A foursome? Are you two off your rockers?'

Far from having a queue of beauties that stretched around the whole of Mayfair, it was slowly dawning on us that we would be dining alone.

'Should we ask Dmitri if we could postpone until he's back from Oinousses?'

'He won't agree to it, believe me. His gesture is already completely out of character. We would be lucky to get a plate of *dolmades* in a taverna when he's back. I'll tell you what. I'll bring a VHS, *Blazing Saddles*. After we've eaten we can watch it.'

In the event, the food was seriously good. Peter Kaufeler, a good friend, lived not so far away. His father was Head Chef at the Dorchester, one of the most illustrious kitchens in the known world, that is.

Gourmets worshipped the ground he walked upon if his feet actually condescended to touch solid ground.

It was his food that Tev and I had shared on our strange stay in his hotel. Plate after plate of ambrosia, washed down with nectar, were delivered by liveried flunkeys.

Only the absence of nymphs sullied our foretaste of Elysium.

*

A week or so later, back at my desk at *CTB*, I was looking in my book of paragraphs for one that dealt with strikes, riots and civil commotion.

An elegant figure was standing beside me and looking at me with faint curiosity. 'I've been told that you speak Italian,' it said. 'For my sins, I suspect, I have our Italian account,' said Simon de Burgh Galway. 'You might be able to help me out from time to time.'

*

Tev had found a flat for sale in Lawrence Street, Cheyne Row, deep in the heart of Chelsea.

'It has three bedrooms', he told me, 'a hall that might become a library, a small dining room, a large kitchen, and an ample drawing room, and it overlooks the Thames.'

It sounded fantastic. It was on sale at £20,000, which was six and a half times my current salary and I could not even afford my half of the deposit. Certainly not my half of the mortgage. But why let reality get in the way of a lucky break? Tev was decisive.

'Just write down your income on this form here. Initial here. And here. Thank you. Now I can raise the entire sum. Don't worry! Just pay half our outgoings and you'll be on the deeds as 50% owner.'

He paid the deposit in its entirety and negotiated the mortgage singlehandedly.

'Tev, there's a place reserved for you in paradise. You have the keys? Let's go and inspect it straight away!'

*

What I saw was daunting, to say the least. It had last been decorated in time for the Festival of Britain.[35] A small antediluvian *Ascot* boiler noisily heated the bath. Judging by the trickle of lukewarm water it produced, Tev and I would have to bathe on alternate days. The bath itself had a strange brown gulch running its length. I hesitated to guess where the stain came from. It had no central heating. The sash of one of the drawing-room windows had come apart and the top half had fallen open. It was not possible to close it and the threadbare fitted carpet beneath had been bleached by an incoming alternation of sun and rain, presumably over many years. The front door showed unmistakable signs of having been jemmied in the not too distant past.

It was not all bad news, however. The church where my father worshipped was a hundred yards down the road and, more important still, the pub was even closer.

'Thirst after righteousness' may be a commandment. It is certainly somewhere in the scriptures. It is also the case in Chelsea. Even the pub's sign depicted the crossed keys to the heavenly kingdom, of which the disciple Peter is the gatekeeper.

*

On a typical Sunday, Fred the Bartender would unlock the door at the third stroke of Big Ben's great bell's tolling of noon and half the parishioners of the Holy Redeemer would be in the pub before the twelfth.

Fr Alfonso de Zulueta, the parish priest, would be there at 12.02. He needed a few more seconds than the rest of us in order to shed his vestments and shake hands

---

[35] 1951

101

with the English and European nobility that he so much liked to garner in his church.

At the table nearest to the garden door my father would sit with the church choir, made up of the pretty Sarah Owen[36] and the extended 'von Trappe' tribe of Bevans, for whom Gregorian Chant was thirsty work. My stepbrother Kevin was also a member of that distinguished caucus.

Crispin Tollast, the property developer, never failed to attend. A very talented fellow - an instinctive negotiator – he was equipped with an infectious sense of humour, the sort that finds the clumsiest attempts at comedy quite riotous. Hilarity being what it is, everyone in his company spent a lot of time laughing alongside like the proverbial drain.[37]

Once his pun was so forced we didn't laugh.

'Ha!' he complained in mock effrontery. 'I see that my witticism is unperceived. I'll quietly replace it in the treasury of my mind.'

John Molony, that same fellow whose picnic party I had joined at that free concert in Hyde Park, had a mother living close by. He would call in when he could. He too was a regular in the Holy Redeemer.

Hugh Vickers, author of *Great Travelling Disasters*, was always there, as were Prophesy and Walter Coles. The industrialist's habits were as predictable as one of Trollope's millionaires. He never missed a Sunday.

Taffy Rhys-Evans worked for *Roneo-Vickers* in Romford, Essex. Someone has to, I suppose, but at least he came into central London to drink. Despite

---

[36] Who would sing Mozart's *Ave Verum Corpus* at my father's funeral in 1986.

[37] Crispin Tollast, now the retired director of a commercial property company, has become the squire of a dreamy 17th-century manor house in the Wylye Valley, Wiltshire, with acres of water meadows, a stretch of celebrated chalk stream and a view over a church and unspoilt village that look like the setting for The Barchester Chronicles. It is a 'piece of paradise' where he and his wife, Ianthe, have brought up three teenage boys. 'We bought it on the basis that we were going to put down roots and slowly but surely restore the house. Cost was pretty much immaterial' he said.

everything he made the effort almost every weekend. He had a great talent, if wasted on Roneo-Vickers. What he didn't know about great music could have been written on a postcard.

The brothers Gervas and James Douglas were diligent devotees of the watering hole; it will have reminded them, surely, of similar watering holes they remembered from them their childhood in Rhodesia.

The only thing missing will have been the mealy beer, to which the Shona and the Ndebele are so partial.[38]

Luke Glass, already a press officer at the *London Stock Exchange*, had been at Oxford with Tev. He was one of our Lawrence Mansions coterie, as was Louise 'Minefield' Mainfeldt who shared a flat in Fulham with Crispin's sister, Feathers, and Louise Allison, the Scottish Lass who had been so kind to me during the occasional English seasons of my 'gap year'.

My current flame, the lovely Adrianna Polenta, would frequently make the journey from Montpelier Square to be there too.

In essence, it was more of a pre-lunch drinks party than a simple quaffing session and, predictably, I became a regular.

The illiberal licensing laws of those days conspired to make us rush our drinks. At half past two, Fred would preface our eviction by grumpily wondering if none of us had homes to go to. Less than a minute later he would refine his impatient mantra to 'time gentlemen, please'. A minute after that, he would inform us that that the 'peelers' were about to revoke the establishment's licence to purvey alcoholic beverages. It was enough.

---

[38] Now Zimbabwe. The Unilateral Declaration of Independence was a statement adopted by the Cabinet of Rhodesia on 11 November 1965, announcing that Rhodesia, a British territory in southern Africa that had governed itself since 1923, now regarded itself as an independent sovereign state. After a civil war, Robert Mugabe became Prime Minister in 1980, and President from 1987 – 2017. He renamed his nation.

Taking the hint, we all left. A number of us to my father and stepmother's house about a mile away. I would sometimes have Adrianna or even Sarah on my arm. The pub had ensured we were a little over-relaxed when we arrived at my father's in Ifield Road. There a sherry would made us even more convivial, despite my father attempts to forbid all further conversation during the closing bars of a Mozart opera. Then could we could repair to the dining room.

Wendy, my stepmother, was a great cook and I always looked forward to lunch. Her rare roast beef would almost set me up for the week. Her boys, Kevin and Gareth, were my step-brother and my half-brother respectively. They were still young but were progressively adept at adapting to the rocket-fuelled banter. They also helped bring down the average age.

*

If getting to the pub was a doddle, the office was more of a challenge. Sloane Square tube station was a mile and a half away, a good thirty minutes walk, and on a good day it took forty minutes to get from there to Tower Hill.

A bus would halve the time of the first leg of the journey, if you could catch one.

If you could actually get on it, which was never possible when it rained. There was nothing to do about the second. I soon realised that I was destined to be under Bob Bostock's little red line for ever, later even than Jimmy Couldrey.

As for the flat, we had no furniture. That aside it was perfect. Being determined to make a go of it, Tev found a couple of camp beds.

'We'll sort the rest out as we go along,' he said cheerfully.

Being a gentleman of property, I had discovered, is not without its issues.

I drafted Wendy's boys into the progressive redecoration of the new pad. They were both at Truro School, a distinguished boarding school in Cornwall. It was the school holidays and they came over frequently. There were acres of wall that needed a dab and expert hand. They supplied the former, but not the latter.

Their frequent presence during the school holidays did not over amuse Tev who felt, logically enough, that a professional painter would do the job in half the time and would not leave a souvenir of Jackson Pollock on the wooden floors or, worse still, on the carpet.

He was, of course, quite right, but it was difficult to tell the boys that their efforts were not welcome. Effort, in the Great Scheme of Things, is supposed to be rewarded. It proved rather harder to liberate the carpet from excessive enthusiasm and concomitant paint. The issue would need tact. The floorboards could be sanded and carpet was ghastly to begin with.

We took it up and secreted it in a neighbouring skip. The next morning it had gone, presumably removed by an admirer of the great American abstract expressionist. Mercifully, the inevitable dénouement coincided with the new academic year.

'Now you're going back to the West Country,' I told them, 'we'll have a professional finish the job. Tev and I want to thank you for all your hard work. Come on, let's go to the pub. I'm buying.'

I know it may not sound much like a reward or thank you for their efforts, but the lads were keener than teenagers should rightly be for a pint of Charrington's *Directors' Bitter* and were as pleased as Punch.

*

The Cross Keys, by our front door, proved to be something of a shrine, at least in the sense it was full of sinners. I progressed from quenching my thirst before Sunday lunch to most evenings.

On my first twilight excursion I saw two of its doyens, Eliot Sage and Johnny Hunter, noisily propping up the bar. Both of them were at *CTB*, in its august marine division.

Also at the bar was the actor Tom Baker, the finest *Dr Who*, right in the epicentre of another little coterie of devotees.

Of an evening the pub could get a little raucous. On one occasion I misjudged my snappy badinage with a wiry little Asian fellow. It turned out he was welter-weight champion in Afghanistan and he effortlessly broke my nose. It certainly taught me a lesson. These days I am scrupulously polite to everyone.

There were occasions when even Tev would find it difficult to walk in a straight line. Finding he had locked his keys in our flat he decided to punch a hole in the glass panelled front door to the block. He came back to the pub, soaked in blood. At St George's Hospital, on Hyde Park Corner,[39] he had the surgeons restore the tendon to his index finger.

What fun, what japes, we twenty-something-year-olds used to have.

*

Around the corner from our place in Lawrence Street was the house of Brian Oates, who generously let his spare bedrooms to a host of interesting people.

One of them, Richard Reinke, was as English as they come despite his Prussian name. At least, he managed to blend generosity with caution which I think is very English.

Sophie von Nagel was another of Brian's Prussian lodgers, a very pretty girl whose aristocratic diffidence

---

[39] Now the Lanchester Hotel.

made people think she was merely shy. She was not, and she is today one of Germany's top photojournalists.

In two adjoining eighteenth century townhouses of Chelsea's Cheyne Row lived Count John Bernard Philip Humbert de Salis. De Salis had a deservèd pride in his ancestry. He spoke so affectionately of the first de Salis to be ennobled, Rudolph von Salis, one had the impression they had actually met. They had not. Rudolph had been ennobled by the Holy Roman Emperor in 1582 and my John was separated from him by nine generations. The family originated in the Grisons, a Swiss canton. John was a Hereditary Knight of the Golden Spur, an honour first conferred on Rudolph in 1571 for his gallant resistance to the Turks at Lepanto.

The family had delivered mercenaries to Popes and emperors for centuries. One ancestor, in the 19th century, had turned down a British baronetcy, considering it inferior to the title 'count' - a view his descendant and my contemporary strongly shared. A proper peerage and a seat in the Lords would, of course, have been another matter.

John's father, the 8th count, had been a lieutenant-colonel in the Irish Guards. He died when John was only two. Breaking its own rules, lightning then struck twice. His Italian mother, Camilla Presti di Camarda, died when he was just five.

An uncle took responsibility for the little boy but he too died young. The poor orphan spent some time with his 'French' godfather, Patrice de MacMahon, Duc de Magenta. That duke's forebear had been a skilled politician, general and had been made a Marshal of France by Louis XIII after Ireland's nobility had taken their 'flight of the earls' to safer waters.

That kindly duke likewise lost his life, this time in a riding accident. This appalling litany of tragedies forced poor John to live between Downside College, his Italian grandmother and sometimes his trustees. He soared above it all to read Law at Corpus Christi, Cambridge, from where he went on to Gray's Inn. Somehow he found time to serve as a reserve officer in the Honourable Artillery Company. He was soon awarded a short-service commission in the 9th/12th Royal Lancers.

When I met him he was playing his part in the long-running soap called Ulster. Speaking perfect French and Italian (with a smattering of German)[40] he and seemed to enjoy the company of someone else who could also speak those languages.

*

Tev often planned to be at home in Wales with his parents. The flat was disencumbered most weekends.

An awkward moment arrived one Saturday morning. I had passed a rather energetic night with an athletic floozy who refused to get out of bed. This was inconvenient as my favourite arm candy, Adrianna ,was about to appear for Sunday lunch. My planning skills were seriously wanting. I was running the risk of being discovered *in flagrante delicto*.

From my bedroom I could hear my adventure of the previous night suggesting in her best Fenella Fielding voice that I - 'lover-boy' apparently - should return whence I had so recently come. Tempting as the suggestion was, the stakes were too high. What should I do? In my pyjama top she was clearly going nowhere. What was now needed was vulpine cunning. If the aforementioned floozy wouldn't leave, then someone else would have to come. Even numbers are always good.

I rang Peter Kaufeler from the drawing room, speaking so quietly he could hardly understand a word I said.

---

[40] John de Salis would return to his roots; he became a Swiss citizen and an officer in the Swiss *Pansergrenadieren.*

'I'm in a bit of a muddle here, Peter. I need your help. Adrianna is coming for lunch and Susie has no intention of going home. I need an alibi in the shape of someone who is prepared to make a fuss of a pretty girl. Susie, that is. Yes, the blonde one I told you about. You will? Brilliant.'

My sigh of relief must have been heard a mile away.

'When? Half past eleven, at the latest. You have to be here before Adrianna. Why? Because, you clot, it needs to appear to her you have been here all night with Susie, or at least that you came together. You're on your way? Superb. You're a scholar and a gent.'

I turned on the shiny new taps in the bathroom.

'Susie, darling,' I shouted over the Niagaran cascade, 'can you stay for lunch? I have a couple of old friends coming over.'

'Lunch?' the temptress sighed loudly. 'That's hours away. Come back in here, right now.'

'I have still got to buy it. I must get dressed.'

'Well, who's coming?'

This was difficult. If Adrianna and Peter arrived together, that would suggest to Susie they were an 'item'. If Adrianna arrived before Peter, I was in deep trouble. I would be guilty as charged. My only hope was that Adrianna arrived last and would mistakenly conclude that Susie was Peter's little piece of Turkish delight. I had set myself up for a fall, I thought, as I peered at my face in the brand new shaving mirror. Susie came into the bathroom, utterly oblivious of the rules of decorum. She had a pee, combed her lovely hair and borrowed my toothbrush. She applied mascara, blusher, hung a string or two of beads or pearls around her neck and gained an instant and remarkable resemblance to the Jezebel of the Book of Kings.

The doorbell rang. If this was Adrianna, I was sunk. I threw on a tie but left the knot an inch or two

109

below the collar. In my foolish head the gesture would imply it had earlier been done up tight. The fear that the world would realise that I was a scoundrel was causing my slumbering brain to engage.

'Sit in the window, Susie. The light there suits you. I want Peter to see you at your loveliest.'

The chair by the window was exactly where a girl would sit if planning forward, not retrospectively. As she sat down I saw – or thought I saw – some stray dogs milling about in the street below. I had never seen them before.[41]

I opened the flat door. To my great relief, it was Peter.

'Come in, Old Man, I was about to open a bottle of Champagne. Stirrup Cup, so to speak.'

I was suddenly and horribly aware of the ambiguity. Stirrup Cup is drunk before a hunt, not afterwards. I glanced at Susie to check but she had not detected the poor analogy.

'This is the lovely Susie.'

'How d'you do?' he said politely.

'Very well I'm sure,' she replied.

Until that moment I had not noticed that her syntax and larynx shared an estuarine bias.

'Peter, would you look after Susie for a moment while I run to the Greek deli. I have yet to buy the secret ingredients for a perfect Sunday lunch.'

Despite it being the Catholic and Orthodox Sabbath, Stavros's shop on the King's Road was always open. I dashed off, hoping against hope they would

---

[41] In 850 BC, Biblical historians have calculated, Jezebel put on make-up, a formal wig and other adornments and looked out from a window. Jehu had ordered Jezebel's servants to throw her from that very window and, on hitting the earth fifty feet below, her blood splashed over the wall and horses. Jehu's horse trampled over her corpse. He then entered her palace, calmly eating and drinking, before ordering Jezebel's body to be taken away for burial. His servants discovered only her skull, her feet and the palms of her hands, the rest of her flesh having been eaten by loose dogs, just as the prophet Elijah had foretold.

have something with which I could improvise a Sunday lunch. A challenge - Peter's father had ensured that his son knew exactly how any such meal should taste.

It was open. I bought some mince. All I could think of, looking around, was 'spag bol', an unsophisticated version of the great Bolognese classic. To wash it down I bought four bottles of Chianti. It was going to be an Italian Sunday, in Adrianna's honour. That, at least, is what I would tell her. There was no point in trying to impress Peter Kaufeler. Growing up in a house like his, even bunting, pressed and flambéed in cognac, would fail to amaze.

On my return from Stavros's I discovered that Adrianna had arrived and that Peter had poured the girls a glass or two. To my relief they were all getting on just fine.

Suddenly I felt I might even get away with it. The insatiable Susie thought Peter, already a successful property developer, well worth knowing. For her part, Adrianna was unalarmed.

The 'spag bol' was edible, if barely, and the wine was better than Stavros's *vin ordinaire*, if by the smallest smidgeon.

I had not been dealt the very best of hands, even if I was the dealer but, in the end, all's well that ends well.

*

At Bowring's I had discovered a likeable cove in Charles Sheppard, recently transferred to 'non-marine' (where I worked) from 'aviation'. He was renting a room in a house in Oakley Street, more or less opposite Oates's and just around the corner from my flat in Lawrence Street.

To shorten the time it took us to walk to Sloane Square I suggested an arrangement whereby Charles and I would share a taxi, paying the fare on alternate days. Expensive, yes, but those extra minutes in the morning and the chance of evading the wrath of The Bostock made it a good investment.

Charles was of such buoyant good humour, at a time of day that more typically lends itself to morosity, that when I saw a policeman going up the steps to Charles's front door I had a malevolent urge.

I asked the policeman his business. He revealed that the previous night a certain Mr Charles Sheppard had left 'a package' in *The Phoene.* [42] He was there to return it.

'It might even be important.'

I told the policeman, who was even younger than me, that Charles and I were playing a little game, surprising each other, and if he told Mr Sheppard that he was under arrest, I would definitely win and we could call the game off.

'Perhaps you could say,' I suggested, 'that he was under arrest for abandoning a package in a public space?'

To my astonishment, this good-humoured copper agreed. So too did the gods, as when my co-conspirator rang the doorbell, Charles himself opened it, dressed only in bathrobe and with his face half covered in shaving soap.

'Mr Charles Sheppard? You are under arrest.'

Charles's face went as white as the lather.

It was immediately obvious to the police constable that he had a whole stash of guilty secrets. The clue was that he didn't say 'on what charge?' He simply said, 'wait there, I'll finish dressing'.

It was time to conclude this silly jape and I stepped into the frame.

'Just my poor sense of humour. Sorry Charles. This kind officer has come to return something you left

---

[42] Now renamed 'The Phene'. Dipthongs ain't what they used to be, as Duke Ellington might have said.

in *The Phoene* last night'. Now it was my turn to feel guilty.

*

When I learned that my colleague Dick Marriott had decided to marry - and that some clearly eccentric member of the opposite sex had been persuaded to accommodate this unlikely ambition - I was thoughtful. Dick was younger than me. I had not yet conceived a yearning for permanence, so I was surprised.

Nor had I ever heard Dick even mention any girl in the context of a companion, a fling or even a simple object of desire. I did not think him gay; no, it was far more likely was that he was still a virgin. He lived with his parents - not a bad idea given a dismal salary and that his father was a well-paid insurance underwriter - an arrangement guaranteed to cramp his style. He reminded of my own fumbling inaugural ineptitude of eight years before.

I decided on a wedding present that would surely be of great use to him in his future life. To deliver it I would need to co-opt my generous friend Mila.

She was from Dusseldorf and was a semi-vegetarian,[43] loved walking in the woods, running marathons and having sex. The clue to a good life, she had told me, was nature itself.

'What could be better exercise than sex? Done properly, it toned the skin. Yes, all that and it was fun as well.'

'Does it matter who you do it with?'

'Of course. He must be athletic. He should be generous and not impatient. He must have stamina.'

'Should he be affectionate and good-looking?'

'These are unnecessary qualities. The first means he is likely to get the wrong idea. He'll start sending flowers or some other nonsense. The second hardly matters in the

---

[43] She did not eat red meat.

heat of the moment. Why care about the mantelpiece while stoking the fire?'

If Mila's attitude was promising, I was not sure how I should broach the subject?

'I have a friend called Dick. Great chap, has all the qualities you admire but lacks, how shall I put it, some of the experience associated with a 'man of the world'.'

Mila was all ears, so to speak.

'He is to marry,' I continued. 'I am concerned his wedding night might be a flop, in a manner of speaking. You would earn your place in Valhalla if you came to his rescue?'

'How will that happen? I have never met him.'

'Leave that to me. I'll give a supper party at my place. You'll be my date, but you will let him know that you think he's nice and that I am not. I shall pretend to be hurt and take myself off to bed, leaving the two of you together. You will work your magic and a mere squire will end up as a knight.'

'Well, it sounds like a challenge I might enjoy. But what if he doesn't like me? What if I'm not his type?'

'No red bloodied man could ever say no to you. This story will end happily, I promise.'

'How should I dress? Stern or sexy?'

'Like a secretary.'

'And is he fit?'

'He looks as though there have always been potatoes on his dining table, but deep within him there lies a snarling carnivore.'

'Oh very well. I don't know why but I'll do it. Just don't tell anyone else.'

*

My one time assistant at Paris's *Aerospatiale*, where I had worked during my gap year, had sent me a birthday present from Paris, where he still worked. It was a beautifully gift-wrapped girl whose name was Marguerite.

I was still friends with Linda Hooton, daughter of an eminent surgeon, who had a large flat off Sloane Square and a spare room. She generously offered it to Marguerite, which ensured that my new *petite amie* and I would walk through Holland Park, go to the cinema, and share some tender moments when we wanted.

She was so dazzling a girl that I could not resist taking her for a brief tour of the City. It included, of course, a chance to show her off to my colleagues, all of whom were most gratifyingly impressed.

*

Friday night arrived. Tev had already taken his train back to Monmouthshire when Dick appeared at my front door.

'Very good of you, Jeremy,' he said, as I handed him a glass of wine.

I had laid the dining table for four.

'Where are the girls?' he asked.

'Marguerite rang me just this second. She is not well and has taken to her bed. We are down to three. Still, all the more *chicken à la king* for us.'

Who was this king? A sovereign? Some chef called King? We shall probably never know.

'Who else is coming?'

'A German friend. Mila. She's very sweet. You'll get on.'

Dick looked very dubious but then the doorbell rang. I let Mila in. She stood in the frame for a moment, letting me assess her, and I was proud of her.

She looked like no secretary I had ever met, not unless the girl had had a substantial clothes allowance and didn't actually need the job.

She was wearing high heels. From there, over the considerable distance to the hem of her miniskirt, two

115

very nicely turned legs worked their magic. That skirt was made of suede, and her blouse was of organdie, a stiffened but fine and translucent muslin, embroidered with a strategically flowering vine. A bolero jacket, also of suede, covered her shoulders while a pearl necklace encircled her neck.

Her lightly freckled face was carefully made up – deep pink lipstick and eyes that had been artfully made to smoulder. Her short hair shone, radiating Germanic health and efficiency. The whole deal was enough to make one wolf-whistle, except one doesn't do that, does one?

Dick, however, looked uncomfortable. As our supper progressed, he became more so.

Mila, in ignoring me, came close to discourtesy. She was focussing her tenderest attentions on Dick, treating him as a starlet might treat a casting director. She laughed at his inept attempts at humour, matched his heartiness when he talked about football, or cricket, or whatever, and had actually seen the film that he had so recently been knocked out by. She showed no discomfort when he banged on about preparations for his marriage.

A broker is a high-falutin' word for salesman and they say that no-one is easier to sell to than a salesman. As usual 'they' were wrong. Dick was not buying.

When the espressos were at last behind us, I put a decanter of port on the table. Not a good move. Mila declined it and Dick took one look and stood up.

'Great evening, Jeremy and thank you. I have to go, train to catch, you know the drill. A pleasure to meet you Mila. I hope our paths cross again.'

With that the poor chump was off like a frightened rabbit. His fiancée would just have to do her own work. I bet she didn't not know the game as well as Mila.

'I'm so sorry,' said Mila. 'I did my best.'

'You were flawless, faultless. A privilege to have watched. Even the best of plans can somehow go awry.'

'Is there any way I can make it up to you?' she asked.

'I think we could have a glass of port next door.' I indicated my bedroom. 'These dining chairs are hard work, don't you think?'

*

On Monday, however, I was in the office at 9.11. I fully expected the full weight of Mr Bostock's untrammelled fury to fall upon me, but instead he told me to report to Mr Galway, straight away.

You might have thought the office manager could fire me without the help of a company director. I felt as if I were going to my housemaster's study to be beaten for sitting on a radiator, or whispering during prep or, extremely improbably, running through a field of wheat.

Discovering that Galway shared an office with two others - Dick Cazenove and Anthony Robertson - made him seem a little less grand. City grandees are supposed have their own offices, pictures of ships on the walls, mostly destined for Davy Jones's locker, with terrifying PAs sitting outside the door like the hound of Hades, ready to devour any interloping underling that dares trespass on her master's turf.

As I went in, all three looked up momentarily, while loading their 'slip cases' with files and case studies to take into the 'market', hoping to persuade Lime Street's reinsurance companies and Lloyd's itself to off-set the risk that troubled an insurance company in some far flung corner of the world.

Galway indicated the chair before him.

'We have an agent in Milan,' he continued. 'Can you be free on Thursday to pay him a call? We'll be back late on Friday. Pack for one night.'

'Of course.'

'No need to speak to me in Italian. I wouldn't understand a word. When they try their singsong on me I smile and, if I judge they have asked me a question, I look thoughtful and say '*dunque*'.'[44]

I laughed.

'Then that's done. Give Freddy in the Car Pool your address. A car will come for you at 5.00 am to bring you to Heathrow. Don't forget to pack a toothbrush. Oh, and you'll need business cards. Obviously there isn't time before this trip, but get them printed anyway. Put your job title down as 'broker'. Well, that's it. You're one of us. Congratulations!'

I had been promoted. Stupidly I had expected that when or if the time came, there would be some sort of fanfare.

Considering that I was going to Italy, a triumphal march perhaps?

---

[44] 'Well then', pronounced 'Doon Kway'.

CHAPTER TWO

Promotion
1975

In which the author goes on a pub crawl by tube. He travels to Milan to discover Negronis and see Michelangelo's prisoners. He sees La Bohème at La Scala. His sister, soon to relocate to Paris, has a blind date with a ship owner. The author meets a famous barrister at the Garrick Club and visits Athens, where he bluffs his way in Greek.

When I arrived at CTB, fourteen minutes late, Bob Bostock had the grace not to fire me. Instead, he shook my hand.

'A broker! Well done. You seem to be on some sort of fast track. Mr Galway is to be your boss, I hear. Take care; he is a stickler for punctuality and has a particular loathing for scrimshankers.' He smiled at some private joke. 'You have a new office. Come and meet your colleagues.'

That smile, such a rarity, made me feel quite emotional. And as for scrimshankers? Must be quite a select body.

The new office was welcome, if aside from being only marginally smaller than where I had previously been, it looked much the same. Jim Cole, Charles Sheppard, Dick Marriott, Gemma Jacques and Roger Huggins were also admiring their new digs. It seemed as though promotion to Scrimshanker Hall was a wholesale process.

*

A telephone call later let me share my good news with Tev, my flatmate, who suggested a celebration.

'A dozen oysters are called for,' he immediately declared with a flourish.

That evening we found ourselves at *Bentley's* in Beauchamp Place where, a few moments later, a

119

plateful of bivalves had been opened and devoured, and an empty bottle of *Pol Roger* stood upturned in its ice bucket.

'Don't worry about the money. It's on me, and I insist.' Clearly he knew the condition of my wallet. 'Now you're a fully fledged broker they'll increase your salary. A little advice, if I may. Ask for the rise. Companies like yours assume that if you don't ask for money you don't need it.'

Tev was right. That summer my salary rocketed from £2,800 to £3,356 p.a. An increase of just under 20%, and it made me feel good. At last I could look a traffic warden in the eye, always provided my gaze did not linger over long.

It was Tev's day for the bath so I made do with a scrub and a shave. My flatmate had ordered a new boiler. The sooner it came the better. He had met a plumber in a pub somewhere and had judged him a good guy. It may have helped that that was also his name.

I joined Tev and Guy for a bevvy or two in the bar under the *Royal Court Theatre* in order to make my own judgement as I was a fifty-fifty shareholder in our property *de grand luxe*. If I were to judge him competent, Tev told me, he might also put in the central heating.

Tev bought a round and I found Guy to be a wry and well-seasoned Londoner. When it was time for him to reciprocate, he suggested instead that we share a glass of Champagne with him in his flat in nearby Cliveden Place.

I will admit being surprised that a plumber could live in the heart of Belgravia but then he probably earned rather more than a junior broker in the City.

Guy's wife, a Parisian, received us with the courtesy associated with that nation's *grande bourgeoisie*. It seemed appropriate for me to acknowledge her courtliness by kissing her hand. The deal was concluded and toasted, Three weeks later we had a new bath, enough hot water for us both to soak in it once a day, each, and even heat our new radiators into the bargain.

*

My career was also warming up. Days later I was in the back of a chauffeur-driven Volvo with a little overnight bag on my lap. Yes, it contained a toothbrush. The driver was a perky sort of a chap but the hour, 5 am, was unearthly and I was not in the mood for chit chat.

What did I know about Milan, I asked myself? I had never been there, but I knew it to be the hub of the Italian fashion industry. It had a very famous opera house. It had a church or monastery where Leonardo da Vinci had painted the Last Supper. Last, but by no means least, Milan was Italy's financial capital.

I found Simon Galway easily enough. He was drinking an espresso in Terminal Two's executive lounge. We had half an hour to go before our flight so we were in good time, if barely.[45] He looked as if this Godforsaken time of day was not in the least unnatural.

'Your first business trip?' he asked.

'I did once escort a package to Croydon,' I replied. It was imperative he did not think me a rookie.

'Then you're an old hand. You don't need my advice.'

Once our flight was called we headed for the gate.

In 1974, *BEA* had merged with *BOAC* to create a new airline. Demonstrating the imagination we have long associated with that company, they failed to call it *Sea-eagle*, *Supermarine* or even *Pterodactyl*. They called it *British Airways* and a Rolls-Royce powered Lockheed TriStar was to carry us to Linate Aerodrome, Milan.

After my 'gap years' I was something of a seasoned traveller but I was still excited. Perhaps I should perhaps remind my reader, if he's still reading,

---

[45] How times have changed!

that back in the old days airlines fawned over their passengers, even in if they had the misfortune to be confined in steerage. There was no corralling as there is today. Nor did we have to take our shoes and belts off and watch our trousers fall down.

Far more important, I was not to travel in the back, not this time. I had bought a *Duty Free* bottle of whisky and as we meandered over the tarmac to climb the mobile stair onto the waiting aircraft, I paused at the top. I decided not to wave to the crowds and paparazzi. It might have amused me but it would have made me look like an *ingénu* in Simon Galway's eyes.

Travelling first class in a commercial airliner was for me a total novelty. Every flight carefully cordoned off the gentry from *hoi poloi*. After all, one didn't know where the latter had been. Air hostesses, lovely girls in dark blue suits, white chemises and blue cravats, hair carefully arranged in buns and contained in their jauntily set pill-box hats, duly ushered Simon and me to our wide leather seats behind the cockpit. The ubiquitous anti-makassars were waiting for us, though it will have been twenty years since anyone had actually used makassar hair-oil.

The passenger in the seat behind need have little concern as British Airways had allotted us four or five feet of legroom. Our seats reclined, should we want them to convert them into a near-horizontal day bed.

'Welcome on board, gentlemen,' said a courteous and sexy aerial courtesan as she attached Simon's safety belt. I was allowed to fasten my own. I needed a better suit, I concluded.

We taxied onto the runway and paused for some unknowable reason. Then we heard the roar of the Rolls Royce engines fire up. The plane began to move, ever more quickly, the nose lifted and we were almost on our backs. I felt my ears shut down but somehow I was aware that a stewardess was murmuring something in Simon's ear.

'Something for breakfast, Sir? An orange juice? Tea or coffee?'

Simon put the menu down. He was characteristically decisive.

'I'll have the fry up. We'll have champagne, Jeremy, and we shall toast your first flight with *C T Bowring*.'

My smoked salmon and scrambled eggs arrived almost immediately on white china crockery emblazoned with a wordmark. The word 'British' was in red, while the word 'airways', written under it in blue, lacked a dot over the 'i', which gave it a cheap feel. At least we had real knives and forks to eat with. All a distant memory these days.

Simon busied himself with his papers and what looked like a phrase book. Small talk was not in order and a couple of hours later, a taxi was taking us from Linate to the *Principe di Savoia* hotel.

This was not student travel, not even close. Not even the *Dorchester* was such an hotel, and first impressions stick. Despite the fact that the hotel was in the centre of town, a few yards from the rather fascist-looking railway station, it backed onto its own park. The principal rooms on the ground floor were panelled in what looked like walnut, while great swags or swathes of curtains cascaded from every window. The rooms were lit by Murano chandeliers and the cream and dusty-blue coffered ceilings contained great oval frescoes, every few yards, in which *putti* besought the gods to grant them a favour or two. Every table had a vase of freshly cut flowers, while every sofa had a businessman reading *La Repubblica* or *The Wall Street Journal*, or a film starlet waiting for Franco Zeffirelli, Luchino Visconti or Federico Fellini to cast her in his new film.

'The streets round here are all named after Italian explorers, philosophers and scientists,' Simon told me.

'You'll have heard of some of them, I expect. Now it's time to freshen up and visit our agent.'

Sergio Corsi proved to be a refined and graceful Italian, one who could even have turned heads in Cinecittá, the hub of the Italian film industry. His No 2, Piero Petronio, had been cast in a more ample mould. Piero was to be my counterpart and my conversations from that day on were to be with him. He spoke near perfect English, after all, a lot better than Simon's Italian, but I saw a chance to liberate the language of Dante from its recent confinement. Piero and I would go native.

Every now and then Simon said his *'dunque'*, but I could see he had relaxed. He could easily have been annoyed but clearly he was relieved there was no language issue. He had found a deputy and could now devote himself to his far more lucrative Japanese account.

The day drew on at its steady, stately pace. The four of us had lunch at a local restaurant where Simon drank water. Watching the Italians follow suit, I felt obliged to do the same. They were used to him but I had been hoping for a glass or two of a *Spada* or a *Barolo*. Never mind the dishonesty of the impression I was obliged to make. I would put things right that evening. The four of us managed to visit a couple of insurance companies before the day was done.

At long last we were back at our hotel, where Simon politely left me 'for a while' to my own devices. He had his progress report to write on every bit of business our company had in Italy. I had no idea who would read it but, having nothing better to do, I headed for the swimming pool bar.

'What will you have?' asked the barista. Always my favourite question.

'What's that man over there drinking?'

'A *negroni*, Sir.'

'Then I'll have one of those.'

The waiter mixed gin, Campari and red vermouth in a flask, added ice and shook it theatrically before pouring the mixture into a Collins glass and adding a splash of soda. It was magic.

An hour passed before the barista reapproached me.

'Telephone, Sir,' he said, passing me the handset.

'Second time lucky. I tried your room first,' said Simon. 'I'm going for a swim. Our hotel has rather a good pool. Perhaps a drink by the pool before dinner?'

'I'll be there in half-an-hour,' I replied, realising that since I was already there I had time for another. That half-hour sped by. Soon I was to have my first drink of the day, ignoring the Champagne on the flight and the two I had already smuggled on board at the hotel's magnificent bar.

Simon appeared in a bathrobe at the poolside watering hole, holding an orange juice and looking like a nobleman from the mosaics in Sicily's Piazza Armerina. I knew that his family had connections to the Irish marquesses of Clanricarde and Sligo and to the former Prime Minister George Canning. There is a portrait of a young Lord Canning, painted by Richard Beard in the 1840s. It could have been Simon himself. His forbears on the Irish west coast must have lent him a soupçon of Spanish blood.

The pool was substantial. Its pale blue water revealed a pair of dolphins in mosaic, laid onto the bottom, copied or looted from some palatial Roman villa. Above us, a barrel-vaulted ceiling gently arched over our heads. In front of us, a classical doorway surmounted by a tympanum led to the changing rooms.

I had been transported to a grand and nautical palace. The pool lacked only a pair of battling triremes. Heaven knows what I had done to deserve this. It must have been good.

I will admit I was rather thrilled that I had somehow landed a role in CTB's Italian business.

'You can buy me a drink,' said Simon, taking a stool and breaking into my reverie. 'It will go on your expense account and I will sign it. That way none of our expense hounds need ever know I enjoy the occasional glass as much as you so obviously do.'

Oops.

*

The next day, back in Blighty, I had a late call from Colin Swan, an old friend who worked for Guinness Peat, the Irish investment bank.

A great-nephew of the brewer Arthur Guinness had founded Guinness Mahon in Dublin in 1836, and it opened in London a century later to merge with Lewis & Peat.

Yes, I would be delighted to see him and Judith again. We had had a wonderful time in Ireland, back in 1970.[46]

Before she married, Judith had spent her time as governess and tutor to two of the daughters of the Earl of Ypres, the ladies Sarah and Emma. In fact, she had provided the entirety of their education. I found this curious but I had read somewhere that the queen had never been to school, so there was clearly a rather grand precedent.

Dinner was very pleasant. One of the guests at their house in Twickenham was the Dominican Republic's ambassador to the Court of St James, a delightful if purposeful lady. Her son, also there, was mad on bridge, a game I also enjoyed, but he insisted on the 'duplicate' version. Part of its thrill is a forensic discussion of every hand after every game, an element of unadulterated joy I could easily do without. I liked 'rubber bridge' with a whisky to enhance the small talk.

---

[46] 'A Gap Year or Two', by the same author, has all the details.

'So Lord Ypres didn't want his girls to go to school?'

'No he didn't. His girls got me instead,' Judith said modestly.

'What did you teach them?'

'Everything I know. Reading and writing, obviously. Sewing and darning. Cooking, lots of that. Flower arranging. The rules of precedence within the nobility. That sort of thing.'

'Very sound. Who needs to spend hours learning the name of the capital of the Faroe Islands?'

Judith looked unsure if I were speaking my mind or gently teasing.

'Have you ever been there?' she asked. 'To the Faroe Islands, I mean.'

'I have this moment decided to put that omission right.'

I must sadly declare that to this day I have not dealt with this glaring omission from my own education.

'Anyway,' Judith persisted, 'Sarah and Emma share a flat. We often see them, usually over dinner,' Judith persisted. 'We're family in a way. You will meet them soon and judge for yourself.'

That would happen very soon, but not in Putney.

*

Tev had a strange favour to ask of me and even he seemed a little embarrassed.

'I told Dmitri that your sister was sensational. He seemed excited and wanted to meet her.'

'I hope you didn't suggest she was easy-going in any way. My sister is a respectable young lady.'

'Well, half the young ladies he knows are anything but that. They mostly charge by the hour. The other half is Greek and that lot make respectability look sinful.'

'Out with it, Tev. What has he got in mind?'

'He wonders what a girl like her would make of a man like him. It's an existential thing. Every Greet maiden knows of the Lemos family; he is a prince of sorts. No one can relax with one of those. He feels his true, generous, affectionate character has been obscured by the accretion of wealth, position, all the gubbins that goes with all that. He wants to pretend he's just a regular guy, like you or me. He believes himself likeable in his own right. He thinks that if we could arrange for him to meet her, and that he could take her somewhere ordinary, taking a real woman who knows nothing about him to a bistro or a pub, he might even learn a little about himself. Grow up a bit?'

'You're asking me to set up a blind date?'

'Would Kate be up for it?'

'She is adventurous. It's not impossible.'

With my fingers crossed I explained to my sister that one of Tev's office mates had been stood up by a prospective client and, having paid the deposit on a table in some swanky restaurant somewhere, asked Tev whether he knew of anyone who might fill the gap. Dinner would probably be somewhere Greek and would end, hand-on-heart, in a safe return home.

'No hanky-panky. Just a pleasant evening on company expenses, no strings attached.'

'What's he like, this sad and lonely loser?'

'Well, he's in his late thirties, quite good looking, I suppose, in a Mediterranean sort of way. I know he's well-versed in the sea-faring legends of ancient Greece. You'll have something to talk about.'

'I don't know...'

'What have you got to lose?'

'Where am I supposed to meet him?'

'Don't worry. He will come for you. He has a car.'

'Just a meal?'

'Just a simple meal. Ten courses if you like, but just a simple meal.'

*

All was settled. Kate made a valiant effort to look as good as possible, which proved little short of sensational.

I admired her courage in agreeing to it all, but then I knew she would be safe. Not particularly because Dmitri was a gentleman but because he could not afford not to be. Anything untoward would get back to me and thence to Tev. Dmitri would lose face in front of his staff. He'd probably lose his deputy and would have to explain himself to his father. He might even find himself ostracised by his little clan in Oinousses. A poor outcome was therefore quite unthinkable.

As my twenty-two year sister old turned around me, showing off her outfit, she appeared quite amused by what by all rights should have been an unnerving prospect, a step into the unknown. Then the door bell rang.

'That'll be your cue. It'll be the man himself.'

We went down to the street door of the mansion block.

Dmitri must have forgotten he was going to present himself as a regular fella. He had sent his 1966 Rolls Royce Phantom V State Landaulette for my sister and, as an added bonus, was himself sitting in the back in his dark glasses, looking for all the world like a film star. The car's lid was down and some local children were already busy interviewing the capped and uniformed driver. This car was black, but another version of the same limousine had recently been made famous by John Lennon, who had had his coachwork illuminated with paisley patterns. Mohammad Resa Pahlavi, the Shah of Iran, likewise owned a Phantom V, so Dmitri was keeping good company.

I waved goodbye to something the size of an ocean liner, my little sister and Dmitri looking to the world like celebrities in the back as it purred its way out of Earl's Court and turned north towards St John's Wood.

*

The third Earl of Ypres may have been a Catholic – it was unlikely, I admit - but his daughters' mother certainly was.

She was born Maureen Kelly and had ensured that the Faith was transmitted to the ladies Charlene, Sarah and Emma.

It may be difficult to believe but Charlotte Despard, the sister of the first earl - the Field Marshal and Lord Lieutenant of Ireland - was an Anglo-Irish suffragist, a socialist, a pacifist, a *Sinn Féin* activist and a novelist. If that weren't bad enough, she was a founding member of the Women's Freedom League, the Women's Peace Crusade and the Irish Women's Franchise League. Over the course of her long life she was an activist in a wide range of political organisations, amongst others the Women's Social and Political Union, the Labour Party, *Cumann na mBan* and the Communist Party of Great Britain.

Quite something, considering her brother's occupation, nursery politics must have been quite dramatic in that household. There will have been trenches in the nursery.

The third earl's eldest daughter, Charlene Milner, lived in South Africa, in what I had heard was a neatly gabled Cape Dutch country house near Port Elisabeth, surrounded by vines and horses, while in London, every Sunday, two devout young ladies took each other to church.

The capital had plenty of temples to choose from. They all differed in their subtle ways. The most readily discernible will have been their self-imposed dress codes.

*

St James's Spanish Place is one of the finest churches in the capital.

Yes, it still has a Spanish connection, and one that is cherished today. King Alfonso XIII's personal standard hangs over the sacristy door, elegantly framed, and the late King and Queen of Spain often attended.

High on the wall above the choir stalls, are two in-built crowns and, beneath them, are pews reserved for the King and Queen of Spain. The historically-informed will not allow their debt to the Zarzuela to be forgotten. During the dark days of Henry VIII, Queen Elizabeth I, Edward VI and the Lord Protector's religious persecution of the Irish, the Spanish Crown established and maintained a dangerous mission to reconvert the English.

Rather more recently, on February 15, 1908, a requiem mass was held at Spanish Place for Carlos I, King of Portugal. Edward VII and Queen Alexandra attended the service. It was the first Catholic mass to be attended by a British monarch since the sadly curtailed reign of King James II.

The Second Vatican Council opened formally under Pope John XXIII on October 11, 1962, and was not closed until Pope Paul VI required all churches to eschew the Tridentine Rite and use the vernacular in an 'accessible' version of the celebration.

That was on the Feast of the Immaculate Conception on December 8, 1965. The Church, the Council declared, was not there for the benefit of Latinists, beauty-lovers and scholars but for the meekest, least-educated and humblest members of our species.

Sadly, this well-intentioned but mistaken perspective admitted the philistines and modernists in the Vatican to reorder the divine office. A tide of insular banality descended on the universal church. Those on whom the Holy Ghost had transmitted that vital link between Art and God were rendered speechless. Traditional Catholic congregations slowly evaporated under a torrent of 'reforms' unleashed by that ill-judged Council.[47] The number of practising Christians declined in inverse proportion to the growing politicisation of the clergy. They would have done better to have remembered an earlier injunction. 'Render unto Caesar the things that are Caesar's and unto God the things that are God's'.[48]

Nevertheless, on Sundays and major feast days, the old Tridentine rite is still in use in St James, Spanish Place. Latin, so evidently God's favourite language, predominates and the smallest of roles is allotted to a horribly compromised English language.[49] The Gothic chancel is reminiscent of the finest French cathedrals and, perhaps predictably, the pretty little church is valiantly supported by the camper elements of the laity, while a very talented choir elevates the celebration with Gregorian chant and polyphony.

The choir wears surplices, the congregation prefers jeans and T-shirts with portraits of *Jethro Tull* or the *Grateful Dead*. Suede shoes and improbable blazers are also tolerated. Strictly surplus to requirements is 'Sunday Best'.

*

This only contrasts with St Etheldreda, in Ely Place off Charterhouse Street in Holborn, London. It was the first of England's pre-Reformation churches to rejoin the Catholic Church.

---

[47] In 1980, the church and its congregation would be partially rescued from the blight of modernism by one of London's best-known parish priests, Father Kit Cunningham, a genial if Chestertonian figure.

[48] Matthew 22:21.

[49] First deformed in the Reformation and then repeatedly 'improved' by well-intentioned idiots ever since.

Its quondam patron, Æthelthryth, or Etheldreda, was the Anglo-Saxon saint who founded Ely's monastery in 673 AD. Her sibling cloister, in London, was built some six hundred years later, in or around 1250 AD. Its outlying palace served the Bishops of Ely as a residence but, in 1534, when the Catholic Church was outlawed in England, the Bishops of Ely were allowed to oversee it as a peculiar.[50]

Such arrangements could not last. The C of E never forgave its parents. They sold it to a cynical heretic, Sir Christopher Hatton. He agreed to pay the recusant bishop a rent of £10, ten loads of hay and one red rose per year. For further revenge against his God, the ingrate then used the crypt as a tavern.

The angels were unimpressed. Count Gondomar, the Spanish ambassador, acquired the complex in 1620. He built an embassy from what could be salvaged from the ravaged medieval palace. He used the upper church as a peculiar. Parliament, worried about Spain's mounting power, declared that the palace and church were on Spanish soil and that therefore the Catholic rite, illegal elsewhere, could recommence. Recusant London flocked to it.

In 1642, well into the English Civil War, the bishops' palace and church were again sequestered by Parliament, this time for use as a prison. Oliver Cromwell personally issued the orders for its erasure and the destruction of its stately gardens.[51]

Despite all this, the Catholic rite survived, largely thanks to a religiously conservative aristocracy and, later, to Charles II's royal protection. Somehow, this Church has remained true to its ancient rubric, and it has become the oldest Catholic Church in England. It is

---

[50] A church outside the parochial system is called a 'peculiar'. Peculiars are practically all royal, the appointment of whose priest is directly in the hands of the Sovereign. Examples are Westminster Abbey and St George's Chapel, Windsor. St Etheldreda's 'living' was for a while in the gift of the King of Spain.
[51] Ely Palace is mentioned in two of Shakespeare's plays, Richard II and Richard III.

one of just two surviving buildings in London that date from the reign of King Edward I.

During the Vatican's ill-judged 'cultural revolution', Fr Baines was the incumbent. He was already an old man.

He'd been young during the Blitz when St Etheldreda's found itself at the centre of the Luftwaffe's onslaught.

He kept a diary. An entry of May 14, 1941, reveals that on Saturday night there came another long and disastrous raid. A bomb hit St Etheldreda, tore a hole in the roof about six feet wide and stripped much of the tiling from the roof. When it exploded, it blew out what was left of the stained glass windows. Three oak beams were sent to the floor. There were people in the Crypt when the bomb fell but, praise be to God, no one was injured.

Restoration was essential, but the church was strapped for cash. Building materials, immediately after the war, were also in desperately short supply. It took seven long years to repair the bomb damage. The job is done and these days the morning light streams through the medieval splendour of the great east window to illuminate an eight hundred year old interior. What is left of the nine choirs of angels is quite breathtaking.

Here the dress code is a nicely cut grey suit, preferably with florescent socks. Buttonholes are mandatory. You are permitted to take your teddybear to mass, though he will not be allowed to take communion.

The Brompton Oratory was the first resort of those wealthier Catholics whose forebears had decided to withhold their last mite from the beggar woman of the scriptures.

It shares its scale with a cathedral. Before the opening of Westminster Cathedral in 1903 it had been the largest Catholic church in Britain. John Henry Newman founded it after being received into the

Catholic Communion in 1845 and built what is indisputably the most strikingly Roman church in the country, an ornate Baroque interior crowned by a great cupola.

As a reward, for services to architecture, piety and the propagation of the faith, Pope Leo XIII awarded Newman a pink hat in the Consistory of May 12, 1879.

It was Newman who persuaded my maternal forebears to revert to the faith of their ancestors.[52] The cardinal opposed 'liberalism in religion', which certainly impressed my great-great-great-grandfather. Their son, John Cardanall Bacon, RA, was 'named' after him.

In building the basilica no expense was spared. Six different types of wood - oak, walnut, mahogany, pear, tulip and cinnamon - were used for the sanctuary floor.

The priests still wear *birettas*, women parishioners sport *mantillas* while its mood, at least, seems quite ante-Vatican II. The mass remains in Latin. London's choir remains Catholic England's most senior and it deserves its international reputation. When I first went, as a boy, there I was transported by Mozart's *Coronation Mass*. If you want a Midnight Mass where you are greeted by excited smiling people wishing you 'Merry Christmas' as you leave the church then this is not the church for you. Solemnity, not happy-clappiness, is its character. It exudes piety, dignity and holiness.

During the Cold War, I have been told, the area between the pillars and the wall at the front of the Brompton Oratory was used as a dead letter drop by Communist spies in Britain, hoping to communicate with the KGB. The fact that the church enjoyed such a close relationship with the Lubyanka beggars belief.

---

[52] My maternal forebears were Bacons, from East Anglia. For members of this family to revert to their ancient faith was a little shocking to the local establishment. My paternal forebears were Irish Catholics, but they too faced difficulties adhering in to the confession of their ancestors.

Dress code, both for men and women, is full length mink or sable coats. Fur hats, in winter, for the ladies. Dogs should be small and kept in handbags during the sacred rite. Smoking during the sermon is discouraged.

The last Catholic Church in this condensed narrative has to be the Holy Redeemer in Chelsea. It first drew breath in 1892 when Canon Cornelius Keens, 'the church builder', gained permission from the Cardinal Archbishop of Westminster, Herbert Vaughan, to found a new parish in the older part of Chelsea, in territory that its rival St Mary's, Cadogan Street, had surrendered. Cardinal Vaughan laid the foundation stone in June 1894 but the then archbishop, later Cardinal Bourne, only formally consecrated it ten years later, on 21st June 1905. Many parishes wanted St Thomas More as their patron but they had to wait until his canonisation in 1935, the quadricentenary of his martyrdom. This was my father's parish and was but a stone's throw from where the saint actually lived, from 1524 until 1535, whence he was taken to the Tower to be decapitated.

The saint's house, later renamed 'Beaufort House', stood astride what is now Beaufort Street. The Cecil family acquired it after More's execution. St Thomas had worshipped in what is now Chelsea's Old Church. It was then Catholic, of course, and he built a chapel there to house the tomb of his first wife, Jane, who died in childbirth.

During the Blitz, on the evening of Saturday September 14, 1940, the church of the Holy Redeemer and St Thomas More sustained a direct hit. A *Panzersprengbombe Cylindrisch* – a cylindrical armour-piercing explosive bomb - was dropped by the Luftwaffe. It crashed through the west window, bull-dozing a path through the organ, very totally destroying it, broke through the floor, into the crypt, a makeshift air raid shelter where between eighty and a hundred people were sheltering. When the wretched thing finally exploded went off, it killed nineteen innocents outright, including poor Bert Thorpe, the church warden. Many more were injured.

The floor needed to be rebuilt but funds were non-existent. A general restoration had to wait until Canon Alfonso de Zulueta, the parish priest, could pay for it out of his own deep pockets. Once Fr Alfonso had become the incumbent, the side chapels, save for Our Lady's and St. Thomas's, were removed and vandal-proofed. A grille was installed but, sadly, too late for the saint's medieval reliquary. It had already been half-hinched.

It was now my local church and, above all, it was a wafer's thickness from where I lived. My father liked to read from the Old Testament from the pulpit, with what he thought was theatrical panache. I wished he wouldn't.

Being in Chelsea, the dress code is eccentric. Tweed jackets, cloth caps, cavalry twills or even jodhpurs and hunter wellies predominate. Since many parishioners believe Chelsea to be in the country, male members wear much the same, though one member of the congregation likes to dress in the dress uniform of the Sacred Order of the Knights of St John of Jerusalem.

His green cutaway frockcoat is indeed very fine.

*

One particular Sunday, however, was not going to follow its well-rehearsed script. Instead, a taxi took Fr Alfonso, my father and me to the Garrick Club in Covent Garden.

The Garrick, founded in 1831, was peopled with men of letters and drama. It only admitted members if they were 'men of refinement and education, prepared to meet each other on equal terms'. It boasted many treasures, one of which was its collection of theatrical paintings and drawings, today the most comprehensive in existence.

The Garrick's governing council had long ago resolved that it would be better for ten ordinary men to be excluded than one bore be admitted. I think they had Dickens in mind but, since his writing has delighted me over many a year, I hope I'm wrong.

I learned that the club had witnessed a famous quarrel between writers - notably Dickens and Thackeray. Dickens's remarks on Thackeray were so offensive they could only have been heard in the privileged circumstance of the club were the author to escape a charge of slander.

'I need a few minutes in private with Alfonso,' my father told me as our taxi drew up. 'Don't fret; this is a club where people speak to one another. I'll present you to someone interesting, I promise.'

If I looked disappointed, my father meant to keep his word and looked around for a few moments before identifying someone he thought might fit the bill.

'Sir Aubrey, may I introduce my son Jeremy. He's quite bright and on rare occasions capable of a *bon mot*.'

This was Judge Melford Stevenson. This awkward moment was made even more so when his lordship generously suggested I might join him for a 'sharpener'.

'I usually favour a gin and tonic at this hour,' he said. Of course I joined him. Of course, this introduction would have been easier if I had remembered where I had heard his name. All too often, my brain lacks nimbility, or is it nimbleness? All I could think of was his passing absurdly long sentences on the eight Cambridge University students who took part in the Garden House riot of 1970. One of them, Dominic Asquith, was not yet twenty-one. He was sent for a term in a juvenile institution. Mercifully, the sentence was almost immediately rescinded. *The Times*, quite correctly, memorably declared that Melford Stevenson had broken a butterfly on a wheel. Asquith, however, came through the crisis with characteristic panache. He has since been knighted and is today a very senior force in our diplomatic service.

But, perhaps, it was not those Cambridge protests that were troubling me? Racking my brain had produced a result. I had remembered Ruth Ellis, a poor creature tried for murder in 1955. She was the last woman to be hanged in the United Kingdom. I was six at the time, but it had been a *cause célèbre*. My parents had discussed it over our dining table, as had the rest of the kingdom. Was this man, whose company I was now enjoying, the judge who had sentenced that sad woman to death? If so, how do you deal with this?

'I imagine you found the Ruth Ellis case deeply disturbing?' I ventured, choosing my words very carefully.

'It was the hardest case I was ever involved in.'

'She was clearly guilty. Didn't she stand over her cheating lover and empty the chamber of his revolver into his chest?'

The judge smiled weakly.

'I was deeply distressed by Miss Ellis's execution. She had no possible defence. Her only hope lay in a pardon from Gwilym Lloyd George, the Home Secretary.'

'Was there really nothing you could do, Sir Aubrey?'

Melford Stevenson sat back, his deep-set eyes moist.

'On the night before she was destined to meet her Maker, I visited her in Holloway. She was dressed in a black suit and white silk blouse. I noticed her untidy bleached blonde hair and asked her if she had any last request. She was still a pretty woman and I was not too surprised when she asked me to arrange for a hairdresser to call on her very early the next morning.'

139

'You succeeded?'

It had finally dawned on me that he was not the judge in the case. He had been defending her.

'At 5.30 the next morning, her blond hair was styled. They tell me she looked terrific. At 8.30, Pierrepoint took her to the gallows. He had the impertinence to place a hood over her coiffured head and, at 8.31, she was reunited with that common-or-garden spiv, David Blakely, for whom she had swung.'

My father at last reappeared.

'Thank you, Judge. I hope he hasn't been a nuisance. We'll take him from here.'

*

I popped over to my mother's flat at the weekend, keen to hear how Kate's blind date had gone.

'I hope you got home safely,' I told her sternly.

'You worry too much. That, and it's none of your business what I may or may not do.'

Those were pretty clear instructions not to press her for any embarrassing details, but she told me anyway.

'We went to a restaurant called *Lemonia*, somewhere in Belsize Park, where the staff all knew Dmitri and kissed him rather too enthusiastically as we arrived. I will admit the food was quite delicious. The place looked good too. Décor, ambience, all brilliant. Dmitri was treated like a prince and I felt like a celebrity.'

'*Lemonia*, eh? I wonder if Lemos has a stake in it?'

'Well, I did. I mean I had a steak in it.'

'Did he ply you with wine all night?'

She pulled a scruffy piece of paper from her bag.

'We had an *Assyrtiko* from Santorini with the *mezes*. Ever heard of it?'

'I'm afraid not.'

'Then you should. It's a belter. Intense, almost briney!'

For a moment I thought I was talking to Robert Parker.

'I'll buy a bottle tomorrow. What came next?'

'He had a *kleftiko* and I had my *steak diane*. Both terrific.' She glanced at a crumpled note. 'We washed them down with a *Boutari Legacy*. Be warned, that's a red that punches above its weight.'

'Sounds as though he knows his wines, at least.'

'Does it? When we arrived, and after he had sent his driver off to park the car, he had a long conversation with the sommelier. When the wine arrived at our table, the only one in the restaurant with flowers, he accepted just one glass of the white and maybe two of the red. Mine, however, was kept full by an epicurean wine waiter. Not that I complained, you understand.'

'What did you talk about?'

'Well, he told me his wife understood perfectly that a man must take a beautiful girl out to dinner from time to time. It is an elixir, according to Dmitri, for you cannot be young unless you feel young.'

'I can see where that line would lead.'

'He told me about the beaches on his island in the Aegian. Naturally, the sand is like talcum powder and, of course, you can safely take all your clothes off, should you choose.'

'I see. He suggested that you might want to see it? That he had plenty of bedrooms in his shore-side mansion and that his wife would be thrilled to see him young and happy again?'

'More or less verbatim.'

'Did he ask your opinion on anything? The arts? The Hellenes? Archbishop Makarios?'

'He asked what I thought of his car.'

I laughed.

'You thought you had never seen anything so perfect?'

'I told him he was too young to have so pompous a car. That he should be driving a sports car like any other successful young man.'

'That will have deflated his ego a little.'

'Well, he called for the manager and said a few words in Greek. Then he smiled. We had our Greek coffee, which up to then I had thought was called Turkish coffee, and that was it, the evening was over.

'We stepped out onto the street and there, parked on the double yellow lines by *Lemonia* was a Lamborghini *Miura Bertone*.[53] Dmitri took the keys from his pocket and held the door open for me. In what seemed a very short time we had driven like a rocket back to Earl's Court, where he attempted the customary kiss, and which I firmly declined. I was home, dry and *intacta*.'

I laughed but I doubted I had heard the whole story. Still, a gentleman does not pry.

*

One Saturday, Tev sprung a curious idea on me.

'Fancy a jar or two?' he asked rhetorically. My reply gave no cause for suspense. 'I have a plan. We are going to have a glass in every tube station on the Circle Line that still has a bar. We'll start at Sloane Square and do the whole circuit.'

'Now there's an idea. How many are there?'

'Nobody knows. No one has ever counted. Possibly thirty?'

'Inside the stations? Actually on the platforms?'

'Well, most are in ticket halls, but at least two are actually on the platform.'

'I know one. The *Hole in the Wall* on the clockwise platform at Sloane Square. The ante is the cost of a platform ticket. We can manage that.'

---

[53] *Miura* is Spanish for fighting bull. *Bertone* is the celebrated car designer.

'Quite right. Platform tickets cost two and a half pence. Since we'll finish back at Sloane Square, that's all we'll need by way of entrance fee.'[54]

And so it was. The next Saturday, at eleven o'clock in the morning, we were in that bar on the westbound platform at Sloane Square, half pints of Guinness on the counter in front of us. 'Best stick to halves,' Tev had said. 'Few underground platforms boast a loo.'

I took a sip. It tasted wickedly good.

'Have you read any Iris Murdoch?' asked Tev. 'No? Well you should. Borrow my copy of *A Word Child*. It's just out.'

'What's it about?'

'Well, la Murdoch uses her consummate narrative skill to summon up her 'word child', Hilary Burde. She spends three hundred or so pages trying to disengage his soul from its troubled past. Her book is stuffed with eccentric, larger-than-life characters who debate everything; redemption, human memory and love for a tarnished soul. It's stirring, witty, painful, joyful and much of it is set here or at this bar's diametric opposite at Liverpool Street.'

'How does she describe these strange places?'

'As sources of dark excitement, places of profound communication with London and with the very source of life. She says they are the 'watering holds of Pluto's Kingdom'.'

'Pluto's Kingdom? Great name for the Underground.'

Our mugs were empty and we caught our train. We skipped South Kensington station whose bar, overhanging the platform, had acquired the ironic nickname of *The Snakepit* for reasons which Tev, despite what was rapidly appearing to have been profound

---

[54] *The Hole in The Wall* was the last of London Underground's pubs to close, back in 1985, which is probably why it is still the best remembered.

research, did not know. We alighted at the stop beyond. This was Gloucester Road.

'The bar is halfway up the stairs,' said Tev, merrily leading the way. 'This one has a loo!'

True, the bar had seen better days, but its Jacobethan façade was still intact. Once inside, sipping our second glass of stout, I ventured an opinion.

'This is a palace of a place. When was it built? Who's it for?'

'The noble firm of *Spiers and Pond* built it in 1886. They built three quarters of the refreshment rooms on the tube. Here people have to change between the surface trains and the tube. A lavatory seemed a good idea. The bar was attached to pay for its construction and attendant.'

Some of the lights had given up the ghost but the mahogany and beer engines still looked great. Sadly, there was no time to dawdle. Ladbroke Grove's ground floor bar offered us a swift libation, as did the station that was advertised as Queens Road (Bayswater). Tev's knowledge of this rather esoteric subject unfurled as slowly as a butterfly does from a chrysalis.

'Railway food before *Spiers and Pond*,' Tev explained as we continued on our unvarying diet of Irish soup,[55] 'amounted to stale buns with a veneer of furniture polish and sandwiches made of sawdust. All accompanied by a scalding infusion, satirically called tea. If you were lucky, they were garnished with an icy stare from the behind the counter where the waitress would insolently ignore your existence. It drove the hungry and the thirsty frantic, if not actually insane.'

'Thank you. I've seen *Brief Encounter*. Aren't these bars limited by licensing hours?'

[55] Guinness

'No. That's because their customers are by definition *bona fide* travellers. The restrictions imposed by General French during the Great War do not apply.'

Paddington Station's *blue room*, so called because the 'front' room in London's semi-detached suburban villas had generally been painted blue, had long been closed. In its day had been reported to have been an elevated establishment, suitable for those able to travel first class. Before the war, even tube trains had a first class compartment and a no-smoking carriage for the delicate or the refined.[56] Nor could we use the bar at Edgware Road. It had been closed for six years, after gaining a reputation for welcoming commuters seeking brief and shallow comfort from ladies of the night.

Baker Street's ticket hall bar, unsurprisingly known as *Moriarty's*, delivered an excellent brew, while *A Broom Cupboard*, the bar at Kings Cross underground station, was a fairly scientific description of its size. The half we had there was shortly followed by another at Farringdon.

Those splendid caterers, *Spiers and Pond*, also operated a venue at Moorgate, a part of the station proper, but the management preferred its passengers to access it from the outside. For a moment or so we thought we would have to forgo the pleasure of another glass of the black stuff but a friendly guard opened a discreet door and ushered us in.

'Strictly,' the guard told us in a noisy conspiratorial silence, 'this door is reserved for staff, but its Saturday and, since you young gentlemen appear slightly the worse for wear, your journey into the fresh air might be a possibly fatal shock to the system. There's a lot of traffic about, even at this late hour.'

Inside, the *Moorgate Street Bar* was an essay in faded charm.

---

[56] There were still first class compartments on the Parisian metro until the 1980s.

'I have heard,' said Tev as we leant on the bar for support, that in the '30s an eccentric nobleman hired an entire circle line tube train and took a hundred chums on a circuit. He dressed the railway staff in his own livery and served Champagne.'

'What bliss! But what did the girls do when they needed to make space for the fourth flute of the day?'

'Curtains and buckets served the truly desperate, and *Spiers and Pond* provided the rest.'

'That must have been a truly memorable expedition. Easily the equivalent of Captain Shackleton's.'

By the time we reached Liverpool Street we had downed ten halves, five pints apiece. We could not plausibly plead thirst to be the reason we stopped at *Pat and Mac's Drinking Den* on the eastbound platform, but we stood unsteadily at the serving hatch that let passengers drink while waiting for their train.

Our last pit stop, almost, was at Mansion House, where a buffet bar had also been built by that considerate company of thirst quenchers. True, the bar was not actually on the platform, but it was tantalisingly close. The important thing was that we did not have to leave the station, as, of course, we only had a Sloane Square platform ticket. The ticket collector heard our tale and waved us through. With that we had completed the circuit.

'One for the road?' said Tev, as we finally arrived home at Sloane Square.

'A bit late for that. Let's try the ditch,' I spluttered as our final beverage was painstakingly decanted into a half-pint mug. 'One day I shall write our odyssey in heroic verse.'

'Hexameter or pentameter?' asked Tev.

'Heroic verse,' I replied. Actually I had no idea what form of verse Tennyson had employed.

On the wall was a poster, an advertisement for Guinness, showing a horse resting on a cart being pulled along an Irish lane by a fit-looking farmer. 'Guinness is Good for You' read the caption.

'Look at that.' Said Tev. 'Dactyls and spondees being brought into the late twentieth century by the horse-drawn carriage-load.'

All that was left of our journey was to brave the open air, assault the loos in the middle of the square, fight gravity back up the stairs to the taxi rank and pour one another into a cab.

'Home, James,' said Tev.

As I slumped into the back seat I half-expected the driver to reply, 'Oh no, it's you two again.'

*

Kate had decided to relocate to Paris. Her French was already damn-near perfect. When at Oxford, reading history, she had zeroed in on the Revolution and the First Empire. With Napoleon governing her heart, the young graduate had found a place on the boulevard Montparnasse, no less. It was not overly grand, but it certainly sufficed. It was a studio flat with a vast salon, two miniscule bedrooms and a kitchen large enough to open an oyster.

I found an excuse to pay her a visit. As far as I was concerned, any excuse would do to be back in the 'city of light', but this time my *agent provocateur* was my old friend and former housemate Nicholas Monson who, coincidentally, was writing a piece on the Grand Ayatollah Sayyid Ruhollah Khomeini. At the time the Iranian was in exile in Paris.

The Ayatollah was in no hurry to go home; there was the minor matter of a death warrant issued against his name. He would have to wait until 1979 to reconstitute Iran as an Islamic republic. In the end, when he deposed Mohammad Resa Pahlavi, Khomeini overthrew two and a half millennia of Persian monarchy.

Nicholas had done his research. He knew the new ruler to be a *marja*, a 'source of emulation' in *twelver* Shia Islam. He was a *mujtahid*, or *faqih*, and the author of more than forty books, even if they preached only to the converted. The Ayatollah accused the Shah of the 'crime' of 'steady and systematic secularisation'. He wanted theocratic rule. 'Democracy', he declared, 'is the political equivalent of prostitution'.

No one in the West has ever understood this but, amazingly, Nicholas got his interview.

Kate's spare bedroom was to house the free-lance journalist after he had done his business. She knew Nick of old; he would not be allowed to be too much of a nuisance.

*

The 14e arrondissement had first become famous in the *années folles*, the 1920s, when Guillaume Apollinaire decided to make it the heart of intellectual and artistic life in Paris. Almost singlehandedly he persuaded his artist friends to relocate here from Montmartre. It had become the breeding ground for a generation of artists, but Apollinaire named his new colony 'Mount Parnassus', even though it could scarcely boast a mound, let alone a mount.

Russians, Hungarians, Ukrainians, Central, South and North Americans, Canadians, Mexicans and Japanese flocked to this reincarnation of the Bohemia of the Martyrs. There was resistance, of course. The 'Dandies' - Zola, Manet, France, Degas and Fauré - refused to recognise the new artists' settlement, but grittier tough-talking, die-hard artists, sculptors, painters, writers, poets and composers took to it as waterfowl do to uninviting ponds. Within a couple of seasons Fernand Léger would write of his time in Montparnasse that a man can relax and recapture his taste for life, his frenzy to dance, his need to spend money. In this explosion, life-force fills the world.

Artists, drawn by the creative zeitgeist, came from around the world. They appreciated the modest rents at communes like *La Ruche*, though they had to live without running water, trapped in horrid, damp, unheated 'studios', and forced to share their workplaces with rats. Some exchanged their works for a few measly francs, just to buy food.

En Montparnasse, la pauvreté est un luxe.[57]

Manuel Ortis de Sárate, Camillo Mori and others made their way from Chile. They were bowled over, *boulversés*. They paid tribute to the 'left bank', *en effet*, on their return to Santiago, and founded the *Grupo Montparnasse*.

The very long list of those who found their way to Montparnasse's metaphysical slopes during the *fin de siècle* includes Pablo Picasso, Jean Cocteau, Erik Satie, Marc Chagall, Nina Hamnett, Jacques Lipchits, James Joyce, Ernest Hemingway, Amadeo Modigliani, Ford Madox Ford, Ezra Pound, Max Ernst, Marcel Duchamp, Henri Rousseau, Diego Rivera, Alberto Giacometti, André Breton, Salvador Dalí, Henry Miller, Samuel Beckett, Joan Miró and, though in his declining years, Edgar Dégas.

Montparnasse embraced each new arrival, more in Seurat than in Ingres, no matter how odd or eccentric they were, and mostly without a qualm. When Tsuguharu Foujita arrived from Japan in 1913, not knowing a soul, he had a glass in *Le Select* and met Soutine, Modigliani, Pascin and Léger that same night. Within a week he could add Juan Gris, Picasso and Matisse to the roll call of his closest friends.

---

[57] In Montparnasse, [even] poverty is a luxury. (Jean Cocteau).

In the ominous summer of 1914, when that wonderful English painter Nina Hamnett arrived, on her very first evening the smiling man at the next table at *La Rotonde* economically introduced himself as 'Modigliani, painter and Jew'. They became instant friends, Hamnett recounted. She borrowed a jersey and a pair of corduroys from Modigliani, went to *La Rotonde* where they danced, inside, outside, in the street, all night.

I knew Paris quite well. I had lived in its Latin Quarter for eighteen months, during my 'gap year'. Yes, Paris was my kind of town, but it was to Milan that *CTB* would send me. No longer as Simon Galway's bag man, I was back in the *Principe di Savoia*, all by myself.

It was clear that from now on I would have to endure in spectacular comfort, but one pesky fly was in the ointment. The expenses system. If not with a client or Petronio, I would have to eat in the hotel, delicious but wildly expensive, or in a café where my official 'per diem' would barely stretch to a sandwich. Of course, if I could find an agreeable client, any restaurant in Milan would do.

Piero's lunchtime adventures were also restrained, but for different reasons. In his case he liked to go home for pasta, a carafe of Chianti and forty winks with his wife, as he put it. It must have been thirty-nine, as he gave one of them to me, but no matter, it meant that Piero and I could not join forces and conduct research into an Italian equivalent of the *Guide Michelin*.

*

Simon had instructed me to prepare and deliver two meetings in the morning and two more in the afternoon. If I went for three days, therefore, he would expect me to have arranged a dozen. I always did, and would show him my itinerary for formal sanction. That done, I would immediately rearrange every one of them. Three before lunch, three after. Lunch would remain as before, but I now had a day to myself, safely concealed in a crowded schedule.

*

As a reward for my cunning, I would treat myself to a visit to the Castel Sforzesco, a huge fortress right in the medieval heart of the city and Milan's most dramatic monument. Over innumerable centuries it has been by turns a fortress, a barracks, a private residence and a museum. It had undergone sieges, demolition and reconstruction under Savoyards, French, Spanish, Austrians and, finally, the Italians.

The core of the castle dates back to the early 1300s when the ruling family of Milan was the Visconti. A hundred years later Francesco Sforza was ruling Milan. He rebuilt the fortress. Considering his predilections, it had to be full of ghosts, and angry ones.

I arrived at 10 am to see little in the way of ectoplasm. Instead I saw a picture gallery, a collection of antique furniture, a museum of decorative arts, an infinite collection of vases, and thousands of unfamiliar, unrecognisable musical instruments. A warehouse worth of tapestries was followed by an armoury full of tin suits, lances and crossbows and a curious museum of 'Prehistory and Protohistory'. From this glimpse into a world before time was invented I was brought up to date in an Egyptian Museum.

All this, of course, was because I had repeatedly taken the wrong turning.

The reason why I was there at all was because my hotel concierge had told me that the prisoners were on day release and could be seen there without going all the way to Florence's *Accademia*. By 'prisoners', I mean of course the 'slaves', each of which Michelangelo had carved from single pieces of marble, each the size of a Neolithic standing stone.

Over a light lunch in the castle's very serviceable canteen, I shook off the museum fatigue that had been afflicting my legs. After an espresso it occurred to me that I might profit from directions. After all, I had already paid the considerable fee for the Michelangelos. On the way to the hall that had long been given over to his last masterpiece, the *Pietà Rondanini*, I passed through a chamber containing some very ancient reliquaries and chalices, silverware and parcel gilt, lifted from European churches over the centuries as the forces of darkness - Goths and Earthquakes, Wars and Protestants - set about destroying our heritage.

Here I was forced to pause in my well-intentioned prison visit. My attention had been grabbed by a crucified Christ, hanging on a wire from the ceiling. His cross, presumably a wooden one, had long since been lost, but He was made of sterner stuff. Ivory, in fact. At nearly four feet tall, some noble elephant had bought himself a ticket to paradise.

The sign beneath him declared that He had survived the Tudor rabble's burning of all such 'heretical' effigies[58] by being sold to a Swedish nobleman in 1542, just before the puritan vandals with their buckets of whitewash had set about dowsing our medieval masterworks. From there it had many adventures before fetching up in Queen Kristina's Stockholm palace.

That queen was one of the most educated women of the 17th century. She collected books, manuscripts, paintings and sculptures while her interest in philosophy, mathematics and alchemy drew many scientists to Sweden. If ambitiously, she had wanted her capital to be known as the Athens of the North. Unfortunately - for posterity at least – not only had she reverted to the

---

[58] In the sixteenth century, almost the entire iconography of English Christianity was taken by the cartload to Smithfield to be burned. Frescoed church interiors were whitewashed. The only 'decoration' permitted by the 'reformed' church were two boards, to either side of the 'table', the Lord's prayer on one and the ten commandments on the other. When, occasionally, a rood screen or a doom survives under layers of whitewash, their very rarity makes them all the more dramatic and the loss of the rest almost too much to bear.

religion of her forebears but, like a priest, decided not to marry. In the fiercely Lutheran and paternalistic culture of the time, this was scandalous.

Her conversion to Catholicism, in 1654, undid the widespread recognition of her intelligence and her loyal ministers now wrote her off as feckless, feeble, fickle and, worst of all, feminine. There are not enough 'f's in the language to describe her. When the pope welcomed her into the bosom of the True Church, her ministers demanded her abdication.

The 'Christ crucified' had travelled with her to Rome, where she would change her name from Kristina Augusta Wasa to become Christina Alexandra.[59] From then the medieval sculpture visited many princely collections before fetching up in Milan's *castello*.

The anonymous sculptor had given our Lord an expression that somehow combined the exquisite pain of His paschal sacrifice with a reconciliation with Higher Purpose. His forgiveness of mankind, His willingness, even in such appalling circumstances, to see in us all that was good and forgive what was not, was conveyed in that facial expression. It was a masterpiece and I was completely transported.

My reverie was disturbed, however, by a voice in my ear.

'That's what we should do to our politicians.'

I turned around to come face-to-face with the attendant.

'Crucify then,' he persisted. 'It would send a message. We'd be better off without any of them.'

Poor fellow, I thought as I left him. He did not only have to live with his politicians, he had to live with himself.

---

[59] Greta Garbo memorably portrayed her in *The Queen Christina*, a 'pre-code' Hollywood biographical film, produced by MGM in 1933 by Walter Wanger and directed by Rubin Mamoulian. The film portrays her life. She was queen at six in 1632 and grew to be a powerful and influential wartime leader in the Thirty Year's War.

At last I discovered the 'prisoners', otherwise known as 'captives' or 'slaves'. Some of the fame of these four great statues - *The Awakening Slave, The Young Slave, The Bearded Slave* and *The Atlas Slave* – is due to the fact that they are works in progress. Some say, apparently, that the artist deliberately left them incomplete to represent mankind's eternal struggle to free itself from its material trappings.

This I don't believe for a minute. Michelangelo was a perfectionist. He would never have voluntarily abandoned these astonishing works.

More likely is that the slaves were designed for some great tomb, a pope's perhaps, and the intended patron died before the work was paid for. Surely the sculptor retained the works in his studio in the ultimately foolish hope that some other grandee would ask him to finish them, furnish the tomb and, of course, foot the bill, arm the sculptor's wallet and leg it.

These works of art show all too clearly how terribly hard it is to excavate a figure from within a single block of marble. Their enormous strength seems a metaphor for mankind's effort to liberate its divine spirit from its mortal captivity, trapped as it is in flesh and blood. Each of the captives seems engaged in a desperate fight to shake off the weight of his stone coffin.

I began with the *Awakening Slave*. Michelangelo's understanding of human anatomy is obvious; the slave is depicted as standing with most of his weight on one foot. His shoulders and arms writhe from his hips and legs. This *contraposto*, or counterpoise, couples the prisoner's immense but impotent power with heartrending anguish. The grooves and marks from the artist's hammer and chisel are all clearly visible. At first, Michelangelo's captive can only have been visible to the sculptor's inner eye. He started from the front of the dolmen and worked further in, around and behind, slowly freeing these poor trapped souls as a hero might rescue a child from a landslide.

Michelangelo himself said his task was merely to remove the extraneous. Giorgio Vasari, in his seminal *Lives of the Artists,* hit the mark when he said that the figures want to climb out of the marble 'as from a pool of water'. Vasari recounts that Michelangelo worked for days and nights without sleep. He also revealed that the master neither changed his boots nor clothes for weeks at a time.

The *Awakening Slave* lay next to the *Young Slave*. The latter figure seems almost to have captured itself, burying its face in its left arm, hiding the right one behind its hips, reminding me of those poor folk in Pompeii, imprisoned by all that pumice, mud and lava. The narrowness of the block exaggerates this *contraposto,* as do his slightly bended knees. Michelangelo's profound awareness of human anatomy is especially obvious in the left elbow and in the careful lines of the slave's flexed muscles, even if his face is only beginning to materialise.

The most finished of the four is the *Bearded Slave*. The sculptor has let a thick, curly beard cover much of the captive's face. His thighs are bound by straps of cloth. The creator of *David* has very finely modelled the torso. The figure is on the very edge of freedom - only his hands and part of an arm, probably about to hold a cloth, are incomplete.

The *Atlas Slave* seems to be carrying a huge weight. Perhaps Michelangelo wanted him to represent that primordial Titan who held the entire world on his shoulders? His head, immobilised by whatever it is that threatens to crush him, pushes down but the brave slave pushes back, creating a breath-taking tension. It is a description in stone of an eternal battle, one of elemental forces that, like a volcano or an earthquake, that threaten to explode and devastate entire towns or peoples.

155

I could almost see the 'prisoners' strain as they try to erupt from their marble sarcophagi. Michelangelo must have believed that a sculpture, like a man, was made in the image of God. He did not simply chip away what was needed to reveal what lay within. He created a form of Man in his own right.

I soon learned that the Louvre in Paris has the two other captives, the *Rebellious Slave* and the *Dying Slave*. Giorgio Vasari explains how they ended up there.

> In Rome, [Michelangelo] finished entirely with his own hand two of the captives, divinely beautiful figures, and other statues, better than which have ever been seen. In the end, they were never placed in position, and those captives were presented to Roberto Strossi, when Michelangelo happened to be lying ill in his house: the captives were afterward sent as presents to King Francis and they are now at Ecouen in France.

*

It was time for dinner and I had definitely earned it. As I had no client I did as instructed and went back to my hotel. Those slaves had taken a profound toll on my complacency and ego. I was humbled, reduced to a sad reality perhaps, to have had it so graphically explained how far my own rather limited creative powers were from real genius.

The thought of a plate of good food worked its accustomed magic. It always does. I left my copy of *Lives of the Artists* in my room and took my place at table with a copy of that day's *Corriera della Sera*.

It would however make a poor companion by comparison, though. Hey ho.

I consoled myself over a *frittata mista* and a glass of *Gavi di Gavi*. A genius on the scale of Michelangelo occurs at most every thousand years. It really was not so very shaming to be excluded from such a list.

*

Having lived in both Pompeii and Rome[60] I felt qualified to comment on Milan's restaurants. You will not be surprised to learn that I concluded they reflect a northern bias. Here, then, is a summary of my advice for travellers.

Even before you read the menu, be sure to have an *aperitivo*. In Italy I favour a glass of *satèn*, a sparkling *crémant* from Franciacorta. It's blended from chardonnay and pinot bianco. It's less fizzy than a supermarket *prosecco,* though perhaps a little more than a *frizzante.* The taste is pleasantly subtle, probably because it's aged for at least eighteen months before bottling.

Now you are ready to start your meal with a small plate of *risotto di quaglia.* The quail and cep mushrooms give the dish an exquisite flavour. Lombardy's rice is named after the town of Arborio, in the Po Valley. It is the most absorbent of these most versatile of grains and the risottos it makes are astonishing.

For your main course, Milanese menus will try to tempt you with *cinghiale* - wild boar. If you can resist that, there is always *cotoletta alla milanese.* That is *wiener schnitzel,* of course, but better.

Ossobuco – marrowbone - is familiar everywhere in the world, but they ate it here first. They do a cabbage and pork casserole, *una cassoeula,* that uses odd bits of pork like the ear or cheek. Because (or maybe despite) this it is sheer heaven.

For pudding, *panettone* is compulsory.

The wine waiter will be breathing down your neck as soon as you sit, so order something from the shores of Lake Garda. *Chiaretto* sounds as though it should be a local claret, but is actually a *rosé*, a *rosato.* Made from barbera, gropello, marsemino and sangiovese grapes, it's deeper in colour than a French rosé and has better

---

[60] For the story of these years, read *A Gap Year or Two,* by the author, Jeremy Macdonogh, published in 2012.

acidity. Lugana's white wines, made from the trebbiano grape, are justly celebrated for their fruitiness and their medium body, while San Martino della Battaglia's whites are made from Tocai friuliano. Garda Mantovano's whites, on the other hand, are based on trebbiano and garganega. Their reds are from merlot and molinara and are among the many Lombardic wines worth a sip. No refined imbiber should fail to sample the sweet *moscato passito* from Valcalepio or the light reds from schiava and barbera grapes - the fruit of the Cellatica and Botticino regions.

In the far north of Lombardy there is an alpine valley, Valtellina, that has been producing red wines for the last two thousand years. These are made from nebbiolo, locally known as *chiavennasca* after the nearby town of Chiavenna. The nebbiolo grape is not cultivated in France and is therefore almost unknown in England. What fools we are! A classic Rosso di Valtellina wine is bright crimson, while its aromatic bouquet nods at dried cherries, tar and rose water. As you might expect for a mountain-grown wine, the body is relatively light but, even so, threaded with tannins. They are weaker in body and power than the more famous and prestigious Barolos and Barbarescos, but be patient. Do not drink them before their fifth birthdays. Over that time, gamey, leather-like notes develop and the crimson turns garnet. Magic in a glass.

*

It was a happy young researcher who fell into his bed that night, but my adventure was not quite over. I had arranged to break my journey home in Paris, giving me a Saturday in Montparnasse without any extra travelling costs, save for a bottle of amarone and a *salami alla milanese*.

CTB had acquired a controlling interest in *Muir Beddall Mise et Cie*. This Parisian reinsurance broker had been born some thirty years, before. Its chief, Hugh Muir Beddall, was in my judgement a terrifying creature. Our paths had crossed in London at a gathering of French-speakers in that part of the building known as the golden mile.

'What's your name, fuck-face', he said by way of introduction.

I really had no way of knowing how to respond. Much later I realised I should have said 'Mr fuck-face to you, Sir.' Realising what it is you should have said, when you're descending the stairs and it's far too late, is what the French call *esprit de l'escalier*.

Roger Huggins landed the French account, though at that time his own French was far from perfect. Perhaps to make his life easier, the secretary that looked after us, Brigitte, was herself from Chartres. We taught her to award everyone not in our team with the honorific 'whippersnapper'. She struggled with this. She pronounced it 'whoppersniffer', an eccentricity of which we all agreed not to disabuse her.

*

I had once shared lodgings in Rome with Sandro Ridomi, during my gap year. Rome wasn't built in A D, as Flann O'Brien observed. Nor had been the Ridomi fortune. He had decided to rent a flat in Rutland Gate, Knightsbridge, one of the smaller streets that lead away from Hyde Park.

I knew the cul-de-sac well. For some years, in fact, when I had been unsuccessfully trying my luck with a girl whose parents lived there. She was only an undergraduate, not yet one of the nation's most senior barristers. Her father had told me that Jacob Epstein, the sculptor, threw away his less convincing works into a skip outside his house. I raided it a few times. Mostly I scored *nul points*, but I do have one small and fractured *maquette* to my name.

Sandro had a fellow émigré friend, Alessandro Torri. Count Torri di Bagnara, who owned a flat in Cheyne Walk, Chelsea, overlooking the Thames. He was a collector, and had just acquired a pair of Tiepolos of which he was inordinately proud. Frankly, they puzzled me. Why should one buy poor pictures by a great artist? The other way round makes far more sense.

Torri would eventually return to his castle near Assisi, his tail between his legs after an acrimonious divorce from his wife, Amanda. She was of Greek extraction and had turned housekeeper. Not as a domestic - more in the manner of Zsa Zsa Gabor. 'I'm a 'housekeeper',' la Gabor once said. 'Every time I leave a man, I keep his house.'

I was soon an habitué. It was bound to happen, as the Italian nobleman's pied-à-terre was only a few hundred yards from where Tev and I had ours and my office colleague, Roger Huggins had his.

The countess turned her flat into a court, and many of those who paid her homage were Italian. I will admit I found it helpful to remind myself of countless colloquial turns of phrase, as it would soon be time for me to make a another trip to Milan.

*

Those were curious days for boys and girls. In some ways people were freer than they had been before or even since. Germaine Greer urged women to be decision makers, particularly in matters of romance. Dr Greer's contribution to feminism - humorous, bold and sometimes coarse - stood the resentful nature of the Lysistratian sisterhood on its head, if only for a while. Women, Greer argued, were being persuaded, even by other women, to hate themselves for blindly accepting male supremacy. To withhold their favours would be coercive and vengeful, but ultimately would be at their own expense.

Male domination, she argued, was because men secretly hate women. Dr Greer was no 21st century *noli mi tangere* feminist, the sort that declares all men to be rapists. She insisted instead that the traditional female willingness to please was turning the fair sex into eunuchs. She instructed women to seek out their partners for themselves; not to wait for some fellow to fancy them. To achieve the freedom they deserved, they should abandon both celibacy and monogamy, to pleasure themselves freely.

> The freedom I plead is freedom to be a person, with the dignity, integrity, nobility, passion, pride that constitute personhood. Freedom to run, shout, talk loudly and sit with your knees apart. Freedom to know and love the earth and all that swims, lies, and crawls upon it. Most of the women in the world are still afraid, still hungry, still mute and loaded by religion with all kinds of fetters, masked, muzzled, mutilated and beaten.

Greer's irreverence towards Freud, coupled with her free adaptation of Simone de Beauvoir's brilliant essays on the same subject, suggested that female sexuality should not evolve. It should revolt.

As for bra-burning,

> what asinine claptrap. Bras are a ludicrous invention, but if you make bralessness a rule, you're just subjecting yourself to yet another repression.

The traditional ambition of the girls in *CTB*'s many typing pools was to be chosen by some lucky chap who would press his suit, with her dad's permission, and be rewarded with an irrational number of children and a semi in Essex. This would change. This emerging and more aggressive frame of mind owed much to the birth control pill which, by 1975, had been available for almost a decade. It also coincided with the strange but popular decision to educate boys and girls together. Males and females do not, after the onset of puberty, mix easily with one another. In the playground, an asphalted equality caused protective scales to fall from adolescent eyes. For those of us who had been raised in single-sex schools, and for whom the battle of the sexes was still moderated by gallantry, we were compensated by the widespread if mistaken (in my case) belief that we had access to salaries, careers, and even inheritances. Many objects of desire still thought that if they gave way to our clumsy proposals they need never worry again.

The times were certainly a-changing. Some modern girls actually took up Germaine's encouragement, and began to hunt on the turf we lads had long thought ours alone.

Nicholas Monson and I decided to indulge in a couple of pints-worth of concentrated chinwag in *The Australian*, a fashionable Knightsbridge public house. We had been there for half-an-hour or so, happy in our insouciant gossip and careless imbibing, when two somewhat overdressed young ladies - not unattractive but certainly over-made-up - came into the bar. They sat at a table near us, sipped for some moments at their Cinzanos and lemonade, before looking at each other, standing, and walking over to us.

'Are you posh?' one of them asked Nick.

The honourable Nicholas Monson, heir to the 11th barony, smiled graciously.

'I suppose we are,' he said, after a thoughtful, even respectful pause. I felt rather pleased by this display of class loyalty.

'We're not common, though, like, but we've never been to Knightsbridge before,' said one.

'We read in *Cosmopolitan* that posh people drink in this pub,' said the other.

'That's how we knew you two were posh.'

'Well,' said Nicholas, improvising wildly, 'you'd better join us. You've come a long way.'

'Bloody right,' said the girls, sitting down hard. 'You boys fancy taking two gorgeous girls out for the night?'

'We're not too hard to get,' said the other.

Nick and I swapped what I hope was the briefest of visual question marks. I think I would have been game for a little 'innocent' fun, but Nick was firm.

'Thank you for your kind offer,' he said with grand courtesy. The girls glanced at each other.

'Well,' said the bolder of the two, 'I know when we're not wanted.'

Had we offended two adventurous girls or had we defended ourselves? One thing was sure. We had experienced role reversal. It was interesting to have heard an ancient story told from the other side. I liked the Greeresque spirit of the two ladies from Dagenham. This was feminism based on real equality, not some idiocy like 'girls on top'. Such ladies were too often demeaningly labelled 'laddettes', which of course was nothing more than an old-school masculine reflex towards self-preservation.

Had Dr Greer's philosophy prevailed, the battle of the sexes would have achieved a truce. Sadly, her message did not carry.

A more unpleasant future was in store for us all, especially for women. Mutual attraction was now to be resisted, not embraced. Feminism was taking a turn for the extreme. It decided that heterosexuality itself was 'sexist'. All men were rapists or potential rapists. This dismal conclusion was long promoted by Jenni Murray in *Woman's Hour*. She may have been infected by the residual Puritanism that characterises the US.

Continental Europe, at least, rejects 'me too'. Its opinion was elegantly set by Catherine Deneuve and reflects the immortal brilliance of Simone de Beauvoir. She published *Le Deuxième Sexe* in 1949 with a great fanfare, a flood of controversy and one admirer in New York, a retired zoology professor, Howard M. Parshley.

He told the world that it was not dogmatically feminist, but 'intelligent, learned, and well-balanced'. He was right and de Beauvoir gave him permission to translate it into English.

*

Meanwhile, in *CTB* it was becoming widely known that I could speak French. This was not always good news.

To my great surprise, Alison, who typed my letters, told me one morning that the police wanted a word with me in a room on the second floor. I did not recall having recently murdered anybody. I said I'd be 'happy' - in principal at least - to help them in their enquiries.

The reception I had might have been penned by Le Carré. Two men in suits were sitting behind a desk, while a third stood to one side. One to read, one to write, and the third to keep an eye on the two intellectuals. Jack Lloyd presented me and then hurriedly withdrew.

'We understand you travel frequently to Paris?'

'As often as I can. What civilised man would not?'

'Mr Lloyd tells us that you can speak perfect French.'

'I do speak French. Perfectly, no. Adequately perhaps.'

'Were you there over the bank holiday weekend of the 5th to 7th?'

I took out my pocket diary.

'I'm afraid not, Sorry to disappoint.'

'You were in England? Can anyone vouch for you?'

'I expect so. I haven't checked. What is all this about, officer?'

The one who could read slid a photo across the desk. It was a fuzzy rendition from a frame of a CCTV, taken in a French bank. The man in the photograph could have been anyone. Including me, unfortunately.

'Is this you?' he asked.

'No. Definitively not. I was in London. I may have said this already.'

The one who could write now showed me a photocopied note. Its message was curiously literary. *'Afin d'éviter un voyage sans escale au paradis, il vous suffit de remplir ce sac avec tout l'argent dans votre caisse. Soyez sage. Je porte un pistolet.*[61]

'That's not my handwriting, officer. That is a French hand. This script is cursive, mine is italic.'

'Is it? Write me a sentence here.'

I obliged. The three looked at it for a good two minutes. In such circumstances, two minutes can feel like an hour, but at last they came to a conclusion.

'Very well, you may go. Do not attempt to leave the country. We know where you live.'

Not leaving the country was a bridge too far.

*

What the reinsurance market calls the 'renewal season' had just finished. I had renewed my Italian accounts before the first of January, as I had to. In the weeks following New Year's Day we had a chance to exploit our competitors' weaknesses and tardiness and our customers' consequent anger. We might even obtain a larger share of their business in the future. A telex to Piero and a dozen meetings were in the bag.

Malpensa airport was fog bound, yet again, so I landed in the early evening at Milan's other airport, Linate, where I found a cab and 'hurtled' into the centre of Italy's 'moral capital'. One hurtles extremely slowly in that city, especially on January 6, a feast day.

---

[61] To avoid a premature trip to Paradise, you need only fill this sack with the money in your till. Be wise, I have a pistol.

Officially the Italians are celebrating the circumcision of our Lord. In practice, paganism has not yet been wholly eradicated. 'Good' children find themselves rewarded by a witch, *la befana*, with 'gold' coins made of chocolate, while 'bad' children get an (edible) lump of coal (also chocolate). Bless her, the *befana* is the nicest kind of witch.

The next morning found me at the eighteenth century *Caffè Cova* for a matutinal coffee and a *spremuta d'arancia*.[62] Piero had suggested meeting him there after I had bored him on the subject of architecture. Piero had his revenge for my appreciation of the mother of the arts. He talked nonstop nonsense about Juventus and AC Milan. My ears folded back into my head. I was impressed by the *Cova*, however, especially when I discovered you can stick your feet out under your table and the shoeshine boy will make your pumps glow before you get them back.

After such treatment, my shoes might have been mistaken for the wonders in the shops in the nearby Via Monte Napoleone.

This famous street is at the heart of the fashion district known as the *quadrilatero della moda*. It is like the Via Condotti in Rome, but it's longer and plays host to Europe's most expensive and exclusive bootmakers and jewellery shops. All the discreet outlets of those Italian fashion designers of which we have all heard are there. Their prices can make a lady faint and her husband cry. In short it has everything that London's Jermyn Street and Paris's rue du Faubourg St Honoré can boast, interspersed with the palaces of the flower of the Lombardic aristocracy, the Melsi di Cusano, the Gavassi, the Carcassola Grandi and the Taverna.

Absent from that little list is the Marliani family. They no longer have their palace here. Up to 1943 it

---

[62] Freshly squeezed orange juice.

had been the finest private house to survive in Italy, possibly Europe, from the middle ages. No longer. Allied bombing sent it to heaven.

Piero had plans to keep me very busy, as he was supposed to, and I had no objections. He was great company, except when straying onto the subject of football.

Piero and I always spoke to each other in Italian. Since those wonderful couple of years in Rome, better known as my 'gap year', I had let it rust a little. Now it was rising like a trout to a fly. Thanks to new Italian friends in London and my business in Milan, every day it grew a little bit better, less rigid, more colloquial.

Rome, however, had not prepared me, philosophically speaking, for Milan. The political capital believes itself to be in the Centre of Italy. Milan, in the north, could hardly be a more different place. Despite a shared language, Milan's spirit is almost Germanic. The trains run on time. They wouldn't dare do otherwise. Some say such officious punctuality owes something to Benito Mussolini. All I will say is that the city is more Teutonic than Sicilian.

Piero was very excited. His boss had just secured the Montedison account and it needed a London broker. This enormous Italian petrochemical conglomerate had refineries all over Italy, plus a few in Libya, Abyssinia (as Italians still liked to call Ethiopia) and Albania. Sergio Corsi, Piero's boss, had packaged them in a cascade of treaties. Could I place them in the London market? Of course I could. Obviously.

*

We went to our meetings before lunch and afterwards we compared notes over a cappuccino in a friendly bar. Piero then went home for his lunch and a nap while I had a delicious *rosetta* stuffed with *porchetto*[63] and a beer,

---

[63] A crusty bun filled with suckling pig.

all by myself. All tightly within those officious expenses guidelines.

Afterwards I went to the back door of *La Scala* where a kiosk sold returns and single tickets. I had seen countless photographs of this unusual palace of a theatre, the most celebrated and magnificent opera house in the world.[64] It had opened in 1778, on the feast day of Milan's patron saint, St Ambrose. To this day, the opera season opens on December 7. The mayor insists that performances must end before midnight, so longer operas start earlier in the evening.

I hit the jackpot. That very night I would see the opening night of a new production of Puccini's *La Bohème*. I was delighted and frankly amazed at my luck. Stalls and gallery aside, the whole house is arranged in boxes. I found myself clutching a 'return', in the first circle, in my sweaty hand. I would be within winking distance of the royal box itself.

Maestro Georges Prétre had cast Mirella Freni and Luciano Pavarotti as the lovers in Puccini's heart-breaking opera. The work blends social realism, intimacy and crowd scenes with the tenderest of duets and solos, the Bohemian way of life and a tragic death, an especially effective formula. I was much looking forward to hearing La Freni sing *Mimi*, but it was not going to happen. She had fallen ill.

Not that I had any idea. I was in the *Obica*, a bar in front of the cathedral, celebrating my purchase of a ticket with a glass of Campari, topped up with frizzante, planning to see Leonardo's *Last Supper* while I still had time.

*

Over that carefully liberated lunch 'hour',[65] I had time to pay the Convent of *Santa Maria delle Grazie* a visit.

---

[64] Actually, that is usually the one I have been to most recently.
[65] Nearer three hours in fact.

It had a late 15th-century mural, commissioned by Ludovico Sforza, Duke of Milan. It is one of the world's most recognisable paintings. It is Leonardo da Vinci's *Ultima Cena*, his 'Last Supper'.

It was not in great condition, despite or because of six hundred years of repeated restorations. Nor can it have helped when we bombed the church in 1943. It spent the last years of the war unprotected from rain, snow and frost, the roof off and a wooden shutter nobly resting against it to protect its modesty. It faded, naturally, but despite such travails, however, nothing has diminished it as a show-stopper.

The wall painting measures 15 x 30 ft, give or take. It took Leonardo a long time to paint, not because he had ADHD (as some revisionaries now claim) but because as he was simultaneously engaged on a huge number of other projects. The monastery's prior complained about the delay, which angered the artist. Leonardo wrote to the abbot, explaining he had been struggling to find a suitably villainous face for Judas and, if he could not find a face that corresponded with what he had in mind, he would use the features of the prior.

The mural portrays each apostle's reaction when Jesus said one of them would betray him. All twelve react differently, and all draw on the complete spectrum between anger and shock.

> First we visited the fading inimitable fresco of Leonardo da Vinci. How vain are copies! Not in one, nor in any print, did I ever see the slightest approach to the expression in our Saviour's face, such as it is in the original. Majesty and love - these are the words that would describe it - joined to an absence of all guile that expresses the divine nature more visibly than I ever saw it in any other picture.
>
> Mary Shelley, *Travel Writing*.

If that was all I would see that day it would have been enough, but my adventure was not yet over. Had I but known, somewhere within *La Scala*, Luciano Pavarotti was advising a desperate Prétre to locate Ileanna Cotrubas.

'She knows the libretto and is not engaged anywhere else.'

Unfortunately, no one had her address. Then Pavarotti himself came to the rescue. He remembered that the head of the Chicago opera, Carol Fox, was in London. She would surely know. The panicking maestro tried to contact her. Eventually he was put through to Ileanna's husband, Manfred Ramin - the conductor and critic from Berlin - in their house near Sevenoaks. It turned out that the soprano was at a routine appointment with her doctor. When she got back, Ramin told her that *La Scala* wanted her to sing *Mimi*.

'That's nice,' she is reported to have said.

'I'm not making myself clear,' Ramin replied. 'They want you to sing tonight!'

La Cotrubas must have found the rest of the day unbelievable. She had yet to pack what she needed, buy a plane ticket for Milan, discover that fog still afflicted Malpensa airport, learn that planes were being diverted to Linate and, even worse, they were stacked in a holding pattern. Circling over Milan, Ileanna Cotrubas started to put on her make-up.

Clearly she knew that I would be in the audience.

*

I had another three meetings early that afternoon, one an hour after 3 pm. I actually enjoyed these intensive agendas, but I was impatiently drumming my fingers at the prospect of going to *La Scala*.

Georges Prétre telephoned the Mayor of Milan, who was suitably shocked. Things in Milan were going from very tense to even tenser. The mayor resolved that his city would do all in its power to keep the show on the road.

When Ileanna Cotrubas's flight finally touched down, a convoy of police cars came right up to the plane, lights blazing, sirens deafening. They put the diva in the back of one of their Alfas with a professional driver who drove like Fittipaldi to the opera house, claxons blaring, and under orders to ignore Milan's traffic lights.

By all accounts La Cotrubas was very calm, though she later confessed to fearing that a disastrous first night at La Scala, of all places, would destroy her entire career.

Jeanette Pilou, Mirella Freni's understudy, had been in wig and costume for hours, ready to take her place. She had been told that 'if *la Cotrubas* arrives before ten to nine, then she is on. If it's after, then it is you.'

Ileanna Cotrubas arrived at *La Scala* fifteen minutes before curtain up. Luciano Pavarotti greeted her tenderly while Georges Prétre worried her by saying he liked to beat *Mi Chiamano Mimi* in two time, not in four.

This was around the time when I pitched up at *La Scala*, bushy-tailed and utterly oblivious of the unfolding drama. We - the audience - had still to learn the bad news. That was when Maestro Prétre stood soberly in front of a hostile theatre to explain that Madama Freni was indisposed. The elegant, cultured crowd did not like him particularly in the first place - he was not Italian - and it liked his news even less. In traditional Milanese style, it hissed and shouted, ready to lynch the messenger.

Notwithstanding, at last, the curtain went up. Like everyone else there I now knew little of the real life drama. It was enough for me at least to wait extra-anxiously for Mimi to discover the boys in their

171

freezing garret, warming their hands by burning their manuscripts.

Then Mme Cotrubas made her entry. Her first aria, *Mi Chiamono Mimi,* is where she introduces herself as a neighbour. Lucky Lucy's *Che Gelida Manina* should have come after it, but there was an ominous silence. As it turned out, no one had needed to worry. Pavarotti generously gave her audience a second or two to collect itself, and when it did the applause was tumultuous. Her rendition had been flawless, magical and desperately moving. After she finished it, there was the briefest of silences. Then *La Scala* shook as in an earthquake. The theatre-goers yelled and screamed their delight. Pavarotti and Prétre let her take the ovation for seven long minutes.

We could see her mouth the words, 'ευχαριστώ Θεέ μου' - Thank you, my God.

The evening proved to be, for me and for all of us, the experience of a lifetime. It had been a huge success; why would it not be? No one yet knew this 'Mimi'. Not even Karl Böhm, who apparently was in the audience. Everyone was whispering to their neighbour 'who is this?' or 'where's she from?' and nobody knew.

Her rendition was flawless, magical and desperately moving. After she finished it, there was the briefest of silences. Then *La Scala* shook as in an earthquake. In a tumult the theatre-goers yelled and screamed its delight. Pavarotti and Prétre let her take the ovation for seven long minutes.

We could see her mouth the words, 'ευχαριστώ Θεέ μου' - Thank you, my God.

Her rendition was flawless, magical and desperately moving. After she finished it, there was the briefest of silences. Then *La Scala* shook as in an earthquake. In a tumult the theatre-goers yelled and screamed its delight. Pavarotti and Prétre let her take the ovation for seven long minutes.

We could see her mouth the words, '*ευχαριστώ Θεέ μου*' - Thank you, my God.

*

Milan's *Piazza del Duomo* can confidently compete with *Piazza San Marco* in Venice or *Piazza Navona* in Rome for Napoleon's famous accolade, 'the finest drawing room in Europe'.[66]

At one end is the gothic cathedral, at the other the eighteenth century opera house, *La Scala*. In between are bars, *gellaterie* and delicatessens. *Gellaterie?* What the Italians don't know about ice cream isn't worth knowing. Start with pistaccio.

I had still to visit the *Galleria Vittorio Emmanuele II*, which adjoins the famous piazza. It is a vast shopping arcade for men, something like London's Burlington Arcade but on steroids. I didn't have much money of my own but I decided to buy something I had never seen in England - a briar shaving bowl, a proper hog-bristle shaving brush in the same wood[67] and a gilded safety razor, all of which hung from a silver-gilt stand. It would sit nicely beside one's bathroom's shaving glass, when one acquired one. We were making a start.

A touch of class, after all, is better than no class at all.

*

Another day, another suite of back-to-back meetings, and I was on the flight home with an order to place three new treaties reinsuring Montedison's petrochemical works in Italy, Eastern Europe and North Africa.

Piero had long been sworn to secrecy about my rescheduling and my consequent days of adventure. The Montedison portfolio easily made up for it. I decided not to reveal to Simon Galway the full extent of my

---

[66] *Le salon le plus beau en toute Europe.* I must add Playa Major in Madrid, Place Vendôme in Paris, and Place des Héroes in Arras.
[67] Which I still own.

rubber-necking. Discretion is the better part of valour, everywhere and most especially in the City of London.

Once home, I discovered that our flat had enjoyed a lick of paint and that our draughty window had been repaired. New curtains and carpets made the place almost homely, while Tev had acquired a appropriately Welsh Dresser and a new gas cooker for the kitchen.

He told me he'd scoured the auction rooms in Lots Road and had bought some flimsily knocked-up furniture at appropriately knock-down prices.

Meanwhile, while I was away, Caroline Swan, whom I had met in both Rome and Paris, had finally come home to England. She had taken up with Robert Booth, a director of well known language school in Kensington.

Robert, looking for me - I presume - rang up the flat and spoke to Tev. Had he ever been to Annabel's, the legendary night spot in Berkeley Square? Tev faithfully reported that neither he nor I had so far darkened its doorstep.

'Then you and Jeremy will be my guests. I have a class of two young ladies and, in an incautious moment, I invited them to come with me and help me make a nuisance of myself on the dance floor. I then realised I would forever earn the unpleasant epithet of being a dirty old man, so I invited my girlfriend Caroline Swan, who knows Jeremy from his Euro-peligrinations. There it is. One of me, and three girls. Your company would protect me from comment on the platform and give me an alibi. Sorry to impose!'

'At least tell us that they are good looking,' said Tev somewhat cautiously.

'Kristina is a German beauty while Fiona is the daughter of an Irish banker. Either that or a general. I don't remember which. They are the ripest fruit on a grocer's counter, one whose sign proclaims 'do not touch me until I am yours'.'

'I'll have a word with Jeremy when he's back from Italy. I predict we're on.'

*

London's most celebrated nightclub was and is Annabel's, deep in the capacious basement of the eighteenth century palace known as the Clermont Club, 46 Berkeley Square. Its membership was set at £750 a year, quite a lot in 1975. It was almost a quarter of my annual income. There was also a five-year waiting list for prospective members.

Once passed the three-headed dog that fended off the great unwashed, one proceeded down a stately blue and golden canopied staircase to discover a smallish bar, nicknamed the 'card room'. One was now in an anteroom, pleasantly furbished with eighteenth century pieces, where one could sit out the dancing for a number or two with a glass and a cigarette. Those were the days.

I had time to admire Mark Birley's picture collection which left little wall space. Great swags of azure velvet curtains reinforced this reinvention of the baroque. In the card room the music was audible but not intrusive. Were it not for the three exquisite sirens on Robert's tentacular arm, I might have sat there all night.

The music in 1975 was rather good. It was still an era of melody. The glam rock band T Rex would be on after 10 pm and, in the meantime, a talented DJ was playing the sounds of the day - Queen, Kinks, Led Zeppelin, Wings - to name but a few.

I had detected a method in the DJ's madness. Four fast tracks were followed by one slow one. Girls will always accept the offer of a fast dance - there are no strings attached after all. If you fancy a smooch, therefore, let three bops go by and only then take to the floor. Let your chosen beauty show off her natural rhythm and only then close in for the clinch. In love, so like comedy in many ways, timing is everything.

The subterranean but celestial stage aimed to reward an awestruck clientèle with a blend of the Arabian Nights and a scene from a Hollywood romcom. I was in there with Fiona before the penny I had tossed for her stopped spinning.

The price I had to pay was three minutes of Status Quo's *Down Down*. Then it was time for a slow number. Mama Cass began to croon a number which I had associated with Doris Day, *Dream a Little Dream of Me*. Fiona was cradled in my arms and I had died and gone to heaven. That song still has a weird effect on me.

The floor was conjured out of *Who's Who* that night. The Prince of Wales was there, dancing with Camilla Shand. Despite our intimate friendship, he did not feel the need to present himself to me and my dancing partner, oddly departing from his usual form. There were so many celebrities on the ground they almost seemed human. It was especially curious to see the former US President Richard Nixon in the arms of a blonde of the platinum variety.

I was struck by all the different generations that were there, like a society wedding, all of us in our evening kit.

Annabel's may be where East meets West, and the Middle East had sent many an envoy. Why not? To me, the club was the *sine qua non* of hedonism. Annabel's was and is an aphrodisiac and it far outranks the common or garden oyster.

'Are you enjoying yourself', Robert asked me as I took Fiona back into the card room.

'I certainly am,' I replied. I was lucky to be there, and Tev and I were to get luckier still, but that's another story.

*

176

Back in the office, Roger Huggins told me in a conspiratorial way that he was bored. Like all of us he had to look busy, even when he was not, and he would load his slip-case with important documents and head for what he was pleased to call the 'flesh pots' of the City of London. In other words, a pub.

He was not alone. Every pub for a mile around Lime Street was packed. We favoured the Lamb in Leadenhall Market, a covered Victorian arcade. If anyone wanted to trap us with tankard in hand they would surely look further away? The Lamb Tavern has been a part of the tapestry of the City of London - since 1780 it implausibly claimed - and is very close to Lloyd's itself.

'What time do casinos open, do you think?' Roger asked me. As I had never been to one I had no idea.

'Why don't we find out? There's no need to play for serious money – the smallest chip in most of them is 50p. Let's jump in a cab and head for the West End.' Which is what we did.

The Pink Elephant Club was just opening its doors as Roger and I arrived and there was no one to ask if we were members. We merely walked in.

'Let's play Blackjack,' said Roger. 'It can't be hard. It's a version of Pontoon.'

We strode up to the only open blackjack table. It had a female croupier. Or should that be *croupière*?[68] Had we been drawn into her web by the prospect of wasting a little time and money or, very possibly, by her dark seductive eyes? Her badge said 'Sharon' and her closely fitting red suit had white piping.

'All the boys love a uniform,' said Roger as we steered ourselves towards her kidney-shaped table. She was shuffling several packs of cards together and, when

---

[68] No. Ed.

we reached her, she put them in a shoe from which she could draw one card at a time.

'Sit down lads,' she said. Her wonderful olive skin somehow gave her voice a backdrop that hinted at every pleasure of the orient. 'Have you ever played Blackjack before?'

Of course we hadn't, but we tried to look sophisticated. The lady graciously smiled at our poor pretence.

'Here, put a chip or two down by your cards and let's see what the cards have in store for you.'

Our fifty pence chips went down and she dealt me a king and Roger a seven. She then dealt herself an eight.

'Now I'll deal you your second card.'

I had a four of clubs. Roger had a six of spades. That meant my points added up to eleven and Roger's to thirteen.

'You both will need another card,' she advised. 'What we do here is say 'card', not 'twist', when we mean to go on.'

My shout. 'Card', I said. I drew a six, making seventeen.

'Stick there,' she said. 'Now you, young sir?'

Roger tapped his cards, like a professional I thought. She dealt him an eight of diamonds. Now she dealt herself a second card. A five of hearts. Her third was a nine of diamonds.

'Twenty-two!' she said delightedly. 'You've both won!'

She put a 50p chip on Roger's and my ambitious stacks. We played for an hour. She suggested we 'stay' or 'draw', according to our cards. Somehow she seemed to know how the cards would fall. By the time we emerged in the street Roger and I had more than £100 each, a small fortune.

'That lady is some kind of angel,' I told Roger on the way back to the office.

'There you are wholly mistaken,' said my sober colleague. 'She is Satan. She knows that she has baited you into her lair and that you'll be back, ready to starve your future children and be evicted from your flat.'

The devil, I had learned, contrary to ecclesiastical rumour, is female.

*

When Tev suggested a trip to Greece, 'to catch a few rays' in Donald Sutherland's immortal words, I was up for it. Dmitri Lemos, wanting to hellenify Tev, had decided he should visit Delos, 'where Greece began'. Dmitri had booked him into the nearby island of Naxos's St George Beach Hotel. There are no hotels on Delos itself.

Tev had to learn something of Greece's long story. Delos was Greece's sacred isle and was where their gods made themselves at home. This, therefore, was less of a holiday than a pilgrimage. The Cyclades were only the beginning. Tev had the courtesy to explain to me how almost every ancient power at one time controlled the Cyclades, that vast spiral of some two hundred islands that sweep out from Delos like a nebula.

'Listen carefully, Jeremy,' Tev told me over the rim of his spectacles. 'By the fifteenth century, Constantinople, the former capital of the Eastern Roman Empire, had been reduced to a shining Christian jewel in a Mohammedan sea. Outside its walls, its former possessions had been taken by the soldiers of the Prophet. Still the city held out, its cisterns filled with drinking water from the domed Vitosha mountain, its foodstuffs smuggled in through countless unprotected gates from the forests of Bulgaria.

'The rest of Byzantium was divided in two. *Latinocratia*, the empire of the Latins, was administered from Ravenna, while *Francocratia* was ruled by the Doges of Venice, whose 'Frankish'[69] warriors were famed for their wanton savagery, cruelty and barbarity.'

I have always enjoyed a good lecture. Tev is a natural scholar and I am a natural pupil.

'I suppose that if the Cyclades had the wherewithal to attract the attention of *La Serenissima*, they will have attracted the Ottomans in equal measure?'

'The history of the Cyclades, appropriately enough, goes in cycles,' he explained. '*Francocratia* would come to a slow and painful end with the Ottoman conquest. The wealth of the Cyclades was weighed in marble, emery and wine. It took the Turks until the 16th century to finish the job. The Turks have long since gone home, retreating to their only remaining Grecian territory, the eastern half of Cyprus. Since then Lord Byron, with various other Romantic poets, countless watercolourists and, these days, at least according to Dmitri, legions of back-packing tourists clutter its beaches.'

'Like us?'

'Of course, though the sartorial details may differ. The good news is that the boss has told me to bring a chum for company. All our expenses are on him. There are conditions, of course. It's down to us to do our bit for Queen and Country.'

'We are to be paid to be tourists?'

'I have a purpose. I am to acquire enough Greek to be courteous in that language. The hotel that Dmitri has booked us into is a few minutes' walk from the waterfront, apparently, not too far from the old town. That's what he tells me, anyway.'

'What will we do there?'

---

[69] They were so-called after the racial mix of the Fourth Crusade of 1204.

I had been to Athens before, in my 'gap year', nigh on three years before. Then I had trodden the steep track up to the Acropolis, and seen the National Archaeological Museum and the Delphic Oracle, mostly in the company of a small troupe of terrifying American teenage girls that I was supposed to be supervising. But no, I had never seen the islands, though Mykonos was on everyone's lips - the in-place to outstrip all others, mostly because of its visitors' propensity to strip off their clothes on the aptly-named 'Paradise' beach.

'We'll take in a few sights, sunbathe a lot, drink gallons of Demestica and come back seasoned world travellers,' said Tev.

The plan was to fly to Athens, arrive before the cockerels had cleared their throats, take a bus from the airport, catch an early ferry from Piraeus and proceed directly to Naxos, not passing 'go'. Well, what more is there? I was on board.

Our plan was to arrive in good time for lunch. Once we were there, local ferries could take us to Delos, Paros or Mykonos; the first for some culture vulturing, the second for simple variety and the third to see whether we could identify Julie Christie without her kit on.

Since we had convinced ourselves that we were not common-or-garden tourists but Noble Seekers after Truth, we thought it appropriate to begin the journey in our Prince of Wales Check suits.

Even before we had landed we had seen from the aircraft's windows that Greece was large and mountainous.

True, we attracted a considerable amount of derision from our fellow charter passengers, but it was readily compensated by the stewardesses with their wonderful in-flight service. So very good was it that Tev, I think, actually fell in love. With all of them.

181

Not so much later, a ferry let us breathe the tasty Mediterranean air, seasoned as it was with a little salt. We arrived on Naxos, clad in our absurd raiment, and were in time for late morning drinks.

We were happy to discover that the warm and gentle air was heavily scented with basil, thyme and oregano. An appetising suite of aromas indeed.

When our taxi deposited us at the St George's Beach Hotel we found it to be a pretty enough two storey building, if a little short of super-luxurious. It lacked air-conditioning and our doors and windows would have to be left open if we were we not to melt in the heat.

St George Beach was right on the beach, (good), and fifty yards from a bar that favoured bouzouki music, (bad), and which only turned off the noise when Apollo tugged the sun back from Persephone's stronghold in Hades. It had a simple dress code.

'Tourists must cover their bits.' The concierge glanced at our three-piece suits and laughed. 'Those clothes, however, may be overkill.'

He then had good advice for us. 'Don't even think of touring the island by bus. Buses on Naxos are there to serve the local population. They leave the most remote parts of Naxos early to drive to the *chora*[70] and in the early evening they return to the villages. It may make life easy for the locals but it doesn't serve those visitors who have not hired mopeds. Get yourselves a couple. Explore the beaches at Kalandos, Hilia Vrisi, Pinelo or Psili Ammos. You will find they pay no service to modesty. Or you could stay here and watch our Beach Volleyball Tournament?'

He winked. There was something, clearly, I didn't know about beach volleyball. But where to begin?

---

[70] The hill-top capital of a Greek island is always called the *Chora*.

We started our systematic investigation that same afternoon. At no great distance, as the crow flies, from our hotel was the *chora*. To get there, as the mountain goat trots, we had so many steps to climb that the path was better suited to apprentice mountaineers than businessmen, even young ones.

Upon our breathless arrival we discovered, to our qualified delight, great bars, dodgy nightclubs, ghastly bouzouki dives, shops both tatty and interesting, average cafés, and any number of promising restaurants. The closer we came to the citadel, or *kastro*, the more picturesque the town became. Cycladic arches lent the town a lot of charm. Its narrow, overhung lanes, were carpeted with underfed but sleepy cats. The shade turned each lamp-lit boutique into Aladdin's cave.

Horribly lost, we repeatedly found ourselves where we had been an hour or so before, until we stumbled upon a hidden garden restaurant. That's where we had a late lunch of dolmades and red mullet, not to ignore those little carafes of chilled retsina. We left healthy, marginally less wealthy and a lot wiser.

Naxos's *chora* is really very urbane. We made a note of several small if interesting museums. There is a Venetian Museum, naturally, and an art gallery - the *Petalouda*. I will readily admit the *chora* has a cultural soul. One example: the privately owned Baseos Tower organises concerts, recitals, traditional Greek nights, exhibitions and concerts throughout the season.

While not late, we were both tired. We had risen very early and flying and its associated shenanigans, especially for cattle-class passengers, are exhausting. A snooze on the beach was warranted. Possibly a perusal of yesterday's *Times*? Or, in Tev's case, another chapter of *Ill Met by Moonlight*?

It was time for us to brave the steps home and take to our rooms, but that was when Tev noticed a place that hired out mopeds. Conveniently, it was open.

'We'll take a couple. If not, we'll slip and break our necks. Come on, let's take to the road; it'll be a damn sight safer than walking down those steps!'

*

Naxos's incomparably lush mountain slopes are littered with unspoiled villages, peopled by country folk who live all year in Naxos. The large chain supermarkets, like DIA and Atlantic, have something of a captive market. They are cheaper but a little less exciting than the local shops.

The next morning we took our little bikes back up to the *chora* to find Greek coffee, yoghurt and honey. That's where we began the serious business of planning the day. Now we had mopeds no qualms remained about exploring the island's interior.

We had seen from our map that there wasn't a circular route around the island so to go inland we would have to brave its hairpin bends. Great fun on the mopeds, though all too easy to get lost. In fact, to reach the villages and beaches to the east, we would have to climb Mount Sas and descend on its steep far side. I may have looked concerned.

'Don't be such a big girl's blouse', said Tev, pointing impatiently at his map. 'Our mopeds will sail along those roads. We could take a look at Agios Prokopios and Aya Anna. Seaside resorts maybe but the book says they're charming.'

Now I too was studying the map.

'Most of Naxos's villages are inland, rather than by the sea,' I observed. 'We should head for the interior.'

'I agree. Nine tourists in ten are here for the sea. In all likelihood the coastal resorts will be over-developed, commercialised into oblivion. The real Greece is inland. I'll bet those villages have not yet reaped the unalloyed joys and delights of tourism.'

'We could start with Lionas, or even Moutsouna. They look hard to reach. Time itself will have been on hold there; they'll be unspoiled.'

'Halki and Apiranthos are also off the beaten track and they may be slightly easier to find. That's where we should look for local character and a slower pace.'

'Why don't we start with the temple of Demeter? The guidebook says the landscape is lovely, and our concierge says the locals are lovable,' Tev told me. He lowered his voice. 'Especially the girls.'

He read a line or two from the guide.

> The temple is a late archaic temple in the area of Gyroulas, about a mile south of Ano Sangri. It was built around 530 BC and is probably the earliest Ionic temple in existence. The temple was rediscovered as recently as 1949, and has been carefully reconstructed from its fallen stones. It had been completely built from Naxian marble. The Ionian order originated here in Naxos.

He closed the book and laughed.

'One universal feature of guidebooks is a peculiar blend of pomposity and nationalist nonsense,' Tev concluded, calling the waiter. 'Σας ευχαριστώ πολύ. Το λαγαριασμό παρακαλώ.'

'The bill, please,' I presumed he had said and, with that, we were off. What seemed like minutes later we found Demeter's Temple two miles south of the village of Sangri. She liked to build her shrines in fertile areas. Or was it the other way around? Could the goddess of grain have made them fertile? Either way, the valley that spread around Sangri was all of that.

Her ruins were not so large. Her box-like structure, with four of its five great columns, either rebuilt or still standing, was an attractive sanctuary a little off the tourist track, though not even a quarter of an hour's ride from the *chora*.

We gathered from the guidebook that the sanctuary had begun here in this tiny temple. Over the centuries that followed, banqueting halls, priests' quarters, and other dependencies had been added until the destructive agent called Time claimed them back. We also saw how impressive the simple site was, set amongst its sentinel pines, shaded but with glorious views over the landscape, and by 4 o'clock we were at a charming if ruinous Portara, well off the beaten track, on a headland by the sea. It had been hard to reach, even on our mopeds. Three thousand years before it will have looked dramatic when arriving by trireme but the little that remained was seriously fragile.

I worried what an earth tremor or a nasty storm might do. The sea spray reaches it easily and the wind was high as we slithered over its slippery slope. Along the highway we took in farms and dairies to either side. We had seen that a fertile interior had kept the island's agricultural traditions alive. Everyone had told us that farming was being slowly abandoned in favour of tourism, but here in Naxos many were determined to scrape a living from cultivation, herding and fishing.

Our road took us past small churches and, sometimes, two or three would huddle together in a single village. Here and there an inaccessible chapel sat defiantly at the top of a crag.

The dominance of the Greek Orthodox Church was underwritten by countless functioning monasteries. The first one we visited was Agios Ioannis Chrisostomos.

It went back fifteen hundred years. It had its early murals and iconostases but, sadly, they had been clumsily restored.

We soon spotted Naxos's 'Venetian' towers, tall and square, and always similar from the outside. The

Bellonia Tower was only a few miles inland from Naxos Town. We knocked its archaic brass hand against the door but it was very private and reply from within came there none. The owners were elsewhere - in Manhattan or Mayfair most probably.

I thought to myself that the millions I was going to make in the City might let me buy one, some day. They were set like jewels, after all.

'Enough culture, already! Tomorrow, young Jeremy,' Tev's voice penetrated my reverie. 'The time has come to tan our snow-white British bodies.'

A good idea. Naxos may have the best beaches in the Cyclades. Nature's laboratory has blessed it with talcum powder - marble ground to dust by nature and natural emery. It was the work of demigods who spread it over mile upon mile of bleached and dazzling strand. This ultrafine white dust sticks to anything damp, especially briny buttocks and bosoms. The emphasis it lends a girl's figure is faintly surreal.

The food on Naxos is terrific. It helps that so many of the necessary ingredients are local, fresher than anything you could ever find in London or New York.

It's well worth buying wine and fruit from the local shops, especially the cheeses. Tev and I bought a sample: *kefalotyri, anthotiro, graviera, feta* and particularly *misithra* and *xinomisithra*. We washed them down with red *Evi Evan*, a wine deliciously derived from the fokiano grape.

A Naxian 'Greek salad' is prepared with the local *xinomisithra*, rather than *feta*, which makes a welcome change.

Tev and I, in our hotel rooms, had no means of cooking meat, fish or vegetables, so all that stayed on the stall. That's what a taverna is for, after all.

As for the local economy, after half-a-dozen millennia, the island's produce has predictably contracted to its best sellers; grape, marble and emery.

Naxos had been a wine producing island before Dionysus was a boy. The old demigod, a great conjuror of wine and revelry, is still the island's principal deity and he still loves his island. His sorcery makes it a merry place. Since the 13th century BC, he has lent both visitors and locals a curious but insatiable fervour.

It's worth adding that wine is still excellent while his liqueur, *Kitron*, a close cousin of *limoncello*, has three or four distinct styles. After much scientific research, Tev and I agreed that *Valindras* was the best.

Naxos's tavernas are everywhere - even the smallest village has one. The one where we decided to bestow our patronage bestowed a pie upon Tev. It was called *misithropitakia*. Who knows its recipe? Certainly not Tev.

My choice turned out to be a chick-pea casserole, slowly baked in a clay oven.

Local pastries and desserts, *amygdalota* and *loukoumades* were everywhere but so were crêperies, pizzerias, sandwich joints; all our western rubbish. The worst offender was Goody's - a fast food chain, possibly better than McDonalds, but struggling. A surfeit of gourmets, perhaps?

If in need of a quick snack, no one should overlook the baker's and pastry shops. They serve great food. Rather solemnly we rated the baklavas in the *chora* A+.

*

We had done Naxos, its history and culture. More, even, than I actually needed. Tev, however, felt obliged to pay homage to Delos, the swirling focal point of a metaphysical world of gods, demigods, nymphs and satyrs. He had been ordered to do so, after all. There would be no fisticuffs. I went along in my most docile way.

Naxos has great ferry connections and we paid Sharon his drachma. We were on our way. Delos, where for the millennium before Olympian mythology began, had been a divine sanctuary. Since its earliest days it has been the single most important mythological, historical, and archaeological site in Europe. Probably the world.

The *École Française d'Athènes* - the French School of Athens - began to dig there in 1872. It unearthed an enormous complex of buildings, outranking those of Delphi or Olympia. Even as we pulled into its Sacred Harbour, we saw three conical mounds.

One has still retained its protohellenic name, Mount Kynthos, and it's crowned with a sanctuary of Zeus. Delos had become a centre of his cult. It then evolved into being an importer of goods and an exporter of magic.

> Delos, if you would be willing to be the abode of my son Phoebus Apollo and make him a rich temple; for no other will touch you, as you will find: and I think you will never be rich in oxen and sheep, nor bear vintage nor yet produce plants abundantly. But if you have the temple of far-shooting Apollo, all men will bring you hecatombs and gather here, and incessant savour of rich sacrifice will always arise, and you will feed those who dwell in you from the hand of strangers; for truly your own soil is not rich.
>
> *A Homeric Hymn to the Delian Apollo*

Stone huts on Delos provide archaeologists with evidence that it had been inhabited since the beginning of history.

Thucydides, arguably the earliest theorist, believed the original inhabitants had been pirates expelled from Crete by King Minos. He declared Delos to have been the birthplace of the twins Apollo and Artemis. Even by the time of Homer's *Odyssey* the island was already famous. Relics of the cult of Dionysus abound, as do those of the Titaness Leto, mother of the

189

twins. The island was to become the magnet for Ionian pilgrimages and the very first quinquennial games were celebrated here. Pilgrims - and their gold - soon ensured that the island was fit for the cult of the gods. As the island had no yarn, no timber, all such stuff had to be imported and food was rationed. Rain was collected in a giant cistern to be distributed to the temples via aqueducts. Its custodians wisely ordered that no women should be allowed to give birth on the island. Being ancient Greeks, this order was on pain of death.

After the Persian Wars, in 478 BC, the island hosted the 'Delian League'. Its meetings were held in the temple, a quarter of which was reserved for foreigners and their accompanying deities. The League's great treasury was kept here until Pericles forced its 'repatriation' to Athens. By 166 BC, Strabo was already accusing the Romans of undermining Rhodes. Delos became a free port, but Roman hostility materialised in the battles of the Third Macedonian War, by land and by sea, after which the Delos was ceded to the Athenians who promptly killed everyone who lived there.

Delos now became a hub for the eastern Mediterranean's slave trade. Roman traders came to inspect tens of thousands of captives, often the booty of Cilician pirates or the survivors of the wars that followed the disintegration of the Seleucid Empire.

The destruction of Corinth, back in 146 BC, allowed Delos to reclaim a little of its former glory as the premier trading centre of Magna Grecia, but its prosperity and population all waned after the island was contested in the Mithridatic Wars.

It hadn't helped that the major trade routes were shifting all over the ancient world. Before the first century BC was over, Puteoli had replaced Delos as the chief focus of *Latinocratic* trade with the East. Even as a religious centre, Delos fell into decline. An unsustainable combination of inadequate sources of food and water and the absence of indigenous inhabitants must take the blame.

Once deserted, it would stay that way for the next two thousand years. Our own little study of the nucleus of the Cyclades was over and it was time for us to move on too.

The time to pay visit Mykonos had come. Naxos ran several ferries every day. The earliest got there at 10.30, and the last return ferry, at 19.55, would bring us home. We arrived in the island's picturesque harbour, beneath its six windmills.

Before it was Byzantine, Mykonos had been Roman. In 1204, when Constantinople was overrun by the Fourth Crusade, Mykonos was briefly occupied by Andrea Ghisi, a cousin of the Doge of Venice. It would prove a fraught century, to put it mildly. Towards its end, the island was ravaged by the Catalans, not generally thought of as an imperial nation.

It was immediately retaken by Venice. In 1537, with the Doge in control, Mykonos was attacked by Hayreddin Barbarossa, Suleiman the Magnificent's infamous admiral. The Ottoman fleet had established itself offshore. Kapudan Pasha threatened to impose a Mohameddan governor and a council of syndics. The Venetians hung on for dear life for almost two centuries but in 1718, when neighbouring Tinos fell to the Ottomans, the game seemed up.

It wasn't. In the event, Mykonos attracted immigrants from everywhere and became a prosperous trading centre. Unfortunately, the British and French fleets met in the island's harbour,[71] the Battle of Mykonos was fought between them. The island's industry was destroyed but the islanders' spirit was not dead yet.

---

[71] June 1794

191

In 1821, Mykonos was to play an important role in the Grecian revolt against the authority of the Sublime Porte. Its leader, a well-educated lady, Manto Mavrogenous, was guided by the ideals of the Enlightenment and put her considerable fortune at the disposal of the rebels.

She equipped and manned two privateers who saw off the belligerents. On October 22, 1822, under her leadership, the Mykonians repulsed an expeditionary force of Ottoman Turks who had disembarked on the island. She then armed a hundred and fifty men to fight in the Peloponnese. She sent men and arms to Samos, enduring a drawn out Turkish assault. That done, she sent fifty men to take part in the Siege of Tripolitsa, and was rewarded when the town fell to the Greeks. Now on a roll, she put together a new fleet, this time of six ships. They, with sixteen companies of infantry, played an heroic part in the Battle of Karystos, late that same year. She went on to fund a campaign to save Chios but could not prevent an infamous massacre.[72]

Another fifty men were sent to reinforce Nikitaras in the Battle of Dervenakia but, when the Ottoman fleet reappeared in the Cyclades, she returned to Tinos and sold her fabulous jewellery. The proceeds served to arm another two hundred Greeks and feed the two thousand who had survived the Siege of Missolonghi.

After nearly six hundred years as a Turkish colony, Greece was again ready to become an independent European state. A statue to the national heroine was raised in Mykonos's main square.

---

[72] The Chios massacre (Η σφαγή της Χίου) saw Ottoman troops kill of tens of thousands of Greeks on the island during the Greek War of Independence in 1824. Greeks from neighbouring islands had arrived there to encourage the Chians to join their revolt. Learning of this, the Ottomans landed and put thousands to the sword. It provoked international outrage, and led to worldwide support for the Greeks.

Heroism, sadly, is never enough. After the opening of the Corinth Canal in 1904, however, the island's economy declined. Many Mykonians decamped to find work in mainland Greece and elsewhere – some as far away as the United States.

If Mykonos was to be reduced to tourism, it would not the end of the world. Closer to the centre, in fact. Twenty five years later, Mykonos had become an international hot spot. Famous artists, politicians and wealthy Europeans began to take their holidays there. Forty years further on, it was our turn.

Kastro's Bar is one of several cafes and restaurants in Mykonos's 'little Venice', but it's the one that plays wonderful classical music. Tev and I had overdosed on bouzouki. It was time to go cold turkey, if I may use that phrase in Greece. That morning we sat on the bar's fragile terrace beside the water, listening to Handel, and watching the pelicans hunt in the shallows offshore.

'It's 11 o'clock. We were up very early,' Tev said persuasively, 'and I need a nap. Let's go to Paradise Beach, find a place to stretch out, watch the girls disport and do the groundwork for tomorrow's headache with a chilled carafe.'

For people watchers, if that's the right term, nudist beaches may sound like paradise, but Tev was certainly not anticipating what would happen next. Having taken in the fleshy landscape, hills and valleys alike, he settled back on his beach towel. God only knows where his fledgling reveries took him when gravity gently pulled shut his eyelids.

Being British, of course, he had left his swimming trunks where they were designed to go, over his wedding tackle. No need to flag up one's old chap, after all. We had seen the sign - *nude bathing only* - but in our well-bred way had decided to ignore it.

I had never quite managed a siesta. I had repaired to a so-called pavilion, more of a wooden frame walled and roofed by vines, and ordered a glass of retsina. From my comfortable vantage point I watched a very large and muscular German spot Tev fast asleep. Unlike the Teutonic traveller, Tev had his trunks on. Horror of horrors! An international incident was unavoidable. The naked German was standing astride Tev's head and shouting at him. I saw Tev wake, and his body language clearly stated that he had no idea what was going on.

Perhaps I should have done something but my glass was still half full. I was amused. Let's see what happens, I thought.

'You swine,' said Tev, when I finally made my way over with a glass of wine as a peace offering. 'Imagine going to sleep in a harem, entertaining every conceivable fantasy, to be rudely awakened by a set of Westphalian genitalia two feet over your nose. I have never ever seen anything so unwelcome.'

'You might have taken your trunks off?'

'Thank you for that sweet thought but I promised my mother under oath that such intimacy would be strictly reserved for married life.'

*

'I don't suppose you speak Greek, do you?' Simon Galway asked me, when I was back in the office. 'You seem to speak every other language. Dutch twice, I suspect.'

'I can manage a few words. Please, thank you and so forth. A least I can read the street names. I was taught Greek at prep school and the alphabet stuck.'

'Well, that's better than nothing, which is the sum total of my knowledge of the language. The bad news is that we're on a hunting party to Athens.'

It was October 1975. I was twenty six and a half years old, already collecting miniature bars of soap from the *Principe de Savoia*, Milan. Now that my business horizon was to be extended to Greece, I was surely on the upgrade path from a stolen miniature plastic bottle of shampoo to a purloined and monogrammed pair of bath slippers.

Simon had booked us into the *Hôtel Grande Bretagne* which, despite or because of its name, is filled with French furniture. It is on Syntagma Square, overlooking the royal palace. I had been there once before, back in 1972, if only to enjoy a Fix (a local beer) at the bar. That had been during the colonels' interregnum. A little after that, on June 1st, 1973, the military regime proclaimed Greece to be a republic and abolished its absentee monarchy. Six weeks later, a referendum confirmed that a civil government would be elected. A second referendum on the monarchy was conducted on December 8th and the people confirmed that the kingdom had fallen.

King Constantine, who had protested the vote of 1973, accepted the result of the second plebiscite with adequate grace, resigning himself to a new life in the bourgeois confines of Hampstead Garden Suburb, of all places. It was not to that *rus in urbis* that my path led. It was to the *Grande Bretagne,* reputed to have been Winston Churchill's favourite hotel in Athens. Curiously he shared that taste with Hitler. The walls had stories to tell.

At least this time I felt comfortable in my Prince of Wales check suit. The girl at reception actually smiled, rather than laughed, and politely greeted two travelling businessmen.

'Καλημέρα,' she said to Simon. Good morning. She seemed to recognise him.

'Καλημέρα,' he replied, 'We're here for two nights. My name is Galway and his is Macdonogh.'

'Here you are,' she said. 'May I see your passports, please? I've booked you, Mr Galway, into the Basilicata Suite, and your balcony has stunning views over the

Parthenon. Mr Macdonogh, your room is on the fifth floor, from where you can see the fire escape.'

What did I expect? As it turned out, my room was clean and comfortable, and its single bed was *Deuxième Empire*. I had a shave and an orange juice, the latter by courtesy of a well-stocked frigobar. Ten minutes later I rejoined Simon in the lobby. He was already there and did a great job of pretending he had spent the last hour reading his newspaper impatiently.

'Your taxi is here, gentlemen,' said the girl on reception. All very prompt. Our cab took us a few hundred yards to *The Hellenic General Insurance Company*. It had a considerable non-life account. We found ourselves in the underwriter's dusty, old-fashioned office. Heavily laden bookshelves lined the walls and every spare square foot held a framed and elaborate certificate. Our counterpart was either a genius or the Greeks gratuitously hand these things out at school willy-nilly. When his assistant, or secretary, or intern, or mistress, put her pretty head around the door, our host told her 'τρία καφέσ με γάλα, παρακαλώ.'

Three coffees. His assistant turned on her heel to return a minute later with a brass tray, a coffee pot in its centre, three glasses in silver carrying cases and three glasses of water.

She fussed around Simon in a slightly brazen fashion, showing off her excellent figure from every possible angle. Why all this fuss over an old man of thirty five, I thought a little crossly. That coquetry should have been for me.

'Ευχαριστώ,' I said, desperate to imply that my Greek was up to scratch. 'Thank you'.

'It is early,' Simon began when he had Mr Spiro's undivided attention, 'but the renewal season is almost upon us and I'd like to check that the treaty details will stay the same and that there have been, so far at least, no claims.'

196

'Καταλαβαίνω. I understand. There are no claims on her. She is uncompromised, as pure as the day she was born. Her suitors in the London Market need have no reservations.'

He was probably talking about the treaty. Probably not his secretary.

'Now, what have we here?' he continued amiably, opening a file. 'Our second surplus treaty, property and pecuniary loss. You have a 15% share.'

'Mr Spiros, Mr Macdonogh here will place the treaty for you in the Lloyd's market. He is one of our most talented brokers. Four legged donkeys live in fear of him.'

Spiros's English was certainly good, but he still may not have understood the exact implication, but he was well-bred enough to laugh heartily.

'Can you handle a larger share?' he asked.

'Of course,' said Simon. 'How much can you let us have?'

'Could you manage half of it? Fifty per cent?'

'Of course we can, can't you Jeremy? Excellent. Send us the stats in the usual way and we'll have renewed our enlarged share of the treaty by December 31.'

We all stood up and shook hands rather formally. As we passed the dark beauty in his anteroom, she looked up at Simon and said 'γειά σας, ασφαλέσ ταξίδι'. Goodbye and safe home.

'Ευχαριστώ,' I said. Thank you.

In the lift, Simon had some detail weighing on his mind.

'Should I have shaken her hand, as you did?'

'I think she would have preferred you to have asked her out to dinner.'

We stepped into Athens' sultry afternoon heat.

'Fancy a Coca-Cola?' he asked me.

'I'd prefer a Fix,' I replied.

To this day I'm not sure if he understood me. He certainly looked at me oddly.

'Anyway, well done. Place that extra share and we've earned our trip many times over. We can afford to coast from here.'

We had another meeting that afternoon before we supped in the hotel's Roof Garden Restaurant. The view, overlooking the first Olympic Stadium, the Acropolis and the Parthenon, was and is to die for. We sampled a fine if sober Mediterranean dinner - just one glass of wine apiece - before Simon disappeared to change and swim a few lengths in the floodlit roof-top pool. The evening was balmy enough and the silky ouzo I paid for out of my own pocket slipped down easily.

Three more meetings the next day and we were on our way home.

*

The following day, back in the office, I overheard Simon remark that I had been speaking fluent Greek all day. Not a bad accolade for the three or four words I had learned on Naxos the month before.

Still, this was not the time for self-congratulation. It was still October and I had little business, other than develop my relationships with London's reinsurance underwriters. I would need their help when December came and I would have to place 50% of a Greek treaty I privately thought impossible. Dining alone on expenses was an unconscionable sin, naturally, but a man with an expense account still needs to do his research.

The *Viceroy*, in Mincing Lane and close to the office, was one of the grandest old-style restaurants in the City of London. I wandered up to the front door, which was defended by a commissionaire in a top hat and frock coat. Presuming I was expecting a guest, he ushered me into a cocktail bar. Aside from the barman the place was deserted. That was a relief. How would I explain a cocktail to my bosses at eleven o'clock in the morning?

'What'll it be?' asked the considerate fellow with the shaker.

'What would you recommend?' I replied.

'At this time of day, most of our regulars need a corpse reviver.'

Churlish not to accept such advice. As I would charge them to expenses, I ordered two. Easier to explain. For the undereducated, a Corpse Reviver is a blend of two parts cognac, one part Calvados and one part sweet vermouth. If ever the phrase 'electric soup' has been better employed I'll eat my hat.

I needed some time and a little craft to consider my working relationship with the chief underwriter of a Brazilian reinsurance company. He would often underwrite risks that I thought unsalable.

Having joined a lunch club called Mytton's, conveniently located between *CTB* and *Lloyd's*, and I went there most days. Now that I was paid my princely wage (actually still the square root of very little) I could take a plate from the salad bar and not face immediate bankruptcy. I went in at noon, already refreshed, to put my master plan into gear.

'I shall be back at 1.00.' I told the assistant manager. 'Please prepare two large gins and tonic. My client likes a stiff beverage before lunch.'

'Of course.' He looked at me oddly. 'How can I help?'

'Well, I'll need a clear head. Can you put three shots of gin in his, plus a slice of lime. In the other, no gin at all and a slice of lemon. I appreciate this involves a slight deception. Would £5 cover the insult?'

A fiver changed hands and I left Mytton's. I went into Lloyd's to do a little business before lunch. There are often adjustments or endorsements that need to be made to treaties during the year and they provide an opportunity to flatter and cajole the underwriters before the big shove at year end.

Then, at ten to one, I was back at *Mytton's*. My client was already there and I saw he was sipping a *G & T*, with that slice of lime. I took mine, with the lemon, and tasted it. Simple tonic water tastes very much like a fully fledged *G&T*, I thought to myself. How clever am I? Ten minutes later, my client told the barman to refill our glasses, on his account, 'same mix as before'. Should I have read more into this turn of phrase? Aperitifs downed, we descended into the basement, into the formal restaurant, where we had a cracking meal. The food there was always great. We washed it down with a bottle of *Mercurey*. I had learned quite a bit about food and wine during the French and Italian seasons of my 'gap year', and I was discovering that my clients were often willing to let me choose the wine and, sometimes, even the food.

We dined well and, when he suggested a cognac to seal the deal, I agreed.

'Let me see your slip.[73] I'll sign it here, whatever it says. Always a pleasure doing business with you.'

I shook his hand solemnly by the door to the club. He went on his way and I stepped out into the fresh air. Suddenly I felt unsteady. A coffee, perhaps would help. I went back in. The inescapable truth was I was horribly drunk. I would not have been able to debate in French with petit fours.

'Are you all right?' asked a solicitous assistant manager.

'I'll be fine. I just need to sit down for a moment. I had more to drink than I had calculated. Sorry!'

'No problem. Take your time.'

'I just don't know how I got it so wrong,' I confessed, feeling sorry for myself.

---

[73] The document on which an underwriter states how much of the risk he will accept or agrees to a mid-term amendment.

'I think I know. You remember you slipped me a fiver to make sure your gin and tonic had only tonic?'

'I do.'

'Well, your client arrived a couple of minutes before you had returned. He took a sip of both and swapped the slices of lime and lemon over. He gave me a tenner not to warn you.'

I had been neatly hoist by my own petard.

CHAPTER THREE

The Iron Curtain
1976

The author, now with a slightly higher salary, is sent to Yugoslavia. He has an attack of tachycardia. His brother Giles gets arrested. He watches, on the news, Montedison's petrochemical refinery blow up. He enjoys St Patrick's Day a touch too enthusiastically and goes on to endure the hottest summer England has known since the eighteenth century.

Despite the fact that I had not a word of Serbocroat, I had been awarded the Yugoslavian account. Not that Marshal Tito's fiefdom amounted to much, business-wise. I think CTB may merely have wanted to add another country to its growing global catalogue of customers.

There is a view, held as axiomatic in public bars up and down the land, that all Northern European tongues are, in round numbers at least, Germanic. All the lingos in the south must be some effete form of Latin. According to such theorists, there are just three languages in the entire continent, Latino-Celtic, Hunnish and the Queen's English. This last is a refinement of the first two, a bit from there, a bit from here; a casserole of slugs, puppy dog tails, liberally garnished with snails.

Infuriatingly, Serbocroat does not conform to any such simplisticism.

The fact that grammar is no longer taught means that this sort of gross generalisation is never questioned. It is an article of faith for those who think a predicate is a priest and a subject is a citizen.

I was about to refine these assumptions. It was excruciatingly early that summer morning when the CTB limo brought me to Heathrow and it was almost lunchtime when an airport bus deposited me and my bags in Ban Jelačić Square in Zagreb, Croatia's largest city.

In 1975 the *Neboder*, then Zagreb's tallest building, had brought a touch of New York to an otherwise humdrum square. Almost all of the largest Croatian companies - industrial, media and scientific - had their headquarters here. I was obviously in the right place.

I already knew that the city had a rich history, dating from Roman days when it had been at the confluence of the Eastern and Western Empires.[74] Zagreb was now reduced to being a seat of local government, a mayoralty and some local ministries.

The little Balkan state had as strong economy as any communist nation could, a barely adequate quality of life and many museums stuffed with treasures confiscated from former capitalists, plutocrats and aristocrats.

Two thousand years before, the city had been Andautonia. Now it was Zagreb. Most of us are content to get from A to B but this pretty city had made the more ambitious move from A to Z.

The city is divided between Gornji, the upper town and Donji, the lower. Gornji is Zagreb's medieval heart. My airport bus obligingly passed in front of the centuries-old St Stephen's Cathedral, its twin spires soaring into the sky. The National Theatre, almost opposite, was a classical building of 1895 and over its lifetime it had hosted such diverse luminaries as Franz Liszt and Laurence Olivier.

I was not there to sample its delights, of course. My task was to insure its property, its industries and its service sector. Saying that, first things first. For everything there is a season, as God and the *Beach Boys*

---

[74] The actual point of division between East and West was at Split, not far away, the one-time seat of the Emperor Diocletian.

had ordained. The sun was fiercely beating down. It all added up to a nice cold beer.

I parked myself at a table in the square, hoping for a glass of the amber nectar and waited for a waitress to come and realise my desires. I would ask her for a beer, but what on earth is a 'beer' in Serbocroat? All foreign words for beer, surely, sound a bit like 'beer'?

No, they do not. An unsmiling apparatchik approached me reproachfully. Capitalist pigs like me wanting to be waited on by the granddaughter of a foundry labourer? The injustice of it!

I offered an unreciprocated smile.

'Good morning,' I said in English. 'Please may I have a cold beer.'

'*Ne rasumijem*,' she replied impatiently, shifting from foot to foot. My linguistic skills were challenged. It could easily have meant 'we don't have any', or even 'I don't understand'.

I tried again.

'*Une bière, bien fraiche, s'il vous plait, mademoiselle.*'

'*Ne rasumijem*,' she repeated.

Hey ho.

'*Ein bier, bitte.*'

'*Ne rasumijem.*'

I was getting desperate.

'*Μια μπύρα, παρακαλώ.*'

'*Ne rasumijem.*'

'*Een bier, gelieve.*'

'*Ne rasumijem.*'

'*Una birra, per favore.*'

'*Ne rasumijem.*'

This was getting ridiculous. I was getting thirstier by the minute and she was determined not to budge. Perhaps the word 'beer' is not universal after all.

'*Una cerveza, por favor?*'

'*Ne rasumijem.*'

Ἄλλοτ'ἀλλοῖα φρόνει, I told myself. Think differently.[75]

A group of four soldiers was sitting at a nearby table and were merrily imbibing their *Klassicheskoe Svetloe*, a tasty Russian beer. A red star in their caps told me that one day, in all likelihood, I, or my children, would have to kill them. Mercifully, this was not the time. I stood up and led the startled hireling by the arm to their table to point at their beers and make charade-like gestures about necking the precious stuff.

'*Pivo*,' she said, shaking me off. '*Odmah!*'

She went off inside, while the soldiers raised their bottles to me in a universal salute.

A few seconds later I had my beer. It seemed to me she might now have proffered me the hint of a smile but she didn't. The Croatian for smile is ten years hard labour.

*

I was in good time for my first appointment. This time with Draža Šuker of the Croatia Insurance Company.

Croatia Insurance had started up in 1884; challenging times which took a long time to get any easier. From there the Austro-Hungarian Empire in general, and Croatia in particular, would 'enjoy' a century of full-throttle historical turmoil – a weak monarchy, two world wars, a nationalised economy, dictatorship and an untrustworthy overseer in the shape of the Union of Soviet Socialist Republics.

My first challenge would be to find their building. Happily the major street signs were written in both the Cyrillic and Roman alphabets.

I glanced at the address I had brought with me from London,

Croatia Osiguranje
Vatroslav Jagić 33
10000 Zagreb.

---

[75] Pindar, *fragment ccxxv*. I was fascinated by Pindar as an undergraduate.

The company had not always been called thus. After the war, Tito had ordered the company to be renamed DOZ (State Insurance Institute), but it had rediscovered its maiden name in 1970. That was a relief. I would not have known whether to call it 'Dozy' or 'Dosh'. At least I had its address, but could I walk it? Did I need a taxi?

*

Austria and Hungary had long battled over the collection of countries we then called Yugoslavia. They began by calling the amalgam 'The Kingdom of Slavs, Croats and Slovenes'. This might imply to the casual historian that its second language would be German or Magyar. In one I could safely order a beer, but I hadn't been understood. I concluded that Russian had replaced both on the National Curriculum. Communication was going to be an issue.

The painful birth of modern Yugoslavia was arguably in the spring of 1941. That was when Nazi Germany, with Hungarian and Italian assistance, invaded. King Peter II, then just seventeen years old and yet to sit on his throne, was implacably opposed to the Tripartite Pact. His uncle the Regent - the late king's younger brother Paul - however, had declared that the Kingdom of Yugoslavia would join the Axis. A crisis on a pan-European scale ensued. The British hastily engineered a coup to unseat the Regent from his throne and replace him with King Peter.

The problem of his youth was easy to deal with. A Juridical Proclamation simply declared the royal lad to be of age.

The Prime Minister, Slavko Kvaternik, declared that Croatia was again an independent kingdom. Colonel-in-Chief Tito was signally unimpressed.[76] He responded by forming a military caucus within the Central Committee of the Yugoslav Communist Party.

---

[76] Later general, secretary, prime minister and finally marshal.

When the independent kingdom was attacked from all sides, it fell apart and it's military, such as it was, folded. A week later, King Peter II and most of the other members of the royal government felt obliged to flee the country.

A few stayed behind to welcome the Nazi generals, officials and politicians in Belgrade. They offered the capitulation of their men, their country and the 'yoked Slavs' of South East Europe. This was not what the Comintern wanted to hear. In Moscow, a furious Central Committee of the Communist Party ordered Tito to unite the people of Yugoslavia against the Germans. Tito, by birth half Serbian and half Croatian, had certainly been browbeaten, possibly even brainwashed in his Russian prison camp after the Great War. Now that he was Commander in Chief of all 'national liberation military forces' - Yugoslavia's Partisans, in other words - he could issue precise instructions for the liberation of the Balkans from the Nazis.

The Führer postponed Operation Barbarossa,[77] much to Stalin's, Churchill's and Roosevelt's relief. Instead, the Wehrmacht attacked Yugoslavia and Greece. Over the days that followed, Bulgaria, Hungary and Italy joined in the fun. Whole regions of Yugoslavia were annexed. Croatia, Bosnia and Serbia saw the Nazis install puppet governments to govern them.

The king and his court reached Greece. From there they went to Jerusalem in British-mandated Palestine and thence to Cairo, the capital of the British Protectorate of Egypt.

At last, in June 1941, King Peter's entourage arrived in London to joined the numerous other

---

[77] *Barbarossa* was the code name for the Axis invasion of the Soviet Union, which started on Sunday, 22 June 1941. The operation stemmed from Nazi Germany's ideological aims to seize the oil reserves of the Caucasus and the agricultural resources of Soviet territories and to repopulate the western Soviet Union with Arians, using Slavs as slave-labour.

governments and royal families already in exile from war-torn Europe.

The handsome young king elected to complete his education at Cambridge University, prior to joining the Royal Air Force. In 1942, a newly commissioned Squadron Leader made a diplomatic visit to America and Canada. He met American President Franklin Delano Roosevelt and Canadian Prime Minister William Mackenzie King. Unfortunately, his charm offensive proved unsuccessful in securing support for the royal cause. The self-made US has an hereditary problem with monarchies.

To make matters worse, Roosevelt and Churchill had adopted Sun Tzu's counsel, that my enemy's enemy is my friend. They needed and engaged the support of the Communist Yugoslav Government in their endeavours to defeat some Nazis.

The Yugoslavian king may have been in comfortable exile but he did not own a white flag. Many of his subjects remained loyal to him and they too found it all too easy to resist the blandishments of Tito's Partisans.

These monarchist freedom fighters called themselves Chetniks, and Tito determined to suppress them. Though the odds were heavily against them, the Chetniks wanted their monarchy, Church and democracy - their core beliefs - restored.

What a choice they faced! The Russian devil to the east, the German Nazis to the north. Neither direction was attractive, and the west was simply too far away. Stalinism meant atheism and the forfeiture, even destruction of their sacred churches, relics and icons. Nazi Christianity versus Stalinist atheism? If that was all there was on offer, it did not take long to decide. They were orthodox Christians and many were 'anti-Semitic', largely because they were unwilling to forgive the Jews for the death of our Lord. Tito described them as fellow-travellers with the Nazis - they were not - but when Tito ordered his forces to help escaping Jews, he out-manoeuvred them. More than 2,000 Jews fought directly for Tito. The marshal became a hero in the Diaspora and in the West.

By now Tito was on a roll. He created and encouraged Proletarian Brigades, sending his Partisans to rename the People's Committees as 'civilian governments'. What's in a name? He established an Anti-Fascist Council for the Liberation of Yugoslavia and, by 1943, the representatives of the resistance had established a basis for the putative post-war reconstruction of his country.

The constituent Yugoslav nations were federated and Tito was confirmed as *President of the National Committee of Liberation*. While the likelihood of an Allied invasion in the Balkans grew, the Axis began to dedicate more resources to the destruction of the Partisans' main force and its high command. This required a concerted effort to capture Josip Bros Tito in person. On 25 May 1944, Hermann Göring ordered an airborne assault on Drvar, Tito's headquarters in Bosnia. *Unternehmen Rösselsprung* failed when the Marshal managed to evade the Luftwaffe's élite *fallschirmjäger*, or parachutists.

Unconvinced of the value of their unreliable Chetnik 'allies'. the Germans rounded them up and concentrated them in Bleiburg.[78] Now what should they do with them? Would the British take them? Churchill refused to accept their surrender, directing them to submit to the Partisans. After some brief negotiations they did just that. Who now can know what they were promised?

In May 1945, just before the formal end of the Second World War, tens of thousands of Chetnik soldiers and Yugoslavian civilians were forcibly repatriated - contaminated by association with the Axis. Columns of Christian Croatians - Chetniks included - began their trek from Carinthia to an uncertain future. The Chetniks were

---

[78] Southern Austria.

marched in columns all the way to Serbia. Few arrived; their melancholy crocodile was regularly visited by giggling Partisans who entertained themselves by shooting a few at random.

Josip Tito was no friendly 'Uncle Jo'. If anyone ever told him he was, the mirror was lying. He was a Balkan Stalin.

Such are the joys of war. Even a week after the German defeat - formally the end of the War in Europe - the Chetniks were still refusing to acknowledge the end of their cause. They were still fighting the Partisans. Perhaps the British might help? Hoping to keep their escape routes open, they fought a retreat to the Austrian border near Klagenfurt where, on May 14th, 1945, the British graciously offered his majesty's protection and accepted their surrender. To be on the safe side, however, the officer commanding ordered them to be interned in the nearby Viktring camp. MI6 sent home reports of gruesome massacres and, on May 31st, 1945, the British cancelled all forced repatriations. There were also some troublesome issues in international law. The legitimacy of Tito's government was recognised by all, while the Chetniks declared themselves to be subjects of the exiled King of Yugoslavia. It cut little mustard. In international law, there was little choice but to deliver them to the local authorities.

The Chetniks were handed over to the Partisans who marched them to internment camps in Tezno, Kočevski Rog and Huda Jama. It was now too late to save the monarchists. Predictably, they were welcomed home with atrocious acts of cruelty and revenge. Tito had repeatedly issued calls for the Chetniks to surrender, offering them amnesty. For some inexplicable reason, his soldiers ignored him and routinely carried out mass executions. Was it that the wording of his communiqué lacked the customary authority of the dictator? He did make one gesture. 'To halt the extermination of prisoners of war' he sent the captured Chetniks in sealed lorries to the USSR.

Uncle Jo was not so merciful. They were sent to labour camps where they were given a menu. They were offered a choice of death by starvation, exhaustion, dehydration, disease or, if they survived that lot, frostbite. The luckier ones were shot.

The British Government remained quiet. Always best not to draw attention to an awkward truth. While Tito pretended to be sympathetic to the widely desired return to monarchy, his republican People's Front, led by the Communist Party of Yugoslavia, won the elections of November 1945 with an overwhelming majority. Not that anyone was surprised. The election had been boycotted by the monarchists, who had demanded but not received assurances that their king might safely return.

'A monarchy without a king is but a masquerade', they averred. Obligingly, Tito proved them right. A few days later he deposed King Peter II, *in absentia*, and the dictator's government was henceforward recognised across the world. From then, the Slavic dictator could flex his muscles with equanimity. He was now declared Prime Minister and Minister of Foreign Affairs of the Federal People's Republic of Yugoslavia. The future marshal could now use force as well as social engineering to unite his country.

Everything henceforward was couched in the seductive but hollow language of 'fair play' and 'equality', so often the slippery siren notes of tyranny.

It all suited the West. Ideological massacres went unreported let alone discussed. Tito had been our ally, after all. The devout and monarchist Chetniks died in silence, like the Christian lambs they were.

The State Security Administration mutated, effortlessly, into the secret police, just as did the Department of People's Security. Yugoslav intelligence imprisoned and brought to trial large numbers of Nazi 'collaborators', a blanket term like 'enemies of the state' that included not just Chetniks but all monarchists and Catholic priests.

This blood-stained list included Draža Mihailović. He had peacefully ruled the Ustaše regime. That was quite enough. Tito ordered a court martial to find him guilty of collaboration, high treason and war crimes that remained unspecified. He was executed by firing squad.

Tito had form. On June 4th, 1945, Prime Minister Josip Bros Tito had agreed to meet the president of the Bishops' Conference of Yugoslavia, Aloysius Stepinač. This was two days after the archbishop's release from prison. Unsurprisingly, the two did not agree. Deceitfully (the word he actually used was 'strategically') Tito encouraged Stepinač to issue a statement condemning Partisan war crimes in September, 1945. It was enough. The archbishop was arrested, tried and sentenced to sixteen years. His crime was to have supported or attempted the conversion of Orthodox Serbs and atheists to Catholicism.

Stalin may have asked how many battalions had the Pope, but his holiness was not completely powerless. In October 1946, in its first special session for 75 years, the Vatican excommunicated Tito and his entire government.

After the war, even our pragmatic West slowly began to realise that Tito was excessively loyal to Moscow. Churchill, better informed than most, described him as 'second only to Stalin in his Slavonic addiction to cruelty'. Tito was in fact completely committed to orthodox Marxism. He introduced censorship in libraries, universities and theatres. Harsh repressive measures against dissidents were commonplace.

The country was characterised by arrests, show trials, suppression of the peasantry, forced collectivisation and of course the steady abolition of Christianity.

Despite this homage to, or faithful imitation of, the USSR, a paranoid Stalin still considered Tito too independent and refused to trust him.

'Neither should you,' said a wise Simon Galway before I caught my plane. 'Be careful not to voice your political opinions in Zagreb or Belgrade.' He lowered his voice. 'If you do we may never meet again.'

I soon appreciated these words of wisdom. My taxi driver frowned as I showed him the address. I had assumed the insurance company was in the middle of town, but twenty kilometres later I had realised the error of my ways.

Half-an-hour late is not the fashion in the Balkans. A commissionaire, or maybe commissar, escorted me to Mr Šuker's office to find him staring impatiently through a window.

On his left was a small black and white photograph of a young RAF officer, a squadron leader with his wings over his heart and the Grand Cross of the Order of the Star of Karageorge over the other breast. To his right was a larger hand-coloured photo of an older warrior, who glowered uncharitably towards the door.

Mercifully, this Šuker was a charitable fellow and could speak a little English, though his assistant, a muscular woman with closely cropped hair, spoke it rather better. After a brief exchange in Croatian, Šuker and his harridan appeared disposed to accept my apology, but neither condescended to smile at their own lofty patronage or at my humility. Perhaps they were aware of François de La Rochefoucauld's throwaway line that 'humility is the worst form of conceit'. I will confess I was growing wary at Croatia's collective inability to smile. I decided there and then to look as stern as I was able.

'I have been sent here by my company to ask you for a larger share of the business we place for you in London,' I began. 'It is also my intention to ask you to consider your evident exposure to earthquakes as meriting a non-proportional treaty that would protect your extensive property portfolio from catastrophe.'

The lady translated and he gave her a terse reply.

'We cannot offer you a larger share of our proportional treaties,' she said on her master's behalf, 'as it is and has long been our policy to share our business with many of London's reinsurance brokers. More for you would mean less for them.'

I must have frowned, as she chose this moment to smile. It was like seeing the Mona Lisa for the first time. Hers was a truly marvellous smile. The clouds rolled back, the sun came out. The air outside, up to now orchestrated with the sound of Zils and Moskvichs, was suddenly resonant with bird song and the hedgerows with the hum of honey bees.

'Nevertheless, I am instructed to ask you to submit your proposals for an excess-of-loss protection together with an estimate of the premium the London market will exige.'

They stood up and Šuker moved to stand under the large and faded photograph of that old soldier.

He shook my hand.

'*Bon voyage*, as they say in France,' he said, via the smiling virago. 'Well done. We look forward to learning the terms and conditions of our new treaty.'

I had done a lot better than I deserved. All I had to do now was to get to my hotel in Belgrade, telex the news to London and prepare for my meeting the following morning.

I glanced at my watch. It told me that if I caught the next train there would still be time at the far end for me to enjoy a quiet bistro dinner of smoked sturgeon, followed by goulash, washed down with a carafe of a powerful Hungarian red. I was beginning to salivate. I had not eaten since breakfast on the plane.

I was at the railway station before two. The timetable said I would be in Belgrade six and a quarter hours later! Had Simon actually realised how much time was needed to get to Belgrade?

A stall on the platform was selling food and wine to a large crowd of passengers but, very sadly, it was too late for me to order what looked like a tasty meat or cheese roll. Maybe there was a restaurant on the train? If not, my train would deliver me to Belgrade's historic station - before the war the Orient Express stopped there *en route* for Istanbul - where there would surely be some opulent palace of a cafeteria?

I was not eligible to travel first class, I vaguely understood from the ticket seller's schoolboy English. I would have needed some sort of pass. Second was not too uncomfortable, however. What I had glimpsed of Third looked truly primitive.

'Might there be a dining car?'

'In second class? Certainly not. The restaurant was reserved for first class passengers.' Thank goodness for communism. I was just able to buy a ticket and catch my train, but I had a window seat and watched the scenery unfold as the train headed across the Croatian plains to the old steel bridge across the Sava which once had linked the Austro-Hungarian Empire with Serbia.

Belgrade (or Beograd) means 'White City'. 'White' is a metaphor for 'new'. It had been almost totally demolished in the Second World War. Over its long history it had been completely rebuilt almost forty times. It has therefore been 'new' for two thousand years. As I looked out over fields, villages and churches I wondered how such a city – a country – can endure such horrific conflicts and still survive so proudly. The answer must lie in the stubbornness or resilience of its people. This long contemplation ended when I discovered that there was no restaurant open in Belgrade's elegant railway station. When I finally arrived, slightly breathless, at the Hotel Moskva, its own dining room was shutting down.

'Am I in time for dinner?'

'Sorry, Mr Madonovič. The kitchen is closing. It's very late.'

'It's barely turned half past eight!'

'Welcome to liberated Eastern Europe, Sir. We do not pay 'overtime', unlike your capitalists. Our staff have families of their own. Would you print your name here, Sir, sign this card? The hotel will look after your passport for the duration of your stay.'

I wrote my name very carefully.

'It's not Madonovič, then? I'm afraid we confused you for a descendant of a hero of the old war with Turkey.'

'I was deeply sorry to read about that war. I was saddened to learn that it did not turn out too well for Serbia.'

He frowned. I was impressed. Frowning in Yugoslavia is their equivalent of a smile.

'I was going to have to put you in a smaller room, Sir, one not reserved for party officials or military officers, but since you have expressed your sympathy for our nation's long suffering you may stay in the room your people reserved.

'As for supper, show this card to a taxi in the rank outside. This restaurant will be open.'

Giving my room a cursory check for microphones, it was not until nine o'clock before I set out. Nothing solid had passed my lips for what felt like a week, save for a rather good Russian beer. It had wetted my whistle and whetted my appetite. That horse I fancied eating would make an excellent hors d'oeuvre. After that, perhaps, a fricassée of elephant?

Now in a taxi, feeling if anything more uneasy, I was aware that something slightly ominous had just occurred. When I had shown the driver the address the concierge had given me, he had laughed. The burghers of Yugoslavia normally need a public execution before they laugh. Naturally I couldn't ask him what was so funny. He had not a word of any known language.

We travelled a long way, passed many post-war buildings in the drab soviet style and among them I had the joy of spotting an older residence called, improbably, the *Public House Hotel*. If one must bother with such English quirkiness, they should have called it *The Case is Altered* or *The Finger in the Till*. Just saying.

Turning into a drive, and passing through a wrought iron gate where a sentry or guardian waved us through, we drove up a steep hill. In the dark I saw strange, windowless buildings to either side. My adventure was becoming surreal. We pulled into some sort of gas-lit plaza. It was set, I was pleased to see, with small tables. As my driver drove off I saw I was alone, except for a hirsute waiter who showed me to a table. I sat for an inexplicable five minutes in the warm evening air before he condescended to return with a menu.

'*Odakle si?*' he asked.

It may have meant 'what can I bring you'. It might equally have meant that my parents had never married? That I had my servants flogged every morning? In short, it could have meant anything. Mercifully, the menu had photographed its offerings.

I plumped for ćevapi which, judging from the helpful picture, was a hamburger minus its bun.

When it came, twenty minutes later, it was thoughtfully accompanied by a huge gherkin and a separate plate of raw chopped onion. Having no idea what the Serbian for wine was, I used one of the few words I felt likely to work.

'Slivovitz?' I tried.

'Sljivovica? Dobar izbor!' He actually smiled! What
the hell had I asked for?

He went off chuckling to himself but soon
returned with a clear bottle of the fiery liquid and a jug of
chilled water, the latter to extinguish the former.

As I dined in this strange place I mused on what I
had expected to eat in Serbia. I had seen something of
Serbia's beautiful country from the windows of my train
and had taken on board its rivers, its green fields and
what I presumed was a mild climate: a good environment
for a flourishing agriculture and a quality cuisine. Its
proximity to the Levant would influence its cooking,
surely? Was I to discover a hearty gastronomy based
around stews, over-boiled vegetables, hard cheeses,
crunchy pastries and baklavas?

My hamburger was lightly seasoned, though the
onion was one of the fiercest varietals of the noble *allium*
I had ever encountered. The Slivovitz, however, was less
of an accompaniment to living and more of an antidote
to life. It may even have been slightly hallucinogenic.
Having time to reflect, I concluded that Communism
must have discouraged the widespread availability of
refrigerators. As a consequence I was destined to live off
jams, jellies, pickles - especially sauerkraut – and cured
meats during my stay. I was still to discover *rakija*, or
fruit brandy, and the wonderful *slatko*, a thin fruit jam
made of wild strawberries, blueberries, plums and
cherries, even rose petals. The Serbians pour this
praiseworthy confection over ice cream, waffle
shortcakes, or use it as a filling for pancakes.

I poured myself a second tumbler of Slivovitz and
sat back. How oddly things can turn out, I thought.
Here I am, all alone on board the Marie Celeste, with
only a cross between a gorilla and a footman for
company, eating a bun-free hamburger and drinking
rocket fuel. For some reason I was as happy as Larry.
Who needs the Ritz-Carlton when you can have all this

to yourself? It was strange, however, that no one else had seen fit to take advantage of this simple restaurant.

Leaning my sturdy wooden chair against a low wall behind me, I imagined myself on the poop deck of the Flying Dutchman on a southern ocean. The roar of the sea below the phantom ship's rail filled my ears.

I put the glass down. I was not at sea. I was in the centre of Belgrade. Two things occurred to me. I should drink less Slivovitz and I should learn immediately what was making that threatening sound.

I stood and looked over the parapet wall. Around six feet below me was a very fit-looking adult male lion, wondering if it were possible that a human should smell so deliciously of lightly seasoned ground beef.

Feeling yet more nervous, I tried to remember how high lions could jump. Six feet for the King of the Beasts seemed not too hard a challenge and this one looked agile, fit and above all, hungry. I had wandered into a Serbian horror story, a tribute to their earlier Roman history and a thoughtful communist way of economising on the high cost of foodstuffs.

I could not leave. First, I was rooted to the spot. Secondly, I hadn't paid. Deserting my post was probably punishable by a generation or more in a labour camp. Meanwhile the lion was clearly measuring the distance for its heroic leap.

At that moment the hairy waiter reappeared and things began to fall into place. I was in a zoo. Not a public one, but a secret one where stray male tourists were fed to lions and a new species of waiter was being bred from female guests and caged orang-utans. I felt the sweat turn cold on my brow.

The waiter-thing was now at my table. It had raised an eyebrow to see me standing but was otherwise unperturbed. It held in its paw a piece of paper on a plate.

219

'*Vaš račun*,' he said, unemotionally. The paper? A prayer? A deed of bequest? The State's official waiver of responsibility?

'No, you idiot. It's the bill,' said my inner voice.

I took it, retrieved a small banknote from my wallet and put it in the waiter's grasp, simultaneously making a gesture designed to imply he could keep the change. He scowled – a good sign - and retreated. I was again the captain of my ship. All that was left for me was to walk the mile or so back in the dark to Marshal Tito Street and find a cab.

Only I didn't have to. The taxi I had come in was in the zoo's car park and, for bringing a victim - I mean customer of course - the driver had been rewarded with a meal. I glanced at all the plates. It had been a more sumptuous supper for him than it had been for me.

*

Back in the Moskva, I thought a nightcap might be a good idea and I looked for the bar. I passed through a great number of stately, old-fashioned rooms, each one hung with vast images of the great and good. What the huge photographs had in common was that they were of the unelected Soviet leaders of the state who liked to stand atop the mausoleum housing the body of the Russian revolutionary and the first Soviet leader, Vladimir Lenin, to watch a Parade of Thermonuclear Missiles pass below them in Red Square and celebrate May Day, the commemoration of the working man's peaceful purpose.

I had already noticed Vladimir Lenin in pole position above and behind the concierge of my hotel. Just inside, Stalin took pride of place. A pale space came next, but a brass plaque beneath explained who the missing man had been. I deciphered the Cyrillic as Malenkov. Whatever had happened to him? Behind the piano was Zinoviev. Was he the one who had written that letter?

Beria looked evil, a sort of Russian Joseph Goebbels. Molotov should have been in the bar, I thought to myself, being so famous for his cocktails. As for Podgorny - in truth I couldn't remember exactly who he was.

Everywhere, small groups of men were engaged in discreet, even hushed conversation and, if they were not in rather bulky suits, they were in uniform. What sort of hotel was this? I would have a word with our travel people when I got back.

I sat down, waiting for the waiter or waitress who must, presumably, have served these important looking people. It was then that I noticed that each table boasted a bottle of vodka, and from time to time, someone in each group would refresh the beakers in front. My eyes panned the room for a fireplace full of shattered glass. Still no waiter appeared. I glanced at my watch. It was eleven o'clock. Oh well, definitely time for bed.

*

My room was huge and lit by chandeliers. It could have doubled as a ballroom. My wardrobe was faced with a pair of full-length mirrors, so I opened it, vaguely hoping to expose a soviet cameraman. I only found a clothes rail.

The bathroom was especially magnificent. I thought a shower before bed, after all that travelling and excitement, might be agreeable and I turned the taps. No water emerged but a low rumbling sound did result. It gradually got louder and louder. I began to panic. Some deluvial cascade was about to drench the centre of Belgrade.

I turned the taps down and the sound of tanks (water tanks that is) receded. Taking my life in my hands I stood under the shower head and turned the taps a bit more courageously. The water that emerged had the sort of pressure that was more usually used on cars in the smartest hotel car parks. By the time I put my pyjamas on I was gleaming like a new Ferrari.

A fretful night ensued before breakfast in the Moskva's dining room. It was agreeable if odd, being mostly pickled fish, and the unsmiling service was efficient and prompt.

Soon I was in a taxi, hurtling at 5 mph along the Marshal Tito Avenue – known locally as 'Oxford Street' – towards the *Insurance Company of the Balkans* and my appointment with a Mrs Janaček. As I walked through the large office that served her smaller one, the silent staff - all male – nodded a court bow in my direction. I was then ceremoniously conducted into her office.

The boss was a large lady, only in her forties perhaps but in her autumn nonetheless. Still, I thought, autumn is the lushest and fruitiest of the seasons. She was well if primly dressed, but there were flaws.

She would have been a teenager in the war. Unsurprisingly, her hands showed signs of hard work. Her fingers were neither long nor beautifully shaped, her nails not perfectly kept. There was no suffusion of pink under a pearly shell, no delicate rounding of the thumb. Nor did she wear rings or necklace. One might expect the ladies from the exotic east, so near the orient, to be bedecked in opal, lapis lazuli, Benghazi myrmum, incomparable cheznook and fahr, but her hair was curled without art. She may even have done it herself.

'Good morning,' she said in her stage-Slavonic English. 'Please take a seat. Do you know, Mr Macdonogh, that your name is strangely similar to a hero of our old war with the Sublime Porte?'

'I heard that, but I must reveal that at the time of that war my forbears were chasing wild boars around Ireland.'

'Boars? That's interesting. We also like to give them, how do you say, a good run for our money.'

I laughed while she indicated a chair, loosely in the style of Louis XV. As I sat down, a waitress had silently entered her office, bearing a tray. The waitress silently prompted me to take a spoon, the bowl of *slatko* and a glass of water. *Slatko* was and is magic. When I indicated I would accept a second spoonful, she beamed. Mrs Janaček was attentive in the extreme. After renewing our treaty, she even offered to take me for a walk down Oxford Street.

'I could show you our tea-rooms, many charming shops which sell glasses and decanters, others that sell food that will easily keep until you are safely back in England. Souvenirs for your children, perhaps?'

'Thank you, Mrs Janaček, but I must decline your very generous offer. I have another appointment in Belgrade for which I must not be late, and then I have a plane to catch.'

'I understand, of course. Here is a jar of *slatko* to remind you of our praiseworthy, freedom-loving country. I hope you may come back to us very soon.'

My second meeting went as well as it might, and the flight was of the best kind; uneventful. Overall, I considered, my first visit to Yugoslavia had gone smoothly and was therefore memorable.

*

Now that I was a *bona fide* card-carrying international businessman, I needed a decent suit. My bank manager agreed.

'Austin Reed is a good gent's outfitter,' he told me.

I looked him up and down. He was not the best advertisement for the clothier. It would have to be somewhere else. Anywhere else. When I asked my father where he would recommend, he replied without ado: Kilgour, French and Stanbury.

'Some very well-dressed people go there. Cary Grant and Fred Astaire, for example.'

That was good enough for me. Americans make the smartest Brits when they put their minds to it. Cary Grant, or Archibald Leech as his parents had Christened him, actually was.

When, after a second and third fitting, I turned up for Sunday lunch around six weeks later at my mother's in my new blue chalk-stripe suit, I looked a million dollars, almost literally. Giles, my younger brother, walked around me, noting my fine jib from every angle, without a comment. He did, however, ask me who had been the tailor. He made a note of the name.

If a bookie had been on hand to take a bet I would have laid £100 that he too would be fitted out, in a few weeks, in another three-fold piece of sartorial magic. The following Sunday it was my father's turn to see and admire this astonishing example of textile engineering. Whenever I put it on I grew an inch, my back straightened and I swear my conversation began to show signs of intelligence.

'So you actually went to Kilgour?'

'I followed your advice, Pa.'

'Good man. Remind me, did I ever tell you I met Frank Sinatra after the war?'

'Frank Sinatra? Really? You never mentioned it.'

'Small bloke. The brightest blue eyes I have ever seen. Kilgour was his tailor, too.'

'Yes. That would explain his photo in the cutting room.'

'It was 1949, the year you were born and I had met him in the Garrick. He told me he had just been filming *On the Town*, a musical by Leonard Bernstein and directed by Gene Kelly. Every one of New York City's most iconic places had played a part - the Museum of Natural History, the Brooklyn Bridge, the Rockefeller Center, and so on and so forth. He had been confident from the outset that the film would be a huge money-spinner at the box office and even then he somehow knew it would bag an Academy Award, a Golden Globe and the Writers Guild of America Award. He would, therefore, have to perform a grand and global excursion shaking hands with the rich and the famous, the great and the good, the merely handsome and the utterly devastating, always looking the gentleman he truly was.'

'So he needed a good suit?'

'The best. He was advised to go to Kilgour. Seeing you I can understand why.'

'Did it go well?'

'Well, of course, the cutters and tailors were thrilled to have Sinatra in their rooms. They made a huge fuss of him and, in his way, he was rather touched.

'He had to have the suit in rather less time than their usual clients but they worked around the clock. The day of his first fitting came, and he was amazed and not a little afraid as they smiled and tore the loosely stitched arms from the coat and made mysterious chalk markings on the fabric.

'A week later he came in again for the second and final fitting. They had ticked every box, dotted every 'i', crossed every 't', tailed every 'q'. Four days after that, the concierge at Claridges telephoned Mr Sinatra to tell him that his suit might be collected and, almost before he had replaced the handset in its cradle, the star was in a taxi to Savile Row to be received like a prince.

'He put the suit on and approached a cheval glass in much the way a protégé might approach a leading lady. The staff would not miss this sight and gathered to applaud. Kilgour had pre-warned the Press who did their thing and snapped away. Someone had seen fit to bring a bowler hat and carefully put it on Sinatra's head at that famous jaunty angle. Another placed a tightly furled umbrella into his hand. A third pressed an ironed copy of *The Times* under his arm. They began to cheer their wonderful creation. The Chief Cutter, on hearing the uproar, abandoned a less important client – a minor royal, apparently - and came to see what was causing the commotion.

'Instead of seeing a delighted customer, however, he saw The Great Carouser looking at his own reflection in the dressing-room mirror, deeply, studiously, long and hard. The architect of the awesome suit saw that ol' blue eyes was not smiling, let alone rejoicing in the ownership of a work of art. Instead he saw a tear well in an eye.

"Is there something wrong?' he asked, utterly aghast.

"Actually not,' said Mr Sinatra, effortlessly affecting a perfect English accent. 'The suit is quite simply terrific. It's just the shame of losing India.'

*

The young friend of Robert Booth, who had been my dancing partner at Annabel's, had accepted my offer of dinner. Fiona was the pretty daughter of a celebrated banker, not a general as previously advertised, and seemed somehow appreciative of my attempts at banter. Since I lived in Chelsea, and she in Barnes, I had suggested a little bistro in Putney and she had readily assented. She was young – twentyish - but then, so was I. Dinner was the classic means of renewing my corporeal overtures.

Across the candelabra, her attention and body language seemed to suggest that I was humming the right song. Not that I couldn't queer my pitch. I would need to pay more attention to the notes.

She was a very pretty girl, nicely built, with a winsome smile. She knew the cinema inside out and, over the meal, we did talk films, for a while at least. She was good at conversation, treating the art as a sport, something like tennis. I did my best to return her serves. When she suggested a coffee at her place, I tried to mask my delight with the nonchalance of a man of the world.

'I have a bottle of Daddy's brandy,' she confided.

We had a magical night...

*

We also had a magical morning. It was high time for me to get dressed and Fiona was already in the bath. Desperate times call for desperate measures.[79] I had no choice – I could not afford to be late in the renewal season. My only chance of being on time was to share Fiona's tub and I simply opened the bathroom door, crossed over to the surprised young lady and climbed in the opposite end to her. Slightly to my surprise, Fiona appeared to take this as a compliment.

'Ship ahoy!' I said, perhaps remembering when, as a toddler, I had played 'Hood' against my sister's 'Tirpitz'.

'Up periscope,' said Fiona, thinking of something else, perhaps. 'Prepare to repel boarders.'

'All hands to action stations,' I cried, realising at last an opportunity to achieve a first in my navel encounters.

God, there was a lot of water on the floor. I left Fiona to it, still throwing on my clothes as I ran to the tube station and up the stairs. I had had too little sleep, too much brandy the previous night.

By the time I fell into a seat in a crowded compartment my heart was racing for Britain. My pulse rate had doubled and frankly I was actually frightened. I managed to get to my office a little after 10 am and I deserved an Olympic gold for the marathon. CTB employed a full-time nurse with a little surgery so I went there directly and was ordered to lie down. I was

---

[79] The expression 'desperate times call for desperate measures' was coined by the ancient Greek physician, Hippocrates, in his work *Amorphisms*: A more literal translation would read 'for extreme diseases, extreme methods of cure, as to restriction, are most suitable.'

shuddering like a leaf in a storm. The nurse took my pulse and rang for a doctor. Ten minutes later he too was taking my pulse.

'Tachycardia,' he pronounced, as if the word changed something.

'You've just said 'fast heart' in Greek, Doctor. Is there anything you can do, while I'm lying here with my heart going thirty-six to the dozen?'

'There's nothing I can do but there is something you can.' He was still feeling my pulse. 'Hold your breath. Breathe in and see how long you can hold it. That's it, good man. Increasing the carbon dioxide levels in your blood will slow your heart to somewhere near where it should be.'

He was right; I did and it did. By half past ten I was upstairs, at my desk, with an unassailable excuse for being late – I had been in the corporate sickbay.

*

The autumn of 1975 had been and gone, and now it was time for London's reinsurance brokers to do some work. Most treaties - all of mine - had to be renewed before the first of January. Everybody else in the wider City seemed to be visiting their families in some remote country fastness, taking a Christmas Caribbean break or even catching the first snows of the skiing season. For our part, we trudged up and down Lime Street or into Lloyd's itself.

Since my family was one of those that lived in London, and since there was no way on earth I could have afforded the latter two, it was not so hard a choice.

As soon as we had our orders to renew and had news of any losses, we could go 'into the market', as we called it, and persuade the underwriters to keep their money on the same horse they had bet on during the previous season.

All earthly temptations were now to be put to one side. As my now married colleague Dick Marriott would put it, it was time to put one's nose to the millstone. This was the inconvenient moment when I had a call from my mother.

'It sounded urgent,' my secretary told me. 'You'd better call her back.'

'It's your brother Giles,' my mother told me a few minutes later. 'He's in trouble and needs you.'

'Ma, I'm very busy. It's our renewal season and I have to move like the lamplighter of legend to get it all done before the new year. It's war out here.'

'That's all by the way. Giles has to be in court tomorrow morning. I can't be there. He may need bail, some kind of surety. It has to be you.'

'Oh, very well. What has he done?'

'Drunk in a public place, he said. Apparently they're dropping the charge of obstructing the queen's highway.'

'Well that doesn't sound too dreadful. Some of my best friends…'

'Jeremy, this is no laughing matter. Be at Horseferry Road Magistrates' Court tomorrow morning. Lend him the support he needs. You're his elder brother and he looks up to you.'

'He'll just get a small fine. I suppose he may be bound over to keep the peace. Either way, it's close to trivial.'

'He's never been to court before and he's panicking. He thinks he'll be locked up, and that he'll never get a visa for the US. Those two scenarios are just the ones he conjures up when he's *not* panicking. Do your duty. Ring me when it's all over.'

Those orders were not to be ignored. I got into my office a little after eight the next morning and saw the telexes concerning Montedison's petrochemical business that had just arrived. These would be new

229

treaties, and before I could place them I would have to agree terms with a leading underwriter and have Montedison agree to them. Only then could I place the treaties in the market.

'Great,' I thought to myself. 'This is not the best time to take a morning off.'

I had little choice. Less than an hour later I climbed out of my taxi at Westminster Magistrates' Court and walked inside. A poorly displayed notice boards reluctantly revealed which courtroom Giles's case would be heard in so I headed in that direction.

Almost immediately I saw my undergraduate brother. He could not possibly be missed in his superb three-piece suit, built for him in the sort of russet tweed that the crofters of Scotland would have gone to war to possess. He looked like a ducal chieftain. Kilgour, French and Stanbury had built him a suit worthy of immortalising in verse. Nor had Giles neglected the details. His shoes shone as though they had been carved from purest jet. His Balliol tie was perfectly knotted under a two-ply Egyptian cotton collar. The cuffs of his shirt were held together by links that looked like Lapis Lazuli set in gold. Giles was the only one wearing a tie. It was clearly a ploy to impress the magistrate. I hoped it would work.

A surly-looking clerk - a Mr Cooper, his name emblazoned on a flimsy tag - came into the general waiting area and directed spectators to the gallery and felons to the business area of the courtroom. I looked over the other miscreants as they shuffled along. They were mostly in the working clothes they wore as MacAlpine's Fusiliers. A truly sorry looking bunch.

A few minutes later we were all in our allotted places. I could not sit alongside Giles, of course, and I was still not at all sure what I was doing there. The magistrate came into the court, his clerk two paces behind.

'All rise', said the clerk, so we did.

'You may sit,' the learnèd gentleman muttered. Turning to his clerk he asked 'Who have we got first, Cooper?'

'MacBride, Dermot, Sir, drunk in a public place.'

The magistrate looked at his clerk as if no one else was in the courtroom. Clearly he did not want to soil his retina with a grim panoply of grimy specimens, waiting to receive their just deserts.

'How does he plead?'

'MacBride,' the clerk asked the accused. 'How do you plead?'

'Guilty, Sir,' the villain replied in the authentic voice of County Donegal.

'He pleads guilty,' the clerk relayed to his boss.

'Very well. Fifty pence. I expect he needs time to pay?'

'MacBride, do you need time to pay?'

'Ten shillings, is it? I could use a month, if it please your honour.'

The judge heard the exchange.

'Inform the accused that he may pay the fine over five weeks. Should he fail to do so he will be in contempt of court. Let him be aware that would deprive him of this court's renowned sense of humour. Very well, tell him he may go. Who have we next?'

'McCormack, Sean, Sir, drunk in a public place.'

The same melancholy performance now ensued almost word for word, except that the villain's accent had shifted to Co Antrim.

'Next?' the magistrate asked his clerk.

'McDermott, Seamus, Sir, drunk in a public place.'

After two or three minutes McDermott slunk off, probably taking his County Moynihan inflection to the pub across the road.

'Next?'

'Macdonogh, Giles, Sir, drunk in a public place.'

231

The judge was still paying no attention to anyone else in the room other than his clerk.

'How does he plead?'

'Macdonogh,' the clerk asked, 'how do you plead?'

'Guilty, Sir,' my brother replied in the accents of County Kensington.

This accent may have been unfamiliar to the bored deliverer of the queen's justice, as I saw him actually raise his gaze to look across the court to the dock.

Giles looked terrific. If he had been going for an audition for some country house drama he would have got the leading role. The woven silk of the tie he had around his neck, however, reminded me that noble murderers in the old days were allowed a silken noose. The magistrate actually smiled.

'May I hear the details of the charge, please, Cooper?' he asked his clerk. The worthy courtroom servant dutifully found the charge sheet. He read out the duty sergeant's report.

'On December 14th inst at around 03.00 hrs the accused was discovered in Eaton Place, London south west, rearranging some loose bricks that had been left by the side of the road in all probability by some workmen what had been earlier engaged in the erection of an extension to an existing edifice.

'On being questioned by PCs Brodie and Doyle, Macdonogh was adjudged to be inebriated and was accordingly charged under the relevant act and brought for his own and the public safety to Chelsea Police Station until the medical practitioner declared him sober enough to be released.'

'I see,' said the magistrate. He put his pen down and spoke directly to his worthy clerk.

'For some time the Home Office has been sending me sentencing guidelines for misdemeanours of this kind. The Secretary of State has allowed me to impose a maximum fine of £50, even encouraging me so to do. Over the years, Cooper, that you have been my clerk you will have seen, as I have, the sort of people it is my sad lot to deal with. £50 would be as realistic as telling these miserable fellows to stick to tea when they were thirsty. At last the police have had the kindness to send me an opportunity to comply with the Home Office's unrealistic suggestion. £50, then.'

The clerk turned to Giles to tell him to go with the constable to the cashier. Once his fine was paid he would be free to go.

'Next?'

'MacDonnell, Joseph.'

I did not wait to hear the dismal process repeated. I found Giles waiting for me and led him across the road to join the other miscreants in the *Barley Mow*, an alehouse already decorated for Christmas.

MacBride was ahead of us, and looked as though he was already on this third pint.

'Well, I shan't do that again,' Giles told me as we got a couple in.

'No need,' I said. 'You'll dine out on this one for all your remaining days.'

*

In the City, the last business days of that December proved a catalogue of clumsily coordinated queuing and cajoling. All my established business had to be renewed by close of play on New Year's Eve.

My one problem - it was a serious one - was the three 'non-proportional' treaties I had with Montedison SpA, one of the largest industrial groups in Europe.
That company's activities included petrochemicals, agribusiness, fluorides, peroxides, engineering, heavy construction and pharmaceuticals, spread over nearly two hundred plants in twenty-one countries, and more than two thirds of its revenue originates outside Italy.

Corsi had designed their new treaties, all due to incept on the first of January. With some difficulty, much to-ing and fro-ing, I had agreed the premium for all three. London's leading underwriters and Corsi had passed the rates onto Montedison. Terms proved agreeable; the policies would begin on the first day of January, the following year. Everyone hoped, of course, that no disaster would befall the industry over the next twelve months. Any catastrophe this side of year-end was no one's problem save the group's.

Unfortunately, on December 31st, I had not quite completed the task. Taking a morning out to see my brother deal with the long arm of the law hadn't helped. The first two layers were done and, therefore, the behemoth could sleep uneasily in its lair. I had not finally completed the third and most stratospheric layer of protection, the one that was only vulnerable to a newsworthy catastrophe. All I needed to worry about was some meteor or nuclear missile straying uninvited into Brindisi's New Year revelries. Nothing less need concern me.

It was seven o'clock on eve of the New Year and the City's underwriters had long gone home. I could finish the job in early January, of course, but January 1st was Sunday and the Monday was the postponed Bank Holiday.

CTB might lose the account if I admitted the business was not placed. That could have been the best thing to do but it would have been the worst for me. My career had seemed to be on the upward escalator but, if I were unnecessarily truthful, it would thenceforward be on the other one, the one going down.

I opted for the little white lie and told Corsi the deal was done. What I didn't tell him was that provided there was no loss to the treaty before January 3rd. Put that way, I still had time to complete the business. Underwriters in the City on January 3rd would be sparse but the job could just be done. Result? Montedison would conclude that Corsi and CTB were their kind of guys while yours truly should earn a white hat and an Iron Cross, with or without bar. After all, we had only got the deal at the eleventh hour and there will have been many who thought it hard to place in such limited time.

That left the gods with two days to punish Corsi, CTB and me with their customary indifference. Now it was New Year's Eve. I had a few glasses of Champagne with my colleagues and set off to my mother's flat to drink yet more with my family. We were due to watch Andy Williams, Stanley Baxter and the Edinburgh Tattoo welcome in the New Year. Festivities now done, my New Year's Resolution (to give up smoking) renewed, at midnight the BBC saw fit to broadcast its first news bulletin of the year.

The melodic voice of the Queen's English came over the waves.

'Good morning, and welcome to the New Year. This is the BBC World Service, broadcasting in English from Bush House in London,' the anonymous announcer pronounced in a perfectly articulated voice – simultaneously unctuous and subtly enunciated. He must have been aware that many of his viewers were foreign and the rest were three parts cut.

'A deafening explosion at the vast petrochemical cracking unit at Brindisi in southern Italy has shaken the entire city. Local radio news suggest that ENI's[80] enormous cracking unit has blown up and that that the sky over Puglia is lit by intermittent orange flashes, strongly suggesting an oil fire is out of control. The silence that the people of Brindisi have come to expect and enjoy in the small hours has been unhappily disrupted by a medley of sirens and klaxons.'

---

[80] *Ente Nazionale Idrocarburi* had become a part of the Montedison Group after privatisation.

True, the wistful phraseology may be just the consequence of an unreliable memory but, all these years later, that's how I remember it.

'When exactly did it happen?' I shouted at the radio. 'Tell me it happened before midnight, please,' I begged the newsreader. 'Please, dear sweet Jesus!'

'We are receiving reports that the disaster occurred some minutes after midnight, local time. Local commentators describe the scene as the worst disaster seen in Italy since the Second World War. We are already hearing of three dead, so far, and more than fifty injured. The good news is that some technicians have been rescued alive from the rubble. Local radio is receiving reports of looting in the town where all the shop windows have been blown in.'

'That's consequential loss! God, I'm in so much trouble!' Indeed, a burning pit was yawning in front of me and the lovely Sharon, the croupier, was beckoning me in.

'We are receiving conformation from the authorities that the explosion is the first catastrophe of this new year. Let us pray it is the only one.'

OK. Let's face it. The game was up. I refilled my whisky tumbler. I could still be a traffic warden, after all.

I didn't sleep at all, I think, until I could be safely back in the City. Not until that Tuesday could I sit at a Lloyds's underwriter's 'box', at nine o'clock, waiting impatiently for him to arrive. I had the 'slip' - the abbreviated details of the treaty - spread over his position. Twenty minutes later he arrived, pointedly ignoring me while he dealt with some wholly trivial back-office matter, he finally condescended to acknowledge my existence.

'You're a bit late with this, aren't you?' the underwriter commented with a cursory glimpse at the slip. He unsheathed his fountain pen and was about to accept a tiny share of the risk. Obviously he knew nothing of the disaster.

'Sir, you need to know that at half-past midnight on the morning of the first of January, the Brindisi plant blew up. Signing this treaty will guarantee you and your syndicate a loss.'

The underwriter put his pen down.

'Then why on earth should I sign it?'

'There is no good reason. Of course, if you don't, I shall probably have to get another job. Outside the insurance industry. That is not your problem. Conceivably you might still want to book the profits that will accrue over the years that follow this freak accident? Possibly you attach a value to your relationship with CTB? I really cannot think of any other reason for you to do me a favour.'

'Well,' said the underwriter, 'I appreciate your candour. In life, rough comes with smooth. One storm does not mean the sea is never calm. I shall take my share and pray that this treaty pays me back in a hundred years or so. Would you mind if I back-date my signature to December 31? Helps with the paperwork, you know.'

This was almost impossibly generous,

'I feel emotional.' I gushed. 'Thank you. I shall tell this story to my children, should I ever have any.'

'If you want my advice, you should get your skates on. Don't tell your bosses until you have placed it all.'

I have to say the remaining underwriters took much the same line and they all signed. By five o'clock, Montedison actually had the cover I had deceitfully confirmed three days before.

Official estimates of the extent of the damage began to roll in on the Wednesday. The sums were colossal. Simon Galway singled me out for some praise.

'Nasty business, that fire in Brindisi. Well done for putting it to bed before year-end.'

'Thank you, Simon. It wasn't easy.'

He smiled. It was a subtle and complex smile. How much did he know?

*

One day a few weeks later, the chief executive of CTB's non-marine division, Charles Cullum, sauntered into my office and asked me if I had plans for lunch. I did but said I didn't, of course.

Did I know Wheeler's? The fish restaurant? It was a Friday after all. I admitted to having heard some good reviews.

'Then you will be my guest. I took the liberty of booking a table for a quarter to one.'

'I'll be there. Thank you very much!'

I guessed that the chief wanted to admit a small party of recent hires into the company's mysteries but, even so, it was flattering to be included. The restaurant, in Great Tower Street, was close to our offices. It was tipping down and I had failed to bring an umbrella. I had to find shelter in Wheeler's doorway, where I tried to brush the rain from my hair and shoulders, before going in. I knew that I was bedraggled and damp. Hardly the stuff of making a good impression but here we go.

As soon as I was inside I was surprised and not a little disconcerted to discover the boss at a table for two. I was his only guest. He had been there a minute or so before me - *noblesse oblige* - and with almost too much courtesy he stood up. It seemed appropriate to shake his hand. Then we sat.

'Raining out there, is it?'

I laughed. Even drowned rats are allowed a sense of humour. We sat.

'You were at Cambridge, I think.' A classic opening gambit. He would not have invited me without a glance at my CV.

'I was.'

'What was your discipline?'

Again an interesting turn of phrase. Most people would say 'subject'.

'I read History and Philosophy,' I replied. 'My efforts were from a scientific perspective. I'm not scared of maths.'

He had already ordered some mineral water. Now he passed the menu towards me.

'Do you like oysters? You do? The sole is good here, but order whatever you fancy.'

'I love sole. I'll have that.'

'On or off the bone?' asked my boss.

'On,' I said decisively. What's the point of having learned to fillet the thing and then let someone else do it? I've always suspected that in their hurry they throw too much of it away.

'I too shall have a Dover sole. What should go with it? Here's the wine list. You choose.'

I had not the faintest idea whether Charles Cullum was a master of wines, an everyday tippler or even teetotal. I suspected I was undergoing some sort of test. I needed something from around halfway down the list but as tasty as the *vignerons* of France were capable of producing.

'This one looks as though it might be OK,' I said, half to myself. 'Sole can be a little buttery. This one is very dry – it should offset the fish well.'

The waiter was beside us and Charles directed him to me.

'We shall both start with half a dozen Colchester oysters, *au naturel*,' I told him, 'and then we'll have the grilled Dover sole. Tell Chef to leave the sole on the bone, and bring a bottle of No 94.'

No 94 was a Chablis Grand Cru, *La Chablisienne*, 1971. The waiter seemed impressed, went about his business and the sommelier returned with the wine, wrapped in a damp cloth.

He poured a little into Charles's glass for him to taste, who sampled the wine with what looked like caution. He seemed pleased with it. Unless he had committed the wine list to memory, there was no way that he could have known what I had chosen. He smiled.

'Why did you choose a Chablis?' he asked me, nodding to the waiter to fill both glasses.

During my gap year at Aerospatiale in Paris, I had learned quite a lot about French wines but I was not sure whether to say too much or too little.[81] Charles was clearly enough of a connoisseur to recognise a Chablis but he still might think me pretentious.

'Chardonnay always slips down easily enough but it is not always dry enough to drink well. They tell me the best ones owe their dryish, flinty character to the microclimate near Auxerre. Winters there are reliably cold and the summers are gloriously warm.'

Charles had again permitted himself a discreet smile. Had I gone too far? He put his glass down.

'Personally', he said, 'I attribute the particular flavour of Chablis to its chalky limestone *terroir*. We often fail to give the region's Kimmeridgian limestone hillsides the credit they deserve.'

The freshly opened oysters arrived with chopped shallots in red wine vinegar, elevating them to their noblest purpose, that of being eaten alive. Next it was time to essay the sole; it was delicious.

'Tell me,' said Charles, his voice quite neutral, 'do you find your career, so far, fulfilling?'

'Much more than that, Charles. I find it exciting.'

'They tell me you're quite a linguist. French and Italian, they say. Any others?'

---

[81] See *A Gap Year or Two* for an account of those years

'I scrape by in English,' I quipped, instantly regretting my fake *insouciance*.

'Yes, yes,' said Charles impatiently. 'You also speak Greek, Simon tells me.'

'A few words. Tourist Greek, in round numbers.'

'So, what about Spanish?'

'No. I haven't been there since I was a boy. It's a little like Italian, they tell me, Latin infused with its own exotica – Celtic, Arabic, Phoenician.'

'Could you add it to your list, d'you think?'

'I suppose I might find it easy enough, but a country's language is more than the result of history. To speak another language you have to understand how another people thinks. Spain is a different place to Italy. Spain has no operatic tradition.[82] It's a harder, more macho world. Even its popular entertainment involves torture and death. It's a bull market.'

Charles had the grace to laugh.

'I understand they have dancing bears in Italy,' he replied easily, wholly unfazed.

The sole at Wheeler's could almost define fishcraft, but we both had business to do. Charles indicated to the hovering waiter that coffee would suffice and waved him away. Five minutes later he would signal for the waiter to bring him the bill.

'I've enjoyed our chat. Now we must both get back to the coal face.'

I looked instinctively at the ice bucket. We had drunk around half the bottle. I had had two glasses to his one. To leave it seemed a sin but a venal sin, in the circumstances, seemed the noblest path.

'We are pleased with the way you're turning out,' he told me as we left. 'Yet a good broker does not

---

[82] I was unfairly overlooking such megastars as Josée Carreras, Placido Domingo, Victoria de los Angeles and Montserrat Caballé. In self-defence, however, I might add that their stratospheric careers owe less to Spain than to the whole wide world.

merely react to a difficult challenge, as you did with Montedison. Yes, we do know the scary details. The good broker also generates new business. Produce a new treaty from our London market and you could yet be going places. But be aware, while you have friends in high places, you are arousing a little jealousy in lower ones. Tread carefully. I shall be watching.'

When we stepped onto the pavement the sun had come out.

*

Why had I had the privilege of this interview? A little introspection gave me the space to diagnose the purpose of our lunch. I concluded I had been given terms. I had just, somehow, got away with the Montedison business.

That's what I thought, at least but I knew it had exposed me to my bosses as a loose cannon. If the sordid details became too widely known, the jealousy that Charles had alluded to would do my future infinite harm.

After all, had I admitted to Corsi and Montedison my failure to complete their business, even the underwriters who had signed up before the 31st would not have paid the claim. Lasting harm? Perhaps not. Markets are commonly said to have short memories.

I could only hope that this vacuous observation might prove for once to be true but what Charles had told me, if between the lines, was that the directorship I had been hoping for was out of the question. Unless, that is, I had made the company substantially richer. There was only one way, realistically, of doing this. As Charles had hinted, it would be for me to create a whole new treaty from scratch in the London market, without a production broker like Corsi to take the credit.

*

That was why I took the boss at the *Dunedin Reinsurance Company* out to lunch a few days later. Hugh Thomson, chairman and underwriter, was a spirited New Zealander and had named his company after the town in which he had grown up. Like many Kiwis his recreation mainly turned around watching Cricket and Rugby - mostly on television, sadly for him. On high days and holidays he would don an antipodean blazer and hop in a cab bound for Lords, or in some other costume for Twickenham.

Sport aside, he had a very keen business brain. He had built up a substantial account over the four years since he had opened the doors to his City office.

Over lunch, we swapped stories about freak catastrophes. I told him of a tornado in the Po Valley that had sucked the cement powder from hessian sacks beside a motorway under construction, depositing their contents over five hundred acres of glazed tomato farm. If this were not bad enough, it had then rained, setting the concrete and causing £10m worth of damage.

He replied with a tale then told me of a hellish hailstorm in New Zealand that had not only destroyed every vineyard in Marlborough, South Island, but had also destroyed every car that had parked in the open air, hoping to watch the Kiwis defeat the Aussies at cricket.

A catastrophe, to an insurance professional, is a single event that causes a claim on two or more policies. Hugh's, however, was spread across two whole classes: motor and non-marine.

By the third glass we were merrily trying to imagine the worst disaster we could come up with.

My tongue loosened, I designed some monstrous scenario, but he won with a nightmarish vision of two Jumbo Jets in collision over Manhattan, one filled with a suit of lawyers and the other with a drill of dentists.

'Well, Jeremy', said Hugh. 'You didn't bring me here to chat amiably about the worst events we could conjure up between us. You want something.'

'I want to reinsure your business, Hugh. We have talked amusingly about disasters that cross the usual portfolio boundaries. Precisely because the risk of such a calamity is slim in the extreme, I could get you a great price. May I have a go?'

'Well, why not? Get a price and we'll see if it stacks up.'

*

I should have been over the moon with my brand new treaty, but all I had done was cover my backside and then, only with the flimsiest scrap of gossamer silk.

A 'friend' told me a rumour was circulating that I might have 'stitched up' the underwriters on the top layer of the Montedison reinsurance programme.

Technically, I was bullet-proof. Every underwriter who had signed the slip, even after the event, had dated their signatures on the 31st but, to some, I was becoming some sort of sorcerer, a spirit of disorder, the force that undermines the very definition of a gentleman-broker.

It was depressingly obvious to me that just one new treaty would not be enough.

*

A courteous and mannerly white Kenyan called Bill had opened his own reinsurance company. It was in Gracechurch Street, so he called it *The Gracechurch*. We got on well. I had many Kenyan friends. Dominic and Nicola French, Hilary Martin, Siba Markham, many others. Through them I had learned a little about Happy Valley. I regularly took my business to the owner-underwriter of *The Gracechurch* and, when not talking business, and when there was no queue for his ear, we dwelled on the vicissitudes of that beautiful African nation.

Bill had been a child there during the drawn-out savagery of the Mau Mau Uprising. It had lasted for a dozen years - 1952 to 1964. The term Mau Mau may have been an acronym for Mzungu Aende Ulaya Mwafrica Apate Uhuru, if others claim that it derives from UMA, a communication code used by the guerrillas. What is beyond dispute is that the Mau Mau were dominated by the Kikuyus, the Merus and the Embus.

White European settlers were their enemy, as was the British Army and the local Kenya Regiment and they would make the activities of our dear, home-grown IRA look like a vicarage garden party.

It only ended with Harold Macmillan's faint-hearted surrender of our administration to Mr Kenyatta. Bill, who had lived through it, was splenetically indignant that a great colonial civilisation had given way to native barbarity without a fist being raised in protest.

I chose to agree with his every fulmination, while in my heart I thought that without the example of muscular support that Palmerstone's gunships had demonstrated, the British Empire would have been relegated to history books long before the Second World War.

If the Suez crisis had been the last heroic chance for our chaps to don their pith helmets, there just wasn't enough money in the kitty. After the Second World War, we didn't have any. Our former colonies saw that without British investment they had no choice but to find alternatives. They would need to persuade the US, the USSR, the IMF or China to step up to the plate.

What an impossible quandary! They would have to pick and choose. No one then had a clue that Europe's wounds might heal and that one day it would combine as a continent. Europe was then a collection of princely states, rather like Germany before Bismarck, and half of them were communist.

It also occurred to the ever-growing-longer list of African demagogues that if they had political parties –

rather than tribes – they would be described by Guardianistas as 'democratic', harbingers of the 'will of the people'. In reality, these gangsters saw that international funding would have to pass through their mistresses, their wives and their 'deputies'' hands. There would be opportunities to build palaces that made Versailles look like a country cottage.

'The working class can kiss my arse', they sang in tuneless unison. 'I've got the foreman's job at last.'

*

The Gracechurch was still relatively new to the international reinsurance market and Bill was always pleased to see a broker from CTB.

My competition was also bearding him in his comfortable lair – his funding and security were excellent – but he was still a little off the main drag.

'If CTB had a treaty with you, Bill, protecting you against some near-unimaginable event, the news would travel fast and all our brokers would call in. I don't know exactly but maybe you could swell your presence in the London market fourfold. The point of a bandwagon, after all, is to be jumped on.'

'You have some sort of proposal in mind? I can tell.'

'Yes. You write marine and non-marine business. What if some coastal ship leaked oil into a bay or a marina? What if a supertanker discharged its entire cargo of crude oil into Alaska or the Gulf of Mexico? You would pay on both accounts. Why not have a treaty that crosses classes? It would be cheap, I'm sure, and you would sleep at night.'

'Thank you, Jeremy, I sleep well enough. Nevertheless, get me a quote, will you? Your idea may yet be good.'

*

Two weeks later, CTB had a second brand-new treaty. Had I redeemed myself? I decided to have a word with Simon Galway, even though I felt he was at best a reluctant sponsor of my cause.

'Two of my colleagues have been offered assistant directorships, Simon. What are my chances of making it three?'

'Meet me half-way, Jeremy. You are henceforward a 'senior broker'. Have your business cards redone. You are now the only senior broker in CTB's international non-marine division.'

''Assistant director' is out of the question, then?'

'Be realistic, Jeremy. There is a shadow hanging over you. There is some irritating tittle-tattle. We can hardly be seen to be rewarding you with a directorship, can we? For that to happen you have to be seen as whiter than white. That may take a little longer.' Since my destiny was in his hands, there was little I could do. Rather like Fotherington-Thomas, to me it all felt a little unfair.

*

March 1976 was at last upon us. March was my favourite month. It was when the Sap of Spring made its customary overtures to the snow queen, who would eventually submit after a show of token resistance.

Winter always seemed a disproportionately long season but, when those green shoots finally found their way into the open air, the whole world rejoiced. We men would leave our coats at home, our ladies would shed layers of unnecessary clothing and they would emerge into the dulcet air like butterflies. March also owns St Patrick's Day.

On that saintly morning, City pubs would open at 10 am, more or less, and Guinness was a compulsory breakfast beverage. Except that I had had breakfast already.

Tev and I had set our alarms early and had travelled to Smithfield Market to have ours in the *Fox and Anchor*, a Victorian hostelry that treated the market's porters and the City's foreign exchange dealers as equals. Traders on the Tokyo exchanges came here for a last swill before going home for a morning's sleep, while their bright-eyed and bushy-tailed equivalents on the Frankfurt markets met here to imbibe an antidote to German rigour before their day kicked off.

That day, everybody there was drinking Guinness. Everyone in the world is an honorary Irishman on March 17th, and I had a better claim to be the real thing than most.

Guinness Extra Stout tastes good at any time, but at half-past six in the morning it tastes very special. The fact that it is slightly sinful adds extra spice. Tev and I limited ourselves to two. It would be wrong to arrive in the office already tight.

Tribute paid, Tev vanished in the direction of the World Trade Centre while I headed for the Bowring Building on Tower Hill. First, a little token business, and then round two; black on black (and I am talking stout, mark you).

I had never seen the City's pubs so crowded so early. I suspect that some of those propping up the bar may not have been Irish. Admittedly they were all quaffing the black stuff but I did not hear the lilt of the Mountains of Mourne. The accent that predominated was the cultivar nurtured in the Thames Estuary and its exponents were clad in blue chalkstripes and red braces. More bray than blarney.

This was a fickle crowd. Today it was the saintly Paddy to whom the glasses were raised. They would also gather in similar vein for the arrival of the Nouveau Beaujolais six months later, yet they pointedly ignored Saints George, Andrew and David.

I am sorry to confess that I rather overdid it. The problem began when I accepted the challenge of 'chasing' my Guinness with a shot of Jameson's 15 year old Special Reserve. It was only fair to offer my challenger a return coupling, a pint and this time a shot of Jameson's 18 Year Old Bow Street Cask Strength. Phew! It was 55% proof! I was in a sorry state when I idiotically went back to the office, thinking I could respond intelligently to whatever telexes and correspondence that would be waiting for me in my in-tray. Of course, whom should I bump into (literally) but Simon Galway. He assessed my condition in a quarter of a microsecond.

'What on earth?' he spluttered.

'St Patrick's day,' I replied. It was all the explanation needed.

'For God's sake, Jeremy, go home. Now.'

The matter was never mentioned again.

*

David Levy and I were returning to the Opera House. He loved rare operas, and so did I, though I was finding it far harder to adjust to modern composers. This is why I had selected *Peter Grimes* for our irregular outing. Not that I am a particular fan of Benjamin Britten, but this time my *ad hominem* aversion could be suspended.

For this opera he had been inspired by George Crabbe's 1810 series of poems 'The Borough'. Britten and his 'partner', the tenor Peter Pears, worked on the scenario for the opera together, transforming Crabbe's monstrous fisherman into a sympathetic outsider, persecuted by a hostile community, just as Britten saw himself.

Britten then asked another friend, the Communist Montagu Slater, to write the libretto, who added many political touches to the text.

The opera was first performed in 1945, just after V.E.Day, with Pears in the title role. The fact that Britten was a conscientious objector may have irritated many a returning serviceman but his unconcealed homosexuality went down well with the 'artistic' madolescents and peterpanjamdrums he cultivated.

Here is the plot. Peter Grimes/Benjamin Britten is a fisherman/composer, living in a small Suffolk town/Aldeburgh. He is summoned to court after the death/loss-of-innocence of his young apprentice on a trawler/rowing boat. The townspeople are convinced Grimes/Britten is a monster/pervert, but he is let off with a caution and warned not to take another apprentice. Ignoring the court's ruling, Grimes/Britten soon recruits a new lad from the workhouse/leading public school. Sometime later the boy falls to his death/goes through puberty. The townspeople gather to hunt Grimes/Britten down, despite desperate pleas for mercy from the schoolmistress Ellen Orford/Peter Pears.

There the overlap ends. Grimes descends into madness. The old sea captain Balstrode tells Grimes to sail his ship out to sea and drown himself. In other words, all good fun, but don't misunderstand me. The opera is truly a great one; its four 'sea interludes' are especially magical.

*

It was turning warm. The general mood was improving, despite petrol rationing and an erratic power supply. Everyone said we were in for a heat wave. They were right. 1976 would see the hottest summer *average* temperature in the UK, ever, before or since. The country suffered a severe and concomitant drought. Very few places achieved even half their average summer rainfall. It was the warmest summer in the Aberdeen area since 1864. In Glasgow it was the driest summer since 1868. Both of these were outranked by

London.[83] For fifteen consecutive days, between June 23rd to July 7th, most of England saw temperatures exceed 32° C. Five days saw temperatures reach 35°. On June 28th, temperatures in Cheltenham and Southampton topped 36°, the highest June temperatures ever recorded in British history, up to that date. There had been nothing even near it in living memory, and we would have to wait until 2003, 2019 and 2022 to see a single hotter day.

With that long dry period came a great drought. It had scarcely rained over the summer and autumn of 1975 and the winter of 1975 – 76 had been almost as arid as the spring. Some months had no rain at all. By August, English fauna and flora were seriously thirsty. Our native seven-spotted ladybirds celebrated the weather with a population explosion.

The warm spring had indulged them with a feast of tasty aphids, their favourite dish but it could not last. As the hot weather unremittingly turned the roses to scented parchment, the greenfly population slowly collapsed. In a last ditch effort to try to find food somewhere else the ladybirds swarmed. The British Entomological and Natural History Society estimated that, by late July, 65 billion of them were rampaging across England.

Drinking water was harder to find than Pol Roger Champagne. The Haweswater reservoir barely had 10% of its water left; people could walk dryshod on parts of its bed, sixty feet below its normal water level. The remains of the drowned village of Mardale were in the open air again, after many decades. Its post office, Red Lion pub and its medieval church were spookily inhabited by the shades of freshwater mermaids and mermen.

After yet another Parliamentary crisis, when ministers were recalled from the South of France

---

[83] Some meteorologists (wrongly) regard the summer of 1995 to be drier. 2018 also saw a very dry summer, as was 2022, but to infer 'climate warming' would of course be statistically silly. Exceptions, as we all know, do not make a rule.

(Tories) or East Germany (the other lot), Denis Howell was appointed 'Minister for Drought'. Why Mr Howell?

'Because he's so wet', *Private Eye* explained.

Howell saw a Drought Bill enacted, but an hubristic House of Commons found, like King Canute had done some years before, it lacked the power to bind God. Devastating fires broke out in parts of Southern England. 50,000 trees were destroyed at Hurn Forest in Dorset alone. Crops were badly hit. £500 million worth of them failed and food prices shot up by 12%.

Yet God, perhaps, did pay some attention to the Minister for Drought. Severe thunderstorms brought rain to scorched earth for the first time in weeks. September and October 1976 were so wet they brought an end to the great drought and the railway timetable.

The latter is always the victim of any unusual weather, blizzards or locusts, hot or cold, wet or dry, Tuesdays or the wife's birthday. Despite the glorious summer, the economy overall was in the doldrums.

The year before, the Government had decided to implement a phased pay policy in both the private and public sectors. Phase I had been announced in the summer of 1975, and it proposed a limit on wage rises of £6 per week for all earning below £8,500 a year.

The TUC General Council grudgingly agreed. In May, 1976, it agreed that increases in salary would be limited to a sum between £2.50 and £4 per week. At its Annual Congress that September, the TUC rejected a motion which called for a return to free collective bargaining.[84] This was Phase II of a progressively desperate incomes policy. We are not out of those woods, even yet.

*

There are times when one meets someone before he, or she, becomes vastly rich and successful. I think it interesting

---

[84] Which meant no incomes policy at all.

to remember that person from his or her early days, if only to observe the quality that would so soon take them to the top of the pile.

Happy families are all alike; every unhappy family is unhappy in its own particular way, while hardship, as Tolstoy almost said, comes in many flavours. Pure undiluted charm only comes in one. Epitomised by Cary Grant, David Niven and perhaps George Clooney, these put their great gift to legitimate use. One of Noel Coward's most magical songs, *Mad About the Boy*, perhaps explains this better than anyone else ever has.

Piers Julian Dominic Pottinger's family circumstances were unhappy, for good reason but, disproving the Russian perhaps, Piers himself was a fully paid up member of the happy breed and was a grand master of charm. Adrian Stroude, a friend of my old chum Roger Turner, had somehow found his adulation of Mr Charm Incarnate reciprocated. Or, more likely, tolerated.

At the time, both of them were working for *Manufacturers Hannover.* Nowadays, people may remember Piers Pottinger as the supremely successful co-founder of *Bell Pottinger* but, back then, Adrian, Piers and I would meet in the *Bow Street Wine Vaults.* Piers told me that he too had spent some time in Rome. I'm not sure that he had, but it was one of Piers' most impressive gifts to identify or even invent what his clients might have in common with him within seconds.

Alongside his magnificent smile, his fabulously tailored suits, his studied languor and a voice that made girls feel pleasantly uncomfortable, he had an amazing ability to create devotees of all who met him.

He flattered everyone effortlessly with his brilliant and carefully delivered aphorisms on every subject, all of which served to promote the illusion in his counterpart that he was as much a genius as Piers himself.

253

'Can it be true you're thinking of leaving Manny Hanny to work in PR?' I asked him. I had heard the rumour from Roger Turner. I heard Adrian's sharp intake of breath and realised, too late, that I had unwittingly betrayed the confidence he had shared with Roger.

'Why not?' Piers replied, batting the question aside like a fly. 'I am one of those fortunate men whose front door mat collects offers from banks and stockbrokers every day. Today I had an offer from *Schroder Wagg*. Yesterday it was the stockbrokers *Laurence Prust*. They are offering two or three times my modest stipend at *Manny Hanny*.'

He checked himself. 'But you're right, of course. PR might be a good idea. It is a neglected sector. I am toying with the idea of founding a PR company that works for great charities. They pay well and, considering the outrageous salaries their bosses like to pay themselves, they are almost as needy of a suit of shining armour as is every Select Committee of the House of Commons.'

Adrian and I appreciated his Swiftian repartee. Adrian himself had been unhappy at his former employer, *Kleinworts*. He asked this Svengali what he thought was the single most important factor for a successful public relations campaign. Perhaps he was hoping to hitch a lift on Piers's coat tails?

'Identifying, aiming for and reaching the relevant audience, however large or small.'

'Are you involved with any charities?' I asked him and was rewarded with one of his lighthouse smiles.

'I am. *The National Society for Epilepsy. The Foundation for Liver Research. The Poetry Society. The Scottish Ballet Company.* Oh, several others.'

This was not an interview. We were in a wine bar, where conversation is supposed to be light. I asked the man with the perfect smile which actor he would want

Hollywood to cast as him in a film of his life? He grinned.

'The Swedish chef from *The Muppets*, though perhaps without the moustache,' he replied genially.

'What will you call your PR firm, when you launch it?' asked Adrian. 'I will want to stag it at its IPO.'[85]

'"*Klareco*'. It's the Esperanto word for 'clarity'. Esperanto is the international language of hope and harmony and that's what I stand for. I will want a name that reinforces the virtue of business within capitalism.'

'So you'll found your own show? You're not planning to join an existing outfit?' I asked.

'If *Lowe Bell*, or someone like that, were to make me an offer I'd join up like a shot.'

'You're not going to stay in banking?' asked Adrian, alarmed at the thought of his hero and mentor disappearing over the horizon.

'Bankers are complete criminals, Adrian. But you know that already.'

Adrian thought it best to remain schtum. After all, Piers knew about criminals. He was the elder son of 'Gorgeous' George Pottinger, nicknamed thus on account of the latter's predilection for expensive suiting.

Three years before, George Pottinger had been sipping his port after a black-tie dinner at the *Muirfield Golf Club* when the Fraud Squad arrived, just before midnight, to arrest him in public. He was charged on the spot with corruptly obtaining building contracts. His trial at Leeds Crown Court took fifty two days and the papers submitted to the court weighed half a ton. Pottinger had already been suspended from his post as Permanent Secretary to the Department of Agriculture and Fisheries.

He and his co-accused John 'Garlic' Poulson, an unregistered architect, were found guilty of a fraud that concerned some very dodgy hotel building in a brand new

---

[85] Stagging a share means buying or offering to buy shares in the grey market that precedes a launch. IPO stands for 'initial public offering'.

ski resort in the Scottish highlands, Aviemore. They were both gaoled for five years on February 11th, 1974. Poulson received a further seven-year prison term (to be served concurrently with the original sentence) while, on appeal, Pottinger's sentence was reduced to four years.

Sentencing Pottinger to gaol, Mr Justice Waller said he had 'let down the honourable [civil] service to which [he] belonged.'

He was then dismissed from his post, his retirement lump sum was forfeited, his pension halved. His 1953 Royal Victorian Order and his '52 Order of the Bath were revoked.

One would be forgiven for assuming that with his father's incarceration, the rug had been pulled from under Piers's feet. I think his actually ambition, boosted by the anger that welled within him. Not that it showed. Outwardly, his defining feature was that great beaming smile, quite as fetching as that of the crocodile of legend.

If the *Bell Pottinger Group* would grow into number one in *PR Week and Marketing Magazine's* league table, its conception may even have been in that conversation. If so it had a long gestation. That said, at the time of writing *Bell Pottinger* has offices in London, North America, the Middle East and south-east Asia. He offers consumer, corporate and financial healthcare. If your strategy for technology, industry, even public affairs needs tweaking, *Bell Pottinger* understands the public sector, corporate social responsibility, internal communication and crisis management, and Piers will undertake lobbying, speech writing and reputation management. He has recently developed a skill he calls 'search engine optimisation'. He sells it to corporates, governments and rich individuals.[86]

---

[86] The last I saw of Piers was in 2010. At that time his fee income made Bell Pottinger the largest public relations consultancy in the UK. He was off to the Far East, planning ever greater things. He has still further to go, of that I'm sure.

I had determined to go back to Greece, and not just to practise the few words I had so far learned. I also meant to darken the melanin tints of my fair and Irish skin.

Someone had told me that the island of Patmos in the Dodecanese was an unsullied foretaste of Paradise and that was good enough for me.[87] In fact, if it were true, it would be a little too good for anyone other than Albert Schweitzer, but I was not deterred by my sinful past. I might not ever see the glory of God in the hereafter, so I might as well have a glimpse while I lived.

Nick Monson was also up for an adventure. He had just met a dark and sultry girl called Jasmine. She looked a little Greek and he thought she would travel well. I had no objection.

Simply getting there was more of an adventure than I had expected. We flew to Athens, from there we took a steamer for Mykonos for a night's shut-eye before taking another to *Skala*, Patmos's port. At last the job was done. The journey from London to Patmos had taken twenty-four hours.

At the end of that last leg I met a striking Greek girl myself and she seemed to appreciate the cut of my jib. Her name was Λέχια, or Lexia, a magical name, and we were all bound for a correspondingly magical place.

As usual, Nicholas had done his homework. He told me that the island's original name had been 'Letois', after the goddess and deer hunter Artemis, the daughter of Leto. Patmos owes its existence to her.

'While the Greek gods were young and mischievous, Patmos was an island at the bottom of the

---

[87] Patmos is situated off the west coast of Turkey and the continent of Asia. It is one of the northernmost islands of the Dodecanese complex, only a little further west than its nearby neighbouring islands. Forbes magazine, in 2009, named Patmos 'Europe's most idyllic place to live', writing that 'Patmos has evolved over the centuries but has not lost its air of quiet tranquillity, which is one reason why people that know it return again and again'.

sea. Artemis frequently visited Caria, on the mainland, where she had a shrine. There she met the moon goddess Selene who, casting her light on waves, revealed the sunken island to the virgin huntress,' he told me. 'Selene wanted Artemis to bring the sunken island to the surface, back to life. She somehow enlisted her brother Apollo in her effort to convince Zeus to allow the island to arise.

'Zeus duly caused the island to erupt from the sea. Apollo dried it and the inhabitants of Mount Letois settled it. These new Patmians were 'Dorians', proudly claiming descent from the military families of Argos, Sparta and Epidaurus.

'It was a slow start. Patmos had to wait until the 3rd century BC, the Hellenistic period, to acquire an acropolis. That was when it invested heavily in defences – mostly a wall with observation towers every few yards.'

This was not the only historical reference to our destination. Indeed, Patmos is mentioned in the Book of Revelation, the last book of the Bible. Nick had read it. He told me that its author, John the Apostle, had been on Patmos when he had his vision. Scarcely waiting for the echoes of the apostle's obsequies to fade away, a conurbation of paleochristian basilicas grew up. Among them was the Grand Royal Basilica, built around 350 AD.

When Islam began to spread, early Christian life on Patmos looked unlikely to survive the Muslim pirates' constant raids. The Grand Basilica was destroyed but, in the 11th century, a far-sighted Byzantine Emperor - Alexis I Komnenos - granted Abbot Christodoulos suzerainty over the island and permission to build his own monastery. Construction began the next year. Even though the Christian Byzantines had fled Constantinople in 1453, the island's Christian population swelled.

It did not take long for it to dawn on the Ottoman Turks that these pilgrims meant money and the best kind of money is an income stream. They allowed the island two key privileges, namely Christianity and tax-free trade with the Sublime Porte. Their rule in Patmos ('Batnaz' in Turkish) was briefly interrupted by the Venetians during the Candian War of 1659 to 1669 and, following the fall of Candia in 1669, Cretan immigrants found shelter here.

A short-lived Russian occupation occurred during the Orlov Revolt of 1770 to 1774, before the Turks got it back during the Greek War of Independence. Then, in 1912, during the Italo-Turkish War, the Italians occupied all the islands of the Dodecanese (save for Kastellorizo). The Italians remained in Patmos until 1943. That is when the Nazis took over the island. They did not leave until 1945. The island remained autonomous until 1948, when the Dodecanese joined the newly independent Greece.[88]

Today, the Monastery of Saint John the Theologian provides shelter to great numbers of pilgrims who pay to see the cave where John had his Revelation.[89]

All in all, an interesting and multinational history, and which provoked Nick, Jasmine and to conclude our best option would be to find rooms in Σκαλα (Skala). My new friend Lexia had prebooked a room in a classic tavern a few hundred yards along the coast on Λάμβι (Lámbi) beach.

Our scrubbed pine tables and wobbly chairs overlooked a blue-and-turquoise seascape. That was where we ate as a foursome, sheltering from the sun

---

[88] On the weekend of September 19, 2018, the municipality of Patmos refused landing to 134 undocumented refugees from Afghanistan and Iraq, in desperate need of processing and care. They had been rescued at sea. Eventually they were sent to the island of Leros where they were processed and given humanitarian aid. The Patmos authorities justified their cruelty by contrasting it to alleged practices elsewhere in the EU: 'Malta sinks their boats and Italy lets them drown', a local leader claimed.

[89] The Cave of the Apocalypse.

and eating wild spring greens and fresh squid, washed down with Vergina beer.

Sometimes we would visit a restaurant in the χόρα, the *chora*. that was owned and run by a Greek American who had repatriated himself and his fortune. This was rather grander, so we took the trouble to dress a little more carefully. There we ate χταπόδι and γάλεοσ - grilled octopus, shark and in garlic sauce.

Life was already panning out rather well and it would be better still. Somehow, in Skala's 'cafeneon', Lexia and I found ourselves talking to an Athenian who had done a deal with an American who wanted to own a house on the island.

In those days, Greek law forbade foreigners from owning a property in its jurisdiction, so the would-be purchaser had identified a businessman in Athens who was willing to buy the house with the American's money and pay a peppercorn rent to the would-be resident.

'So you share it? Do you have some sort of roster?'

'He is a New York banker. He has ten days holiday a year and another ten days takes off 'sick'. He spends them here.'

'Every year?'

'Every year. And when he's not here, I can use the house, only provided I keep it clean, take care of the fabric, restock the fridge before his arrival, pay the cleaner and make myself scarce. This before he even sits in the front cabin of a Pan Am Boeing 747 at JFK, awaiting take off.'

'Great arrangement! Where is the house?'

'Up in the *chora*. Would you both like to see it? I'd be more than happy to offer you a glass.'

Since I had not yet set foot in any of the houses that surround the great monastery I jumped at the chance. I glanced at Lexia. Happily she too was pleased to come along.

Constantine had a little car and soon we were in it, passing the sanctuary of St John half-way up the hill.

Our new friend's house nestled against the grey stone walls of the impressive religious house that sat atop the hill, dominating the island.

The house was stunning, whitewashed without and within while its wooden elements, beams, floorboards and antique furniture, were all in polished olive wood. There were some *objets*, great sea shells, an Attic vase or two, a painted panel from the sixteenth century, where the bees had made the place smell of polish and wild flowers.

Up a flight, a dining room could seat eight in comfort; ten at a push. Two good bedrooms had carved testers and perforated, embroidered bedspreads. The kitchen had been recently fitted with every known and some unknown appliances.

'Now let me show you something you will never have seen before,' he said proudly. 'Bring your glasses.'

We had reached the top of the stairs in our guided tour, to be shown into a small dressing room. It had a fine cheval glass, a seven-drawer serpentine chest of drawers and a wardrobe.

'It's not what it seems,' said our host. 'Go on, open the wardrobe door.'

Lexia did exactly that. It held a few shirts on hangers and a couple of pairs of trousers.

'Push them aside. Do you see a catch?'

We did.

'Then pull it to the left.'

Lexia did as directed, and the back of the wardrobe now swung open to reveal a narrow stair beyond.

'After you,' said Constantine.

I felt like one of C S Lewis's characters. The three of us walked through and up a flight. We reached a master bedroom, adjoining a stupendous marble bathroom that could have been mistaken for a temple. 'French' windows opened onto a roof terrace with awesome views over Patmos's *chora*, the great monastery and, of course, the Aegean.

'Turkish pirates would never find a family or its women in here. Their slaving parties went away empty-handed and disappointed. Penthouses[90] such as these are everywhere. They are our island's secret bunkers.'

As I gazed over the astounding view, listening to a silence only disturbed by cicadas, I resolved that I would return to Patmos as often as God permitted me. In a word or two, it is the loveliest place I ever saw.

*

---

[90] 'Penthouse' arrives in English from German but ultimately derives from the Latin word 'appendix', or building appended to the main structure.

CHAPTER FOUR

Four Candles
1977

The author explores his Irish heritage and stays in the venerable Kildare Street Club. He attends four weddings, one French, two Italian, and one Scottish. The odd one out, so to speak, is the marriage of Venice to the Adriatic.

My flatmate Tev had some commercial business in Dublin.

'I have to go to Ireland. Business. It's one of the world's greatest seafaring nations, second only to Wales.' Tev is Welsh.

When Tev suggested I tag along it took me but the tiniest fraction of a millisecond to agree. He had discovered, moreover, that his club in St James's had reciprocal rights with the Kildare Street Club, of which I had heard tantalising tales. But what would I do in Dublin? I had decided to seek advice/

'You should go to the Royal Dublin Horse Show,' Colin Swan told me over dinner. 'You're in luck; I'll be there on the first day. You can't buy a ticket - it's far too late and they've long sold out. No matter. We'll be in a private box and you'll be my guest.'

Tev and I came to an arrangement. While he strutted his stuff, I would watch the horses strut theirs. A 'royal' horse show? In Dublin? I had absolutely no idea of what I was in for.

The Kildare Street Club was, as one might cleverly deduce, in Kildare Street.[91]

---

[91] Anyone foolish enough to replicate my adventures should know it is there no longer. It has moved to the University Club's premises on the north side of St Stephen's Green. I'll warrant, however, that its new location is still the focal point of the Anglo-Irish Anglican Ascendancy. As for its old building, where I went, it has been leased to a Heraldic Museum and the Alliance Française.

'It's one of the most eccentric institutions in Dublin,' Tev told me. 'It plays host to, if not actually defines what was once called the 'rent party' within the four walls of Ireland. It represents those who with an oyster-like capacity for understanding just one thing: that they should get fat in the bed they were born in.'

'All that was long ago,' I protested.

'You think so? They don't. Our B & B is the landed gentry's oyster-bed.' Tev had certainly acquired an Irish accent.

'It is their redoubt, their enclave, their secure haven in which one drinks cognac and exchanges absurd views in the pantomime dialect they call 'Georgian'.'

'Really? It doesn't sound that awful. I look forward to having my copy of *The Times* ironed before it's delivered to my room.'

'You'd do better to order *The Racing Post*.'

I knew I was in clover, and of the four-leaved kind.

*

Tev and I found ourselves booking into an L-shaped building whose terracotta façade was an unlikely half-way-house between the Gothic and the Byzantine. Its large arched windows were divided by thin columns, their curious bases ornamented with by whimsical creatures playing billiards.

The entrance lobby had a glazed cubicle to shelter the porter, under a huge oil of Her Majesty the Queen. Yes, in Dublin. Further in, beside the bar, a framed cartoon by Pont showed a man in a loud check suit talking away happily while a group of gentlemen in pinstripes look on appalled. The caption read 'the man who spoke Gaelic in the Kildare Street Club'.

Tev was a little less impressed by the club's blue-blood.

'If this building were a temple, its resident demigods would be Claret and Whist. Look at these self-elected members of the Ascendancy! The whole effect suggests to me what the Reform Club in Pall Mall must have been in the days of Phileas Fogg.'

The two of us had demolished a full Irish breakfast in the club before Tev and his attaché case went somewhere else.

The club was almost next door to the National Library and that's where I was going. It is a fine old building with a domed reading room, a smaller version of the British Library in London.[92] I would begin to research my genealogy with a perusal of the censuses of the Irish people, taken every ten years, from 1821 to 1921.

The west wing of the Four Courts had become the Public Records Office in 1922. It housed many treasures, including originals wills, some dating back to the 16th century. It also held more than a thousand Church-of-Ireland parish registers, replete with baptism, marriage and burial records.

No Catholic ones, however. That year, 1922, was when a two-day bombardment ravaged the noble pile. Almost every record had been burned to cinders in an incendiary bombing of the Four Courts, inflicted by the English during Ireland's civil war. It was horribly damaged and, adding insult to injury, its dome fell in. Funds for the building's restoration at last became available in 1924. The good news is that today the Four Courts is once again one of Dublin's many architectural gems.

I thought I'd begin with the censuses. The earliest complete census is now that of 1911, while there are

---

[92] London's great copyright library used to be housed within the British Museum. It has recently been replaced by a featureless modernist 'assembly hall of an academy for the secret police', as Prince Charles satirically but accurately observed.

incomplete fragments from 1821, 1831, 1841 and 1851, but it took hours to find even the smallest mention of my family. Being Catholic and living 'beyond the Pale', the relevant details were not documented. Probably never had been.

The military might have something. I persevered and discovered a tantalising mention of a Major Macdonogh of the 8th King's Royal Irish Hussars, living at Wilmont Park in Portumna, Co Galway. There wasn't much. If he served in the Crimea, it will have been as a very young man. He may have served in the Boer War but by 1911 he will have been an old soldier. Tracking the regiment, it turned out that three years later, on the outbreak of the 'great' war with Germany, his regiment was in India playing a noble role in the important business of pig-sticking.

Though the major was way too old to fight, his regiment was brought back from the subcontinent to man the trenches on the Western Front. They made themselves as comfortable as they could, but they arrived on December 9, 1914, too late to play a part in the Retreat from Mons. Most of their losses were not from enemy action as much as from the unsanitary conditions of these hellish dugouts.

The regiment was almost always in reserve, impatiently awaiting 'the gap'. The English generals may have thought that a regiment of Papist squaddies, better suited to building roads, should be digging trenches. Not until the Battle of Givenchy did they see action, where their success gave their commanders some confidence.

That may be why the Hussars were ordered into Flanders. In May 1915, however, they endured disaster at the Second Battle of Ypres, where the Germans first experimented with chlorine.

Not until July, 1916, did the Irish fight again, this time at Bazentin, at Flers-Courcelette and, the following month, at Villers-Faucon - all infamous battlefields in the Valley of the Somme. Their mission was to clear the residual nests of machine guns the Germans left behind to defend their retreat. The Irish regiment's two squadrons conducted a last 'mounted' charge in their two armoured cars, supported by a limited battery of howitzers and attacked a heavily defended German position. Their armoured cars, however, were soon disabled. The Irish continued, but this time on foot. Nevertheless, in a costly action, they managed to capture two Maxim guns. After the 1918 Armistice those weapons were brought back to Ireland and proudly used as guardroom trophies.

The censuses did reveal several McDonoghs in Galway City. I learned they were established merchants but I could not find enough to draft a family tree. I did learn, however, that my coat of arms had been granted in the thirteenth century. That was when all Irishmen were Catholic, an impressively long time ago.[93]

*

Tev and I had drinks that evening, in the club bar.

'Went the day well?' I asked him.

'Definitely. Excellent piece of pathfinding. It turns out that shipping between England and Ireland accounts for a sizeable proportion of all European maritime freight. There may be a strip of water between the England and Ireland but that won't stop us. It will be a great opportunity for Dimitri. C'mon, enough business. Let's go and explore Temple Bar.'

I am easily led.

*

The next morning, when I joined Tev downstairs, I was feeling a tad fragile. Odd that too little sleep and too much of the demon drink should have such an ill effect, when at the time it had seemed such a good idea.

---

[93] Back in London I would show my father the photocopy. 'Ah, yes. I had it as a signet ring. It was quite old. It may have been my grandfather's, or possibly his. I was forced to sell it in 1946. Shame to have let it go.'

'I'm off to the Horse Show with Colin in a minute or two,' I told him. 'What will you be up to?'

'I've been asked to identify and list the customs formalities here in Ireland,' he said. 'Rather a dry old day for me, I'm afraid.'

It was unlikely to be so dry for me.

'If the Republic would only join us in the Common Market it would help,' Tev continued. 'I have had to lay my hands on a sample of the official forms and I'm not sure if sending goods to our partners in Europe, or anywhere else for that matter, should incur duties or taxes. Those will be the bones of my day. I shall endeavour to put flesh on them.'

*

As for me, and as arranged, I met Colin Swan and his friend Diana Pickersgill. Colin was jauntily dressed in tweed, topped with a fedora. She was less showily clad in a sensible frock. Our rendezvous was at eight o'clock in the bloody morning, by the RDS's Concert Hall entrance. The official opening time was 9 am, but on production of Colin's badge we were waved in. We found our way to a large box in the grandstand, bang on the arena. The word 'Presidential' was neatly painted over a faded but discernible 'Royal' on the door.

I had been led to expect the Horse Show to be a 70° proof cocktail of show jumping, fashion and, of course, upperclass banter. This year was set to be very special as it was the one hundredth such show. Very few years had been missed, despite an Easter Rising, a Civil War and two World Wars.

'The Royal Dublin Horse Show is the summer fixture that no Irishman will ever miss,' Colin told me quietly. 'Some of the best horses and riders in the world compete on Arabs and thoroughbreds, just as their children do on their ponies. It's a place where magical memories are forged.'

Once we had threaded name tags through our buttonholes we could look around. The Royal Box was already filling with some very well-dressed people, men in dapper suits, ladies in gown-and-hat combos, the sort most commonly seen at weddings. Its ranged seats were on a steep incline. Only the front row was cushioned. Clearly we would not be sitting there. They already smelled of Very Important Posteriors.

Basing my ideas on Royal Ascot, I was not surprised that a goodly sample of the Anglo-Irish and Gaelic nobility would attend. While we milled about, I read a few badges. My efforts were rewarded with one that identified 'The Reverend the O'Connor Don'.

Chiefs of the Name, at least a handful of them, had only been formally recognised by the Irish government in 1943.[94] That recognition, curiously, had been provoked when Queen Victoria had recognised an early O'Connor Don as Prince of Connacht in 1861. Of course the 'recognition' was merely a romantic gesture. Irish princes had long lost any semblance of real power in their (former) demesnes.

Colin quietly pointed out racing royalty; George Boyd-Rochfort and Walter Haefner had just arrived with their wives. The box was beginning to fill.

I reflected on famous Irishmen. Is it the 'gift of the gab' that ties the Irish together? There really is a great inventiveness in Ireland, and I don't mean the pedal-powered wheel chair or the solar-powered pacemaker. From Joseph Murphy's potato chips to Robert Percival's soda syphon the sons of Erin have immeasurably contributed to our lives, sometimes in prodigious ways. Those ways can be unfathomable, literally so in the case of John Phillip Holland's eighteenth century submarine.

The land of saints and scholars can boast a terrific catalogue of literati, of which I list a smidgen in the

---

[94] This courtesy was discontinued in 2003.

random order they occur to me; Oscar Wilde, George Bernard Shaw, W B Yates, Edna O'Brien, J P Donleavy, Maeve Binchy, Flann O'Brien, P J O'Rourke, Mary Costelloe, Jonathan Swift and James Joyce will just have to do. Even W M Thackeray deserves an honorary mention in that his wife was Anglo-Irish and he spent four glorious months in a grand tour of that kingdom. Thackeray wrote that 'to love and win is the best thing. To love and lose, the next'. If that's not an Irish sentiment, what is?

Music, too, as I would be reminded. One of the guests in the Royal Box was Christy Moore. He looked a wreck. Years of heavy drinking, sleeping crippling hours, continual travel and living off takeaways cost him even more than his genius could earn.

He was terpsichorean descendants of O'Carolan, who has a plausible claim to have invented modern Irish music.

As was John Field, the pianist and composer, whose nocturnes were of such immortal beauty that they excelled those of Chopin.

His father and grandfather taught him music at home in Dublin, before sending him to London to pursue his studies under Muzio Clementi.

Clementi was, in turn, impressed. In 1802 the maestro took Field to Paris, Leipzig and finally St Petersburg, where before long the pupil had secured recognition as a virtuoso pianist and composer. While there, he wrote seven piano concerti and four sonate. His nocturnes are perhaps more concise and intimate than his larger works, but all his music is revolutionary. He is said to be the first musician to use or possibly invent the sustaining pedal.

Seamus Heaney and Michael Gambon now took their seats, side by side. Colin was especially delighted to espy the owner/trainer Vincent O'Brien. The empty seat on my right was taken by Richard McGillycuddy 'of

270

the Reeks, Lord of Doonebo', or so said his badge. Colin obliged with an introduction and an explanation.

'The McGillycuddy's Reeks is a mountain range in County Kerry, known in Irish as *Na Cruacha Dubha*. Don't be fooled by the word 'reek'. It has no connotation with some untoward aroma. It is a Hiberno-English version of the word 'rick', meaning a stack.'

The man in question was tall and dashing, rugged, auburn-haired and about my own age. It was obvious that the young McGillycuddy of the Reeks would be much in demand among London's Sloane Rangers.[95] The chief warmly shook my hand. 'The show will soon begin,' this eligible young man assured me. 'You will never have seen the like, that I promise. There's just time to fetch something from the bar. May I do the honours?'

While Richard McGillycuddy went off in search of a stirrup cup, Colin took advantage of his absence to usher me into Ireland's history.

'The McGillycuddys go back beyond the dawn of recorded history. They were here before the dinosaurs. They fought the Viking, Norman and English colonisers for many a century and, for a while, they held back the tide. Inevitably, I suppose, the Gaelic order was systematically crushed in the 17th century. Unlike the famous earls, the McGillycuddys eschewed exile to stand their ground. A bumpy ride, shall we say, but at the Battle of the Boyne in 1690, their chieftain craftily sent two sons into the fight, one for King Billy and the other for King James, thereby hedging his bets. A racing man, even then. Only a few years later the survivor swore allegiance to the victorious William of Orange and consented to conform to the Reformed Church. By the opening decades of the

---

[95] Feeling that he had little in common with the local people in Kerry, McGillycuddy decided to sell the Reeks and moved to France, where he acted as a property consultant to prospective British purchasers of châteaux and lesser French properties. Eventually, in 1983, at the age of 35, he married Virginia Astor, granddaughter of the first Lord Astor of Hever and a cousin of David Cameron.

new century the family was forming alliances with the English Ascendancy and, in due course, they became part of it. The nine-bay country house they built - Beaufort - is a handsome testament to the value of adaptability.'

It occurred to me that the Irish upper class is versed, if not immersed, in each others' histories.

'The McGillycuddys still had 15,000 acres as late as the end of the 19th century,' Colin continued. 'Richard's grandfather distinguished himself in the First World War, winning both the DSO and the *Légion d'Honneur*. He sat in the Senate of the Irish Free State, a supporter of the moderate W T Cosgrave and an opponent of the republican Eamon de Valera. His father died in 1959 from the wounds he had sustained during the Second World War. Richard was only ten years old at the time, still at prep school, before setting off for Eton. I don't think his English mother ever felt quite at home in Ireland, but she dutifully preserved the family inheritance. Every August she organised a rather gentrified cricket match on the lawn at Beaufort. She was forced, sadly, to abandon the tradition when Richard, who had little interest in cricket and was not paying attention, was knocked down by a mighty drive from one of the Cambridge Crusaders' top batsmen.'

'So what does he do these days?'

'His passion is cars. After a short sojourn at the University of Aix-en-Provence he joined the motor trade. His uncle Dermot is a Dublin solicitor, beloved of every class and creed, but Richard is impervious to all efforts to interest him in Ireland.'

This expiation was interrupted by a forty-something-year-old, who greeted Colin as an old friend.

'Jeremy, may I introduce you to Diarmid McCartan of County Down? He and General de Gaulle used to be as thick as thieves!'

Both McCartan and I were a little startled, if the former merely smiled.

'Colin, you're an old mischief-maker, are you not,' said the Ulsterman, 'but there is always a whisper of fact behind your every casual assertion.'

'It must have been a few years ago,' I said, slightly baffled. The general had gone to a better place in 1970.

'De Gaulle harboured a deep-seated desire to visit Ireland,' McCartan explained. 'When at last he arrived in Dublin he demonstrated an astonishing awareness of his Irish ancestry and a profound knowledge of our history. Josephine Maillot, his grandmother, had already published a dazzling biography of Daniel O'Connell, the Liberator, and during his visit the General ensured that the McCartans were invited to a reception given for him by the President in *Aras An Uachtarain*, the viceregal lodge in our Phoenix Park. It was a memorable occasion.'

'There was some connection, then?'

'That will have been De Gaulle's great-grandmother, Marie Angelique McCartan, daughter of Andronicus and sister to Félix. The General was accordingly proud of his Irish roots.'

Colin, the banker, was still whispering in my other ear.

'Those two, over there, are Tony Ryan and Michael Sobell. We are bankers to them both. I must say hallo to them, let them know I'm at their service.'

He swept around with his binoculars.

'And that chap at the back is Desmond Guinness. That's one you're going to have to meet if you are ever to reclaim your ancestral seat at Kanturk. He runs *An Taisce,* the National Trust for Ireland.'

A military band struck up the Irish National Anthem and a pair of ceremonial gates the far side of the arena were opened by a couple of flunkeys to let four strolling figures walk with a studiously casual gait towards our box.

Colin was back and he nudged me.

'That's President Carroll O'Daly with his consort on the left,' he said through the applause. 'The other two are Taoiseach Liam Cosgrave and his.'[96]

The grandees graciously acknowledged the full-bloodied cheer and the percussive applause of the crowd, continuing their saunter to our, or their, box. A footman opened a door for them and the foursome stepped inside. No sooner had they sat themselves down than the gates opened again, this time to admit an open Landau, drawn by four greys, which began to make a circuit.

'That,' Colin told me though the renewed applause, looking through his field glasses, 'is the Earl of Iveagh and his countess.' I may have raised an eyebrow, as Colin leant into my right ear to announce 'the chairman of Guinness.'

I felt, rather than noticed, Richard McGillycuddy flinch. 'That man's forebear did my family out of a fortune,' he spluttered into my left ear. 'And now he's an earl, some sort of High King. It's a disgrace!'

My surprise obliged Richard to explain. 'As early as 1720,' he began, 'even before we had even moved into our new house, we gave permission for a country fair to be held in the grounds. We meant to say thank you to our retainers and peasants. Every Midsummer's Day, all five hundred were invited to a country fair. It became a tradition. Our comptroller, a certain Arthur McInness, illiterate but ambitious, brewed the beer according to a formula my family had owned for centuries. It was

---

[96] Cearbhall Ó Dálaigh was a *Fianna Fáil* politician, judge and barrister who served as the 5th President of Ireland from December 1974 to October 1976. He served as a Judge of the European Court of Justice from 1973 to 1974, Chief Justice of Ireland from 1961 to 1973, a judge of the Supreme Court from 1953 to 1973 and Attorney General of Ireland from 1946 to 1948 and 1951 to 1953. His Taoiseach was Liam Cosgrave. Cosgrave was an Irish Fine Gael politician who served as *Taoiseach* from 1973 to 1977. He was Leader of *Fine Gael* from 1965 to 1977, Leader of the Opposition from 1965 to 1973, Minister for External Affairs from 1954 to 1957, Parliamentary Secretary to the Minister for Industry and Commerce and Government Chief Whip from 1948 to 1951. He served as a *Teachta Dála* (TD), equivalent to the English MP or the American Congressman, from 1943 to 1981.

brewed once a year with meticulous care. It was justifiably famous. We called it 'stout', as it was not as thin as a 'porter', and it was good for our people.'

'You have to mean Guinness?'

'In 1759, that swine McInness, so poorly educated that he thought his name was Guinness, secreted the formula and took it to Dublin. There, on the site of a former leper colony, he began to brew our ale. He secured the land on which he built his brewery for the princely sum of five shillings a year, and in perpetuity, mark you! No one else wanted it.

'A shrewd move, I am forced to concede; especially from a man who hardly knew his own name. I am forced to admit he made a fist of it. His marketing skills were extraordinary. 'Guinness is good for you' was his first slogan. He sold it to everyone who felt a little untoward in the morning. What a constituency! The pregnant and the dipsy, the thirsty and the incontinent, the clergyman and the politician. That thieving ingrate made his own family a fortune to outrank all others in Ireland, possibly in the whole of the United Kingdom. And what did we see of it? How much you got in your pocket? We saw less than that!'

*

Tev and I caught up later at the Kildare Street Club. We had time to trade some amusing banter about our very different days. We were fed a decent offering of lamb cutlets, mashed, boiled, roast and fried potatoes and something green and translucent that may once have been cabbage. On the matter of wine we were circumspect. We had a plane to catch and work of the paid variety the next day.

Aer Lingus got us home in one piece. I realised, on the plane, that my Irishness had experienced some sort of revivalist crash course. In the early '50s I had been in Ireland with my parents. I remember little, save for a huge red setter called Oonagh. In 1970 I spent a week with Colin and Diana in Dublin, in Tralee, and at the Curragh. Now I had completed a three day study-fest and had 'met' (which translates as having been at the same event) some of the country's most iconic people. I must have been getting something right. The leprechauns, I fancy, were trying to tell me something about a crock of gold.

I had set off near penniless. By the time we were back in England I was the pretender to a ruined castle, the scion of a military family, one of which may have charged the Russian cannons in the Crimea.

Still potless, though.

*

Back in London, the quotidian business continued as usual.

One Friday, a month or so later, on my way home from Milan, I stopped over in Paris, to stay with my sister as was my wont. I had a wedding to attend.

My brother Giles, while not invited to the wedding, was also in Paris, so the three of us had supper across the road from my sister's studio on the *boulevard Montparnasse*.

For some strange reason, Giles was wearing a cable-knit pullover and a string of pearls. While Giles was no friend of Dorothy's, he found the camp manners of Quentin Crisp appealing, or at least amusing. There will have been some disappointed gays in his corner of Oxford who had discovered this strange affectation to be merely skin deep.

Le Select, where we went for drinks before dinner, was (and is) guilty of living beyond its social means but, while its clientèle no longer reflects its name, it's very large and selfish tabby cat did. This beast, Félix by name, lived on the zinc.[97] It would only move when physically

---

[97] The bar.

threatened, but when it did so it would exact revenge by barging half a dozen *pastises* and two or three *coups de Champagne* into an irreversible beyond. Most cats would have endured some appropriate or even disproportionate punishment for so grave a sin, but Félix had achieved the quasi-Egyptian status of the semi-divine. Had Apollinaire lived he would have surely celebrated Félix in verse.

Then, across the road in the *Coupole*, the three of us would set about a great dish of *fines claires*,[98] stung into a final salute with neatly chopped shallots in red wine vinegar. The *Coupole* had been declared an historic monument. The building, while by no means ugly, was typical of the pomposity that epitomised the 1920s. What lent it distinction was the large number of frescos on its walls, painted by some of the most celebrated artists of the early twentieth century as a means of settling their tabs. It was a little like dining amid the impressionist collection of the *Tate*.

After the oysters, we swapped our Champagne for a serviceable red – chosen by Giles[99] – to help us digest our *plats du jour* before returning to raise a cognac or two as a tribute to the imperturbable Félix back at *Le Select*.

*

Very sweetly, Caroline de Bartillat - Charles-Henri's[100] sister - had invited my sister Kate and me to her wedding to Gilles de Navacelle. The marriage would be celebrated in an eleventh century Romanesque church in their village, to be followed by a reception at the de Bartillat manor house beside the Loire.

We were in good heart that morning, fragile but successfully togged up in our wedding finery. Kate donned something chic and floral, a huge hat obscuring

---

[98] Oysters. Fines claires may be the best of them all.
[99] Giles was later to become a food and wine writer for both the FT and Decanter Magazine.
[100] Charles-Henri de Bartillat was my first and closest friend when I arrived in Paris in 1973. *A Gap Year or Two* has all the details.

most of her face and I was in my tails, yellow waistcoat, topped with a topper. Our arrival at Paris's brand new railway station at Bercy was timely.[101] The train was about to pull out. Possibly a little overdressed by the standard of the commuters surrounding us, we boarded our train.

Kate had made friends of a plump American called Eugene, almost the only example of that Christian name I have ever met outside France and, since he was wearing a grey silk hat, we found him easily enough. We were to share a compartment and, finally at Tours, the three of us would pile into a taxi and asked to be whisked to a monastic chapel on the borders of the Bourbonnais and Berry regions, where the waters of the Loire mingle with those of the Allier.

Our taxi driver is assured a place in heaven. To find the church he took us across featureless grassy prairies, down country lanes and up rolling hills. After an age this great navigator pointed out a slate bell tower, topped with a cockerel, the symbol of vigilance. '*Vous y êtes*,' he proudly announced in a quite unnecessary triumphalist tone. '*Voilà*'.

It was a beautiful chapel of ease, whose door was flanked by primitive Corinthian columns, crowned with a semi-circular tympanum reflecting the canopy of heaven and, in *bas relief*, a young woman giving alms.

Inside, a spiral stair led to a gallery that featured an oaken balustrade. Since the nave was already full, up we went but the steep climb was for once rewarding.

---

[101] How I hate that station! Such an ugly place, built by modernists to handle the trains to Lyon and Dijon! How dare they build a railway station like that over the last vestiges of the Neolithic peoples of Gaul? It handles the mainline intercité trains to Vichy & Clermont Ferrand, the TER regional trains to Lyon and Dijon as well as a few local trains. It's full title is 'Gare de Paris-Bercy-Bourgogne-Pays d'Auvergne'. Unsurprisingly everyone calls it Paris Bercy. It's barely a quarter of an hour's walk from the Gare de Lyon, and it feeds into the same tracks out of Paris as the Gare de Lyon - indeed, it was originally built as something of an overflow station to help solve capacity problems there. The terminus has six platforms, which is the nicest thing one can say about it.

From the 'dress circle' we had an unobstructed view over the pulpit and the shell-shaped font. Wainscoting covered the chapel walls, while the choir still had its vaulted ceiling. Some faded murals had left hints as to the grandeur of the original conception.

The congregation began to quieten. The Benedictines were about to partake in a great piece of divine comedy. They filed in, censers swinging, chanting a Gregorian psalmody with impressive dignity, while their abbot followed them at a stately pace before oblating himself before the altar.

The monks fanned out into a semicircle before us. They sang *a cappella*,[102] which was when I realised that term did not derive from the efforts of Ivy League songsters.

Caroline and Gilles were already married, of course, in accordance with French law. That dry, legalistic rite had happened the day before. It will have been a civil and secular business, redolent of the demystification of the infinite favoured by bureaucrats and materialists world-wide. The couple before the altar were about to deliver an *amende honorable*.

A debt to the Holy Spirit and to Poetry was to be repaid in this thousand year old setting. The many words of the long ceremony were in high Latin, not in legalistic French, as were the responses of the standing, sitting and occasionally kneeling couple. At the end of the long ceremony, the Abbot solemnly told us to go.

'*Ite*,' he pronounced. '*Missa est.*'

'*Deo grátias*,' we all replied, and meant it.

'*Benedicat vos omnipotens Deo, Pater et Filius et Spiritus Sanctus.*'

We replied with a great shout of '*Amen*' and let the happy couple proceed down the aisle. The nuptial

---

[102] 'A cappella' music was used in religious music long before it became 'barber shop'. By the renaissance it had become the favourite vehicle for secular vocalising, known as the 'madrigal'.

mass was over, its Gallo-Latin inflections left to echo around the rafters.

Caroline and Gilles fell into the tender ministry of the local press and the family's photographers, who had been lying in wait outside.

*

Now to the de Bartillat's manor house, locally but lazily known as a château, had been fitted out with a marquee.

Once inside we saw it had been arranged for the wedding breakfast in the traditional way: a top table for the family, the abbot, the mayor, a neighbouring duke and his duchess with a number of descending trestle tables for mere mortals.

An army of caterers now waited on us. An *amuse bouche* of a *tartin* of crab on a bed of watercress was served while our glasses were filled with Champagne. Waiters held the bottles in damp cloth to maintain their temperature, but there is no disguising the shape of a bottle of Dom Perignon.

The *hors d'oeuvre* that followed was a *parfait* of foie gras, paired with a plum and fig compote and a warm brioche.

A sorbet of passion fruit cleansed our palates before we embarked upon a fillet of seabass *en beurre blanc*, topped with asparagus spears and served on crushed new potatoes. By now a white Sancerre had replaced the Champagne.

The main course arrived to a spontaneous ovation from the assembled guests. Sixty fillets of beef, wrapped with smoked bacon and accompanied with *chanterelles* in a truffle sauce, were revealed upon the choreographed raising of the silver domes that kept them warm. The wine that came with this wonderful dish was a red Menetou Salon, *domaine de l'ermitage*.

Cheese, and then creamed-filled profiteroles under a warm toffee sauce, brought 'breakfast' to a close. As we sat back our Champagne flutes were refilled, ready for the speeches and the toasts.

The abbot was the first to speak, an eloquent exhortation, both to God and to exemplary demeanour, urging the couple to produce as many good Catholic offspring as Love could conjure. We cheered that couple volubly.

Count Henri de Bartillat, Caroline's father, spouted almost inaudibly about the great joy of having a new son and being just nine months from a new grandson. We toasted that putative grandchild.

Gilles welcomed the alliance between the Navacelles and the Bartillats that had been forged that day and we toasted the union of two ancient families.

And that was that.

The tables somehow vaporised, the spindly gilt chairs rematerialised against the curtain walls and a band appeared on the vacated dais.

It was barely 3 pm and, after the solemnities of the day, it seemed somehow odd to be applauding a progressive-rock *zeuhl* band, barely minutes after they had got out of bed by the look of them, but *Zao* put on a great show. The drummer, who appeared to be the band's leader, claimed his music extolled a spiritual and ecological future not just for France but for all humanity. A reasonable ambition, I thought. A pity, therefore, that the President of France and his ministers could not be here to hear a rock opera of massed and chanted choral motifs, outbursts of martial and repetitive percussion, explosive improvisation and unexpected lapses into eerie, minimalist silence.

Everyone over the age of thirty found an excuse to go home or retreat to the château but in its way the experience was worth pursuing. Watching the corpulent Eugene attempting to dance to *Zao's* eccentric rhythms was well worth it. A memory to treasure.

This was France. At around 5 pm, a table was laid for a Gallic version of afternoon tea (Champagne and/or coffee). *Zao* joined in, looking incongruous, reminding me of the terrorists in *The Discreet Charm of the Bourgeoisie*.[103]

Then, at eight o'clock, a 1910 *Gregoire Triple Berline*[104] appeared and Gilles and Caroline clambered aboard to be taken to Tours Val de Loire airport and on to Senegal.

The next day was a Sunday. Kate and I were to be among the twenty or so guests that stayed the night at the château. We were allowed to retire quite early and we were grateful. I, anyway, needed a good dose of sleep before my rail-bound destiny took my sister and me back to Paris. Thence I would travel by air to London.

*

I arrived, almost on time, in my office on the Monday to discover that Charles Cullum, my chief executive, had sent word that I was to 'pop my head around his door'.

'Jeremy,' he asked apropos nothing, I thought, 'do you know which is Italy's largest insurance company?'

'I think so, Charles. Isn't it the *Assicurazione Generali*?'

'Spot on. By a country mile, in fact.[105] I mention it is because I have been asked to give what I believe Americans call an 'internship' to the son of one of its shareholders.'

'One of its shareholders? There must be millions.'

---

[103] *Le Charme Discret de la Bourgeoisie* is one of my favourite films. Louis Bunuel's surreal, virtually plotless series of dreams centred around six middle-class people and their consistently interrupted attempts to dine together.

[104] A very early French Motor Car. It looked a little like an early nineteenth century railway compartment.

[105] 'A country mile', surely an Irish turn of phrase, refers to the winding manner of the country roads and the distraction of wayside hostelries. A given destination may be a mile away, as the crow flies, but it might take rather more time and shoe leather to arrive by road.

'This particular shareholder has 3% of the company.'

'I see. Lucky fellow.'

'Quite. He's called Baron Alberto Baldiserra, and his son is called Giacomo. I've no idea whether he can speak English, but I want you to field the lad. Take him with you wherever you go. Lloyd's. Lime Street. The pub, if you must. Take him out to dinner. Take him home. Let him meet a pretty girl. Show him how we do business, how the market works, how we live.'

'When does he get here?'

'He's here now. Clearly you failed to see him on your way in. He was the fellow in the loud sportscoat, impatiently sitting outside, buried in some Italian financial newspaper.'

*

'So you're the poor beggar commanded to reveal to me what you call 'the market',' said Giacomo in near perfect English.

'Yes. This is not the renewal season, so there's not too much to do, but if there is a change in the terms and conditions of any of our treaties we will have to get the underwriters to agree an endorsement. This one is a good example. The *Delta* has had a claim, so the whole thing needs to be reinstated. There are forty underwriters on this slip, so we must trudge around the market getting the thing back up and running and not let them charge us too much for the privilege. We will start with the leading underwriter, and in this case it's the *Generali*, so you're on home turf. Once Bernard Spark[106] is on board we'll go for the rest.'

'Very good. Let's go. I'll carry your bags,' said Giacomo.

It takes a great deal of to-ing and fro-ing to get an additional premium for a foreign treaty agreed in London. The *Generali* wanted rather a lot, so we returned to the office and telexed the details to Piero Petronio at *Corsi*. *Delta*, the insurance company refused

---

[106] The lead underwriter.

to pay. Giacomo and I had to return to Spark and try and squeeze a better deal out of him.

We succeeded. Finally London and Milan could agree. Now we could begin to tour the 'following market'. It was relatively quiet and the queues to see underwriters were short. Nevertheless, forty signatures – averaging six before lunch and three after – meant we would need a few days. There was also a risk that there might be a second loss while we were still arranging cover. We hoped that the gods were too bored, decrepit or old to be so mischievous.

I took to Giacomo straight away. He was an intelligent and thoughtful man with an interesting take on all matters philosophical. He had many Italian friends in London and was keen to introduce his mentor to them. All were bright and some were very pretty, a welcome bonus.

Baldiserra had graduated from the University of Padua, not too long before, where he had read Political Science. While racially a member of Venice's Jewish tradition, his Catholicism was strong. I suspect he derived some comfort from the metaphysical dimensions of both religions, he embraced both the *caritas* of the New Testament and the stern commandments of the Old.

He (or his father the baron) had arranged for him to lodge with an orthodox Talmudian family close to Regent's Park.

Giacomo certainly had a healthy appetite for everything to do with the fair sex. He was frequently mounting a charm offensive across the better restaurant tables of the capital. Over the weeks that followed I never saw any evidence that his generosity was repaid with theirs, but was he down-hearted? Perhaps he had not paid enough attention at the footstool of his namesake, Giacomo Casanova?

The two were both Venetian and shared the name of James, the soldier-saint. In some strange way, one was the mirror image of the other.

My Giacomo was a scholarly businessman, honest and rich but, socially, all elbows. That he was indulged by the opposite sex was due, to some degree, that he lived in his family's palace and owned a bulging wallet.

Giacomo Casanova was the obverse to his reverse. He was one of the most famous lovers in history and owned not a brass razoo. This previous Giacomo was, in no particular order, a scamster, an alchemist, a spy and a prelate. He was also lucky and talented; qualities useful both in business and in bed. He wrote satires, fought duels, and escaped from some of Europe's most secure prisons. This last would almost become a habit.

As children, both these Giacomos had been as bright as buttons. Though born in Venice a couple of centuries apart, they had shared their undergraduate years at Padua, if the first did so at just twelve years old. After graduating, my Giacomo took up travelling, while the other took a gap year or two to acquire and practise the vices that would make him a household name in Europe. Both enjoyed gambling and female company, but the first one had a superabundance of wit, charm and style that the second one could only dream of.

While the earlier one powdered, scented and curled his hair, the younger's naturally wavy locks had no need of heated tongs. Both, I expect, smelled of manly 'royall' bay rhum.

As far as girls were concerned, my Giacomo just talked the talk. The former, on the other hand, walked the walk. He had an affair not just with a sixteen year-old girl but with her fourteen year-old younger sister, and at the same time. If that weren't enough, many years later, Casanova would later wind up in bed with one of those two sisters again – this time with her daughter who, incidentally, was also his.

They also shared an interest in the divine. My Giacomo talked profoundly about it while the other actually professed a vocation. It didn't last. Gambling debts landed him in prison. He would try again for the Church, but after a couple of false starts he thought about a new career. As a soldier!

He was only twenty-one, but he quickly discovered just how dull was life in the military. Again and again he was drawn to the green baize like a moth to a flame, only to discover that luck is an inconstant mistress. Owing yet more money, he was 'asked' to resign his commission.

> I bought a long sword, and with my handsome cane in hand, a trim hat with a black cockade, with my hair cut in side whiskers and a long false pigtail, I set forth to impress the whole city.[107]

Both Giacomos loved music, the first becoming a violinist and an enthusiastic follower of the 'red priest'.[108] The other had a penchant for Billy Joel.

Lady Luck, fickle as she is, revisited Casanova. He was in the right place and the right time to save the life of the noble politician, Count Bragadin. A grateful count was easily persuaded to become Casanova's patron.

It should have been more than enough but of course it wasn't. In trouble again, Casanova had to flee Venice. He escaped to Parma, only to fall in love and, inevitably, have his heart broken.

Both Giacomos would travel widely, to London, Paris, Vienna, you name it. The earlier one seduced dozens of women while the later one thought about it a lot.

---

[107] *The Story of my Life*, by Giacomo Casanova.
[108] Antonio Vivaldi.

Casanova, meanwhile, wrote a play, became a freemason and, in 1753, returned to Venice. Unfortunately, exaggerated tales of his gambling, illegal Masonry and romantic escapades – mostly brief and tawdry affairs with married women, nuns and fledgling virgins - caught up with him. When the philanderer was thirty he was detained by the Venice Tribunal's carabineers.

> You are under arrest, primarily for public
> outrages against the holy religion.

Despite his persuasive ways, he was sentenced to five years in solitary. He was taken in chains to 'The Leads', the cells under the roof of the Doge's Palace, so-called because of the lead plates that served as roof tiles. It had long been held to be inescapable.

It was also extremely uncomfortable. Casanova's cell lacked any natural light and had so low a ceiling that he could not stand up straight. A guard was appointed to stand outside his door, day and night, adding insult to injury by charging his time to the prisoner's account. As in England at that time, prisoners were not discharged until they had settled their debts to the authorities and the wardens.

The rake was confined in this discomfort for thirteen long months. It took his friend, the lordly Senator, that time to convince his captors to move him to a larger and better lit cell.

Casanova was not exactly grateful. He had been on the verge of breaking out. Ages before, on a carelessly escorted walk - his gaolers showing him a little compassion - he had found a piece of stone and a piece of iron bar. He spent the next few months sharpening the metal into a chisel, rubbing it for hours at a stretch against the stone, before he could start to dig through the wooden floor beneath his bed.

His cell was directly over the Inquisitor's chamber - another problem to overcome - but his unexpected transfer to a new cell meant he never got the chance.

As it transpired the prison's unhappy chaplain lodged immediately above Casanova's new dwelling. The prelate loved reading and the jailers were indulgent enough to allow him and Casanova to exchange the books and newspapers that Bragadin loyally sent him. Using as ink the mulberry juice he claimed was for refreshment, Casanova wrote a note and stuck it into a book's spine, which led to a covert, epistolary friendship.

Under the seal of the confessional, Casanova admitted to the priest that he planned to escape and begged for help. All he needed, he wrote, was for the priest to break through his floor into Casanova's cell. Then he and the priest would both disappear into the eventide.

Casanova's suggestions fell on fertile ground. Casanova sent him the 'chisel', hidden in a Bible. Religious obedience and the practice of indenture ensured that Fr Balbi, if not technically a prisoner, was certainly a captive. He was no more free than the wastrel below. He too needed an escape hatch.

Unfortunately, their freedom remained elusive. A new problem had arisen. The Doge's Council of Ten had awarded the libertine a companion, who was in fact a profoundly religious, gullible and inept spy. Casanova found it simple to exploit him. He told his credulous cellmate that, in a dream, an angel had revealed to him that he was coming to deliver him from prison. Him alone, mark you.

When the two of them heard the priest above, digging away, Casanova explained to his cell-mate that this was his angel. The poor fool believed him.

Fr Balbi, as agreed, broke through as quietly as he could in the small hours, while Casanova's fellow inmate, a remarkably heavy sleeper, was in the pleasant thrall of a rhum-induced stupor. Balbi's room was directly under the roof of the palace. The priest lowered a 'rope' he had fashioned from sheets, blankets and even the mattress cover, and Casanova climbed into the attic space. The two of them dislodged a few lead plates and, using their 'rope', made their way onto the roof.

Their bid for freedom was neither done nor dusted. Though they had hauled themselves onto the roof, it was far too high to risk a jump.

There seemed to be no way off until they noticed a dormer window, two-thirds of the way down the steep slope. Using his 'chisel', Casanova prised open the grate over the dormer and, after a perilous attempt that almost sent him sliding to his death, he was able to get both himself and the priest into the palace. Once inside, the pair broke a lock, walked into a corridor, and simply strolled out into the *Piazza San Marco*. By sunrise they had escaped by gondola.

> Thus did God provide me with what I needed for an escape which was to be a wonder if not a miracle. I admit that I am proud of it.[109]

Whatever became of Fr Balbi is lost to history, but Casanova fled to France. He pretended to be an alchemist, claiming he could create diamonds from scratch. As a reasonable historian, he told the world that he was three hundred years old and recounted stories to corroborate. He was a consummate liar and was accordingly believed. Every Parisian patrician (male and especially female) wanted to meet him.

One day, however, he contemplated duping one unusually rational aristocrat. The nobleman saw straight through him. Far from denouncing him, he had seen - given the Venetian's ability to say anything with a

---

[109] Ibid

straight face – that Casanova might prove an excellent spy.

Casanova immediately agreed and, characteristically, insisted on a fat fee for his labours.

The lives of the two Giacomos would now coincide a second time. My contemporary would come to the City of London and explore the financial community, while the earlier did exactly the same in Amsterdam.

The earlier one was soon wealthy men, while the modern one started that way.

Sadly, the former was quick to lose his easily won fortune, mostly by spending it on the seduction and retention of his many lovers. Fresh debts and new enemies occasioned grave dangers and wild solutions. In Paris in 1760, yet again penniless, Casanova carved a new personality for himself. Calling himself the 'Chevalier de Seingalt', he convinced an unbalanced noblewoman he had the occult power to turn her into a young man, should she pay him enough. Immediately after his purse was recharged he travelled to England and contrived an audience with King George III. He was in no way hamstrung by simple matters of geography. His next stop was St Petersburg where he had an audience of Catherine the Great and sold her his idea for a national lottery.

There was a moment's worry in Warsaw. He had to fight a duel with a colonel over an Italian actress. To the maiden's relief he won.

Not until 1774, after more than a dozen years in exile, did Bragadin win his protégé Casanova the right to return to Venice. It should have been in triumph and the play he had written so long before was at last performed. It turned out, however, to be a blistering satire of the Venetian nobility. It did famously at the box office but it got him expelled. Again.

In later years, Casanova would calm down a little. Count Joseph Karl von Waldstein[110] employed him in Bohemia as his librarian, a position he found so lonely and tedious he even considered suicide. Only the urge to write his memoirs kept him alive.[111] It took him a year to submit his manuscript to a publisher.

He was seventy-three. With the advance he celebrated his success with a little Champagne, lay down and died.

There was one more strange overlap between the two Giacomos. On April 5, 1797, while Casanova was still alive, Venice was seized by a General Napoleon Bonaparte, a member of the five-strong 'Directory' which had governed France from 1795.

The French were in desperate need of money - the revolutionary *assignat* was suffering a run - and the Directory required the Doge to seize the possessions of the fabulously rich Duke of Modena. He did as he was told but was thought too slow - too serene, perhaps.

Bonaparte declared war. The Doge fled for his life and the Republic immediately capitulated. What else could it do? The Venetian administration was replaced by a French 'provisional municipality'.

On April 18, the future emperor signed the preliminaries for peace. On May 3, that same year, Venice's Minister for France was ordered to leave the city 'for his own safety'. Bonaparte's commanding officers would now occupy the palaces of the Bride of the Adriatic and were ordered to treat the Venetian militias as the enemy.

This was a coup. Bonaparte 'persuaded' the bankers to transfer the bullion in their strongrooms to the bankrupt Directory in Paris. A jubilant conqueror needed a palace in which to stay and celebrate his overlordship of the Most Serene Republic but he could not allow some

---

[110] Waldstein was also a patron of Beethoven.
[111] *The Story of My Life*, by Giacomo Casanova.

aristocratic member of the Venetian establishment the privilege of being his host. Instead, a rich and young merchant, a certain Baldisare Treves de Bonfili,[112] a Bonapartist and a Jew, offered the ambitious 'first consul' his magnificent palace in the heart of the *Ghetto Nuovissimo*. It was complete with a warehouse giving easy access to a sailing nation's ships and barges. This gesture impressed the Corsican and an overarching peace treaty was signed there, on May 16, 1797.[113]

By now, Napoleon had crowned himself Emperor. By way of thanks to his Venetian friends, he rewarded the merchant Treves family with a vast amount of franked bills of exchange[114] and, in 1811, he elevated them to a barony, almost unheard of at that time for a Jewish family,[115] or indeed any Venetian family.

It was only possible because all religious 'boundaries' within the French Republic had been dissolved. Napoleon even declared France to be a secular state.

The family now moved out of the ghetto into the splendour of the twelfth century Palazzo Emo, on the corner of the Rio de San Moisè[116] and the Grand Canal. Their merchandise was now stored in and despatched from the ancient *Fondaco dei Tedeschi*.

---

[112] Baldisare is the Italian spelling of Balthazar. In Venetian this becomes Baldiserra, which may appear less Jewish to the casual observer.

[113] Venice paid the ultimate toll; it was never again to play a significant role in Europe's political history.

[114] Later to be called 'francs'.

[115] The English Rothschilds had their barony only in 1865, but in Austria, the Council of Francis I recognised the nobility of the Rothschilds on 21 October 1816, permitting them to use the 'von'. The Treves dynasty therefore, may be the first Jewish family to be formally ennobled, after Baron Peter Shafirov (1670–1739). In 1723, Peter the Great deprived Shafirov of all his offices and sentenced him to death. His offences were embezzlement and disorderly conduct. The sentence of death would be commuted to banishment and on the death of the Czar, Shafirov was released and commissioned to write his late master's biography.

[116] Ironically, perhaps, the little canal's name translates as 'the Canal of Holy Moses'.

A newly ennobled Baron Alberto Isaac Treves de Bonfili had the gothic exterior wall of the Grand Saloon, high above the canal, demolished to allow two colossal statues of Hector and Ajax to be admitted. Their sculptor was none other than the wonderful Antonio Canova. Once the great marbles were inside, the wall was rebuilt in the latest Palladian style.

The banker Baldasare, Treves's younger son, would reluctantly adopt the Catholic religion but since he had been instrumental in ending the Doge's unreliable stewardship of the Bride of the Adriatic he was rewarded. Napoleon singled out the former Jew for favour in the Italian and French banking concordats. As a result, the lad was able to build a new palace near but outside the ghetto on the Ca' San Lorenzo. There he could to house the handsome pair of Sevres vases the Emperor had sent his father and which I would soon see on either side of the canal stairs.

In 1914, his grandson the lawyer Giacomo Baldissera, Baron Treves Bonfili, married Anna Maria Mordo. Alberto and Adolfo Baldissera Bonfili Trier were born of this union.

The Treves family loved the theatre and built three of them. The *Apollo* and the *Goldoni* were for stage plays. The Opera House, very sadly, was razed in a fire in 1774. They rebuilt it and renamed it *Il Fenice*, 'The Phoenix', since it had risen from the ashes. *Aficionados* of the roar of the grease paint and smell of the crowd, they embraced the exorbitant costs and pleasant duties of the *Apollo* and *Goldoni* theatres and the *Fenice*.[117]

---

[117] Teatro La Fenice is one of the most famous and renowned landmarks in the history of Italian theatre. In the 19th century, it became the site of many famous operatic premieres at which the works of several of the era's major *bel canto* composers – Rossini, Bellini, Donizetti, Verdi – were performed. That was the year that Giacomo Baldiserra's forebear paid for its rebuilding. They had to do so a second time in 1836. They still owned it in 1996, when an arsonist destroyed the house, leaving only the exterior walls. This time, huge public subscription and Italia Nostra paid for its rebuilding. It was re-opened in November 2004 and, in order to celebrate this event, the tradition of Venice's New Year Concert began.

Their palace was not topped out until the 1820s. It is the most modern building in all of Venice, excluding only Mussolini's imposing railway station on the Grand Canal and Piazzale Roma's Bus Station.

*

Quite out of the blue I had another piece of news from Italy. My old friend N.D.[118] Violante Brandolini d'Adda was to marry her fellow Italian, the Sicilian Marchese Gaetano Sersale.

The letter that brought me the news was addressed to the *egregio signore Jeremy Macdonogh*. If at first I felt a little affronted to be called 'egregious', it is one of those words that means the exact opposite when moving from one language to another.

Opening it, I read that a wedding was to take place in one of Rome's most historic churches and followed by a reception in the *Casina Valadier* on the Pincian Hill above *Piazza del Populo*. Dress would be formal, in *frac*, which is how the word frockcoat has passed into Italian.

Obviously, this was not to be missed. I showed the invitation to Giacomo, who suggested that I might stay with him in Venice before the wedding. That way I might participate in Venice's carnival before heading south to Rome. He thought that there was no way on earth that I should miss either event, and he was right.

I had to plan for around a week. There were three days between Ash Wednesday and the nuptials. My friend Adrianna had sweetly suggested that I could stay at her villa in Bellagio on Lake Como. Why not make an event of it all? Venice, the lakes and Rome all in one go? There was only one word for this proposal: sublime.

---

[118] N.D.: *nobile donna*. Doges did not grant its citizens noble titles, save for N.D and N.H., *nobil homo*.

An itinerary was needed. Fly to Venice. Train it to Lake Como. Then another train to Milan and find a connection to Rome. After Violante's wedding, a flight from Fiumicino would carry me home.

Planes and trains, hills and lakes, villas and palaces, what more can a man want? I even had a little money in my pocket, now that I was a 'senior' broker. This would pay for my plunge into Italian high society.

Though I was almost the man who has everything, I realised I lacked an amanuensis, a witness to retail stories on our return. These should be euphuistic tales of glory, romance and opulence, conjured up to spare me the need to swank on my own behalf too objectionably. Who did I know who was lyrically self-effacing? Ah yes, my step-brother Kevin. He could neither speak Italian nor hog the limelight. He would be the perfect travelling companion.

For some obscure reason, Kevin seemed to accept that a glamorous holiday was a Good Idea. He agreed to fly to Milan. From there, a car would find him and bring him to our houseparty in Bellagio. A hungry theatrical type, he anticipated the foothills of the Alps would serve as a backdrop as he filled his face with river trout or wild boar. Before he could arrive, however, I would have another chance to descend on Venice.

The first had been five years before. Then I had been effectively friendless and penniless. Despite that, the experience had been wonderful, but now I had an invitation to stay in a private palace on a canal.

*

For unexplained reasons of his own, Simon Galway, my boss at *CTB*, resolutely opposed this journey of a lifetime. We were not in a particularly busy season and I was equally stubborn. I was going. The odds of a similar invitation at some later date were a billion to one against.

With hindsight, I can see that my insistence may have cost me something in my slow progress as a broker. Even so, tell me just who could refuse such an opportunity? Not a young man with fully functioning eyes and ears, a lust for magic, and with the scent of adventure in his nostrils.

As a consequence, and obviously, I agreed with Giacomo that I would arrive at Venice's Marco Polo Airport on the Saturday before Ash Wednesday, 1977. For most of us, back then, flying to Italy meant booking a ticket to Milan or Rome. That would be a mistake. Venice's Marco Polo Airport is a far more interesting portal into that wonderful nation.

My plane made its approach on a clear day, and the views from the air were breathtaking. I saw the Dolomites, the Adriatic and, at last, the Lagoon. Land seemed to come and go with the tides, somehow suggesting a northern Atlantis. From the right hand side of the plane, I easily identified the *Rialto*, the *Campanile di San Marco* and the Grand Canal running alongside.

It was late on Saturday morning when we touched down and I was bright-eyed and bushy-tailed, ready for anything. The Alilaguna airport boat took its cargo of carnival-goers through the lagoon, passed the *punto della dogana* and discharged us at the jetty beside Harry's Bar at the edge of the *Piazza San Marco*. I had a fabulous view of the lagoon, the Doge's Palace and, across the Grand Canal, the Jesuit *Basilica di Santa Maria della Salute* on the far bank in the Dorsoduro *sestiere*.[119]

Giacomo was already inside, waiting for me on a stool by the bar.

Harry's Bar was wildly famous but it struck me as curious. It was filled with round tables, too close together and barely able to accommodate three or four revellers. It was crowded but, as Giacomo had warned

---

[119] Literally, 'a sixth'. Odd that we English only use the word, 'quarter' for describing a part of a city. New York has two 'sides'.

me, it always was. The visitor has a choice of first impressions: the astonishing prices or the humdruminess of the furnishings.

Giacomo was clearly well-known, as the white-jacketed waiter addressed him as 'signor contino'. He had already secured two Bellinis. One he had sipped, the other not.

'They're the best things in this place,' said Giacomo, passing me the pink aperitif. 'The only alternative here is a Pritz, the house cocktail. Which is horrible, by the way.'

In truth, the Pritz - a prosecco beefed up with Aperol - is both refreshing and stylish. Giacomo is not really a drinker. I had long before decided to ignore his opinions on all such Bacchic matters.

'Come on, drink up. We're expected for lunch. Ever been on a gondola? No? Then we'll take one home.'

Our gondolier took us to the *Ca' San Lorenzo*. As he found his way through the canals to the relatively unfrequented quarter of *Castello*, between the *Fondamente Nove* and the *Arsenale*, I expected him to sing.

He must have been shy or tone deaf. I was a little disappointed. I had wanted to hear a *barcarolle*, ornamented with echoes from the palaces to either side.

Giacomo's *palazzo* turned out to be a discreet mansion, severe in its muted neoclassicism. My host had arranged for its waterside doors to be unlocked and open, so our gondolier conducted us inside the building directly from the canal.

On ascending the stone steps that climbed out of the water in our private cave, we passed between Napoleon's urns. Up another two flights and I was received with old-fashioned courtesy by his father the baron.

Small talk in the salotto let me discover that Baron Alberto had some interesting perspectives on the Church in general and Life in particular. For some reason we talked about St Francis of Assisi.

'What a wretch that man was! An ingrate of the first order. His father, a leading silk merchant, adored and rejoiced in his handsome, witty and gallant son's high-spirits. Francis mixed with troubadours, delighting in fine clothes as every wealthy young man should. He spent his father's money lavishly like any spoiled brat.'

Nevertheless, Francis's father thought his son's sinews needed stiffening. He bought him a commission in the army of the Holy Roman Empire and, in 1219, Francis was sent to Egypt as a Christian officer, his mission to convert or bring the Crusade to a victorious close.

*

On his return to his regiment's base in Sienna, some wretched beggar asked for alms. Francis, the Christian soldier, gave the man the small fortune in gold he had in his purse. The gesture was not unnoticed. Rich kids in tailored clothes were never going to defeat Satan or the Sultan.

'Not unnaturally, his father and friends all mocked him for his overblown act of charity but the angry lad stripped off his fine clothes in front of the town hall, handed them to the undeserving poor. He fled half-naked into the ruinous lands around Spoleto to restore a few dilapidated country chapels. What a reward for a son to give his loving father!'

The lad went on to found a mendicant order, the Franciscans, and it would grow to such an extent that its primitive organisational structure was no longer sufficient.

*

We could not continue this interesting narrative, as we and everyone else in Venice were already counting down to the carnival's crescendo. The old grand dame had already loosened her stays, readying herself to kick over the traces as were a quarter of a million tourists.

After a simple lunch, Giacomo and I walked through the town to Piazzale Roma, where his car was parked. Though it was Monday, with days to go, almost everybody we passed was already in costume. The common denominator was masks. The classic was the *Bauta*, covering the entire face, only leaving a little space at the bottom to allow eating and talking. The *Columbina*, made popular by *Commedia dell'Arte*, only covered the eyes. The Plague Doctor's mask, with its striking beak-like nose, was another a carnival favourite.

We allowed an uncomfortable reveller - wearing shoes like gondolas - to pass and, moments later, let a couple in 18th century garb stride past, on their way to St Mark's Square. It was chilly. They must have been wearing thermals under their courtly robes.

Most of these revellers would be at the *Ballo del Doge* the next day. A privileged few would favour the ball at *Ca' Vendramin Calergi*. In St Mark's Square a costumed woman was soon to take off from the bell tower and 'fly' above the packed square. The 'Doge', at the *Festa delle Marie*, would bestow twelve local virgins with dowries.

Little children had costumes squeezed over their ordinary clothes, releasing a chaotic swarm of miniature Michelin men. On the *Riva degli Schiavoni* a funfair let the little Pulcinellas and Cenerentolas enjoy the rides and the candy floss. *Campo San Giacomo dell' Orio, Campo Santa Margherita* and *Campo Vienna* had mostly unpleasant music belching from huge PA systems.

Everywhere, stalls sold *frittelle*, doughnuts, either 'plain' (with currants and candied peel) or 'filled' (with such delights as custard or whipped cream). I was assured there was a 'healthy' version filled with apples. Giacomo and I declined repeated opportunities to scoff *galani* – light pastries covered in icing sugar.

'Where are we going?' I asked, aware that we were about to leave the best party on Earth.

'Be patient. And be ready to be delighted,' came the tantalising reply.

He was, as usual, wise. Soon we had crossed the causeway onto the mainland in Giacomo's modest motorcar. He turned north into Treviso, somewhere in the general direction of Austria. After forty miles or so, we were driving alongside the walls of a castle, so immense they might have encircled a small town.

'This is the place I wanted you to see,' he said.

'It looks like a ruin,' I said. Realising I might have appear unappreciative, I added 'but a handsome one.'

'This is the twelfth century *Castello di San Salvatore*. Long held to be impregnable, it was the capital of a county that extended from Falzé as far as Refrontolo. The family that lived here, until the Great War when the Austrians shelled it and destroyed much of the wealth of art within, are called Collalto.[120] They still live nearby. After we've visited the ruin we shall call on them. You will discover a long history of love of the region, one that has woven itself into the fabric of a great family.'

'A great family?'

'Yes, truly great. How many other families can you think of that have lived on the same land for a thousand years?'

'You're right, there can't be that many. What do they do?'

'You like Prosecco, don't you? Theirs is thought to be the best in the world.'

In 1977 this great fortress was being patiently restored. A word from Giacomo and the contractors admitted us through a three storey pedimented marble gate, once extremely grand. In fact, it still was. Its stone

---

[120] The Austrians shelled it in 1915. The restoration began in 1919, and is today (2019) almost complete. Of course, the furniture had been replaced *'com'era, dov'era'* but its statues and paintings have not. Nor, sadly, can they be.

walls were curious. Around forty feet tall, they were built of a pale stone that may have been granite, with a repeated striation of red bricks a storey apart.

We climbed a stone stair to the top of the walls from where the views were phenomenal. 'Behold the Veneto! Wine country.' He extended his arms like a preacher. 'Vineyards!'

'I thought the Veneto was too soggy and flat to produce a decent wine?'

'You know a little less than I thought. We produce the finest Pinot Grigios and Proseccos in Europe,' said Giacomo proudly. 'Come on, jump in the car. It's time to meet the family.'

We drove a few hundred yards to a large country house. Though tiny by comparison with the ruined castle, Prince Manfred Collalto received Giacomo as an old friend. He took us indoors to greet his wife, Princess Trinidad Castillo de Jura Real, and his two daughters. How well I remember Isabella Collalto, then seventeen years old, and her younger sister. An easy feat as they were both utterly beautiful.

'These two young princesses,' said Giacomo, 'will be joining us tomorrow in Venice for the Wedding.'

'The wedding?' I said stupidly. I knew of no wedding.

'The Wedding of Venice to the Sea. We shall be at the *Circolo del' Unione* to watch the gondoliers accompany the dogal barge, the *Bucintoro*, and witness the 'doge' throw a wedding ring into the Grand Canal. We Venetians take these matters seriously.'

I asked Prince Manfred - a German name? - if his family had always lived in Lombardy.

'A few documents from before the year 1000 AD have survived. On good authority we believe that our name is cognate with the House of Hohenzollern, and that we are the Romanian branch of the margravate. Last year, Isabella and I travelled anonymously to our old castle near Bucharest. Ceausescu has converted it into a lunatic asylum and, sadly, it produces an undistinguished wine on the slopes beneath the parterres. We were given a tour of the vineyards, while the guide spouted the usual drivel about the merits of collectivisation. Little Isabella here asked an ancient, fly-blown peasant if the wines he made were any good. The good fellow replied that they were, 'but not a patch on when his old masters, the princely Collaltos, had run the place from 'upstairs'.' We were most gratified.'

Isabella turned out to be a brilliant linguist, already coming to grips with Italian, English, German, French and Spanish. She was on her way to becoming a top interpreter.

Eastertide was rushing at us. Shrove Tuesday, the last feast before the privations of Lent, was upon us as preordained. The good news is that, before the *quarantesima* of self-denial commences, eggs, cream and fellow perishables have to be consumed. They will not keep as long as Easter. Shrove Tuesday, or *Mardi Gras*, or *Martedi Grasso* - not Christmas, not Easter - has become the ultimate bacchanal in the Catholic world.

Of course, all these delicious temptations cannot be sated in one short day. The Voiding of the Larder has became a long, drawn out carnival, beginning almost as early the Feast of the Three Kings. It always reaches its climax on the day before Ash Wednesday. English Catholics refer to the season as Shrovetide, since it is the season for the faithful to make their annual confession and be 'shriven' of their sins.

The Carnival is famous in Rio de Janeiro, in New Orleans, in Colombia's Barranquilla, in the Cayman Islands' George Town, in Trinidad and Tobago's Port of Spain, in Quebec City, and in Mazatlán, the capital of Mexico's state of Sinaloa.

In Venice, however, the Carnival has altogether another dimension. An early lunch saw us at the *Circolo del' Unione*, across the Piazzetta from *Harry's Bar* and just by Sansovino's library, in good time to witness Venice being spliced with the Adriatic. This was to be my second marriage of the year and it remains the most unusual in my life (so far).

As we crammed the ample balconies above the Grand Canal we saw the dogal barge, *il Bucintoro* (the Bucentaur) hove into view as it emerged from the Cannaregio.

It had been used every year, on the *Festa della Sensa*, up to Napoleon's reduction of the Republic in 1798. Even though there is no longer a Doge, nor yet an Emperor of France, the practice has refused to die.

Nowadays, the mayor dresses up in pre-Napoleonic robes and symbolically does the deed and the accompanying applause will have been heard as far away as the Dalmatian and Hellenic coasts.

That afternoon, strolling happily in Piazza San Marco, Giacomo told me that he wanted me to meet Francesco da Mosto. He had told me that the da Mostos had been part of the city's history since the beginning.

'Perhaps the first to arrive was one of those fishermen the Romans referred to as *incolae lacunae*?'[121] I ventured.

'Unlikely. Too early. More probably they were winemakers.' Giacomo was Venetian and I gave way.

'The very word 'mosto' refers to the juice that is pressed from the grape before vinification can begin. 'Must', I believe, in English. You're quite interested in wine, I think? Mind you, since those heady days, the family have been traders, explorers and politicians.'

---

[121] Lagoon dwellers. The traditional founding date is the dedication of the first church, that of San Giacomo on the islet of Rialto (Rivalto, 'High Shore'), which took place at the stroke of noon on March 25, 421 (the Feast of the Annunciation).

We walked across the Rialto bridge to take in the early 13th-century Ca' da Mosto from the outside. It's the oldest on the Grand Canal, has high narrow arches and distinctive capitals. They reflect its beginnings as a *casa-fondaco*, house and workplace of its first merchant owner. The second floor was added at the beginning of the sixteenth century, the third in the nineteenth. Yet even though Ca' da Mosto was on the Grand Canal, it looked forlorn.

'High waters have breached the basement quay,' Giacomo explained, 'but it is *the* building we Venetians most want to see restored.'

We were welcomed by n.h. Ranieri da Mosto. His countess, Maria Grazia Vanni d'Archirafi, came from an ancient Sicilian noble family. Older Venetian palaces combine splendour with functionality, at once warehouses and living quarters for large families and their staff. This particular family seat was a stupendous piece of architecture. The wall that rises from the *rio* beneath should naturally enclose rooms and offices. Instead, it stands free of encumbrance, something like a cinema screen, on which is an immense map, in mosaic, of the voyages of Alvise da Mosto, the ancestor who discovered the Cape Verde islands off the west of Africa. It can be studied from all the internal windows of the palace that overlook it. There is even a viewing balcony.

The family had carved out a comfortable apartment within the monumental sequence of frescoed halls and palatial reception suites. Even in the domestic quarters the ceilings were impossibly high with wall-sized windows of leaded glass at either end of the *piano nobile*. One chamber was wallpapered in leather – another first for me.

Yet another was arranged as a chapel. Thrones for the nobil homo and his nobile dama, chairs for their children and guests, pews for the employees. The family took its Catholicism seriously – Francesco took his first Holy Communion in St Mark's itself and, a few years later, was confirmed by none other than the future Pope John-Paul I.

Now the man himself, Francesco, made his appearance.

'How lucky you are to live like this,' I told him, hoping the sweep of my arm would indicate the whole of Venice, not just his palace.

'Francesco isn't particularly optimistic about the future of this city,' said Giacomo. 'Are you, Francesco?'

'At least Venice can be saved from drowning. More disturbing is what kind of city will it become? Every thirty years or so the population halves. When I was born 170,000 lived here. It's half that number now. Aside from a perennial tourist trade we have little employment. True, you'll have seen the odd workshop, a furniture maker here, a paper maker there, but even such traditional crafts are in decline.'

'Is there a remedy?' Giacomo asked him.

'One has to be found. The city has its share of entrepreneurial young people. Such people must remain. We need to offer tax breaks for start-up businesses.'

'Tourism?'

'Not everyone can work in tourism. It would ultimately fossilise the place itself.'

'There are some places that tourism has preserved,' I ventured. 'Most of Europe's most adorable are in Italy. San Gimignano, Positano, Alberobello, Bellagio, the Cinque Terre and the Civitá di Bagnoregio come readily to mind. They harness the seasonal tides of business reasonably successfully.'

'No, Jeremy, they do not. Put those rose-tinted spectacles away. Tourism denies any living for those whose ambitions exceed waiting at table. Have you been to Carcassonne in the south of France? I have never seen so many souvenir shops selling plastic tat. It made me shudder. Tourism merely puts a place in aspic and expels its talent. It is a curse, not a blessing.'

This talk was depressing. I caught Giacomo's eye, had a last glass of *Prosecco Collalto* and bade our adieux.

We were heading for Piazza San Marco which, like the *statua della commendatore*, was coming to the party. It was filling with revellers while a masked orchestra delivered Respighi to the *Florian* and to the *Quadri*. To find a seat in either of these famous cafés you would have to have been there since daybreak and even then you would have to have climbed over backpacks and assorted luggage.

This was Shrove Tuesday, the zenith of the Carnival, and Giacomo and I were at its epicentre. In the late '70s the carnival was not yet the extravagant monster it has since become. The visitors numbered perhaps a few hundred thousand, not the millions that go today. Nevertheless, St Mark's Square had an enchanted atmosphere.

Thousands of regular folk let their laughter fill the great square while a few privileged Venetians made their way to masked balls in the city's private palaces, the most traditional of which would throw their doors open to the public after dinner.

St Mark's Square, had become a stage for an endless parade of revellers. I had bought a cheap mask at a kiosk that had colonised a street corner. Did I care that there were far grander ones than mine? I saw some works of artifice that ancient ateliers had produced, according to the rules of tradition, with papier-mâché and streams of ribbons, some of which were so elaborate and beautiful they were destined to become collectors' items and future antiques. The oddest mask was the *moretta*, the 'Moorish Girl'. It was made in a dark velvet and was held in place by a button in the mouth. As the poor lady inside would be unable to speak, it was also called a *moretta muta*.

'In 1162, after the victory of the Patriarchate of Venice over that of Aquileia, The Carnival of Venice began,' Giacomo patiently explained as we paused to enjoy an iced tea. 'Our people gathered and danced. They have commemorated the event every year since, but it was not until the Renaissance that the carnival became official and given a fixed date. In the seventeenth century, the *Palazzo Dogale* promoted the carnival as a means of propagating a prestigious picture of the place to the whole continent of Europe. By the eighteenth century it was even more famous but, sadly less for its joy but more for the licence it turned a masked eye to.'

'The Pope banned it, didn't he?'

'The Pope has little sway here in Venice. We have our Patriarch. In fact it was the Holy Roman Emperor and his successor Austrian Emperors who outlawed it. Masks, thought to hide depravity, were banned.'

'Not exactly successfully,' I said, looking around. There may have been liars among the crowds but none were bare-faced.

'They only began to reappear in the nineteenth century, and then only for short periods, for fancy-dress balls and nostalgic feasts. Only in recent years did it spread into the Piazza. There is talk of restoring it to its full ancient grandeur.'

'I hope they do, Giacomo, but it's pretty grand as it is.'

Giacomo sighed.

'We should be careful what we wish for, Jeremy.' Any pessimism as dispelled by the arrival of the Collalto princesses, Francesco da Mosto and a healthy sample of Giacomo's circle. We listened to the music, sipped our astronomically priced prosecco, ate the rich foods that the stands had on offer, and danced when the music and crush allowed. Finally, and at long last, an exhausted Giacomo and I headed for his discreet 'modern' house on the *Ca' San Lorenzo* to surrender to Morpheus's embrace.

Even so, slumber and wickedness do not readily combine. Barely were our knives and forks closed over our breakfast plates than we were in church, to have our foreheads marked with sacerdotal ash.

After a surprisingly austere lunch we were on our way inland, this time in the westerly direction of Lake Como. We turned off the main road into the *Parco delle Orobie Valtellinesi*, passing countless small lakes, carelessly annoying herds of cows and goats, photographing furious waterfalls and silvery rivulets, only to stop outside a large and rustic farmhouse, one that its farmer owners had evidently added to or subtracted from for centuries.

I had already experienced the frantic pace of life in Milan, Europe's international fashion capital. Or was that Paris? But Lombardy was growing on me.

I had crossed the paths of rustic Cremona and its swarms of cyclists in spray-on Lycra. I had seen the snow-covered mountain tops around Bergamo and the steep hills of Brescia and had eaten the cheeses of Valtellina and drunk the wines of Oltrepò Pavese.

Now Giacomo and I had driven into the courtyard of a ramshackle farmhouse, ranged around a large courtyard. Some of it was rather grand, some apparently unplanned, while another side was arranged in galleries, just as if it were an Elizabethan theatre. On the attic floor, solars had given its nineteenth century female occupants space to enjoy the breeze and shyly loosen their stays while retaining a modest dignity, while a twentieth century open air swimming pool did the same for the horny-handed sons of toil who earned a hard living there. At last, the proprietor finished shaking Giacomo's hand He turned to me.

'*Spero vi piaccia tacchino?*' he asked me. You like turkey?

'I love it,' I lied. I don't dislike it but I have never quite seen the point of it. If you're lucky it tastes of cranberry sauce.

'He likes wine too,' Giacomo said helpfully.

'Good,' said the farmer. 'We have a few hectares of vineyard. Do you have a particular favourite?'

'*Buttafuoco*,' I said. I was bluffing but I had a clue. The wooden wine case in the hall had that word written on it. It had to be the wine the family drank at home.

'Good,' my host smiled. 'We believe our *riserva*, whose plot fully faces south, to be unique.'

'Which grapes go into it?' I asked, pushing my luck.

'Mostly *Croatina*. Also *Barbera* to give it some acidity. A little *Ughetta Canneto* to lend it elegance. Would you care for a glass?'

'I certainly would.'

Giacomo snorted.

'We have already opened a bottle. It's by the pool,' the owner continued. 'Come, let's enjoy the weather and greet my girls.'

Two minutes later I had a glass in one hand and was shaking hands with his plump and pretty wife with the other.

'Well? What do you think?'

The first sip seemed promising.

'Mature and warm, a robust body and intensely perfumed. Promising in the mouth and I think persistent.'

I saw Giacomo raise his eyes to heaven.

'We call it '*Pozzo della Tromba*' after a medieval well below Castana Castle,' said the owner, taking neither umbrage nor (even) notice.

His daughters came over to say hallo. Federica was dainty and graceful, Francesca striking and athletic. Both were in their early twenties, though it was hard to judge which was the elder. Since they were in bikinis I felt overdressed. Oh well, of all the problems to have...

It was a cool white wine that accompanied the bread-crumbed escallops of turkey that evening; a *pinot grigio* from Redavale, our host explained.

'We are not marketing this wine. Not yet, anyway. It's something of an experiment. What do you think of it?'

'Light and refreshing,' I said, thinking it bland and thin.

'We think that *pinot grigio* may show us the way ahead. We calculate we can produce it in industrial quantities, selling it on to the sort people who ask the sommelier for a 'glass of white'. They should find it drinkable, at the very least. People like that outnumber people like you.'

It was my turn to feel embarrassed.

'Good idea,' I mumbled.

At last it was time for some shut-eye. The bedroom that I had been assigned was vast. Its windows overlooked the most wonderful hill-strewn scenery, while a few sticks of painted furniture gave it the semblance of an inflated doll's house. It was as if charm itself had been made fact.

The next morning the family were up early and I went with them to see the turkeys, housed in a vast barn close to the house. The birds scrambled noisily to let the farmhands walk through them, and every few feet the workers would stoop to pick up a dead one. God alone knows how many cadavers they carried out.

These huge black fowl were prone to heart attacks. So would I be if someone crowded me into a shed like this, I thought. I found London's Underground hard enough.

A good thing we had eaten their turkey the night before. I might have lost my appetite had we seen how they were farmed. Lunch, mercifully, was a scrumptious *carbonara*, washed down with a little more *pinot grigio*, unambitious but excellent. There is a lot to be said for simple fare.

After this fine repast Giacomo and I were on our way again, this time to the celebrated village of Bellagio, where Adrianna, her family and my step-brother Kevin awaited us.

Villa Polenta proved to be a classic lakeside mansion. It resembled a film set; its wrought-iron portals leant the Pearly Gates an earthly rival. We drove in, disembarked from the little car, retrieved our bags and walked up to the front door.

Kevin had arrived as planned and a call from Giacomo had alerted Adrianna to our own arrival and they were on the steps with hugs and kisses.

On entering the state rooms we were enveloped in comfort, style and elegance. They were filled with indescribable, even priceless antiques and beamed with olive wood. Sadly, most of the paintings that had once adorned the walls were in safe-keeping. I would later learn that they were stacked in the family's London house in Montpelier Square. In Italy it is apparently inadvisable to keep a house filled with *objets d'art* for an occasional visit.

Happily, the family was in residence. Grandma, mum, dad and the two daughters were already there. As the commodious villa only had four bedroom suites, Giacomo, Kevin and I were sent to a guest lodge to unpack, all of fifty feet way across a manicured lawn. Things looked good and the days ahead had promise.

Kevin and I immediately realised was that we were in the most sensational strand of Lake Como. The *salotto* looked over the lake, while the snow-capped Alps towered over the little hamlet of San Giovanni and its quaint harbour, pebbled beaches, ancient church, restaurant, grocer and all-purpose post office. We were a mile, if that, from Bellagio's lakeside habour, in one of Italy's most beautiful towns. Even the walk into town was a bit of an adventure, but that was because we had to walk along a narrow, winding road with little room to either side. Never mind, along the way it revealed every charming nuance of Italian life. The only problem was that we had to hug the walls or risk the ditches to avoid being eradicated by a lunatic in a souped-up Alfa Romeo.[122]

Refreshed by our walk, we returned to the villa for drinks, our neckties done up again. After a glass or two, just before supper, the evening light began to fail, but compensation for the removal of the view came in the form of a stunning fireworks display over the lake.

'What do think we should do while we're here?' I asked Adrianna.

'Tomorrow we could take the boat. The mooring is only fifty metres from here. Why don't we take her to San Giovanni? There is a great lakeside restaurant there; *Mella*, it's called.'

Giacomo smiled knowingly. 'Failing that, there's always the beach with its snack bar. That's barely two minutes away.'

*

Our time in the villa was amazing. Bellagio is a paradisiacal city, full of everything I love - mornings with cappuccino and a brioche at *Bar Rossi*, strolls along the lake, leisurely afternoons in the Melzi gardens, dinners in the villa with the finest food and wines.

Adrianna and I had been close in London, but a little light flirtation was never going to blossom into a full-blown romance. I had been dreading this, a dark cloud over a sunlit week, but she made it easy for me. She knew the difference between a dalliance and a proposal. Her behaviour, in these difficult circumstances

---

[122] Were these narrow lakeside roads built by Mussolini to see off enemy tanks?

was magnificent, her family's hospitality never compromised.

As for Kevin, he was the perfect guest. Always charming and well-mannered, he was easily able to affect the impression of a keen understanding when the table switched into Italian. He was acting - and with great skill - but with a sympathy to the general company that could not have been gainsaid. He had to be back in London, and Giacomo had to return to Venice, but I was off to Rome. I had to see my old friend Violante married.

I knew she was dynastically engaged to be wed to a marquis. Her fiancé, the Marchese Gaetano Sersale, was a year older than me. He had been born in Rome, but his line had origins in the South. I had first met her during my 'gap year'. Violante Brandolini d'Adda was an intelligent and diligent Venetian (even if born in Milan) and was (mostly) living in Rome. Her palace on the Grand Canal was leased to IBM, for some obscure reason. Obscure for IBM, that is. You can never have too many houses. Her family also owned places in Paris and Munich.

She was at most a couple of years younger than me and loved photography, skiing, films by Woody Allen and the Cohen brothers, music by Keith Jarret and Django Reinhardt, books by Georges Simenon and Irene Nemirovsky. She was thereby qualified for the affection of any gentleman. I just hoped was that Sersale was one.

Her degree was in English Literature, her thesis had been on Katherine Mansfield, the prominent modernist and short story writer from colonial New Zealand.

In 1973 Violante had given me a typed quotation. I had kept it carefully.

> Risk! Risk anything! Care no more for the
> opinions of others, for those voices. Do the

hardest thing on earth for you. Act for yourself. Face the truth. Make it a rule of life never to regret and never to look back. Regret is an appalling waste of energy; you can't build on it; it's only good for wallowing in. I always felt that the great high privilege, relief and comfort of friendship was that one had to explain nothing.

After graduating, Violante had moved on to England's *Textile Conservation Centre*, whose purpose was the restoration of antique tapestries and fabrics. A good call, since in her family's many palaces were exquisite pieces that needed expert conservation and someone to assess if the price were right. She also began to write.[123]

*

Her marriage was so Roman it might have been planned by Gabriele d'Annunzio.

He once wrote that 'one must make one's life as one makes a work of art'. *Pleasure*, first published in 1889, was his first and greatest novel, set in a townscape of the Eternal City's most sumptuous residences, churches and gardens. It walks the reader through the marvels of Palazzo Zuccari, Palazzo Barberini and the Villa Medici.

I felt as if the Brandolini-Sersale marriage was lifted from its pages. Of course, the marriage was processional, and in full dress. Why have a priest if you can have a cardinal? Why have an acolyte when you can have twenty?

You will have seen *Tosca*. Imagine Sant' Andrea della Valle, with its processions and secrets, its organ supplemented with a string quartet and a trumpet. Incense filled the atmosphere as in a film set, and the

---

[123] La Marchesa Violante Brandolini d'Adda Sersale went on to publish a collection of short stories *Frammenti di Paura*, in 1995. Her anthology, *The Look of the Medusa*, was published in 2005. A second collection *Incontri* came out in 2009. In 2014, she published a digital edition of *Hidden Nodes*.

stately rhythm of sacred Latin made its way through the haze. The sequence of bows and open armed prayers followed as in Noh, the classical Japanese musical drama. Then it ended and we were released into reality.

Not the starkest of realities, however. The reception was in the Villa Borghese – not a house but a park, bang in the heart of Rome. There is a restaurant there, the *Casina Valadier*, and we the congregation were reborn as wedding guests.

Despite my years in Rome, I had never been there. Perhaps I thought it too touristy, too American? I was so wrong. We were received in its ballroom with elaborate courtesy. We were each of us given a little bouquet of flowers and a box of sugared almonds. The Casina provided the best and plumpest black olives ever nibbled. Finally, we were all were assembled, we were invited by the *maitre d'hotel* to take our seats in the banqueting hall for the wedding breakfast.

The park, the terrace view and the building itself were the core ingredients of the most memorable evening. I think I must have been at one of the best tables since, as Apollo slowly descended into the underworld, the flood lights came onto the Vatican. The *Scalinata de Spagna*, beneath us, was lit by the cleverest and most discreet lighting in Europe. As an added bonus, the girls to my either side were utterly ravishing.

Perhaps the noble couple were rehearsing similar thoughts. They have since had two sons, Francesco and Nicolá, the elder born nine months to the day after their marriage.

*

Back in the UK, and slowly coming down from an overindulgence in weddings, I thought I'd tied enough knots to last a lifetime. That was before, while flicking through the Daily Telegraph my eye caught an announcement.

The engagement is announced between Mr Richard Newbury and the Hon. Julia Hamilton, only daughter of Lord and Lady Belhaven and Stenton of Islay, North Britain.

Not only would this one be worth going to. I had never been to Islay, the Queen of the Hebrides and its most southerly island. Good things, I sighed, are like buses. They tend to come all at once. I approached a few friends for advice. Gervas Douglas told me that the island had countless distilleries,[124] whose characteristic peaty single malts are very definitely a treat.

If this weren't enough in itself, Dick Newbury revealed that in its northeast there are the remains of an ancient settlement, including a prehistoric fort and some crusader tombs.

For his part, Richard Turner vouchsafed the island's stunning scenery, friendly people and edible wildlife. 'Huge flocks of barnacle geese,' he said, 'in fact almost half the world's population, overwinter in Islay, but you won't see them. Nor will you see the white-fronted geese. By the late spring most of the birds will have finished breeding and are off on their various migrations. The ducks return to the floods for the winter, the waders find their way to Africa. The geese will not yet have returned from Greenland for their autumn holidays.' He sighed.

'Had you gone in late autumn you'd have seen them fly down Loch Gruinart to spend a week or so regaining their energy on the 'flats' before dispersing. In the third week of October the air fills with the calls of skein after skein of barnacle and white-fronted geese. There can be twenty thousand geese on the mudflats, turning the fields black and white.'

I pictured him, gun under his arm.

---

[124] *Ardbeg, Bowmore, Bruichladdich, Bunnahabhain, Caol Ila, Kilchoman, Lagavulin, Laphroaig, Port Askaig* and *Port Ellen*. Yes, since you ask, I have sampled them all. 2018 brought an eleventh: *Ardnahoe*.

'October, that's the best time,' he persisted. 'That's when the Brent geese and Whooper swans fly in. They're on their way from Iceland and stop where you're going for a day or two's rest before heading on to Ireland.'

*

Clearly, my own research was nowhere near thorough enough. It had, however, informed me that the island is mentioned in Adomnan's *Vita Columbae*, a biography of that bad-tempered Irish Saint, written around 720 AD. Adomnan made particular note of its thriving and healthy population. The saint 'visited Islay on his journey from Ulster', he wrote, 'prior to founding a Celtic monastery on Iona, off the south-west tip of the Isle of Mull'.

I noticed that the historian wrote 'Islay' as 'Ilea'. He was writing in Latin. In Gaelic the island's name is spelt 'Ìle'.[125]

Gervas assured me that Islay's west coast was especially dramatic. 'Stunning bays and impressive sunsets await your pleasure at Machir, Saligo and Sanaigmore with a courtly bow.' He told me that Saligo Bay in particular has the most luminescent sundowns in Scotland.

When Willy Peto told me of the round church at Bowmore, I was convinced. As a Cambridge man, I approve of round churches.

Yep. It was time for me to don the old pith helmet and head north. I booked a week in the Islay Hotel in Port Ellen, a fishing village that proudly called itself the capital of the island.

Between you and me, I will admit that I was drawn by the fact that the distilleries of Laphroaig, Lagavulin, and Ardbeg were but a short ride from the hotel's front door. Like a moth to a flame, in fact.

---

[125] The word 'Gaelic' is pronounced 'Gallic' in Scotland. In Ireland, the same word is pronounced 'Gaylic'. The island is 'Aye-la'.

Everyone I knew seemed to have had the same idea. When I checked in and unpacked, an unreserved chambermaid advised me to visit the bar. It was open and since I was a *bone fide* traveller, she assured me that I could drink outside the licensing laws that 'Sassenach politicians' had arrogantly imposed on the Scots. And, yes, she too would appreciate a wee noggin, should I care to buy her one. It seemed like a good idea, but one needs to look smart in Islay's top hotel so I changed my tie and headed downstairs.

There were five days until the nuptials, so I expected to be in the delightful company of local crofters and sheep shearers, speaking heavily accented English and downing vast amounts of Caol Ila, heavily cut with milk.

As usual, I was wrong in every detail.

There were a couple of locals propping up the bar, but they more closely resembled Sir Alec Douglas-Home than Rob Roy. I deduced they were not trawlermen; it was their unaccented speech that gave me the clue. Clad in tweed, sporting cravats, they carried walking sticks with elaborate bone handles. The only props they lacked were Inverness Capes and Meerschaum pipes. They sipped their whisky from small pewter cups, while the dreadful Glaswegian habit of adding milk to scotch had clearly not travelled as far as the Hebrides.

I felt rather underdressed, but then, Peter Kaufeler admitted feeling the same as I joined him at his table.

'You're here early,' I commented unnecessarily. 'Here for the whisky?'

'Actually, a little fell-walking. Perfect country for it.'

We were joined by John Molony, fielding his suitcases.

'Many painters have eulogised about the Islay light. Edward Arthur Walton, Robert Sivell and Eric

Auld among them,' he said as he sat. 'The junk shops may have some paintings or drawings my shop should acquire.'

John was working for a small gallery – 'shop' he called it - around the corner from the Cavendish Hotel in Jermyn Street.

One of the gentlemen at the bar came over to our table.

'May I buy you lads a drink?' he asked.

We were flattered if not a little surprised. Generosity is famously not the Scots' longest suit.

'Very kind of you,' said John, taking the bull by the horns, 'but why would you want to?'

'Well, you're obviously in Islay for The Wedding, so we are already friends, just ones who have not yet met. Lady Belhaven will sort that bit out on Saturday. More important, and far more urgent, it will soon turn two o'clock. Being locals, we can't buy a drink after that, but you can. We'll buy you this one and then you can buy us one back in around a quarter of an hour.'

I had thought that Scottish licensing laws were more observed in the breach. This method of getting around them smacked of the justly renowned Scottish inventiveness and, of course, we agreed.

Then Dick Newbury made his entrance.

'I thought I might find you here. What are your plans for the week?'

Peter Kaufeler answered first.

'Wild life. That and walking. There are roe deer all over these hills, good looking animals with little upright horns.'

'You stand a good chance of seeing an otter, too,' Dick confirmed.

'Brown hares,' said one of our new friends from the bar. 'And seals, if you like that sort of thing.'

'The pests eat the fish,' said his drinking companion.

'Your prize will be our feral goats,' said the other. 'See one of those and you'll believe yourselves in Afghanistan.'

'You're looking down, Hamish. You should be looking up. There are sea and golden eagles. Some can carry off a sheep.'

'Peregrines and hen harriers are sometimes seen hunting. You may even see a barn owl scanning the roadsides in the gloaming.'

'You'll see oystercatchers and razorbills if you walk along the strand. That's where I'd go.'

'Why not take a look at the folded metagreywackes of the Colonsay Group near Saligo Bay?'

'Metawhats?'

'It's a strange geological formation. Unique to Islay. That's where you'll find the 'artists' light'.'

'Then that's for me,' said John. 'I'm up for the metaphysical and grey whacky thingammies.'

'…and don't overlook the orchids.'

'Orchids? You have orchids?' asked Peter. 'Aren't they tropical?'

'Orchids? You are in orchid heaven. We have Pyramidal Orchids. The early and the northern orchid. Fragrant ones, marsh ones, early purple, common and heath spotted ones. This is an orchid hunter's paradise.'

'So why have you left out the Common Twayblade, Iain? It's the finest of them all.'

'So sorry, Hamish. I do apologise. To make amends, I hope the Frog Orchid and the Helleborine will hear me plead forgiveness for a clumsy oversight.'

'You are forgiven, but you should take care not to undereducate our young English visitors. They will need to talk about our island at its best, and for years to come.'

Inevitably, we agreed to do a bit of everything.

We would begin our adventure that very afternoon, after a plate of cheese sandwiches. We decided to start with Loch Gruinart. Islay's famous oysters had my vote.

'Go there very early and wait for the dawn,' Iain or Hamish had advised us.

'That's when you'll see the thin mist, hanging in the air, turning the yolk-like sunrise into a dull glare on the horizon.'

'Take a deep breath of Islay's air,' said the other. 'Watch the pale light catch the tips of the grass as it shuffles in the wind.'

Sadly, such poetry was wasted on us. We would never have had the self-discipline to be anywhere before dawn. After half-an-hour's drive our hire car delivered us to a parking area close to an old bird hide. It was apparent that Loch Gruinart was one of the most exquisite parts of Islay. Very possibly the world.

A track took us through some sheltered woods from where we had sudden but terrific glimpses of the loch. We followed the path along its banks to stumble upon Kilnave kirk and cross. Wherever it was, it was indisputably remote. The heaviness of the clouds threatened rain. While such squalls last only minutes before the sun re-emerges, to keep dry we sought sanctuary in the church.

Inside, a poorly-printed leaflet told us that in 1598 a fierce battle had been fought here, the Battle of Traigh Ghruineard. This was the last significant clan confrontation to be fought on Islay. Like all the best battles, it was a family affair - Sir Lachlan Mòr MacLean, 14th Chief of Duart, took on and killed his nephew Sir James MacDonald of Islay.

They had squabbled over the ownership of the Rhinns in Islay. Lachlan Mòr claimed them as the dowry given to his wife in 1566 by her brother Angus MacDonald, chief of Clan Donald South, and the most powerful branch of Clann Dhomhnuill.[126] Not everyone agreed.

When the fighting was almost over, thirty MacLeans had sought sanctuary in the old chapel. They had backed inside, bolted the door and waited. They were not confident, as their lives would depend on whether the MacDonalds had respect for holy ground. Alas, their enemy was half mad with grief and anger at the demise of its chief and, lusting for vengeance, set fire to the chapel's thatch.

Everyone inside was killed, save for one man, a Mac Mhuirich who managed to climb through a hole in the burning roof and made good his escape.

*

Our own situation was not entirely dissimilar. After an impressively powerful but intermittent suite of showers the sun cautiously ventured out. As it looked likely to remain that way, we judged it safe to take the Ford Prefect a few miles to Bruichladdich, home to the first whisky distillery I had ever seen.

We drove for a quarter of an hour through the most dramatic country. Scudding clouds delivered shadows to the hills to our right while otters swam in the shallows to our left, hunting for waders and ducklings. Theirs was not the easiest of tasks, as lapwings dive-bombed and yelled abuse at them in an attempt to distract them from their chicks. While the redshanks made themselves scarce, more elusive corncrakes called out their strange warnings from patches of nettles and irises[127] while curlews contributed a plangent descant over their demesnes.

'Here we are,' said Dick.

---

[126] The Rhinns: hills that dominate a peninsula attached by a narrow isthmus to Islay's northern end. It is a deformed igneous complex that forms the base of the Colonsay Group of metasedimentary rocks.
[127] Islay's fields have long been harvested or mown from the centre outwards to allow corncrakes to escape to the field borders.

Bruichladdich's Victorian distillery was built as coal was beginning to prove an alternative to peat as a fuel for pots and stills. The 'Laddie' also used it to dry the malted barley. Inside, and a little poorer for having paid what seemed an extortionate 'admittance', we were surprised to see that the original Victorian machinery was still in use. We were offered a shot glass of the first distillate, to be followed a minute later with a venerable twenty-year-old. The first was almost a pungent vodka, though there was already a faint hint of the miracle that Age would bestow. The second shot was an essay in the subtlest hues a distiller can impart to a sophisticated dram. Any artisanal, living product should speak of the place whence it comes, of the people who have created and nurtured it, of the soil, the air, the geography that influence it; in short, its *terroir*.

Its signature salt-citrus tang came through decades of Islay maturation. It is as much a portrait of Islay as any of John's artists might achieve.

We were encouraged to buy a bottle apiece - which we did, of course – before swooping into the centre of Bowmore.

*

On our wonderful journey the more knowledgeable among us identified beef-suckler cows and black-faced ewes. These creatures maintain or even structure habitats for Islay's wildlife, and had been moved off the wetlands to prevent the nests of wading birds from being trampled.

'A journey on Islay is like driving through a movie location', I said, quite truthfully. We drove through mile upon mile of open grassland, fenced in by forest and hills, giving way, here and there, to a stunning coastline and the open sea. We had been advised to keep our eyes peeled for birds of prey - hen harriers, sparrow-hawks, merlins, peregrines and, of course, eagles. They all have country houses in the inner

Hebrides. Everywhere small birds were feeding in the stubble.

If we did not catch a glimpse of an eagle, we did see flocks of redwings strip the berries from the rowan trees, while choughs pulled cowpats apart in their hunt for dung-beetle larvae.

*

Islay is not just an aviary. Just as promised, we saw plenty of roe deer. As we journeyed on, tiny fawns raised their heads to us from the loch-side reeds and rushes while their magnificent stags mounted guard.

Suddenly we were alighting in Bowmore, home to Islay's oldest distillery and caretaker of the world's oldest whisky maturation warehouse, its No. 1 Vault, and our timing was perfect. The staff were already preparing to celebrate the start of their third century. They planned to release a rare and limited edition in reproductions of the original Mutter bottles the elixir had first been sold in. *Bowmore*'s founder, David Simpson, had bought the land in 1766.

There are 'plausible rumours' that distilling may have started here even before that. Illegal distillation was popular among croft settlements, thanks to the prohibitive tax on legal spirits. It therefore came as no surprise to hear that by 1779 the island was already equipped and ready for the future and legal development of a commercial whisky industry. Simpson had not been sitting on his hands.

'I'll no keep the secret from ye. It's our sweet Hebridean air,' explained our virgil, handing us all a pewter cup. 'That and the lazy passage of that old waster Time. Between them they impart its character. This whisky is thereby heir to the exquisite heritage of our first-fill Bourbon casks. Take it into your lungs, my lads, breathe it in. Can ye no smell the vanilla fudge, the sea air, the peat smoke, all handsomely balanced by honeycomb and cinnamon? Now take a wee sip. Good.

If am no mistaken you'll be getting a rush of citrus, gentle saltiness, vanilla and maybe flakes of coconut. Right, that's enough foreplay, it's time to swallow. Aside from the pleasant warmth you'll savour the smoke, the lime, the artifice. What do you make of that? One to smuggle over the border, I'll warrant?'

I, for one, felt a little sinful drinking whisky so early on the Sabbath.

*

There was a remedy for guilt. It was time to take in the round church.

We found it in a commanding location at the head of the village. It dominated its surroundings, and the views from its porch only ended when Loch Indaal took them to the ocean.

Distilleries aside, Kilarrow Parish Church may be Islay's best known building. It was built in the mid-eighteenth century by Daniel Campbell of Shawfield, who at the time owned every square inch of the island. He did not just build a church, he planned and extended the settlement at Bowmore, determined to turn it into a small town.

His motives were not altogether altruistic; after the clearance of the area's main settlement of Kilarrow[128] his principal purpose was to generate rental income. He also meant to clear the area around his home, Islay House, and extend its gardens and grounds.

Some sceptical folk believe that in building a church he was offering the previous dwellers of Kilarrow a sweetener, a fine reason to move to his new village at Bowmore. Even if so, his successors have continued to modernise the island roads, develop a fishing industry and build schools.

*

---

128 Or 'Wheelbarrow', as Molony teasingly put it.

His church is certainly handsome. Its architect is undocumented but I was firmly told that it was John Adam. It seems he had been specifically commissioned in 1758 by a Duke of Argyll to design a round church for the new settlement of Inveraray. The original design was never built because, apparently, it wasn't practical to divide a church in a way that allowed services in both English and Gaelic.

Campbell was related to the Campbells of Inveraray, which may have given him access to John Adam's plan. If so, it certainly found a fertile plot in Bowmore.[129]

Sixty feet across and with walls three feet thick, the church is certainly large. A massive oak pillar, almost two feet thick, is at its heart, raised on a sandstone slab. It supports the roof with eight radial beams. It's so light and airy one could be forgiven for thinking it much younger than its two centuries.

One last ecclesiastical anecdote. We would learn that evening, at the bar, that the circular design was intended to ensure that the devil could find no corners in which to hide.

*

It was now approaching five o'clock and we were getting hungry.

On our way back to our hotel and supper we saw a million ducks, mostly blue-winged teals and wigeon, but also mallard, shoveler, golden-eye and pintail. Each tastier than the last. We also saw egrets, marsh harriers, wood sandpipers and female hen harriers that flew up from their nests in the deep heather to catch the morsels their hard-working partners dropped in their dramatic fly-pasts. Butterflies and dragonflies, in herb-rich meadows and ungrazed moorland, danced a spectacularly choreographed ballet

---

[129] There is an alternative theory. The architect may have been a Frenchman, recruited during Campbell's grand tour of Europe in the 1750s.

among the wildflowers. Sir Frederick Ashton could not have managed better.

No better plan had occurred to me so we stayed in our hotel to check out who else would pitch up and, after supper that night we headed for the bar where Louise 'Minefield' and Penny Rippon had joined the party.

My new friend, the buxom chambermaid, was now on my side of the counter. 'I'll wager you do a lot of cycling,' she told me with a saucy wink.

We enjoyed an hour or so, sipping our pints of 'heavy' but, at ten o'clock, closing time, a policeman, helmeted and in uniform, came in. Was the game up?

He looked around the thirsty collection of topers and smiled. Taking his helmet off, he went up to the bar and said 'It's ma bell'.

There was a cheer, but it had to be explained to me that this odd phrase meant he was buying a round.

'Whit ur ye fur?' asked the bartender.

'Scotch muffler, laddie,' he said, taking his whisky to the piano. He raised the lid and began to play *Danny Boy*. We were in a local pub, with friends and friendly locals, quaffing real ale or Scottish wine, beside a roaring fire and hearing the village bobby paddle the Joanna - it was idyllic, even after a picture-perfect day. It was also only the first of a number still to come.

Islay is the teeming womb of smoky, peaty single malt whiskies and I was an eager student. At 10 am the next morning, a taxi took me and my camera into Port Ellen and thence to Laphroiag. Half an hour later I was enjoying my first dram of Island Malt Whisky. It was akin to an interview with an angel.

Ambitiously, I was planning to do Ardbeg that same morning but, when at last I got there, sadly for my research, I discovered the distillery at Ardbeg was closed for restoration. There was some consolation, however. Its café was open. I ordered lunch and opened my guidebook.

I read, while I ate my bread-crumbed fresh-water trout, that

tools and implements, discovered in archaeological digs have confirmed that Islay's history reaches back to around 8000 BC, the Mesolithic era. Scholars agree its earliest major settlements were Celtic.

By the sixth century AD, Islay was part of the Gaelic kingdom of Dál Riada, which stretched from Ulster to the West of Scotland. The 16ft-high Kildalton Cross was erected in around 800 AD, and it still stands.

Much of this would change with the Viking conquest. The Norsemen defied the ancient Gaelic kingdom and fought for the independence of the Western Isles from the mainland.

In the mid-12th century, a Scot called Somerled Mac Donald rebelled against Islay's Scandinavian settlers, but not on behalf of the Kings of Scotland. His descendants would rule Islay as 'Lords of the Isles' – independently - for hundreds of years. They based themselves at Loch Finlaggan near Port Askaig, and ruins of their settlement are still visible today.

Not until the late-15th century did Islay come under Scottish rule. That was when a plot to help the English king conquer Scotland, in return for Islay's independence, was uncovered. The Lords of the Isles - the MacDonalds - controlled the waters with their fleets of galleys or birlinns. Notionally vassals of the Kings of Norway, at the height of their power they were the most powerful lords in all Britain, after the king of course.

Finlaggan was their seat on Islay and their era would only end in 1493. MacDonald II had his titles and estates seized by Scotland's King James IV who awarded their stewardship to the Campbells of Argyll, the largest and most dominant of the Highland clans.

Despite their leading position on mainland Scotland, on Islay the Campbells were absentee lairdy. The island would fail, its inevitable if sad economic consequence meant that by the early 18th century, the Cawdor Campbells were struggling to maintain power over their estates. The island provided them with little income. The lairdy had faces on them as long as a hare's back leg. Worse still, famine was killing or exiling their workers.

That was when the aforementioned Daniel Campbell of Shawfield, a business man and politician, came to the rescue. On becoming Laird of Islay he introduced new farming methods and a thriving textile industry. Fortunately, these introductions took firm root.

Three generations later, in 1816, Islay was again flourishing, its population recovering. Walter Frederick Campbell had taken over its ownership. New villages - Port Ellen, Port Charlotte and Port Wemyss – had sprung up and a new source of income, the distilling industry, took to the air.

Alas, it proved a false dawn. In the 1840s, the contagion of the 'Irish' potato famine reached the Hebrides. Landlords and locals were faced with a choice between disaster or migration. All save the very most stubborn, the infirm or those with elderly parents chose the latter. Between 1841 and 1861, a third of the population of western Scotland emigrated to Britannic colonies; chiefly Australia, New Zealand and Canada.

Sadly, in 1848, Walter Frederick Campbell went bankrupt, his estates dismembered and sold off in parcels.

Today, almost all the island is owned by just five owners: Dunlossit and the Islay Estate are the two largest landowners. The others are Ardtalla, Foreland and Laggan, all perpetual trusts whose members shelter behind anonymity.

*

We all learned that from Islay's early human settlement through to an empire independent of the Scottish crown, its settlers had forged the island's unique landscape. It is home to romantic ruins of the past and the burgeoning of a thrusting future.

Today's Lord of the Isles is the Duke of Rothesay. He is the eldest son and heir apparent of the King of Scotland who, since the creation of the United Kingdom, is also His Majesty the King. Confusingly, Rothesay is also known as Prince William of Wales.

The MacDonalds still contest the right to the Lordship. It's all good natured these days but, for a long while, uprisings and rebellions against the Scottish Monarch were commonplace.

The history lesson was over, and it was Friday. Louise Allison and some of the other girls we knew were now installed at the Islay Hotel. Everyone had been infected by the mood of the place and we were *bona fide* travellers. We were buying until the small hours. The policeman-pianist and the thirsty chambermaid were floating on a rising tide of drinks.

I will admit to feeling none too agile the Saturday morning and we had some way to go to get to the church in Kildalton. Like the opening scene in *Four Weddings and a Funeral*, there was a lot of cursing as we struggled into our kit for the great event.

Julia and Dick had known each other for around a year. I had known both of them for rather longer. I had known Julia since my return from France to England in 1974, while Dick and I had been at Cambridge together. I may even have introduced them. If memories like that are of their nature unreliable, seeing two old friends marry was to be the climax of my time in the Hebrides.

Julia's mother Lady Belhaven had sent a bus for us and, ever nearer to the hour that spells L.A.T.E., we were finally on board. Twenty minutes later we alighted at what had seemed - at first sight - to be a very severe

330

church. Its stern exterior, however, belied a carpeted interior. At the east end, an Italianate altar in green marble was lit by a stained glass window above, depicting the Kildalton Cross and some appropriate Celtic motifs.

The ministry was contested by those distant cousins, the Episcopalians and the Roman Catholics. Canon Kenneth MacKenzie, the Catholics' Diocesan and Itinerant Priest, was to conduct the rite.

Since Lord Belhaven could not be there, the bride was escorted to the altar by her brother Freddy. Dick was already there, in his grey morning coat, patiently waiting for his handsome, strongly-featured bride, a woman with amber eyes, a transforming smile and formidable feminine charm.

The wedding service was admirably brief; great hymns, a short sermon. What seemed like minutes later we were back in the open air, waiting for the photographers to do their bit. Then, at last, we were again aboard that bus and on our way to Ann Belhaven's surprisingly modern house.

I remember knowing almost half the guests. The 'breakfast' was less formal than most - it was what some call a 'finger buffet' but the champagne flowed like water. It is remotely possible that I may have over-indulged. A little. After what can only have been around an hour, Lady Belhaven told me, firmly, even bluntly, that I was drunk.

'Leave now. Find your own way home.'

I wanted to object. I was only as drunk as anyone would be who has skipped his own breakfast and downed the best part of a bottle of bubbly, mitigated only by a tired sausage roll.

Still, it was not my place to be objectionable, either literally or figuratively. The wedding had to be flawless. I wandered along the hall, opened the front door and stepped into the cool air, without the faintest idea of how I might get back to the hotel.

I had been standing there for half a minute at most, feeling foolish and clueless as to what to do next, when the door opened and a man three inches shorter and thirty years older than me stepped out to join me.

'I've just been thrown out,' he said. 'Drunk, she said.'

'That makes two of us,' I rejoined.

'My name's Alasdair. I manage the bank in Port Ellen. I think I can drive safely enough. Would you like a lift?'

'I'm at the Islay Hotel. This is really very kind.'

We got into his car and set off. Alasdair certainly didn't drive conspicuously badly or appear drunk, and I was fairly sure I wasn't either.

'We're both a bit the worse for wear,' Alasdair disagreed. 'Don't argue. We'll stop at home where my wife will fix us up with some cheese sandwiches. Her platter is truly sobering, let me assure you.'

He seemed to shudder at the very thought.

'That's very kind, Sir.'

Just as the bank manager had promised, some minutes later I was faced with a great dish of cheese sandwiches – classic Scottish ones; pre-sliced white bread filled with a rubbery variety of cheddar. A chubby and diminutive Scots lass was holding it for me to take one. Alasdair had poured me a serious whisky, putting a finger to his lips as he did so.

'Hair of the dog,' said Alasdair. 'You know, you might want to transfer your own account up here. Cheques take three days to clear in London. On Islay they take four. A great local advantage. Your wealth will immediately increase by 0.3%.'

An hour after this pleasant interlude, Alasdair and I regained the bar of the Islay Hotel. John Molony was already at the piano and my coterie was standing around, glass in hand. Perhaps they had all been thrown out too?

All adventures must end. We would all be heading home the next day.

*

The next time I saw Julia would be in London. She had divorced Dick and had married a second time. This second husband, Stephen Hobbs, had given her two very pretty, very bright girls.

Since then, Julia has become a serious novelist. Her intelligence shines through her every word. Eventually she married a third time, to Trevor Mostyn, a significant author in his own right; a traveller, a philosopher, an Arabist and a committed Christian.

May God bless them and grant their prayers. On the subject of her first marriage, Julia wrote that

> Dick was a nice, intelligent man, but I should never, ever have married him. I made the mistake of telling Dad 'Dick would like to marry me'. In no time at all I was on Islay getting married, pumped full of valium in an attempt to soothe the headache I had suffered for days. It was not a joyful event, not for me. People still talk about it because of the magical setting and how everything was amazing, but I feel as if I wasn't there.

CHAPTER FIVE

The Reign in Spain
1978

After a gourmet expedition to Bologna, the author begins to learn Spanish. An opportunity to be paid to see Spain's tourist attractions arises and he takes his 'neglected' sister and a friend to Marbella, Tarifa, Puerto Banús, Sotogrande, Cádiz, Jerez de la Frontera and Seville. He works a trial position in Madrid, where he meets a supposed 'nephew' of the Duke of Medina Sidonia.

At one of Jack Lloyd's celebrated 'French lunches' at CTB – delicious buffets where not a word of English was allowed – I found myself talking (in French of course) to the head of Bowring's Overseas.

'I don't recall if you speak Spanish?' Andy asked.

'No, I don't,' I said firmly. 'French, Italian and English.'

'Well, would you care to add Spanish to your little list? We think you might help with our Spanish account.'

'I would prefer to help with the French one. I can speak French already so it would be a lot less effort.'

'France is in Northern Europe, in this company at least. Spain is in Southern Europe, along with Italy, Yugoslavia and Greece. We are thinking of offering you the account. You can't have France. That belongs to your chum Roger Huggins.'

'Must I repeat myself? I do not speak Spanish!'

'Trust me. We can fix that.'

*

No sooner said than done. A month later I found myself at the Regency School of Languages, just off Regent's Park, enrolled into an intensive course. 'Intensive' was an understatement. I was down for three hours of one-to-one tuition in the morning, the same again in the afternoon. All this would make for two weeks of brain-numbing slog.

I had had an idea. In Ireland, according to Flann O'Brien, when you ask directions, you are told 'I wouldn't start from here.' Well, that applied to me. Spanish was said to be a lot like Italian. I would start from there.

I decided to give this challenge my best shot. If I could pass muster in that noble tongue at the end of the endurance test, then Spain would be added to my growing portfolio, and southern Europe would be on my plate in the palatable form of an oyster.

*

Those two weeks passed fast. They may even have been wearing roller-skates.

I crammed so much Castilian into my head it was trying to burst out again. It leaked out while I slept. I would wake up shouting *¡Ai no corrida!* Still, the job was done as best as I was able. The first Monday I was back in the office, I greeted my colleagues with a breezy *'¡Ola! ¿Que tal?'*

None other than Charles Cullum announced himself as a spokesman for 'the many' who purportedly wanted to congratulate me on what my tutor had apparently described as an exceptional performance. I felt accordingly smug, even though I was of course aware that the school's highly flattering stuff about my supposed gifts was in their financial interest.

Cullum was already on my list of angels. When he breezily informed me that 'it takes more than a gift for languages to make a country manager,' he rose higher on my honours board. 'You need to understand when to stand or sit, kiss hands and send flowers.'

'Naturally,' I said cautiously.

'General Franco popped his clogs last November,' he continued. 'The Board believes the new king will bring Spain back into communion with the rest of the world. Everyone should gain from their newly minted globalisation. Other things being equal, you'll be in Spain in a few weeks' time. You need not be in our Madrid office from Day One – you must explore Spain and digest what makes them tick. Six weeks should do the trick.'

'What will I do for money?'

'You are employed by CTB. You are, therefore, on expenses. Get an advance from the relevant people. You'll manage.'

Six weeks on full expenses? No duties? My cup was running over.

*

But first I had to go to Bologna and I had never been there before, either.

The little I knew of it was that the place had been a major conurbation for more than two millennia. Everyone seemed to know that the Etruscans had founded it. After the infamous 'rivers of blood', the Romans took it over, using political sleight of hand to rename it *Bononia*, the happy place. During the early Middle Ages, as a free municipality and *signoria*, it became Europe's largest city, housing something like a million people.

Its university, established in 1088, is the oldest European University.[130] It numbers Thomas à Becket, Dante, Nicolaus Copernicus, Boccaccio, Petrarch, Albrecht Dürer, Carlo Goldoni, Umberto Eco, Guglielmo Marconi, Pasolini and Giorgio Armani among its alumni.

It's a city famous for towers, churches, porticos and food. And yes, I forgot, the beauty of its women. I was looking forward to a little window-shopping.

---

[130] While not in Europe, Cairo's University of the Flowers may be even older.

336

I felt sad (and vicariously guilty) to learn how much damage we Allies had inflicted on this venerable city during the Second World War. Air Chief Marshal Harris had categorised it as an industrial and railway hub, connecting (as it does) northern and central Italy. Apparently, that made it a suitable candidate for the treatment known as demolition. On July 24th, 1943, the RAF flattened most of the city's historic centre. On just one terrifying day, more than a thousand years of history were ravaged. Hundreds of men, women and children – the 'enemy', Bomber Harris called them - died in the flames.

The city, therefore, had good cause to resent us. Up to the War it had been a thriving commercial and industrial centre. At least, that had rebegun but its aggrieved citizens had now made it the political stronghold of the Italian Communist Party.

Bologna was constantly in the news, if for the darkest of reasons. The 'Movement of 1977' saw dreadful riots. The police had shot dead a far-left activist, Francesco Lorusso. Days of murder and mayhem ensued.

From there it got worse.

On one dreadful day, at the height of the rush hour, terrorists detonated a bomb in the railway station. It took a dozen lives.

Many years would pass before the neo-fascist group, the *Nuclei Armati Rivoluzionari*, could be safely convicted of the outrage. There is no longer any question that the legal process was wilfully hampered by Licio Gelli, Grand Master of the infamous Freemason Lodge *Propaganda Due* (P2). He was finally charged with wilfully stalling the investigation, along with three agents of the Italy's secret military intelligence service, SISMI.

'Years of lead' was the sinister phrase coined to describe the era that followed.

Nevertheless, I had business in Milan, as always, so I would shop there. When done I could travel from Italy's 'moral capital'. A train was waiting for me at *Milano Centrale*, the second largest railway station in Europe, to carry me the two hundred miles to Bologna, the other side of Italy. Bologna's smartest neighbour is Venice itself.

Milano Centrale deserves to be a tourist destination in its own right. It was opened in the early 1930s with the intention of reveal the imperial magnificence of Mussolini's vision. Questionable politics aside, it's Benito at his best. It has an ornate grey stone classical portico, with four sets of twinned columns, over which hangs every European flag. Inside, a soaring glass roof sails over its twenty-four platforms.

Now that I was a 'senior broker', I was allowed to use my corporate credit card to buy a first class ticket. That was a smart move, as the fast train from capitalist Milan to communist Bologna only carried first class passengers. An antidote to the Soviet Union, perhaps? Or maybe an echo? In Moscow, so-called 'Zil lanes' on high streets were reserved for the use of important apparatchiks in their limousines.

I will admit that the train connecting the two so different political worlds was wonderful. My compartment felt more like a gentleman's club than a British Rail cattle truck. I was rewarded with majestic lakes and mountain ranges as they unfurled outside my window for an unforgettable couple of hours.

The *Ferrovia Nazionale* had tempted me with a restaurant car but, since I was heading for the 'gourmet capital' of Italy, I rejected its overtures. I would find somewhere when I arrived.

To add a certain *no so niente* to my whim, and when only a few miles out of Milan, the conductor made a routine announcement over the train's public address system.

'Gentilissimi signori, signore, questo servizio ferroviale si fermera solo alla sua destinazione finale, il comunale di Bologna. Il nostro tavola calda è aperto per il vostro restauro', came the perfectly reproduced dulcet tones of a trained public speaker.

I thought that would be that, but now a dulcet French lady repeated the call to action.

'Messieurs, mesdames, ce train ne s'arrêtera qu'à sa destination finale, Bologne Centrale. La notre table d'hôte est ouverte pour votre restauration.'

I smiled. I have always loved the singing tone of French.

Only a moment later the PA system crackled back into life - the cabaret was not yet over.

'Meinen Damen und Herren, diese Zug haltet nur an ihrem endgültigen Bestimmungsort, Bologna Centrale. Unsere Speisewagen ist offen für Ihre Hochgenuss.'

It was wonderful to be a member of the European Economic Community.

I could not have predicted, however, that when the English version came, it would emerge from the ether in the lilting accent of South Dublin.

'My lords, ladies and gentlemen, this train will only stop at its final destination, Bologna Centrale. Our restaurant car has opened for your delectation.'

Mussolini's trains always ran on time; that was his boast. Despite the dictator's cruel demise, by and large they still do. We arrived at Bologna's multilevel railway station precisely two hours after we had left Milan. Climbing down onto the platform I stepped into what had been for so long the last completely walled city in Europe.[131]

I had a tough job ahead. Not the relatively simple business of trying to drum up business for CTB. No, my real challenge was to study my guidebook for some

---

[131] Apologies to York, Lucca, etc, etc.

stylish restaurant where I might digest the blend of medieval, renaissance and baroque urbanity in this antique settlement.

I set off at a brisk pace along the Via Emilia. The streets of central Bologna are laid out on a grid, a predictable outcome of its classical heritage.

The original ramparts had been supplanted long ago with medieval ones and it had not taken the proud burghers of Bologna long to ornament the city's defences with a hundred and eighty defensive towers, twenty of which remain. Even today, two of the medieval skyscrapers, the leaning *'due torri' Asinelli* and *Garisenda*, provide the city's icon.

Miles of elegant, covered walkways enrich the place. While I walked along the *Portico di San Luca* I had no idea that was the world's longest arcade. Overall, there are twenty-four miles of them in the Bologna's centre alone. Even in the fiercest of deluges, the people of Bologna stay dry. To open a shop selling raincoats or umbrellas would be to court bankruptcy.

The Sanctuary of the *Madonna di San Luca* in central Bologna has a vaulted path all the way to the Porta Saragossa,[132] one of the twelve gates through the ancient walls. A portico of 666 vaults, no less than four miles long, has led many a visitor to the Emilian countryside from the great city's heart. It provides a sheltered route for a procession. On every Feast of the Ascension since 1433, a Byzantine icon of the Madonna with Child[133] is carried along it, in state, to be blessed in the cathedral.

As I walked towards the centre of town, the town's prosperity radiated like heat from a fire. I found its communist predilections hard to comprehend. Dressed as I was in the court dress of capitalism, the pinstripe suit, I soon saw I was alone in wearing a tie. I collected a few glances from amazed pedestrians who

---

[132] A corruption of Caesar Augustus.
[133] Attributed to Luke the Evangelist.

appeared never to have never seen one before. Behind my back, in all likelihood, some will have fallen to their knees in shock.

Eventually I arrived at the *Basilica of San Petronio*, the tenth-largest church in the world. It's built of bricks. The other basilica, that of Saint Stephen, may even be the oldest in the world, according to its implausible claim that it was offered to the Egyptian goddess, Isis. Both churches would repay study but, given that I had forsaken the delights of the dining car, my priority was food.

My stomach was sounding an alarum. With no particular plan, recommendation or strategy, I fell upon the most ancient, trusted and near infallible method of all. Pot luck.

Passing a hotel, predictably called '*i Portici*',[134] I noticed a framed menu beside the door. Like a moth to a flame I drifted inside. At Reception I was intercepted by a dragon, handed to a short-tempered head waiter, led into the restaurant and then sat in a corner by a pretty but sulky waitress. I felt like a baton in a relay.

The restaurant was certainly elegant, while strangely modern. I studied its playful menu while whetting my palate with a Pritz (apologies to Giacomo). What I desired was *spaghetti alla Bolognese*. I had to know what it should taste like, but to my surprise it wasn't even listed. I asked the waiter. '*Un menù turistico non ci conviene,*' he loftily replied. I was out of luck. They don't serve tourists? What sort of restaurant was this?

Well, render unto Caesar, etc. I decided on an *insalata di funghi* - a mushroom salad - and a *Cotoletta Petroniana*, a local variant of a *schnitzel* and named in honour of Bologna's patron saint.

Pot luck was again on my side. The mushroom salad was a revelation. Six different types of raw

---

[134] 'The Porticos'

mushroom had been carefully sliced and arranged on my plate in concentric circles. Chanterelles, Penny Buns, Blue Legs, Fairy Rings, Shitakis and Field Blewitts revolved around a finely sliced Black Truffle, as the solar system might appear to a hookah-smoking caterpillar. A tiny jug of some wonderful dressing, loosely based on balsamic vinegar, was there to set the thing on fire, which it duly did.

As for the *Cotoletta Petroniana*, it turned out to be veal, breaded in egg and fried, moistened with a spoonful or two of broth, and released from its captivity in the kitchen with a slice of ham and liberal shavings of Grana.

I am writing and you are salivating. Hold on, you can't possibly read about food without knowing the wine I plumped for, admit it? Authenticity meant local - a wine from Emilia-Romagna. Butter and veal leave are fatty on the palate and some would balance this with a sparkling wine. With advice from the sommelier, however, I decided on a glass of *Malvasia di Candia*.

Malvasia is a still, dry and exquisitely fragrant white wine. It proved a half-wise choice. It was Wise, as lunch was extremely tasty, and Unwise as half an hour later I was due to meet Guido Frangipane, Chief Executive of *Bologna Assicurazione SpA*.

Time to pay and be on my way. The half-hour's walk to the insurance company that had originally summoned me to Bologna was pleasant enough. I passed countless cafés and bars, and the sun shone in an encouraging sort of way. Girls of inestimable, unconjurable beauty sat gossiping with one another, their figures accentuated with their fabulous posture. Valentino would have jumped for joy. Well, I did.

'Calm yourself, boy,' I told myself. 'Have a coffee on the way back.'

My meeting was going to be a challenge, given the female distractions, radical politics and an encore in the form of a second glass of Malvasia. All three might have undone me.

As I walked I breathed deeply, a technique my motoring friends told me was often effective on the way home when stopped by a constable in his Mk 7 Jaguar.

I did know there was no point in going into the lion's den with the intellectual equivalent of a water pistol. I would have to depend on the font of stoicism on which every man of the world must rely. It was my only weapon.

About to enter another world I steeled myself.

A white jacketed fellow conducted me to the first floor office of the big white chief, I saw immediately just how an unfamiliar a sort of CEO was Frangipane. A thin beard encircled his face - he could have doubled for Manfred Mann.

His lower limbs bore fawn corduroy trousers, while his upper ones were mostly hidden beneath a Fair Isle pullover. His sockless feet were sandaled, his shirt open at the collar. Of tie was there no trace, present or historical.

I sat in front of an autographed photo of Fidel Castro. On the wall behind was a photogravure of *L'onorevole* Sig. Berlinguer, General Secretary of the Italian Communist Party. True, he had distanced his party from the Soviet version of that absolutist creed, and pursued a more moderate line. He had successfully repositioned his party within the Italian political spectrum.[135]

---

[135] His 'eurocommunism' would come to be adopted by Western Europe's other significant communist parties, in Spain, Portugal and later France. Its significance as a political force would come to be cemented, in 1977, when Enrico Berlinguer, Santiago Carrillo and Georges Marchais met in Madrid. Berlinguer chose to describe his 'alternative' model of socialism as distinct from both the Soviet bloc's and the socialised capitalism practiced by Western countries during the Cold War. He called it the *terza via* or 'third way', a phrase Tony Blair would later adopt.

It may have helped me that Berlinguer was the eldest son of a immensely rich Sardinian marquis. This was an embarrassment for some of his more radical supporters but for me it was a source of sardonic amusement.

On the desk at which I sat was a cigar box. Embedded in its lid was a small brass oblong, engraved '*Recuerdo de Cuba, 1970*' and the ashtray, next to it, was engraved with the hammer and sickle of the PCI.[136] Even now, with all those years of finely tuned hindsight behind me, I still think of these Bollinger Bolsheviks, as my father liked to call them, as simple hypocrites, draped in corduroy vestments perhaps, but earning enough to buy and lease out a street's worth of peasant hovels.

No, I am not in the mood to apologise. Of course, the directors may be devout Christians, or Jews, or Seventh Day Adventists, for that matter, but in office hours at least they should keep that stuff under wraps; the same applies, and in spades, to their politics. In the end, insurance and reinsurance companies are businesses, there to repay the shareholders who created them in the first place.

The majority in every parliament, anywhere, are professional politicians. They have little choice. Elsewhere they would be lucky to get jobs minding mice.[137]

Yet here I was, in the uniform of an *obergruppenführer*, in front of a leftie who felt that I was personally responsible for Mandela's imprisonment, the repression of the Mau Mau and an inept attempt to retake the Suez Canal. Given the above, the meeting went well. It helped no end that that I spoke Italian.

I came away with a new top layer in their reinsurance programme, a much needed filip.

---

[136] PCI: *Partita Comunista Italiana*.
[137] I am misquoting Flann O'Brien. Again.

I had fared sufficiently well in my intensive Spanish course for the director of Bowrings Overseas to offer me a date for the onset of my Spanish adventure.

My domestic affairs were becoming more complicated. Tev and I had fallen out. I will admit it was entirely my fault but I plead for a merciful judgement. The issue was about money, the most corrosive issue of all, and I was in a psychological trap. On the continent, where I could charge my time and expenses, I was some sort of millionaire, while in England those about me had to listen to my tales of this opera house or that racecourse while impatiently waiting for me to buy a round.

All those shiny shoes and silk ties come at a cost. I was blinkered enough to think that future hikes in income would retrospectively solve my problems. It didn't happen, or at least it didn't happen fast enough.

When Simon, my boss, refused to make me an Assistant Director, the next rank up, he had neatly side-stepped the issue by calling me a 'senior broker'. If I had been more politically astute I might have seen even then that my cause was lost.

I had to move out of Cheyne Row, selling my share of the leasehold back to Tev. Charles Sheppard offered me a room to rent in his house in Battersea. It was a lot cheaper so, given the circumstances, I leapt at the offer. I was hardly going to sleep rough, was I?

Yet was the game up? I was only in my mid-twenties, and Andy was offering me Spain.

Madrid was worth a mass, wasn't it?

*

I had an idea. I could let Rome come with me. It was still spring, after all. Sandro Ridomi, with whom I had shared a house in Rome, had just bought a flat in

Rutland Gate, close to the Albert Hall. I asked him if he wanted an Iberian adventure.

'Yes,' he said. 'You'll do the talking, I'll do the listening. Italian and Spanish are close. Between us we'll manage.'

*

Now for the itinerary. Not knowing Spain, I thought the South Coast could get us started. British tourists went there in large numbers and most of its shopkeepers, barstaff and restaurateurs had mastered English. If this holiday was to be another attempt at immersion, let it start in the shallow end.

I also approached my sister, which meant weekending in Paris. I have so much to endure.

'Fancy a few weeks in Spain,' I asked her. 'You seemed to enjoy Rome all those years ago.'

'Plan? Details? Expenses?'

Sometimes, from the way she talks, I think she must have been a quartermaster in a previous life.

'We'll fly to Marbella before it gets too hot. From there we make our way west, via Cádiz, until we reach Seville. Then we come home. You'll like Cádiz. It overlooks Cape Trafalgar.'

It really wasn't too hard a sell, but the defeat of Napoleon's navy might be controversial. Kate thought the diminutive Corsican slightly taller than God.

'General Franco died last November', she soberly adjudged. 'Whenever a lid comes off a pressure cooker, mortal danger results. A holiday in Spain will be dangerous.'

'What nonsense. King Juan Carlos has mounted a successful charm offensive and is busy dismantling the *Franquista* regime', I replied with feigned confidence. 'He has announced a 'Transition to Democracy'. All Spain eats out of his hand.'

'I don't know. The Spanish are cruel, stubborn and not a little mad. I'm afraid Franco was typical of his race,' my sister opined. Since these are the very qualities that real women love in a man, I knew then the game was on.

The three of us were soon booked into the Marbella Golf Resort Hotel, which had more stars than a bottle of Metaxa.[138] Deciding I should not be spending CTB's money too wantonly, I thought to alternate between expensive and cheap accommodation. That would average out the bills. Sandro was paying his own way, and he and I would share a room. We would manage Kate's surcharge between us. It would be trivial.

The facility to play a round of golf cost a lot extra but, since only Sandro could play, he nobly waived his rights. His eyes were on a different sport. I had not reckoned on his wanting to hook up with the Hotel Hooker, but even that turned out all right. He played away while I had a good night's kip.

As always, the fates wanted a role in my new adventure.

*

The sum of my knowledge of Marbella was that (a) that Sean Connery lived there and that (b) *The Daily Mirror* had mischievously rebaptised the Costa del Sol the 'Costa del Crimm'. In short, not a lot.

Intending to soak up some rays the next day beside the hotel's Olympic pool, I found myself in deepest chinwag with the editor of the *Sunday Mirror*.

'You've missed him,' the tabloid chief told me.

'That's a shame,' I replied, clueless as to what or whom he meant.

'We played a round yesterday but he's had to go to Pinewood.'

That should have been enough of a clue.

'What a pity. I would have liked to have met him.'

---

[138] Metaxa, the Greek brandy, benefits from the generosity of its distillers by having stars in inverse proportion to its digestibility.

'Yes. It turns out to have been a bit of a wasted trip for a groupie. Sorry!'

'Perhaps, but meeting the editor of a national newspaper amply makes up for it.'

The editor smiled. 'You'll join me in a beer? We start drinking at 10 o'clock over here.'

'That's very kind.'

My new friend and I were joined by Kate and Sandro, who both looked a little disapprovingly at the two decadent alcoholics quaffing their St Miguel at a godforsaken hour. I was unrepentant. I was in Spain precisely to learn how to do things differently. Kate and Sandro were similarly inclined to broaden their minds.

Puerto Banús was our next port of call but it was still some way away. We would have lunch *en route*. Sandro, who had hired our car, insisted on his rights. He would do the driving. A fanatical motor-sports enthusiast it was a shame he was not a professional. He would have put Emerson Fittipaldi into second place. Given that he and I had been to Le Mans together, Kate and I gave way.[139] That and the fact that neither Kate nor I had a driving licence.

The road that runs along Spain's south coast desperately needed to be replaced,[140] especially since Marbella and its satellite resorts had decided to house a goodly number of ex-pats, many if not most of whom were bank robbers, who drove their Ferraris or Lamborghinis like getaway cars.

Not every inhabitant of the Costa del Sol had made his pile, however, and horse-drawn carts would share the road.

To be as safe as possible on this race track, farm vehicles normally drove in the middle, their wheels straddling the thin white line that divided it in two. Not

---

[139] For details of this adventure, see *A Gap Year or Two*, by this author.
[140] That was then. There is now a shiny motorway beside which, every few kilometres, are signs declaring it was funded by the EU.

that this was anything other than a challenge to Signor Sandro 'mph' Ridomi. We threw up a lot of dust from the kerb as we rocketed past these wagons.

Kate was beginning to protest that she would rather walk. Even Sandro felt put out by being forced to undertake a cart on the left-hand-side of the road, especially when some dolt in a Bullitt Mustang came straight at him at a similar speed. Estimated collision speed: 230 mph, I read in my obituary. Kate had become adamant that Sandro should pull over for a minute or three. We did as instructed, in the carpark of a restaurant, *El Libro Amarillo*.

'It's an omen, a signal. Time for The Bite is upon us,' Kate pronounced in the twin spirits of relief and appetite. It would take more than a glass or two, however, to recover from the Grim Reaper's unwarranted overtures.

We had struck luck. *El Libro Amarillo* was no amateurish roadside café. It meant business. Once inside we discovered the whole place, bar, cloakroom and restaurant, had been done up as a library.

'You can order an aperitif at the bar,' a seriously camp waiter told us as we went in, so we did.

Sandro thought his manner had something to do with the *Commedia del'Arte*. I was simply puzzled. Looking about I soon saw that many of the customers were a little overdressed and, yes, I do mean the men. Extremely tight trousers seemed *de rigeur*. Earrings were clearly sold singly in Marbella; one unlucky lobe would just have to go without. Jewellery weighed heavily in bulky chains around a collective neck, wrist and occasional ankle.

Kate, who has a 'thing' for gays, warmly approved and even my brain slowly engaged gear. A library? It was beginning to add up. Oscar Wilde's beloved copy of Huysman's *À Rebours* had been bound in yellow pigskin.

Aubrey Beardsley and some of his friends had published a quarterly review of curious literature, calling it 'The Yellow Book' and it had become a gay bible.

When our designated waiter minced over to us to take our order, Kate put her White Lady down and solemnly pronounced she would have *'una ración de jamón ibérico'*. Sandro plumped for *'gambas a la plancha'* and I went for the *'anguilas jóvenes'*. I had never eaten elvers before and I had heard they were quite delicious. My sources had again proved reliable. I had thought of asking if he had frogs' legs, but I already knew what his answer would be.

'No, Sir, it's just the trousers they make us wear.'

As a main course we all had pigs' trotters – a nice joint in a nice joint, quipped Kate - and we washed it down with a *Faustino Quinto*. So far our Spanish sojourn was panning out rather well, and it was to get better still. Between us we had done some damage to the carafe. We finished the wine and paid up. Sandro seemed rather more relaxed when we clambered into the car for the next leg of the journey.

Puerto Banús is one of the Costa del Sol's playgrounds for the rich. As we pulled in it reminded me a little of the Cala de Volpe hotel in Sardinia – a brand new 'fishing village' with an impressive mountain hillscape.

The port was in fact designed and built in 1970 by José Banús, the eponymous property developer, as a luxury marina and shopping complex. Not a great period in architecture, however. Too much concrete. Famous for its beaches, beach clubs and buzz, all of them especially appealing to Sandro, its shops seemed to be designer outlets for Gucci, Ralph Lauren, Balenciaga, Yves St Laurent and the like.

The restaurants catered to a supposed 'celebrity' lifestyle. It is a place where people-watching can be rewarded with periodic sightings of pop-stars, disc-jockeys and reality-TV icons if, Sandro said loftily, all 'a bit B-list'.

Sandro was no groupie, but sports cars and big boats still worked their magic on him. The sight of so many Ferraris and luxury yachts let him think he had arrived in heaven. My sister affected a noble disinterest but, tacitly, even she was impressed.

We were lucky to find rooms. It took us an hour, but then the great and the good had been there ahead of us.

Thank goodness most of them were to sleep in the staterooms of their ocean-going craft. The beneficiaries of God's largesse were of course not the only ones to rough it on board. Their crew did too.

While Kate powdered her nose in the loo of the *Astral Bar y Cocktail*, Sandro had already intercepted a ravishing girl of what he considered the perfect age; probably her late teens, possibly her very early twenties.[141] The melody that a well-spoken Italian can infuse into the most banal of exchanges had her eating out of his hand. It was with a spring in his step and a smile on his face that he brought a shy Flemish maiden over to our table.

'Jeremy, this is Astrid. She is from Antwerp but lives in Tehran. She works as an *au pair* for the wife of the chairman of Iran National,[142] the motor manufacturer.'

'How do you do?' I said, holding out my hand.

'Pleased to meet you,' Astrid replied politely.

'Are you staying here?' I asked.

---

[141] Late 'thirties, most likely.

[142] Iran's new government would take hold of every industry. According to the Islamic Revolution Council law of Iran Industries Protection and Development, 'Iran National' was to be sheltered by the National Industries Organisation and managed by Ministry of Industries. When Iraq went to war with Iran, the currency sank. There were shortages of raw materials, machinery wore out and product quality consequently deteriorated. The nationalised corporation would have failed in a free market. It did not. It is now known as 'Iran Khodro'.

'Not exactly. We are moored out there,' expansively indicating the sea. 'I asked for a day off to see the village. I have to call the ship for a launch to come for me.'

Kate chose this moment to reappear.

'Who's this?' she asked, rather bluntly.

'This is Astrid,' Sandro replied. 'Her task is to speak in English to four Persian children. I am hoping to add an overgrown Italian boy to her charges.'

'Hullo,' said Astrid, addressing Kate. 'Are you from one of the yachts in the port as well?'

'Would you care for a glass of cava,' I asked her, signalling to a waiter to bring another glass.

'Thank you, but no. I do not drink.'

Kate rolled her eyes. 'Maybe Astrid has to get back on board to look after her master's children?' she suggested.

'No, there is no hurry', Astrid replied. 'The children are in Marbella tonight. They and their mother enjoy the nightlife. It's a bit better than in Tehran.'

'Well, then,' said Sandro. 'Time to party!'

'Wonderful!' said Kate without enthusiasm.

The word 'party' to my sister inevitably involves music written after 1950, all of which is rubbish. It is probably redundant to reveal that Kate and I had to endure what was left of the evening together, in the bars along the Calle Ribera. Sandro and Astrid were 'making shapes' in TIBU.

We had agreed to hook up again at midnight, check all was well and to sit out for a breather in the balmy evening warmth. In the end, it was almost 2 o'clock when we met up again outside *Pangea*, at the end of the marina next to the tower. Where Astrid and Sandro had spent the time inbetween we had no idea. Sandro was there, proudly sipping his glass of wine, Astrid with her innocent Coca Cola.

She must have used the ship-to-shore walkie-talkie she had in her handbag as the Persian crew of her employers' motor launch now arrived to help her on board. Her goodbye to Sandro was quite emotional.

It took the rest of us a while to up sticks. We had been hoping to visit Gibraltar but the roads in and out were closed. Sandro unilaterally decided we would head for Sotogrande instead. Sotogrande, being at the western end of the Costa del Sol, is convenient for Tarifa and Gibraltar.

It really is one of the most luxurious sports and residential developments in Europe. It's a large, privately owned residential development which started out as a gated community in the heart of San Roque. Even at first glance we saw it had every imaginable necessity, including polo and golf clubs. Its marina housed incredible bars and restaurants. The views alone were to die for; over sea, hills, cork forests, green fairways, the Rock and even Morocco. Even when crowded, the resort was certainly not unattractive.

It was an architectural showcase. Its houses varied in style from the traditional Andalusian, including a number of Moorish or mudejar-style homes, to adventurous modern stuff, even a Swiss chalet. Not too much concrete this time.

Puerto Banús, eat your heart out. Sotogrande combines ritzy glamour with aristocratic sophistication. Some of its buildings had already been listed as being of significant importance, protecting them from modification or demolition.

They included the Biddle House, by Francisco Javier Carvajal and the Zóbel house by José Antonio Coderch and the Real Club de Golf, by Luis Gutierrez Soto. The residents play polo, too, and the resort has a certain nautical aura. It seems a little detached from the frenetic pace of the rest of the coast.

A few miles away, across the gulf, the great Rock of Gibraltar rose majestically out of its seas, even more dramatically, perhaps, than South Africa's Table Mountain from its oceans. While the weather was perfect, there was a cloud in the sky. Just one single, stationed over the Rock, its task to remind its apes and people that they were British.

Sandro had some sort of mysterious purpose and, since he had control of our wheels, no negotiation was possible. Not that we were all that unhappy to be stranded in paradise.

'You'll be fine. I have to see an old friend nearby. It will only take a few minutes,' he said, making it seem like a Bond film, 'or at most an hour or two. I'll leave you here. Try the seafood.'

Kate and I soon found a hotel in the *puerto* that let us change for the beach. Its windows let out over the marina's busy taxi boat service. It didn't take long to learn that some of the richest and most powerful families of Spain and the United Kingdom had their summer homes in Sotogrande. It amused us to learn that Peter Caruana, then Chief Minister of Gibraltar, was a resident. He was famous for wanting to have nothing to do with Spain. A bit like a modern Nigel Farage having a fabulous retreat in Germany. HRH Prince Louis Alphonse, Duke of Anjou, pretender to the throne of France, had a house in the *conurbacion*. A clever young politician called Tony Blair was also housed there. I wonder what happened to him?

If the sand was coarse, the Med was not. It was shallow, warm, clean and inviting. The wind drove the waves into the large stones at the water's edge, raising fountains of spume. The shore had something for everyone: surf for antepodean skinny-dippers, a sunlit platform for German body-builders and, of course, bars for the Brits.

We thought about testing the 'waters' at the *Santa Maria Polo Club*, but Sandro had suggested we met him in the *Club Real de Golf* and its œnophilic hideyhole, *The Nineteenth*. When Sandro eventually returned he looked as pleased as Punch.

'All went well? The Soviets are ready to deal?' Kate asked him.

'MI6 is ready to confirm your appointment, Mr Bond,' I told him formally, continuing the theme.

Sandro merely winked.

'No questions, no pack drill,' he said, amused and conspiratorial, while we watched, amazed, his near perfect English grow ever stronger.

'Come on, guys. Put some clothes on. We are going to Tarifa. It's recommended and it's on the way to Cádiz. I've booked us into a hotel.'

I had a look at the map. Tarifa is about as far south as you can go and still be on the mainland. It's on the Costa de la Luz, where the Atlantic and Mediterranean collide.

'We'll adore Tarifa,' Sandro was saying. 'A sweet old town with fabulous food. There are some decent bars for Jeremy, and shops and cafés for Kate. Come on, hurry up. There's no time to lose.'

At the speed that Sandro drives, nowhere is very far. Tarifa was an excellent decision; it's a fairytale city, directly on the sea.

Even at sea level we could see the peaks of Morocco's Rif Mountains across the Med, barely ten miles away. Half-expecting to bump into Sinbad, Ali Baba and his forty thieves or more likely, Suleiman the Magnificent and his Saracen hordes, we suspected an even greater likelihood of a few hundred package holiday makers from Scunthorpe.

Sandro had booked us into the Kook Hotel and, since it was not too ambitiously priced, he had booked a couple of nights. I checked in with a clear(-ish) conscience.

When the concierge told us that we might even see a sperm whale, we needed no further enticement. We changed back for the beach and took our towels with us. Despite the lure of an unbelievably long and wide strand of fine white sand we saw few Germans. Sadly, neither did we see a sperm whale.

We could, however, see the oceanic frontier between the Mediterranean and the Atlantic. The collision of currents was creating some sort of submarine vortex, in which dolphins danced, playfully springing from the water into the air above. We also caught a glimpse of Tarifa's famous orcas, or killer whales.

Kate, characteristically, had somehow acquired a guidebook.

'The Moors settled here in 711 AD, just thirty years after the death of the Prophet. It was their first footfall in Europe, in fact. Tariq ibn-Ziyad's army, wanting to invade Visigothic 'Andalus', had crossed the Strait of Gibraltar from North Africa. That castle we drove past as we came in is the Castle of Guzmán el Bueno. He's the fellow who founded the ducal dynasty of Medina Sidonia. Not that he built the fortress. That had been the work of one Abd-ar-Rahman III, the Caliph of Córdoba, in 960. Guzmán acquired it in 1292 when Tarifa was taken over by the King of Castile, Sancho IV. In 1296, Guzmán refused to hand it over to the besieging forces of the evil Infante Don Juan, brother of King Sancho, even in exchange for the life of his son.'

'So the Moors had already been here for five hundred years! No wonder the place feels so Arabic,' said Sandro.

'You said Guzmán,' I said. 'Isn't that a Jewish name?'

'Semitic languages share a lot, but to infer that the dukedom has a Hebrew origin is simply mad. The

356

seventh duke, after all, was the admiral who led the Spanish Armada to disaster in the English Channel,' said Kate. 'Spain had once tolerated the Jews but they had been expelled by then. That must imply he was a Christian, surely?'

I laughed. The Duke of Medina Sidonia could not possibly have been Jewish. The very thought! Then again...

'Tomorrow morning I'd like to see some of the history of this place, before it gets too warm. The Gate of Jerez, and the castle, if its open. That church looked interesting, too,' said Kate.

'That leaves us with tonight. I shall take it upon myself to guide you through the city's tapas bars and nightlife,' said Sandro.

'Your assistant,' I volunteered a bow. 'I'll carry your wallet.'

'Then you must walk five steps behind,' laughed Sandro.

'It says here that there are Roman ruins,' said Kate. She was still immersed in her guidebook. 'They are a few miles away, so Sandro, you'll have to drive us. You are Roman, after all.'

'Florentine,' said Sandro indignantly.

'Same thing!' said Kate. Her word was his command.

The next morning found us in Baelo Claudia, Andalusia's best-preserved archaeological site.

It's set on a gentle incline some ten miles north of Tarifa, close to the little town of Bolonia and its lovely beach. It will have been strategic for trade routes between Europe and Carthage.

At their narrowest, the Straits of Gibraltar are just ten miles wide. Baelo Claudia, of course, was there for a reason.

As in all imperial cities, the streets and avenues had been laid out in a grid. The remains of an impressive temple, a forum, a basilica, baths, an aqueduct and a fish-salting factory are all still there. Kate read aloud a passage from her guidebook.

'Baelo Claudia connected Europe with *Tingis*, or Tangier. It dates from the Republican period, the 2nd century BC,' she declaimed in her best professorial manner. 'Augustus built its forum but not until Claudius did the monumental complex become a *municipium* and gain its urban and economic splendour.'

I wondered when and why the city was deserted.

'It survived until the 7th century,' Kate promptly replied. 'So, if it wasn't the Arabs who put paid to it, who did?'

'Look at this wall,' said Sandro, who was studying a wide crack in the masonry. 'Only an earthquake would do this.'

He unfolded his map and looked about. The landscape that once lent Baelo Claudia its strategic maritime position now served as a backdrop.

'Over there, to the East, are the San Bartoleme hills,' he explained, 'and there, to the West, are the Higuera and Plata mountains. Combined with those dunes they will have sheltered the harbour from winds and tides. Roman ships had a shallow draft.'

'It does nestle prettily into the coast,' Kate agreed.

We spotted what was left of the Eastern entry gate and a small stretch of ancient aqueduct. It had once brought the city water. Traces of *opus signinum* were detectable inside,[143] used to line and waterproof both baths and pipes. We saw the external furnaces that had heated the aqueduct's water.

---

[143] *Opus signinum* is an ancient building material, a waterproof mixture of lime, sand and broken pottery, occasionally decorated with tiles. The Romans inherited the technique from the Phoenicians.

Kate found some large, luxurious *thermae* and smaller, private *balneae*,[144] decipherable traces of their sports arenas and leisure halls.

We could still admire the twelve remaining columns that stood around in the forum, where the basilica delivered justice to aggrieved or wronged citizens. The amphitheatre was arranged on a natural slope and its seating and *caveae* (the vaulted entrances) were being restored. A sign told us that it was soon to be used to stage a production of some piece of classical Spanish theatre.

The edge of the site had 'saucers', salt baths where tuna would be layered with salt for their preservation. They provided the city and *Baelo Claudia* with funds and purpose. Tradition dies hard. The fixed net fishing method favoured by the Romans continues in the *almadraba* nets of today.

It was hot, and getting hotter. When we were back in Tarifa we felt we deserved a decent lunch. Paella was the simplest of most obvious answer.

Our coffees were not a patch on Italian coffee, according to an irritable Sandro. Kate and I thought the 16th century *San Mateo* might repay a visit, but Sandro set off in a huff for a bar on the Bononia Beach.

St Matthew and its striking baroque façade was (and is) Tarifa's principal church. It had a bell tower with a square, robust base, topped with a small fluted cupola. The sacristy was also domed, but soared magnificently over giant scallops that began on the ground and rose to form three semilunar chapels.

The guide repeated an unsubstantiated legend that in 1506 it had replaced an ancient mosque. It was adsorbing.

---

[144] *Thermae* usually refers to the large imperial bath complexes, while *balneae* were smaller-scale facilities, public or private, that existed in great numbers throughout the Roman Empire.

After an hour or so, Kate and I walked back to the beach in search of Sandro. We found him with a pretty Spanish girl, batting their divergent versions of Latin at each other like opponents in a tennis match. Spanish and Italian may have long shaken off their classical origins, but Sandro and Alejandra could just about make out what the other was saying. Not that it was over-complicated. Nor was it that flirtatious. The girl's *duenna* was five feet away, pretending not to listen. He was going nowhere and he knew it. When we joined him he looked less indignant than relieved, saved by a long drive ahead.

Tarifa to Cádiz is a little over a hundred kilometres or, as our guidebook had it, a little under a hundred miles. Given the state of the roads, Sandro estimated we would need a couple of hours. At the very least, Kate and I hoped.

By the time we had settled our bill it had turned four o'clock. We were on the road again. We drove like startled and supercharged bats from a dark and hot place. Our driver - his brow corrugated on his forehead, his hands clenched on the wheel - rocketed along a road that had been designed for those who had never sought nor experienced the thrill of unadulterated frenzy. Unhurried traffic, in plain English.

Our car whizzed past craggy mountains, pine forests, fields and countless beaches – all wild and empty. The afternoon sun beat down, reminding us just who is Boss in the Costa de la Luz. Air conditioning could only be achieved by opening all the windows, which in the heat, noise, dust and wind, admitted hundreds of small, repellent, blood-sucking insects. They seemed particularly drawn to Kate.

Sandro, meanwhile, was either enjoying it or determined to get the ordeal over as fast as possible. It was hard to tell which. Kate and I, even had the noise allowed for conversation, were not inclined to debate the matter. He rocketed through old walled towns, on roads obstructed with watchtowers, Arabic forts, medieval churches and renaissance palaces.

Fittipaldi (or whoever was in control) ignored our inaudible pleas to slow down. We hurtled past bars filled with incunabula and curios.

Beguiling *bodegas* sold bullfighting paraphernalia, while tobacconists were stocked with Cuban cigars. Roadside restaurants were filled with people eating fish at rickety tables while unsteady scooters with two lovers on board erratically carried their children in the front baskets.

At these speeds, however, all we reliably saw was an expressionist wash of colour, all we really heard was the terrified cries and screams of those we overtook.

Sandro treated us to a flickering glimpse of Bolonia, Valdevaqueros, Zahara and Zahora. At last we saw a sign announcing Vejer de la Frontera and Kate, who was sitting in front, managed to penetrate Sandro's dogged determination to be the fastest man on Earth. He slowed down.

'You're after another bar?' he asked her.

'No. I want to catch my breath. It will be with us in a quarter of an hour.'

We had arrived at the bottom of a ravine. Sandro now meant to show us what he could do with a narrow road up a steep escarpment.

Vejer turned out to be a whitewashed village - about six miles from the coast - perched high above a steep gorge. We found a space in the Plaza de España, parking the car in the shade of its giant palm trees. Even this was a challenge, since the car shared an aversion with its driver to do anything at less than fifty mph.

Nevertheless, when our feet touched the ground, we found ourselves in what might have competed for the title of prettiest village square in Spain. At its heart, a wonderful old fountain featured ceramic frogs which spouted cool water high into the air. Even Sandro seemed reasonably happy to use his feet and stroll from the plaza into the old walled sector through a rather dramatic gate. There we discovered a stunning hilltop town, replete with quiet, cobbled lanes that meandered through a maze of wistful patios, narrow streets, large brick archways, all the way up to the Alcázar, where vines and bougainvillea climbed the raw castle walls that stood as a witness to a remote and belligerent past.

There were many bars, seemingly ordained by God to take the weight off our pins. In one of them, selected at random, Sandro ordered a glass of wine, Kate a cup of tea and I a cold beer. The wine and beer came with a miniature pizza on top. Some sort of seal to keep the insects out? Or was it that one should not drink without eating?

'Why is it,' asked Kate, replacing her cup in its saucer, 'that no one in continental Europe knows how to make a cup of tea?' She pulled the bag out of the cup. 'Liptons? They are supposed to be good. Bringing the water to the boil might also have helped.'

'It's nearly five o'clock. Surely you should have considered a beer?'

'And have the car stop when I need it to? With your mad friend at the wheel?'

She had a point. Meanwhile, my mad friend was already beginning to show signs of impatience.

'We need to get back on the road if we are to find a hotel in Cádiz.'

'We could stay here, couldn't we? That would give us plenty of time to find a hotel in Cádiz. That guest house we all noticed, *El Cobijo de Vejer*, it looked charming.'

I expected Sandro to resist, but I was wrong.

'Good idea,' he said. 'This is as fine a place as I ever saw outside Italy. Yes, let's stay.'

None of us needed further persuasion and we were rewarded with *El Cobijo*, a 19th-century house ranged around a pretty courtyard, a few yards from the church. It occupied a picturesque corner of a quiet alley on Vejer's hill. Probably still does.

The place was in the *moresco* style, the rooms comfortable and quiet. Jesús and his wife Isabel - our hosts - were friendly, their prices not too terrifying, and Kate, Sandro and I were soon on the hotel's lovely roof terrace, admiring a wonderful view over a whitewashed town. We could see all the way to *Sahara los Atunes*. Bliss upon joy, a fresh breeze had found its way from paradise and cooled our superheated cheeks.

'This being Spain, the tourist attractions will be open well into the evening. All Vejer is in walking distance. As for supper, only the tourist restaurants will open before nine or ten this evening,' Sandro warned us solemnly.

'We could see if the Alcázar is open?' said Kate.

'It's always open. Lizards and buzzards get in free.' teased Sandro. 'No human has lived there for five hundred years!' He had a point. The town was dominated by its ruins.

The vast grey 'castle' had once been a great mosque, dating back to the 10th or 11th centuries. Some of Vejer's houses had been built directly into its walls. We found a well, hidden in a corner, just where its façade stood intact. Vejer is a fusion between the distant past and the-not-so-very-long-ago. We loved the ancient windmill, proud in its glorious setting. So too, the colourful and inviting boutiques and shops, bars and restaurants.

'Gastronomy must be in the corporation charter,' I suggested. 'It's obvious that food is taken seriously here. Let's give the tapas bars a miss. We need somewhere with something finer on offer. You must have seen how many excellent looking butchers and grocers we passed? Food must be this town's great secret.'

'Sound thinking, boyo,' said my hungry little sister.

We happily pottered about in this enchanted place for an hour or so we found a restaurant that appealed to the three of us.

Roman, Saracen, Sephardim, Berber and Gaelic cooks have left their marks on the tables of the South of Spain, just as they have in Sicily. In Andalusia, food has to begin its journey to the table in the mountains or in the sea. It draws its recipes from tradition, folklore, grandmothers and *duennas*. These are the 'godparents' of its culinary magic and the results range from spicy dishes that napalm the palate to chilled soups, where ice cubes float in a manner suggestive of the Arctic.

'Did you know,' said Kate between mouthfuls of the *gazpachuelo* we shared, 'that our national dish - fish and chips - was invented here?'

'Really?' I mumbled, as I stirred the shellfish and shrimps into the fragrant stock in front of me. It had been thickened with white of egg and diced potatoes.

'Yes, really. That's why I've ordered the *pescaito frito*. Those unfortunate Spanish Jews who were evicted in the 16th century brought it over to us in England. It is a Shabbat dish. Sephardim eat it after attending their synagogue on Friday night or on Saturday. They may not cook on the Sabbath.[145] They buy it from Christian kiosks in the market places, where it's served in paper, just as it is at home.'

'So what did you order? Cod? Haddock? Dogfish?'

'Dogfish? I think not. I'm having the sole. Coated in the purest flour, *a la andalusa*, and fried in olive oil from Jaén. Yes, and with chips.'

---

[145] The Sabbath starts at sundown on Friday and ends with the appearance of three stars on Saturday night.

'A curious choice so far from home?'

'Think of it as a tribute to an old friend. So what did you order?'

'*Perdiz*,' said Sandro. 'Partridge. Casseroled with beans. Garnished with hard-boiled eggs.'

'Sounds yummy. And you?'

'I thought I'd try the *riñones al jerez*. Kidneys, sautéd with garlic and onions, flour and paprika and finished with sherry. Brilliant.'

It was indeed a first-rate supper, steeped as it was the richest savours of Greater Araby. A 'sufficiency' of Rioja ensured we would sleep well that night.

We spent two nights of self-indulgence in Vejer. On both mornings, our batteries were recharged by a cooked breakfast.[146] All very English.

Also very English was the difficulty of getting on the road again. Kate had the map and was readying herself for Cádiz.

'I mean to visit the exact location of the Battle of Trafalgar,' she declared.

'Quite impossible,' said Sandro. 'It's out at sea. I suppose we might hire a rowing boat?'

'The battle was fought close to the shore,' said Kate. How she hated even the most trivial deviation from historical fact. 'We needn't even get our feet wet.'

Soon we were in a pleasant little café and had ordered coffee. I knew a little of the life of Horatio, Viscount Nelson. Inevitably, really. I had admired his swords, tunic and medals, preserved in a little museum deep inside Lloyd's of London. Sandro appeared to be happy to be included in Kate's plans.

'Forgive me, but not being one of your countrymen I know little of your little pocket admiral,' he admitted.

---

[146] The Spanish appreciate a cooked breakfast, just as we do.

'Well, I can tell you a little about how he started out,' I said. Bravely in the circumstances.

'Don't listen, Sandro. He'll make it up as he goes along,' said Kate, the family historian.

'Go on Jeremy. Pay no attention to your sister. Tell me all.'

'Very well, here I go. Block your ears, Kate.' She duly pretended not to listen. 'Sandro, Nelson was and is Great Britain's greatest naval hero. He defeated the French, Spanish and Danish fleets and had enough energy left over to grapple with Emma Hamilton on his days off. He was not tall, but was still a greater man than Napoleon.'

'At most by two inches. God preserve us,' said Kate, unable let me tell the story my way. 'Here we go. Ignore him, Sandro.'

'I'll start at the beginning,' I said, overriding Kate's objections. 'He was born in a little Norfolk town, Burnham Market, the sixth son of the Reverend Edmund Nelson and his incubator of a wife. While still a boy, he ran away to join the fishing fleet in Lowestoft, where he learned all there was to know – bawdy shanties, how to stay standing when drunk, how to kill a polar bear and not how not to pay for beer in Calais.'

'Calais?' Sandro was surprised.

'The fleet liked to put into Calais. It had its distractions.'

'Distractions?'

'More even than Portsmouth. Nelson said, rather later, that his experience with a 'lady of leisure' had 'worse consequences than taking a musket ball in the arm'.'

Sandro laughed but Kate rolled her eyes.

'Over a mug of ale in Great Yarmouth he denounced the Rebel War in the United Colonies. The king was not impressed, he said. 'He, Nelson, was ready to see 'George Washington, Thomas Jefferson, Benjamin

Franklin, John Adams and Old Tom Cobbley hanged from the yard arm of HMS Incontinent'.'

'When the Americans were joined by the French, the Spanish and the Dutch, Nelson enlisted.

> Nothing would please me more than to catch
> sight of their ships ablaze on the high seas.

'Reports of this taproom braggadocio reached someone with scrambled egg on his bicorn, who took a chance on him. It was a shrewd move. He proved an exceptional midshipman[147] and was soon invited to captain his first frigate, *The Boreas*.

'Soon enough, Horatio Nelson found himself on the island of Nevis in the West Indies. That was where he met Frances Nisbet, a judge's daughter. Fanny was an heiress, true, but duller than a rainy day in Burnham Market. Nelson married her, nonetheless. Nelson asked Prince William Henry, who happened to be in the Caribbean at the time, to give the bride away, and naval officers presented him with a silver watch.

Thomas Pringle, his friend and colleague, declared the navy to be in peril of losing its 'greatest ornament. A wife just gets in the way'.

Prince William Henry, however, said he was all for it. 'I wish him well and happy and that he repents not the step he has taken.'

Once his posting was completed, Nelson returned to England. He directed Frances to follow on later.

'Being used to the warmth and luxuries of life in the West Indies, she would find life in England a challenge. When Nelson returned to sea, he wrote regularly and affectionately to his poor wife and, in one of her replies, she disclosed the sad news that the doctors had discovered that she could not have children.

---

[147] Midshipman: the lowest grade of officer, below sub lieutenant. At the time it was offered to gentlemen as they joined up.

'It was now a couple of decades since the Americans had begun to fight the English for their most noble cause, the pursuit of wealth.

'With time, like most of us, Nelson aged. The lean and agile youngster had become white haired, haggard and, after the Navy's attack on Santa Cruz in Tenerife, in chronic pain from the loss of his right arm.

'Even so, he and Fanny still appeared happy together. Whenever he had shore leave, she nursed him devotedly. They bought a home together in Roundwood,[148] near Ipswich, and Fanny would divide her time between Suffolk and Bath. Then, that same year, came good news. France declared war on Britain and Nelson set off for Portsmouth to find a ship.

'In the harbour, some French traders were still preparing to make sail for their homeland. Nelson claimed he could hear the dockside ladies encouraging the French tars.

"A l'eau, c'est l'heure!" they cried.'[149]

'For God's sake,' said Kate, either in despair or in pain.

'Nelson was back in the thick of it. His men thought the world of him; he was obviously courageous and competent, but was he officer material of the most senior kind? The Admiralty found him uncouth and rather uncompromisingly heterosexual. He was still commanding the worm-eaten *Boreas* in 1797, when he demonstrated skill and nerve by steering directly into two Spanish galleons in the Battle of Cape St. Vincent.

'The Spanish were so amazed they let Nelson crash his ship between theirs and fire a cannonade from

---

[148] His country home Roundwood House, was situated in what is today east Ipswich. A philistine council agreed to its demolition in 1967. All that is left today of the house is in St John's Primary School, in Victory Road. A plaque there reads 'the brickwork to which this panel is secured was taken from Roundwood House which occupied this site from 1700 until its demolition in 1967. It was owned by Horatio Nelson between 1795 to 1800.'

[149] *To the sea, it is time:* an approximate translation.

either side. The battle was won and his reckless seamanship was thought a terrific example of British brio. Commander Nelson was made a Rear Admiral.'

Kate was getting restless.

'Nelson was not an effete English gentleman, Jeremy. You know that. The man you're describing didn't call on his opponent to leave the pub and settle the matter in a traditional fashion,' she said. 'Nelson was the sort of man who fells whoever disagrees with him with a barstool before his victim has even realised he is in danger.'

'Well, Kate, if Nelson didn't always bow low and lower his hat to his feet, England liked the fact that he never ducked a scrap. The Admiralty reluctantly concluded they had better look after 'this Nelson chap' and stop him from losing any more limbs, but this brief essay in kindness was indirectly curtailed by Napoleon. Nelson received orders to take a few ships to Aboukir Bay and rid Egypt of the French.

"I can beat them with one arm tied behind my back,' the admiral declared. His crew knew Nelson's right hand was in a surgeon's bucket somewhere in the Canaries and everyone laughed at his macabre jest.

'At sunset, Nelson ordered his fleet to attack. He wrote in his journal, if I have it right, that

> we arrived in the early evening in the bay. The Frenchies were completely unaware we were there. I could hear them having wild Parties on their Ships and that there were Women on board. I had to smile - we had caught those Revolutionaries with their Bell Bottoms down.
>
> I signalled to the other Ships in the Fleet that 'Gentlemen! We have Bonaparte's Balls in our Hands'. If Boney's Fleet can be destroyed, the Corsican Adventurer will have to stay out here and fry his Arse in the Desert.

'The Rear-Admiral pounded the hapless French. One of their ships blew up. Unluckily, the French Vice Admiral François-Paul 'Stumpy' Brueys d'Aigalliers was still on board, waving his arms, desperately urging the boys on his burning decks to keep firing.

'The British crews cheered and taunted the French with the popular drinking song 'You're Not Singing Now', fighting on until the enemy had surrendered or scuttled its own ships and, on learning of the victory, the king ordered the admiral to be elevated Baron Nelson of the Nile, who celebrated by heading off to Sicily for some urgent infidelity. He had heard that the British Ambassador to the Two Sicilies's wife there was the hottest totty our side of the Mediterranean. Her name was Emma Hamilton.[150]

'Despite the admiral's battered body, Emma Hamilton fell for the naval hero. Even more remarkably, she persuaded her husband William Hamilton to stay in his library, or greenhouse, or somewhere, while she right royally entertained Nelson. She wrote to her friend Lady Jersey that

> he arrived in my bedroom wearing only his admiral's hat. Nelson looked magnificent, all five foot of him as he stood to attention at the edge of my bed like a proud 100 gun Ship-of-The-Line. I beckoned him and asked him to show his legendary Nelson touch as he caressed my bare body. When that moment came of mutual happiness, it was like a broadside aimed at the centre of my heart.

'Tales of Nelson's sexual vigour got back to London where some wondered if it was wise to leave him in command of the Mediterranean Fleet. They were overruled, and Nelson and Emma were left in peace to pursue a life of happy cupidity.

---

[150] I make no claim to the lofty tone of an academic.

'Eventually Nelson (with Emma and her cuckolded husband) returned to London to receive a hero's welcome.

'The Admiralty now ordered the Hero of the Nile to deal with the Danish in Copenhagen, as second in command to the Admiral of the Fleet. The action started badly. Some English sailors jumped ship, to be picked off by Danish snipers. Several British ships ran aground and, at the height of the battle, Admiral Parker signalled Nelson to withdraw. Nelson somehow missed the message.

I have but one eye. That gives me the right to
be blind half the time.

'In the end the Danes threw in the towel and Nelson had won again. Our admiral returned to Britain in 1801 to have his barony upgraded to a viscountcy, but Fanny objected to having to share what was left of Nelson with 'that brazen floozy Emma Hamilton'.

The strategy failed. Nelson left Fanny on Christmas Day, no less, after she had unwisely knitted him a jumper with two sleeves. Upset and angry, Nelson said he wanted to fire her from a cannon. Their marriage was over.

'In 1802, Britain and France signed a peace treaty. Nelson's purpose seemed over. Thinking the armistice a betrayal he decamped to Taormina, Sicily, where he lived openly with Emma and William Hamilton. It was an odd arrangement but by now, Nelson was exempt from petty public morality. It all became a little less scandalous when Hamilton inexplicably died, a year later.'

I felt I had dealt with the story well enough but Kate told Sandro that everything I had said was an historical farrago and he was to ignore it all. I was a little miffed. I had told the preamble to the Battle of Trafalgar as best I could.

We were heading for Cádiz, which sits on a narrow spit of land, hemmed in by the Atlantic Ocean. Sandro drove our car at an eye-watering speed through the wide avenues and modern buildings of suburban Cádiz, through the city walls, into the *Casco Antiguo*, the Old Town. Inside it, its *barrios* - or quarters - consisted of narrow winding alleys, interrupted with large plazas, forcing Sandro to reduce his speed to a bumpy trundle. The old town was rather smaller than I had expected. This part of Cádiz had buildings which, due to their age and historical importance, were not suitable for what modernists call 'urban renewal'. Just as should be the case in every European city.

Cádiz may even be the oldest continuously inhabited city in Western Europe. Archaeological remains go back 3,100 years, making it half-a-millennium older than Rome. A few Phoenician numismatic inscriptions remain. They suggest that they knew Cádiz as a *Gadir* or *Agadir*, meaning 'wall', 'compound', or (by metonymy) 'stronghold'. Indeed, the Berbers still call Cádiz the *agadir*.

Sandro had booked us into the *Senator Hotel*, right in the heart of that curious city. The cathedral soared into a cloudless sky, minutes from the hotel door and, beyond that, was La Caleta beach and then, Cape Trafalgar itself. A good man that Sandro.

Kate seemed spellbound by the vista. In her mind's eye, Villeneuve's Franco-Spanish navy was at anchor before her, while that buccaneer brigand Nelson was bringing his fleet to fight the most important battle in the annals of European naval warfare.[151]

---

[151] There have been countless great sea-battles. The Battle of Leyte Gulf between Imperial Japan and the Allies in the waters around the Philippine islands of Leyte, Samar, and Luzon was the largest naval battle in history. On September 11, 1814, a US squadron under Thomas Macdonogh defeated the British under George Downie on Lake Champlain. In Europe, on September 2, 31 BC, Octavian decisively defeated Antony and Cleopatra at Actium. In 1263 a Venetian fleet of 38 ships under Gilberto Dandolo defeated a joint Byzantine-Genoese fleet of 48 ships off the Peloponnese coast at Settepozzi, and in July and

Kate's eyes were moist, her breath was quickening. She remembered how she had once had defied the laws of space and time to find herself in the back of Notre Dame in Paris as a witness to the bizarre coronation, when her heroic emperor had crowned himself. It was little wonder she was so emotional.

Now she was using her time machine to visit Cádiz during the Revolutionary Wars, when it had been blockaded by the British. She already knew every street in the town. This was not her first visit. That had been in 1802, at the Peace of Amiens. She had witnessed our renewed efforts in 1803, and again at the outbreak of the Peninsular War in 1808. She had seen stubborn Cádiz hold out against the invading French and their commander Joseph Bonaparte, before it became the seat of Spain's military high command and Cortes.[152] The liberal Spanish Constitution of 1812 was proclaimed here. Kate's Tardis had let her watch the citizens rebel in 1820 and secure the constitution's reinstatement. She knew that when Ferdinand VII was imprisoned in Cádiz, it had taken nothing less than an intervention by Louis XVIII to secure his release - the 1823 Battle of Trocadero - and suppress its ill-judged liberalism.

As for the match on the boating lake of Cape Trafalgar in 1805, she relived it when she slept if, that is, she wasn't already engaged on the playing fields of Eton - by which I mean, of course, the Battle of Waterloo.

Kate and I planned a trip to the cathedral, while Sandro declared he would attempt his own adventure on the beach. Cádiz's baroque, rococo and classical cathedral is a triumphal eighteenth century celebration of Spain's trade with the Americas. The earlier basilica, dedicated to the Holy Cross, proved too small to

---

August 1588, Sir Francis Drake defeated the Spanish Armada off southern England.
[152] Parliament.

accommodate the port's burgeoning population. Building the new one began in 1722, only to finish a century later. Its architects changed, died or were poached by other projects.

The cathedral's flamboyant façade has an intriguing colour palette, the lower half a dark brown, the top in cream. The whole ensemble is crowned with a yellow dome.

Everyone always wants the latest style and in this one building every style of the post-gothic world competes for the joy and elevation of the faithful. To either side, its towers look like baroque lighthouses. Perhaps, in some metaphysical way, they are. I wanted to take the ramp to the top of its Levante Tower to see Cádiz from above but Kate doesn't do heights. I had to park my high-flying ambitions.

Inside, directly beneath the dome, the high altar is a miniature temple in its own right. Its tabernacle rises twenty feet from the altar's surface. In the rococo style it somehow recalls the circular temples of the classical world.

A spectacular baluster stair leads from the sanctuary, flies up around the walls to lead the archbishop up to an extraordinary gilded, canopied pulpit. By way of contrast, the choir is almost mediaeval. Pedro Cornejo carved it from Spanish oak, most likely. Kate thought it was odd that in a city and cathedral that sparkled with New World gold and silver, it should be in plain wood. At its centre stands a stern, unadorned chair for the archbishop to preside over his clerics, as in a chapter house.

The Latin word for a chair with arms is *cathedra*, once reserved for an emperor in his palace or basilica. Back in the fourth century, the Church's earliest bishops highjacked the idea. They sat in them themselves.

Above them, overlooking the *scola cantorum*, ranged cherubim play musical instruments of every kind - a mute and endless oratorio, while below them, in a huge undercroft, we learned we were below sea level and the Atlantic was a few short yards away, its surface over our heads.

Most crypts are small with low ceilings, but not in Cádiz. This one was seriously large. It had no obvious means of supporting what was going on above. It contained, however, a museum and the mortal remains of the usual suspects, mostly bishops, but also those of Manuel de Falla, the composer.

The museum brims with gold and silver chalices, sacred vessels that powerfully attest to the immense amounts of precious metal that poured into Cádiz from the looted treasuries of the Incas, the Aztecs and the Mayans. The glitter there represents plunder on an industrial scale.

Of course, the stolen metal had been remodelled with infinitely noble propose. Particularly striking was a vicious thorn, taken from that cruel 'crown' that our Lord was made to wear and set into a solid gold circlet, held aloft by joyful gilded cherubim.

On resuming fresh, less sepulchral, air in the cathedral square, there was (of course) a restaurant-cum-bar and, since we had been so earnest, we needed to recover. The weather was perfect, possibly too much so. It had reached some 35°. We pictured Sandro stretched out, his skin glowing with Protection Factor No 5, caressed by a cooling breeze, or better. Well, if you can't beat them, join them. A few minutes later we had retrieved our cozzies and were headed for La Caleta. Cádiz is home to some very fine beaches. Playa La Caleta may be the best of them. Two ancient fortresses, the Castillo de Santa Catalina and the Castillo de San Sebastián serve it as bookends.

Being so close to the centre of town, it was inevitable that the shore was crowded and busy. The transparent water proclaimed its cleanliness. The beach is not huge but even so it boasts a goodly number of expensive bars, *chiringuitos*, worrying showers, filthy loos, muscular lifeguards, the scantily clad and all the other trappings of a modern idyll. Naturally enough, we discovered Sandro surrounded by a bevy of secretaries taking a three hour siesta away from the bustle of the streets. He pretended to be pleased to see us.

'Well, out with it,' he said by way of a greeting. 'Have you been forgiven?'

'You obviously have,' replied my sister. 'Looks to me as if you've died and gone to heaven.'

'Reports of my death have been greatly exaggerated,' he said, misquoting Mark Twain, just as we all do.

'A glass of holy water should return us all to life,' I suggested in my Irish way.

The nearest dispensary of the precious elixir was about twenty feet away. No one could be in a better temper than me. Lotus eating is addictive, as Homer had long ago revealed. To think I was being slowly turned a chestnut brown by the ultry sultry powers of the Creator and being paid for it! True, somewhere in the back of my mind a thin strand of conscience would occasionally throw off its torpor and remind me that I was here to learn about the Spanish way of life.

I remembered, all the time, that when I had lived in Rome I had begun to bring my Italian from proficient to fluent by watching films in Italian that I had already seen in English. The playground method, true, not the classroom one, but it worked then and it would work again.

Huge picture-palaces were everywhere, but the choice of viewing was quite mad. Two were not far from our hotel. One was showing Visconti's *The*

Damned, a pornographic frolic set in Nazi Germany, the other Fausta Borja's *Erotic Adventures of Alice in Wonderland*. Perhaps it was not surprising that Kate had not the faintest urge to visit a cinema. Sandro, smiling like Jack Nicholson, told us he preferred the real thing.

Over a coffee we concluded that Franco's death had unleashed some long pent up frustrations. Spain's recent liberty had provoked an unbuttoning that verged on the grotesque. The whole nation was on speed, pornography was everywhere, its churches standing empty. The mood in the country reminded me of the King's Road, ten years before, just after the general availability of The Pill had loosened English stays and turned adolescence from an ordeal into the most joyous of times and for the first time in the history of the world.

At breakfast the next day, Sandro did not join us. One of those secretaries must have taken him home to see her etchings. He reappeared around midday and, being keen to avoid packdrill, we asked no questions.

On the rooftop terrace of *The Senator*, overlooking Cape Trafalgar, I asked Kate about the battle. I felt her narration might provide us with a topical monologue. I also knew her account would be closer to the truth.

Sandro and I settled back in our recliners. In the intense heat we looked over the narrow stretch of blue that divides Europe from Africa and sipped at our frosted beer glasses.

It was easy to picture the confrontation of sixty huge men-o'-war - the English ships each with more than five hundred souls on board, some of the French ones with closer to a thousand. I was ready to hear the closing bars of Admiral Nelson's derring-do.[153]

'You told Sandro about his rise to fame', she replied, allowing a bored tone to infuse her voice. 'He needs to know why he is England's greatest hero. You

---

[153] HMS Victory, Britain's largest ship, had 700 hands on board during the battle.

left off where Nelson's future was passing him like 'a Ship-of-the-Line in the night'. Sandro, Nelson was far more than a great sailor, and it was not just Emma Hamilton who loved him. His men did too. His taste for wry amusement endeared him to the common man. It served him well and he exploited it for all it was worth.

> I could not tread these perilous paths in safety,
> if I did not keep a saving sense of humour,

she quoted effortlessly, if avoiding the temptation to put on a Norfolk accent.

Kate is such an eloquent Bonapartist, even if her European perspective played a familiar tune in a different key, I allowed my eyes to close. An image of Cape Trafalgar, just over the parapet, firmly transferred from my retina to my mind.

'By 1805, (she continued), Nelson was already a national hero, the ultimate naval commander. With every battle he resolved a major strategic impasse. His long list of successes meant that even the Admiralty considered him the only British officer able to outmanoeuvre Bonaparte's admirals. Nor, apparently, did Napoleon disagree - he kept a bust of Nelson in his Parisian *amirauté*.

'Nelson took the art of war at sea to a new height. He planned nothing less than to destroy Napoleon's war machine and reward England's twenty-two year long struggle with a great victory over Revolutionary and Napoleonic France. He had adopted Admiral Sir John Jervis's system of command[154] and was finally senior enough to reveal and deploy that genius for vision and action he had demonstrated under Admiral Lord Hood. Nelson could combine a flair for strategy with exemplary management. Somehow he knew that invasion by France

---

[154] The tough old sea lord who had taught him how to keep a fleet efficient.

378

was not Britain's greatest threat - far more devastating would have been the loss of her nascent trading empire. International trade was conducted by ship, and victory over the French would give Britain a leading role *in the world* for at least a century.

'When in 1793 Spain protested the execution of Louis XVI, an unabashed Robespierre declared war on her. Portugal and Spain signed a treaty of mutual defence against the *sans culottes*. Unfortunately, in 1796, Spain's Prime Minister, Manuel Godoy, allied with France to declare war on the United Kingdom.[155] As a result, Spain's great navy fell under Republican France's command and, by 1804, the Franco-Spanish fleet was ready to challenge Britain's maritime supremacy.

'Napoleon's projected invasion of Britain still lacked the means of ferrying a *grande armée* across the channel without having to face the Royal Navy, so the reduction of the latter was a precondition to invasion. In England, a panicky Admiralty awarded *HMS Victory* to Admiral Lord Nelson. Unfortunately, she was still undergoing extensive refitting in dry dock, in Portsmouth, where she had put in after the 1803 Peace of Amiens. The French First Republic was replaced by the First Empire in 1804, but Britain remained on the defensive.

'The Sea Lords had long expected the French Navy to make the first move, but in the spring of 1805, Vice-Admiral Pierre-Charles Villeneuve, Commander of the Franco-Spanish fleet, was in Toulon where he received orders from Paris to break out into the

---

[155] Manuel Godoy y Álvarez de Faria, Prince of Peace, was Prime Minister of Spain from 1792 to 1797 and from 1801 to 1808. He had many titles, including *Príncipe de la Paz* by which he was widely known. He came to power when still young as the favourite of the King and Queen and, despite many disasters, he stayed in power. Many Spanish leaders blamed Godoy for the disastrous war with Britain that cut off Spain's Empire and ruined its finances. The prince is one of only two people in history (the other being Baldomero Espartero) to have held the title of 'Prince' in the Kingdom of Spain, other than the heirs-apparent.

Atlantic and draw the English into the middle of nowhere.

'The emperor wanted to keep the British fleet busy, out of harm's way and far from the Channel. Under Admiral Collingwood the British chased the French admiral all the way to the West Indies.

'By September, Villeneuve's fleet had new orders. It recrossed the ocean, putting into Cádiz. From there, Villeneuve could control access to the Mediterranean, compromising Britain's lucrative trade with Italy, the Levant, with North Africa and with Russia.

'The *Victory* was at last refitted. Nelson took her through the Bay of Biscay to join the British fleet off Cádiz - at the sharp end of 'our sea',[156] as the Romans had liked to call it. When he explained how his battle plan was pivotal he alarmed, thrilled and electrified his men by turns. If and when the enemy put again to sea, the Royal Navy would annihilate it. Britain, not Napoleon, nor even Neptune would rule the waves.

'News of Nelson's imminent arrival must have rattled Admiral Villeneuve, but the Frenchman believed his combined fleet of thirty-three ships of the line, versus twenty-seven flying the White Ensign, was sure to gain the day if only by force of numbers.

'He was wrong. Both Napoleon and Nelson had ordered or anticipated Villeneuve's every move. Neither needed a crystal ball to know what would happen next.

'Napoleon decided to replace Poor old Villeneuve with François Étienne de Rosily-Mesros. This man was to bring his predecessor back to Paris to account for his dire performance. His prospects were not good. The emperor had written to his Minister of Marine that 'Villeneuve does not possess the strength of character to command a frigate. He lacks determination and has no moral courage.'

---

[156] *Mare nostrum.*

'When Villeneuve learned of Étienne's mission, he gave the order to make sail on October 18, well before his replacement could arrive. Even so, I'm afraid he was a little disorganised and his inexperienced crews took two days to get his thirty-three ships out of port in any sort of order.

'On October 21, 1805, Villeneuve's eyeglass revealed the British fleet. He immediately turned back, meaning to put into harbour. Too late. He was intercepted by Nelson, off Cape Trafalgar. Planning a head-on approach,' Kate resumed, 'Nelson had divided his warships into two columns, an inverted 'V', a risky ploy as it exposed the unarmed bows of the flagship and the ships of the line that followed. Nelson knew, of course, that these were narrow targets and ships' cannons were notoriously inaccurate. As soon as Nelson saw the Franco-Spanish fleet he ordered his fleet to sail straight at them.'

England expects that every Man shall do his Duty

Leading from the front, Nelson's flagship, *Victory*, crossed the line of the Franco-Spanish fleet to engage the enemy.

'Trafalgar was never going to be any ordinary battle,' said Kate, settling into her yarn. 'The battle on October 21, 1805, transcended any prosaic counting of ships and men, the accountant's mundane method of predicting victory or defeat. This, however, would be a battle between philosophies, the wills of entire peoples, a test of that elusive magic that defines nationhood. It would neutralise the greatest threat to British security that we had faced since we were conquered by the Romans in 55 AD, the Normans in 1066 and the Dutch in 1688.

'On the horizon swelled ballooning clouds. Nelson had seen that a storm was brewing and that time was running out. The enemy would have to be swiftly dispatched.

'Nelson's vessels drew up on *The Victory*'s stern. Admiral Lord Nelson walked around her decks, talking and laughing easily with officers and men alike. Nelson was not in armour, unlike his French and Spanish counterparts. Instead, he had had his medals and chivalric orders reproduced by an embroiderer. The Admiral of the Fleet looked the business but was in fact in comfortable clothes.

'The British sailors had even had time to eat a good meal in preparation for the battle. Nelson, while his salts and tars tucked into bacon and eggs, had to wait for Villeneuve to show his flag.[157] He needed to know which ship to strike.

'Their enemy may not have had such healthy appetites. Villeneuve hoisted his colours and *Victory* led the British fleet onto the enemy line, on the receiving end of heavy fire from the Franco-Spanish, but was unable to reply.

'Round shot came smashing through the flimsy bow, killing and wounding many. John Scott, for example - Nelson's Public Secretary - was standing on the quarter deck, talking with Captain Thomas Hardy, when he was cut in two. At the same time, the wheel was smashed and a double-headed shot scythed down a file of eight marines on the poop. Nelson casually reassured Hardy that 'this is too warm work to last for long'.

'Nelson and Hardy still paced up and down on their chosen ground, the starboard side of the quarterdeck, while lethal oak splinters flew around them like bullets. One of them tore the buckle off Hardy's shoe.

'Nelson continued to stroll with Hardy, even though the captain of the *Redoutable* was trying to clear

---

[157] Orders to other ships were given with flags, which is why the commanding vessel is called a flagship.

Victory's upper deck with musket ball and grenades. Before the Victory could even open fire, fifty British hands were already dead or wounded. The enemy's concave line allowed *Victory* to sail hard into the morass. Shrouded in smoke from the canons, the ship ran right under the stern of the French flagship, the *Bucentaure*, shortly after noon. Only then did she fire such a double-shotted broadside that the enemy vessel visibly shuddered, leaving it rudderless. Two hundred of the enemy were instantly killed or wounded and Admiral Villeneuve found himself the only man left on his quarter deck. Floundering, the enemy was now at the mercy of Admiral Cuthbert Collingwood's column, while Nelson had the relatively simple task of wiping out the rest of the Franco-Spanish fleet in the remaining hours of daylight.

'The *Redoutable* blocked Victory's way through the enemy line, leaving Nelson stuck on a ship that was simultaneously fighting three opponents in the middle of the combined fleet. Even so, he knew he had delivered the fatal punch. Villeneuve was trapped on board his crippled ship. The Franco-Spanish centre was in chaos, lacking the leadership it needed to coordinate an irresistible British thrust. Our gunners steadily wore down the enemy and the Franco-Spanish force began to teeter. Stamina was the key. For three more hours, Nelson's plan was faultlessly executed, breaking every supposedly inviolable rule of tactics, treating an enemy spoiling for a fight as one running away, swapping speed for mass and precision for weight. Conventional commentators at the outset would have offered him impossible odds but they were dramatically shortening.

'When battle began, the first British ships were heavily outnumbered but, as had happened in 1588 with the Armada, pace and flexibility won the day. When the front line weakened the second wave came in to administer a *coup de grace*. Nelson's enemy at the Battle of

Trafalgar had more ships and twice as many guns. There were more than a thousand deaths and injuries and even the slightest wound proved fatal.

'*Victory* herself was the target of enemy snipers and, at around 1.15 pm, Nelson himself fell to a musket ball. A Spanish marksman, high in a crow's nest, had shot the admiral though the collar bone deep into his chest. The round severed an artery in his lung and lodged in his spine. The admiral still lived but it was obvious that the wound was mortal.

'Hardy had his chief carried below. William Beatty was hard at work on the growing list of casualties. He was a skilled surgeon but faced a daunting challenge, as did his patients. The only anaesthetic was rum. His patients were told to hold a musket ball between their front teeth. If it fell, Beatty moved on to the next. By the time Nelson got the news that the French and Spanish were in flight he was close to death.

'A crowd of sailors gathered around the wounded admiral to witness his end. His journey to the next world would take about three hours. Outside, the struggle with the *Redoutable* had reached a crescendo. The French repeatedly tried to board the *Victory*, only to be driven back by cannon and musket fire.

'At 2.30 pm Hardy returned below to report to Nelson that a dozen or so of the enemy fleet were taken, and that not one British ship had surrendered. Hardy could not linger as the leading enemy squadron was trying to rejoin the battle but was outfoxed by Edward Codrington's brilliantly handled *Orion*, *Minotaur* and *Spartiate*.

'After horrific bloodshed on the *Redoutable*, her captain had finally put up the white flag. At 2.30, so did Villeneuve on the *Bucentaur*. Nelson's genius, the flexibility of the Royal Navy and the failure of the Franco-Spanish leading squadron to come to his aid had doomed the Frenchmen.

384

'Hardy returned to Nelson's bedside at 3.30 pm to confirm a glorious victory.

"Weigh anchor, Hardy. Weigh anchor and find shelter!' commanded the wounded man as the rising sea told him of an impending storm.

"You are dying, Sir.'

"*Kismet*, Hardy.'[158]

'Hardy knelt and kissed him, as Nelson struggled to breathe, infrequently repeating the phrase: 'Thank God I have done my duty.' Unable to contain his grief, Hardy went back to the upper deck, hoping to bury his feelings in the fight.

'Nelson died shortly before 4.30 pm, but he went to his Maker knowing he had won. His transition was attended by his officers, all in tears, and by his chaplain, who had been vainly hoping to provide the old sinner with the password to paradise. His body wasn't thrown overboard like lesser casualties.

'Instead (despite some protests), his body was put in the lead-lined coffin the admiral had insisted should share his cabin. Spanish brandy filled the sad container which was then lashed to the mast. A humorous tar improvised a label which he attached to the barrel. *Fundador Nelsonio Vieja Riserva, 1805*. This tactless tribute was immediately removed.

'The triumphant fleet made sail for Portsmouth, to be met with joy and grief. The eighty-mile route of his catafalque, saw the admiral's mortal remains slowly borne to London in a stately sarcophagus designed but never used for Cardinal Wolsey. The road was lined with mourners, two or three deep every inch of the way. The progress was slow but never faltered. Thirty one hours later the admiral reached St Pauls and his obsequies had full military honours, the memorial service being conducted by the Bishop of London.

---

[158] Destiny (from the Arabic).

'Victory had guaranteed Britain's control of the oceans, granting her the basis of her commercial power, certainly not dimmed until the Great War. It can be argued that it did not evaporate until 1948 and the dissolution of the Indian Empire.

'His estranged widow Fanny sent her condolences and a letter to the admiralty, confirming (or demanding) that all prize money owed to Nelson should go to her and not Emma Hamilton. The luckless Emma only received the blood-stained tunic her husband had worn on the fatal day.'[159]

*

Kate had concluded her sorry yarn. The admiral's death completed her account. It was not quite the end of the story, however, and I took up the theme a second time, directing the narrative at Sandro.

'You Italians are good at memorials but it took our bureaucrats a while to agree what sort of monument best suited Nelson's memory', I persisted. 'Some suggested that an erect Corinthian column with two large hemispheres at the base, possibly representing the southern and northern halves of the world, should be raised in London's Whitehall. Eventually, in 1840, an area nearby was cleared and renamed Trafalgar Square. The spheres were never built, and four bronze lions were cast, the metal coming from the captured brass bedsteads of French and Spanish officers, or so the wags declared. They were placed around the base.'

Kate put her glass down and got up. I refused the hint.

'Once finished, it was supposed to be topped with a statue of the admiral, but his pose had still to be decided. Many thought that Nelson should be shown looking through his telescope. That was not done, though Nelson stills looks towards France, the source

---

[159] It is now in the Lloyd's of London Museum.

of an early humiliation and a later triumph. Nelson now has to deal with a different type of manure everyday: pigeons have colonised his hat.'

Kate finally decided to leave us and headed for the stairs. I heard her say 'enough', as she departed.

I pressed on.

'According to Victor Hugo, filled as he was with splenetic Gallic irony, Nelson was just lucky in his battles. It was the French who gave the English admiral a sporting chance. He wrote that Napoleon had wanted to know if this 'man who beats me on water' might come across the channel to join the winning side. Hugo hinted that Emma Hamilton was a Bonapartist agent but had spoiled his plans by falling for the old sea dog.

'Officially Nelson died 'childless' which is why his trophies and pension went to Fanny. That was how the Law dealt with children out of wedlock back then. In reality, Nelson and Emma Hamilton had two daughters. The British government insisted this all be hushed up to avoid equipping gossips with scandalous assertions. In death, then, a sanitised Nelson became the perfect hero.

One of his drinking chums, Vice Admiral Charles Thompson, was awarded the credit for being the girls' father. The British press duly bought the story, reporting that Thompson had named 'his' elder girl Horatia in 'admiration' of Nelson.

'A hereditary pension was voted by parliament, £500 a year. Since the viscount had no male heirs, his noble title should have become extinct on his death. Parliament, however, passed 'a special remainder' to allow the 1801 barony 'of the Nile and of Hilborough in the County of Norfolk' to pass to Nelson's father and sisters and thence their male issue. Nelson's older brother, the Rev William Nelson was, in November 1805, created Earl Nelson and Viscount Merton 'of Trafalgar and of Merton in the County of Surrey'. He also inherited the dukedom of Bronté.

'By comparison, Marlborough got Blenheim and Wellington got Stratfield Saye. The inheritance dwindled in real value until 1974, when Prime Minister Wilson finally cancelled it. A sad and wholly unnecessary retrospective slight.'

So endeth the lesson. My sister had reappeared with a refilled glass.

'So, in the end, Napoleon came out of it rather better,' she stated, triumphantly. 'Little Horatia was confused as to her real parents and refused to believe Emma Hamilton was her mother, preferring to believe she was the daughter of a European princess. Those who met her were not deceived. She grew up to look almost exactly like her famous father, given that she was a girl.

'To the victor the spoils?' Sandro suggested. His English still amazed me.

'Britain took nineteen enemy ships as spoils of victory; the few that escaped fled to Carunna or Brest', Kate replied. 'Victory was at a cost. Probably fifty thousand men, overall, were involved in the battle. Some seventeen hundred British hands were killed or wounded. The enemy suffered far worse, losing six thousand. Twenty thousand prisoners were taken, and many of these were lost in the storm that followed the battle, as was Villeneuve's crippled flagship.'

'...and Napoleon was history?' asked Sandro. 'In 1805?'

'Not quite yet,' I said. 'but the *Battle of Trafalgar* saw the end of his plans to invade Britain. It confirmed little Englanders in their delusions of superiority to Europeans.

'For two centuries it would deny the country the use of the metric system that made the sciences so accessible to European school children, it eliminated the will to write a written constitution, one that explained the rights of man, not merely the wrongs, and it meant we would drive on the left for the rest of time. England would come to be the soldier who thinks the army is out of step.

'Admiral Collingwood brought Villeneuve to England, where the Frenchman was given leave to attend Lord Nelson's funeral. Released on parole, he stayed in the *Crown Inn* in Bishop's Waltham, in Hampshire. His surviving shipmates, two hundred of them, were put up nearby.

'The following day, Horatio Viscount Nelson's oldest friend, Admiral Collingwood, addressed the British fleet with an Order of Thanks.

> The ever to be lamented death of Vice Admiral Lord Viscount Nelson, Duke of Bronte, the Commander in Chief, who fell in the action of the 21st, in the arms of Victory, covered with glory, whose memory will ever be dear to the British Navy and the British Nation; whose zeal for the honour of his King, and for the interests of his Country, will forever be held up as a shining example of the British seaman.

'His powerful speech was printed and reprinted until almost every literate man in England had read it and every illiterate one had heard it. For many Britons, however, what should have been exultation was qualified by the loss of their hero.

'Nevertheless, *The Battle of Trafalgar* had crushed a deadly enemy and the threat of an invasion could at last be dismissed. Britain could relax, at least until Napoleon escaped from Elba. *Trafalgar* was the product of one man's obsessive genius and an unequalled commitment to his country.

'Later in 1805 the admiralty freed Villeneuve who returned to France. Once home he tried to go back into military service. His pleas fell on deaf ears. On April 22nd, his body was found at the *Hôtel de la Patrie* in

Rennes, with six stab wounds in the left lung and one in the heart. A verdict of suicide was recorded.'

Sandro raised an eyebrow. 'Nobody suspected that Napoleon had ordered his murder?'

'Not in Napoleonic France,' my sister replied. '*Cui bono?*'

*

It was time to move on; our next destination was Jerez de la Frontera but Sandro had made some excuse and vanished. We agreed to let him be. He was a big boy and could look after himself. Years before I had lost him in the crowds at Le Mans - I knew the form.[160] He was probably busy showing a Spanish maiden something she had never seen before.

Without him, however, we were obliged to take the train to Jerez. Sandro had the car, after all. It's less than thirty miles, but the train felt it necessary to stop en route every couple of miles to let us appreciate the beauty of *Al-Andalus*.

The driver paused, presumably to let us admire the view at the yachting haven of El Trocadero. It was where, in a battle in 1823, King Louis XVIII had secured the release from captivity of Ferdinand VII, King of Spain.

We didn't stop at Puerto Real - the Royal Portal - named after the 'Catholic Kings', Ferdinand and Isabella, but chuffed weakly through acres of flats whose marsh reeds were used to weave mats. We could have been overtaken by a peasant encumbered with a wheelbarrow. We then came to an unexplained halt, perhaps engineered to let us admire the lagoons and flocks of migratory birds, presumably *en route* to their second homes.

The railway company gave us the time we needed for an in-depth arboreal study of pine forests. Had we

---

[160] Details of our adventures at Le Mans are in *A Gap Year or Two*, by this author.

pen and paper we could have written a lengthy dissertation on Spanish marshland. Another on quarries. Considerably older and wiser, and well over an hour later, we limped into Jerez.

'You do know why this place is called Jerez de la Frontera?' Kate asked me as we struggled with our cases towards the historic centre of town.

'*Jerez* is the Spanish for sherry', I replied. 'They make it here. As for the frontier, I've no idea. We're some way from Portugal.'

'Then let me enlighten you. The current name of *Jerez* came by way of the Arabic شريش, or Sherish'[161] said a pleased sister. 'Descendants of the Phoenicians, deprived by their Prophet of the vinous product of their wonderful shiraz grapes, uprooted them and transplanted them here. They took exceptionally well. Aging and fortifying the base syrah liquor gave us sherry. As for '*frontera*', it refers to the border between the Moorish and Christian kingdoms of Spain, a dangerous place of frequent skirmishing between the more boisterous adherents of the two religions. After the Castilian conquest of Granada, in 1492, the town was no longer a frontier town, but its name proudly immortalises an old memory.'

'What a mine of information you are! Henceforward, my schooner of sherry will never taste the same.'

'Talking of which, we had better find a hotel before we down one. The *Feria de Caballo* starts tomorrow.'

'A pony festival?'

'Don't tell me you didn't notice the loose boxes? We are in for a treat! They breed Palomino horses here. The Spanish Royal family gave them their name, or

---

[161] The word is cognate with *sheikh*, or 'royal'. From this word we have 'checkmate', or 'kill the king'.

didn't you know? You need to put in for a refund on your college fees.'

After a good ten minutes walk we had arrived in a large square, *Plaza de las Angustias* to find ourselves outside the Itaca Hotel. Our bags were heavy, awkward and did not have those wonderful little wheels that they all do nowadays. I for one was ready for my first libation of the day. We would probably manage one inside the odd-looking building. It looked as though it had been a palace and a monastery at the same time.

Then, perhaps in Spain, that arrangement is not so strange. Was I learning and, by extension, earning my keep?

We were a little startled to discover a large marble statue of Jesus on a plinth in the reception area which, I thought, rather confirmed my brilliant theory about palace-monasteries.

Amazingly, a pair of single rooms were still available. Mine was barely big enough to pen a postcard on its little desk. There was a leaflet explaining that the *pension* had been, in the 19th century, the Convent of Maria Auxiliadora. The convent's awesome chapel, I read, was now a relaxing and exquisite breakfast area, *el bocado*.

It was not breakfast time, however, but it was sherry time and when in Rome...

The festival began early after a very good night's sleep. It was a cheerful event. The streets were awash with humanity as early as 9 am; girls dressed as Elena Montero and little swash-buckling Zorros steered their similarly clad fathers and mothers into the fray.

The *feria* would go on for ten days, twenty-four hours a day. We were glad we had remembered to pack our reserves of stamina. Mercifully, our rooms were quiet. Should we be in need of a little peace we could retreat to them.

Everywhere there were *casetas*, or stalls, possibly two hundred of them, where we could eat or drink or both, to our livers' alarm. Some even had live music, mostly in the shape of a guitarist and a dancer with castanets.

The streets began to glorify the famous Palomino ponies and Andalusian horses. True, some of them had a serious job to do, pulling carriages around the venue, and their drivers, *hidalgos* and *damas*, were haughtily dressed and as grand as grand can be. Some of the horses had to have been taught their business by the *corps du ballet*, or at Vienna's Spanish Riding School, and the show they put on had to be seen to be believed. You saw them dance and half-expected them to sing.

Kate had found a colourful frock from somewhere and had put a red gardenia in her hair. Not between her teeth, but she looked great and unexpectedly Spanish.

What a time we had, surrounded by hordes of happy people; ladies and daughters in flared dresses, and many of their consorts in bum-freezers... Their joy was infectious.

The restaurants that commanded a view of the pageant were understandably packed, while the kerbside *casetas* sold tapas, beer and, of course, sherry without the need to book.

Immersed or submerged in a riot of colour and noise, the historical *Feria del Caballo* was a superb junket and the entire city of Jerez was behind it. Noise? It was at levels associated with Runway One at Heathrow during a Jumbo's take off. Nor was it just people and music. A fairground for the local children had the obligatory Ferris wheel and its organ made a terrible racket, just as they do everywhere. Naturally, the children shrieked with pleasure until their lungs could exhale no longer.

'Do you actually like sherry?' my sister asked me, her eyebrow quizzical.

'I'm not sure,' I replied frankly. 'That stale and cloudy rubbish the dons used to let us have wasn't much to sing and dance about.'

'The same at Oxford. I think we should do some research, since we're here. It can only be better than it is back home.'

'I agree. I've been ordered to adsorb so much of Spain that the natives will think me one of their own. I can't do that without knowing a bit about the national drink, can I.'

'Should we make a plan?' Sound logic was behind her question. 'Go from the youngest to the oldest, or the driest to the sweetest?'

'Yes,' I answered unhelpfully.

The *casetas* were owned by *Gonzales Byass, Sandeman, Lustau,* and all of the other great names of this very Spanish industry.

In '70s England, sherry was becoming something of a rarity. It had been one of the world's most celebrated drinks, yet it was no longer available in most public houses, nor even many private ones.

As with wine there were many styles to choose from, and frankly I didn't know what a good one should taste like.

'Perhaps we should start with *manzanilla*. That and *fino* are the ones that we see most often. Let's go to that Hidalgo *caseta* and have one,' Kate enthused.

The *manzanilla*, theatrically ladled out of the barrel into traditional glasses from a great height, was fresh and dry but had an oddly dusty flavour.

'*¿Te gusta?*', the waiter asked me. '*Debiera*. We have been producing sherry since 1792 in the seaside town of Sanlúcar de Barrameda. The warm sea breeze has found its way into our wine.'

'What's lovely about this *La Gitana*,' I suggested, 'is that its flinty saltiness seems to include a hint of pear?'

'*Eres astuto, mi amigo,*' said the waiter. 'Maybe you can taste maybe some apple? Or some fresh baked bread?'

'I can,' said Kate. 'I think this would go well with cheese, seafood, anything salty in fact.'

'*Es uno de los jerez más secos y picantes.* The important thing is that you serve it chilled.'

We effusively thanked the good fellow and moved on. There was a parade of local bulls which we could not miss. Mercifully this was not Pamplona; they were expertly corralled.

'Time for another sherry?' I asked my sister as the sound of the bovine stampede began to recede.

'Why don't we go over there and try a dark one', she replied. She pointed at *Bodegas Brabadillo' caseta*. We decided to try an *oloroso*, not for any other reason except that neither of us had ever had one before. The concoction was dark, rich, complex, nutty and not too sweet.

'What subtle aromas linger under your nostrils?' I asked my sister in an attempt to mimic the style of a seasoned wine buff.

'Possibly a generous helping of walnuts, figs and raisins,' she replied, playing the same game. 'I detect some toffee notes.'

'Yes,' said I, not expecting to be topped. 'They lend the wine a rounded finish.'

'It would go very nicely with a slice of fruit cake.'

'Then we had better find some. Let's try that tea room. Let's not rush our glasses, we'll take them in with us.'

After a good morning's research, a glass or two and the many *tapas* and slices of fruit cake *en route* we had to go back to our hotel to rest a little When we arrived in our nunnery, the receptionist had a message. It was from Sandro.

'I've found you!' it read. 'Only the fourth hotel I tried! I'm booked into another but I'll see you here for a glass at six.'

In my opinion Siestas are peculiar. They are definitely an acquired taste. If one is used to being beaten into consciousness by one's alarm clock and then staying in the woken condition until around midnight, the idea of an afternoon nap is wholly alien. That said, when Kate and I bade each other a fond forty winks I, at least, let myself into my little cell to open the window – the air conditioning seemed to be taking its own little kip – and lay down. My mind was over-stimulated. I tried to concentrate on the dullest things I knew, but my imagination persisted in straying onto herds of wild beasts rocketing along the *Avenida del Generalissimo*. The fact is I was in the deepest end of a blur of colour and *alegrìa*. It would be amazing if I slept at all.

I was still determined to learn how to enjoy a spot of Egyptian PT in the traditional Spanish way but, in the end, I gave up. This challenge would have to wait upon another day. Nor was the next day any easier as early afternoons are hot in Jerez de la Frontera. The Spaniards had deserted their streets, taking with them all their wonderful costumes.

The only people left out there were in jeans or tracksuits, all of whom carrying cameras and guidebooks. Some were drinking beer from the bottle.

Well, I was reduced to my first duty, to learn about Spain and all its ways, so I returned to the bar. I was surprised but relieved to find it open. I thought I might have a small glass of *fino*. The barista offered me a glass of *Gonzalez Byass*'s own brand. This *delicado*, he told me, was a limited production of well-aged *Tío Pepe*, and made with liquor taken from three casks in which the layer of flor yeast was still alive and then left in its oak for six further years.

'It has a lot of orchard character and an unexpected freshness,' he told me accurately.

I wondered about *fino* as I sipped this great example and began to speculate where the most careful elaborations of this classic aperitif might lead. On the shelf was an unopened bottle of *Tres Palmas*. It was presumably unopened for a reason. Cost would seem most likely.

I put the empty glass down and glanced at my watch. It had turned four. Oh well, sometimes it's hell or high water.

'¿Te gustaría probar un moscatel?' asked the barman.

Bill Bryson defined *moscatel* as a wine with flies in it. *Moscatel*, particularly in the USA - being inexpensive and sweet - is mostly dismissed as a wine meant to be swigged from a bag by a derelict. I am not so easily put off.

'Me vendría bien al planeta Tierra,' I clumsily replied. Dreadful Spanish. I was trying to say that it 'would suit me down to the ground'. There are perils in starting out in a new language.

Moscatel's starting point is the Muscat of Alexandria varietal. Its juice is fermented until brandy is added to halt the process. Then, before its natural sugars have entirely vanished, the resulting liquor is then aged in Spanish oak. Timing is the essence.

California may one of the world's leading producers of *moscatel*, but it could be that the wineries out there no longer recall their Spanish heritage. Or was it that it had been easier to make a bathtub version from supermarket grapejuice during Prohibition? It's not all bad, however. The Ferrara Winery in Escondido, California, still produces a halfway decent *Nectar de Luz*.

I was in Jerez, however. Sipping at the brown concoction in front of me, I was surprised by its intense flavour, redolent of burnt caramel and vanilla. It was something like an ice cream topping, but better. The taste finished like toasted nuts.

'*Bébelo despacio. Seguirá mejorando en la copa*', suggested the helpful fellow across the bar. Drink it slowly – it will even improve in the glass, so I did as instructed. When I finally replaced my glass on the counter it was six o'clock, on the dot. Sandro was supposed to make his appearance, but I was only too well aware of that heightened sense of urgency known only to Latins. Kate, too, was probably still pushing up the zeds. Irish girls can be even less given to helter-skelter than their swarthier cousins. Yet I was wrong. They both made their entrances within seconds of each other. My glass and bowl of crisps had been cleared away but the fragments that had surrounded them strongly evidenced that I had been in the bibulous business for some time.

Kate looked half asleep, but Sandro was as perky as it is possible to be. Nor was he alone. On his arm was a very pretty girl.

'*Jeremy, te presento a Ana Sofía*'.

His Spanish sounded good to me, but then he had had the best part of two days and night's intensive tuition.

'*¿Como estas?*' I offered.

'*Muy bien, muchas gracias,*' she replied.

'*Ciao,*' said Kate. That word is universal, of course.

'*¿Puedo ofrecerles a todos una bebida?*' My formality derived from my honorific position in the chair.

'*Me gustaría un vaso pequeño de pedro ximenez, si eso está bien*', Ana Sofía said promptly. She would welcome a small glass of sherry.

'Make that two,' said Kate. She and Ana Sofía were clearly destined to be the best of friends.

'Make it three,' said Sandro. He led the ladies to a table and patiently held their chairs for them to sit. I sat unaided. The waiter brought this new (to me) sherry to our table, this time with olives and roast almonds to decorate our table. The wine that Ana Sofía had asked for was deep, dark and rich.

Its base material, I would learn, was overripe or sundried grapes. They were the starting point for something that exploded on the tongue.

'Mmmm,' said Kate. 'Thick and velvety, if a bit chocolaty.'

As it seeped into the more remote corners of my palate, cherries and plums began to reveal themselves, rendered more sophisticated by their pleasing hint of bitterness.

A surfeit of leisure in sunny Spain made it hard for me to decline a smidgeon more. Our table was booked for dinner for 9.30, the moment it opened. That left us with nearly two hours to kill. I felt the need to taste a *palo cortado*, a sherry that had so far remained elusive.

Palo cortado is an ambiguous type of sherry. It combines the aromatic refinement of an *amontillado* with the structure and body of an *oloroso*. Or, to put it another way, *amontillado* on the nose, *oloroso* on the palate. It is a wine that exists by accident, the barman explained.

'*Es una especie en peligro de extinción*', he declared, both theatrically and pessimistically. 'It is becoming too popular and its production is drying up.'

Technically, a *palo cortado* is an *oloroso*, but it starts with the juice that would ordinarily have been destined to end as a *fino*. Its flor is killed by the sturdy fortification that takes the wine to 17% or 18%. Like Diogenes, it will thenceforward continue its life in a barrel, endeavouring to mature gently, while unknowable mysteries – hidden beyond the reach of science - work their magic within the yeast, the grape, or even the cask itself. Only when the genie has done its stuff can the casks be taken from the *solera* and a vertical chalk mark, a *palo*, could then be crossed with a diagonal *cortado*.

Palo cortado is the rarest of sherries. Fewer than a hundred thousand bottles are sold a year, compared with sixty million bottles of sherry overall, yet among *aficionados* it remains the very pinnacle of desire. Ours was served a little warmer than I (at least) had expected, but that was all to the good. It was a treat of the first magnitude.

The lovely Ana Sofía, however, was a little circumspect. Her next glass was *horchata* - almond milk. The barman gave us, or more likely her, a qualified approval.

'*La horchata debe consumirse en uno o dos días porque no fermenta*', he said. Drink it quickly before it goes off, I think he meant. Perhaps sherry schooners are larger than they look. I felt a touch relaxed. Even standing up might prove a problem.

'*¿Existe tal cosa como un jerez sin fortificar?*' I asked the barman. I was seeking a peaceful and kind wine, one with the courtesy to take prisoners. I was sure there had to be such a thing. A great climate, usually mild, makes this land an ideal place for great wines. Good as gold, he recommended a red Ronda, a Chinchilla *doble doce cosecha* from Doña Felisa, aged for more than a year in oak. Its nose suggested ripe black fruit, while its body hinted of cedar and spices.

Kate, Sandro and I had booked a table and rooms for the night at *La Mesón Asador Las Pachecas* and, before long, we were on our way. The restaurant, on the banks of the Medina Lagoon, was seven miles from Jerez de la Frontera. Our agreeable barman had suggested the four of us should eat there. Of course, it belonged to a cousin.

We found the *Mesón Asador* in a narrow street. From the outside it appeared to be little more than a roadside diner, but at least it was quiet. Its menu looked surprisingly good. My problem was that I had to shut one eye to read it. A huge grill, front of house, made it an obvious haven for carnivores.

Our starter was a *parillada*, made up of various meats and *patatas panaderas*. The pork cheeks were particularly good. There was a fine *pisto*, and the tapas of *bacalao* with tomato were excellent. The bread, too, was fresh and warm. For a main course I essayed an oxtail in what I judged to be a Roquefort sauce,[162] beefed up with sauté potatoes. With its accompanying lettuce hearts it was more than enough. Kate opted for the Burgos black rice pudding with fried egg and chips. She declared it amazing. It had no lumps of fat in it, as it would have done in the UK. Sandro and Ana Sofia plumped for a *cazuela* of cod with chickpeas.

'A great casserole,' Sandro grudgingly opined, 'but in Italy it would be better.' We washed it all down with the house *ribera*,[163] and toasted the Mediterranean and all who dwelled there. Our pudding involved engorging a strawberry cake with whipped cream.

Completely unnecessarily we ended with coffee and brandy.

I wished him, Ana Sofia and my sister a rather emotional goodnight. As I somehow managed to stumble my way upstairs I thought the hotel must be one of Jerez's the best kept secrets and that my condition should be one too.

Whether I managed to get my pyjamas on – the likelihood is not - can only be conjecture. My room was probably comfortable, I don't recall, but I do remember sleeping badly, dreaming that I had been shipwrecked. It was a long and troubled night, all that my subconscious would deliver was the awful sound of sea crashing onto a beach.

---

[162] Almost certainly it was not. There will be a suitable ewe's milk cheese in Spain. Ed.
[163] *Ribera del Duero* – a fine red wine from the banks of the Duoro.

A Spanish beach, too, probably that beach off Cape Trafalgar, where so many English tars had ended up, which up to then I had believed benign. I had no idea that the punishment for overindulgence could be audible.

When I woke my hangover was something no living man, no matter how evil, should ever have to endure. I nursed my head, holding it upright with both hands. I had to. I staggered onto my balcony to breathe some clean air and take in the scene beyond. If that should have sorted me out, it didn't.

La Laguna de Medina is the largest lake in the province of Cádiz and, after Fuente de Piedra, the second largest in Andalusia. We were in a landscape, studded with farmhouses, each one set in a rounded quilt of cultivated hills, patched with fields of cereals and sunflowers.

Smooth slopes direct the rain in Spain into the plain. Everybody knows that. There is a song about it. The soil it passes over, rich in gypsum, slay and marl, must take the blame for the salinity of its waters. The wetland this creates can be an inland sea in winter but, in summers with little rainfall, it will dry out completely.

Beneath my balcony, around the hotel and the lake, were reeds, bulrushes, tamarisk and *bunium incrassatum*. Between them they housed many an endangered bird. The white-headed duck and red-knobbed coot were enough in themselves to guarantee a pilgrimage of twitchers. Nor did it end there. Other stage-struck birds, notably garganeys, geese, pochards, ducks and even flamingos liked to make their appearance.

Mediterranean scrub - wild olive, mastic, palmetto and rockrose - was everywhere I looked.

Sadly, I was not in the mood to be properly appreciative. I'm not sure I can speak for Kate, and I know I can't for Sandro, but I have never before or even since had quite so much to drink in a single day.

Idiots, over the years, repeat the absurd mantra that 'a coffee will sort you out'. My condition was more in need of brain surgery than caffeine. Nothing known to man is quite as dreadful as a nuclear *gueule de bois*. Any inability to think coherently is sabotaged by a quagmire of loud and rude noise and glaring primary colours. Even this torture is dwarfed by a thirst that all the tears in purgatory cannot slake. At that time of day a healthy appetite for croissants or eggs benedict is irreversibly cancelled. Nullified. *Distrutto. Ecrasé.*

I looked morosely over my untouched coffee on the breakfast table, realising that the whole awfulness of The Hangover has a moral dimension, too; a searing guilt leisurely tumbling from the darkest recesses of one's mind into the forefront of a gradual recollection of the night before.

'Oh no! Tell me I didn't say that!'

Kate was saying little. Ana Sofía had to be back in Cádiz. Sandro decanted us into his car to take us back to the Jerez Itaca. That done, he could take her back to her parents' house, himself to Marbella, return the car to Hertz and fly home.

'Arrivederci!' His cheerful shout reached us on the hotel doorstep as he screeched his tyres in a wheelie and rocketed off with his new friend. Now we were down to two. The last leg of our epic adventure was upon us and Kate and I, brother and sister, were to be bound in a Seville partnership.

I had been told that its largely mudéjar[164] cathedral was actually larger than the great basilica[165] of St Peter's

---

[164] Mudéjar: Originally the term was used for Moors or Muslims of Al-Andalus who remained in Iberia after the Christian Reconquista but were not forcibly converted to Christianity. It was a medieval Spanish borrowing of the Arabic word Mudajjan مدجن, meaning 'tamed'. The term was probably a taunt, as it was often applied to domesticated animals such as poultry. In this context it merely means Moorish,

[165] It is not. By volume, St Peter's is larger, but is not a cathedral. A 'basilica' was a building in the classical world used for the administration of justice with

in the Vatican City. It seemed unlikely but we would find out in a few hours. A few? Our train took three hours to cover the seventy miles inland and, on arrival, would feel just as dusty and exhausted if we had walked.

We reached Seville and, what with one thing and another, my expenses were mounting up. I felt slightly guilty about the bills my employer would have to pay. I made an unilateral, well-intended but, in the end, idiotic decision to stay in a very ordinary hotel. Within a few minutes of arriving we saw that the huge thermometer on the façade of the station was registering an astonishing 45°C, and in the shade.[166] That's not merely hot. In a city with no lakes, no parks, no grass, no lungs, that was scalding.

We did not have far to walk, but in that heat? We took an air-conditioned taxi to our B & B, checked in and found ourselves a place to sit outside. If I allowed my hand to stray from the awning's shade, I could feel my skin burn where the sun shone directly onto it. Curious to be sitting in an oven at gas mark 8? Curious? Correction: read unbearable. The idea of exploring the city without tropical gear and a pith helmet was patently absurd.

'The cathedral,' Kate said wisely. 'It's our only hope.'

Its ancient walls had nobly adsorbed a degree or two of the heat to avoid parboiling the faithful. That will be why we stayed inside it for almost four hours. We were close to comfortable in its five naves, the largest of which houses the mortal remains of Christopher Columbus. Those four hours guarantee Kate and me to be among the world's leading experts on that wonderful house of God.

---

the authority of the ruler. The word *basilica* is Latin for βασιλική στοά, or royal house. It is not the primary seat of a bishop.
[166] 113°F.

It stands on the site of what had been, as recently as the 12th century, Seville's Great Mosque. The Almohad caliph Abu Yaqub Yusuf wanted to supplant an even earlier one, built around 830 AD by Umar Ibn Adabbas. His new prayer hall had seventeen aisles, directed southward at right angles to its Qibla wall, as with so many mosques in Al-Andalus. Its great minaret soars upward of three hundred feet, built in homage to the Koutoubia Mosque in Marrakech. Its girating weather vane is known as the Giralda, while the statue right on the top, El Giraldillo, was put there in 1568 and is said to represent the Reconquest, the earlier triumph of Ferdinand and Isabella's muscular Christianity.

Today, the world's two largest ecclesiastical temples are the Basilica of the National Shrine of Our Lady of Aparecida in Sao Paolo, Brazil, and St Peter's Basilica in Rome. Since neither is the seat of a bishop, formally speaking, Seville's is the largest cathedral in the world. It gained that status in 1248 when the city was conquered by Ferdinand III of Castile and that most Christian king ordered Yaqub Yusuf's mosque to be put to Christian use.

Legend has it that the newly elected bishop declared, '*hagamos una Iglesia tan hermosa y tan grandiosa que los que la vieren labrada nos tengan por locos*'.[167] His architects began by reorienting the mosque east-west, reorganising its spaces and adapting them to the Catholic rubric. Bays along the northern and southern walls now served as chapels while the entire eastern half of the cathedral was turned into a royal chapel, ready to receive the bodies of King Ferdinand, Queen Isabella and King Alfonso the Wise, when the muffled bell tolled.

The King of Castile, León and Galicia – better known as Alfonso X - was chosen by a faction who

---

[167] Let us build a church so beautiful and so grand that those who see it finished will take us for mad.

wanted this likable man to be King of the Germans or, perhaps more correctly, the King of the Romans.[168] That would not happen: a jealous Pope vetoed this nomenclature. But what's in a name? That King of Spain established Castilian as the language of higher learning when he founded the two great universities of Salamanca and Toledo but it was his prolific writing, which included much Galician-Portuguese poetry, that won the proud monarch him the soubriquet 'the Wise' - *el Sabio* – and 'the Astronomer' - *el Astrelogo*.

He was not the most humble of philosophers. *'Had I been present at the creation, I would have given Him some useful hints for the better ordering of the universe'*, he declared immodestly.

Six centuries ago, Seville's 'new' cathedral overtook Istanbul's Hagia Sophia as the largest in the world. While it became a place of Christian worship it still looks like a mosque. Seville Cathedral towers over its rivals by around a hundred feet. The rectangular floor plan measures 350 feet long by 250 wide. For the kind of comparison so regularly employed by *The Daily Mirror*, the overall length of a football pitch is 200 feet, and its width 150. Hagia Sophia measures a mere 250 feet by 215 and, in any case, Istanbul's great church is currently deconsecrated and the Turks are in the process of re-establishing it as a mosque.

St Peter's in Rome is a basilica, not a cathedral, but the seat of a Basil (or king). The Pope may be Bishop of Rome but his cathedral is San Giovanni in Lateran, where the Holy Father sits as a bishop. In St Peter's he is merely a monarch.

The world's two largest churches are the Basilica of the National Shrine of Our Lady of Aparecida in Sao Paolo, Brazil, and St Peter's in Rome. Neither is formally the seat of a bishop. Seville is therefore the

---

[168] The Germanic Empire was the name given by many to the Holy Roman Empire. Rome itself, counter intuitively, was seldom a part of it.

largest cathedral in the world. A bishop sits *ex cathedra* and a pope does not even have to be a priest. In the renaissance at least one was not.

We began our tour of the immense temple in the principal nave. Seville's cathedral has eighty, yes, eighty chapels. The grandest is the royal one, *la Capilla Real*. In 1896, some sort of a record for piety was achieved when five hundred masses were offered in the cathedral, its naves and its dependent chapels, and on just one single day.

Kate and I agreed that we should attempt to trace the church's evolution from mudéjar, gothic, renaissance, baroque through to neo-classical. Fifteen doorways pierce its four façades and, given the oppressive heat outside, we decided to 'review' them all.

We thought it would be appropriate to start with the 'Door of the Conception'. It opens onto the Patio de las Naranjas - the 'Court of the Oranges' - a courtyard formerly used by the Moors for ritual ablutions. Today it houses ranks of orange trees. We were both struck by this.

Kate remembered that Queen Victoria liked oranges. She had the grace to explain to my raised eyebrows that 'the queen would leave them in a fruit bowl outside her bedroom when she wanted Albert to visit. Her bedroom door was thus another fruitful 'Door of Conception'.'

The one in Seville is kept closed, except on high days or holidays. It was built in the Gothic idiom to harmonise with the 'newer' parts of the building. Our progress was logical, at least. It began with 'conception', moving through the 'Door of St Michael', better known as the 'Door of the Nativity'. It depicts the birth of Jesus but it was locked. The archbishop only opens it in Holy Week to allow processions to pass through. We moved on to the 15th century gothic 'Door of the

Baptism', to reenter the cathedral via the *Puerta del Perdón*, another survivor from the old mosque.

Inside again we admired a carved scene depicting the baptism of Jesus, transplanted from England to Spain by King Philip. Our pre-reformation Benedictine monks had given it to the Spanish king upon his marriage to Queen Mary Tudor. It was an ancient English work from 'Laurence the Merchant's Winchester workshop'. Representations of the English monks St Isidore and St Leander and the nuns Sta Justa and Sta Rufina had been worked into its elaborate tracery.

The 'Door of the Sanctuary' admitted us into the church's most sacred area. Corinthian columns flank it while a statue of King Ferdinand III of Castile sits on top, next to Sts Isidore, Leander, Justa and Rufina whom he had petitioned to secure him a place in Paradise. One can only hope they did their stuff.

The 'Door of St Christopher' has a replica of the Giraldillo in front of it, while the 'Door of the Lizard' – *la Puerta del Lagarto* - is named after the stuffed crocodile that hangs over it for no obvious reason.

The Main Door, in the centre of the cathedral's west façade, lies under an elaborate nineteenth century Assumption. It is called the 'Door of Forgiveness' and opens onto the street, the *Calle Alemanes*. It is not really a door to the cathedral at all, but another survivor from the ancient mosque. It retains its horseshoe arch shape from that time. I went through it slowly - it had a lot of work to do.

The 'Door of Sticks', otherwise known as 'the Adoration of the Wise Men' – *la Puerta de Palos* or *la Puerta de la Adoración de los Magos* - has a sixteenth century relief of the Magi at the top. The name Palos - 'palings' - derives from the wooden barrier which separates that area from the rest of the building. To me it suggested Ireland. English Ireland was once protected from the Gaels by a fence, *The Pale.*

When the 'Door of the Bells' – *la Puerta de las Campanillas* – was being built, its bells were rung to summon the workers. It has a Renaissance relief on its 16C tympanum: Christ coming into Jerusalem on an ass.

'Its name is hard to forget,' said Kate with her characteristic arch smile.

'That's because it will always ring a bell,' I said, predicting her punch line.

At last we had done the lot.

'I never did care much for *The Doors*', said Kate.

'An overrated band,' I agreed.[169]

There is much else to admire. A staggering altarpiece, built over many centuries in an impressive jumble of styles, somehow works despite having the odds stacked against it. harking from the second half of the 16th century, the Chapter House was once the cathedral's parliament. For all I know it still may be.

We made a headlong rush through a sacristy, festooned with flora and fantastic creatures, realised in ornate bas relief, all in the peculiarly Spanish plateresque manner, a decorative style that imitates in wood and plaster the work of Spain's early Renaissance silversmiths.

One of its chapels, the baptistery, houses Bartolomé Esteban Murillo's 1656 painting of 'The Vision of St Anthony'. Not only was its art miraculous; the picture's story is equally so. In November 1874, thieves cut out the section that depicts the saint. Two months later, the following January, a Spanish emigrant tried to sell the fragment to a commercial art gallery in New York City. The man declared it was a complete

---

[169] …but I did visit, much later, Jim Morrison's grave in Paris's *Père Lachaise.*

original by Murillo. Saint Anthony (he claimed) was one of the artist's favourite subjects.

The owner of the gallery, Hermann Schaus, agreed to pay a price of $250. Claiming the picture needed a specialist's attention, he immediately contacted the Spanish consulate. The Consul-General rushed the ransom over and Schaus sent the picture to his benefactor, who promptly shipped it home to Seville, where it belonged, via Havana and Càdiz. The subsequent restoration of the masterpiece is immaculate. No one today could possibly detect the slightest hint of the ordeal the masterpiece had suffered.

Overall, the cathedral is a key, a compendium of all Spanish art and history. There is but one way a traveller can understand Spain in a single trip. He should come here.

*

Our B & B had no air conditioning. Unwisely I had been trying to economise. That baking night we had no choice but to leave our windows open. There was scarcely a breeze and if the temperature, even in the dead of night, dropped below 40°C[170] I'll eat my hat.

In my little single room I tried to sleep stark naked on top of my narrow dormitory bed, knowing at last how chickens feel when we roast them. True, if unlike those chickens, I was still alive, if only just. I had never experienced such a night before, and I sincerely want never to do so again. God help the natives, who have to endure it for six weeks a year.

Kate and I had determined to do Seville justice. The city has plenty to do and see, but at that temperature, motivation – or its absence - challenged us. Air conditioning, ubiquitous nowadays, was in the '70s confined to the most expensive and seriously chic restaurants. This, therefore, is where we went.

---

[170] 104°F. I ate the hat. It tasted of finest raffia, since you ask.

'Can we try suckling pig?' asked Kate.

'Of course we can. It counts as research.'

Our concierge directed us to a place called *Mama Bistro*. A glass of Sangria, with *jamon iberico*, fresh figs and warm, herb-infused bread kept us busy for a while. *Iberico* is a hot-smoked ham of exquisite flavour (and significant cost). It is the legacy of the little black pigs of the region. If these ill-fated animals lead but a short life, it is one of exceptional privilege. Those afflicted with vegetarianism should have more respect for those porcine hedonists. They are raised under Spanish oaks – those very trees that built the Armada and whose cork seals so many a bottle of fine wine. The pigs receive a daily massage, rather like Kobe beef, and I would not be surprised if they were played Joaquín Rodrigo's enchanting *El Concierto de Aranjuez* while sniffing and snorting their happy and nonchalant pastoral paean. If not for their future date with the headsman they would never lead such blissful lives and would survive in a few zoos or, more likely yet, be extinct.

Our first course devoured, the waiter delivered a huge plate of suckling pig on a bed of perfect roast potatoes and blueberry risotto to our table. This most wonderful meat is a curious treat. Fatty, tender and slightly salty, it is delicious but Kate felt pity for the poor sow who had sacrificed her piglet for our pleasure. She tucked in enthusiastically enough, but maintained a pained air of general melancholy until her plate looked brand new.

We finished with a simple salad of passion fruit, the ripest strawberries and fresh pineapple, drowned in *chinchon*. It was beyond compare.

We had, yet again, been on the receiving end of a magic spell.

*

After another futile attempt at a siesta, at least for me, and we set off to experience an Andalusian flamenco in

411

the historic El Arenal quarter. Many of the city's cultural attractions are there.

We took our seats at the esteemed *Tablao Flamenco*, possibly one of the finest flamenco bars in the world and, praise be, air conditioned. Curro Vélez, the owner and a good humoured fellow, politely welcomed us in. He had only founded it only the year before but it was already talked of as a marvel. Vélez was a renowned *bailor*, a flamenco dancer. He took a good-natured fancy to my sister and rewarded her indifference with sneaky, surreptitious glasses of *palo cortado*.

Thank goodness for air conditioning. In enormous comfort we watched an intense flamenco, spellbinding in its choreography and music, realised by sublimely talented dancers, guitarists and singers. How they can click their fingers in syncopated percussion to the music was weird but wonderful. I practiced all the way back to our hotel while Kate pretended not to know me.

*

There is an anti-Newtonian law that anything set in motion will inevitably grind to a halt. It does not apply in Seville. We carried ourselves back to our sauna - 'hotel' it laughably called itself - where we failed absolutely in our efforts to get any recuperative shut-eye whatsoever.

All told, however, our adventure was incapable of being surpassed. It had been a three dimensional, panoramic and total immersion in the culture and tradition of a great nation. Even so, it was time for us all to leave this enchantment and return to the quotidian business of the every day.

In the morning, Kate needed to be at the airport to catch her flight to Paris, while I had to travel to the capital and introduce myself to my office with a plausible pretence to be an expert on all things Iberian.

CTB had arranged for me to stay at the *Hotel Europa* on the Calle Carmen, somewhere between the Plaza Mayor and my office the heart of Madrid. It was comfortable; not luxurious but at least it boasted a bar and restaurant. My fourth floor room was blessed with a balcony, but should one open the shutters, not just light but heat would flood in alongside a fine view of the Puerta del Sol.

The long bar on the ground floor, however, had tables in the shade outside where I could indulge in a little people-watching, eating olives and nuts, sipping a *Sangría* and planning my visit to the Prado, the Royal Palace, the Gran Via, El Rastro (the Sundays-only flea market) and at least a trillion tapas bars.

CTB España's office was easy to find. It was just off the Plaza de España. At the centre of the square was a monument to Cervantes, behind which rose the 117 m drama known as the *Edificio España* - 'the Spain Building'. It had been built in 1953 and looked for the world like a transplant from Soviet Moscow.

*

On Monday morning I rose early. I had had little or no preparation for the office protocols I was likely to encounter. I would just have to wing it. Before I leapt in the deep end, however, I felt the call for breakfast. Not in the Europa's breakfast room. It was clinically functional but was not included in the bill. I decided to sit myself down in the Bar Roma, *en route* to the office, where I ordered a coffee and a pastry. I looked about. Strange. Not many customers. Newspapers were on poles I took one from a rack.

When it came, the coffee was excellent, if not quite as they do it in Italy. Struggling to read *El Pais*, a local chap tapped on my newspaper. He registered a determination to clean my shoes. When I agreed, the good fellow got on his knees, disappeared under the table and turned my beaten up old brogues into the shiniest, newest pair I had ever seen. Meanwhile, I had found the paper's cartoon strips. If anything, they were harder to decipher than the journalese.

What did my sojourn in Spain portend? Let me see the menu. A choice, it seems of sweat, tears, or perhaps both?

I arrived at CTB's Madrid office at 8.00 am. I had the impression that no one was expecting me and the confusion came close to a kerfuffle. I politely tried to look the other way. After a while – the few minutes seemed longer – a youngish bloke came up to me with an outstretched hand.

'My name is Paco,' he announced in English. 'You can sit here, opposite me. We understand you are going to work with us for a couple of weeks. Can you speak Spanish?'

'*Por supuesto,*' I bravely but inaccurately replied. 'Of course'.

'*Bueno.*' He continued in Spanish. 'We are currently bidding for *Banco Mare Nostrum*'s insurance business. Here are their stats for the last five years. Can you design a first and second surplus treaty?'

'*Creo que puese*. Where is *Mare Nostrum* based?'

'In the Canaries. In Tenerife, in fact.'

'You're sure we are talking non-marine business?'

'Yes. I am.'

'I suppose that some of the giant yachts that pitch up in the Canaries will be insured facultatively.'

'Who cares? That's a marine matter. Well, it's turned eight o'clock. We have breakfast at ten o'clock and you can tell me how you're getting on over a *postre.*'

I thought it prudent not to mention I had already had breakfast an hour before.

'*Estaria feliz de hacer eso,*' I clumsily agreed. If the stats were good the business should not be too hard to promote.

At the stroke of ten o'clock, Paco was again by my side. *'Pon esa pluma abajo. Estamos saliendo.'* Put your pen down. It's time to go.

I was about to learn that the entire office staff of every enterprise in greater Madrid took twenty minutes off mid-morning to stretch their legs. Not to have a cigarette; no, they were encouraged to do that in the office, and they did it with so much enthusiasm that the resulting clouds of smoke posed a real danger of collision with the furniture.

Paco and I fetched up at a crowded café just off the Plaza Castilla. It seemed to specialise in sweet cakes, but it did have air conditioning - the most essential constituent of creature comfort in a Madrileño summer.

'When we have finished our coffees we shall return to the office. You will work at those statistics until two o'clock. That is the end of your day.'

'Sounds a bit short?'

'That's *your* day. Senior staff have to return at five and work until eight. We work *oras españolas*. We do not work *oras americanas*.'

'Does everyone go home for a siesta? They must all live locally?'

'They do not. Mostly they have to look for a taxi when they leave the office. Our taxis have three-way signs on the roof. They say *alquilar*, which means they can be stopped, *non alquilar*, the opposite, or they show a destination, such as *Puerta Hierro*, a smart suburb. That last one means that's where the driver is going for his own siesta and only if you want to go there too will he help.'

I still hadn't got my head around this siesta thingie. Perhaps I could trade the shut-eye for the Prado and its awesome collection of Rubens? Then I might have an early supper, ready to be up early the next day, bright eyed and bushy tailed.

It was not to be. The Prado was firmly shut until 5 pm, while Madrid's restaurants did not open until 10 pm. It was finally dawning on me that a siesta is not a luxury. Wandering in the heat, almost as far as the Plaza Mayor, I noticed the *Casa Revuelta* was open and had put a sign on the pavement outside saying *pescado fresco esta mañana*. 'Fish fresh this morning.' Since Madrid is some three hundred kilometres from the nearest port I thought this odd, but I would chance my luck. Ferdinand and Isabella had sensibly decreed that their capital should be as far from the sea as humanly possible, while their Moorish adversaries confined their raids to the coast.

It was an unpretentious restaurant. Despite its hard benches and wooden tables, it was crowded – always a good sign. I ordered *gazpacho*, to be followed by a *tajada de bacalao*, which turned out to be deep fried cod with fried potatoes. Yes, fish and chips again, but very good and authentic fish and chips in the country that invented the dish. A glass of *albariño*, a fine white from Galicia, helped it on its way.

How could this be? Did they fly the fish in? Did it come that huge distance in chilled lorries?[171] It was a puzzle.

Once I had settled the bill I made my way into the square. I had no clear idea of what to do with myself. It was now four in the afternoon. I had no commitments until the following morning. Plaza Mayor carefully, even romantically, melds the magnificent with the magnanimous. Philip II had wanted his subjects to have a palace of their own and had the wonderful idea of building an outdoor one in the form of an urban square. At the centre is Giambologna's 1616 equestrian statue

---

[171] It comes by train.

of Philip III and around its rim are the *mesones*[172] that encourage the townsfolk to chat, flirt and plot in creature comfort.

I took a seat outside the *Homenaje a Cervantes* and ordered another coffee. Perhaps the writer had dined here? I reflected on the weird coincidence that he and Shakespeare had died on the same day, the feast day of St George. Over a beer I wondered why the Calle O'Donnell, the road that led from the Parque del Retiro to the square, was so called. Why, in the very heart of Madrid, should a street bear so Irish a name? I was bowled over by the plaza's unparalleled splendour. I thought to myself that maybe only the Place des Héros, in Arras, compared with it.

Arras's Place des Héros was formerly known as the *petit marché*. It had been laid out in the XIIth century, and rebaptised in 1945 to pay tribute to those members of the French Resistance who had been lined up against a wall there and shot. Still a market, it meets every Wednesday and Saturday morning. They tell me that the mayor of Arras is determined to prohibit the square to motor cars. Let's hope he wins his battle.

Paris's Place Vendôme comes a good second, however, if Piazza Navona in Rome doesn't count as it was not purpose-built. It arose from the wreckage of an ancient hippodrome. I also disqualified the Grand' Place in Brussels, since it was built as a suite of separate palaces for an ex-pat Spanish nobility who ruled the Netherlands at the time, even if the square it encloses has ended up as a popular palace in its own right. The idea was catching on. Only a little later, London's squares would reflect this new-found ancient tradition.

*

I thought I might watch a film. What I was looking for was one that I had already seen in English, but one that

---

[172] Cafés and the like.

had been dubbed into Spanish. My old plan, the one by which I had learned Italian had been, I modestly considered, inspired.

There was an Entertainments Guide in the pub, a freebie. I had a choice of *Lawrence of Arabia*, *The Dambusters* or *The Italian Job*. That last was the film I plumped for. It was an excellent film and my lazy brain would somehow simultaneously translate the Spanish back into the original English without my making any particular effort. Secondly, it would allow me to lose a boiling afternoon in an air-conditioned cinema, while the Madrileña intelligentsia were pushing up the Zs.

*

At 10 am the following day, Paco and I exchanged a few words. Kind ones, as it turned out. He was keen to further my transition into a hispanophone and I was grateful. While he greedily chomped away at his pastry, he revealed that Spain had always been a difficult country for those - like him - that had been denied by birth of a foothold on the social ladder. He was already a director of CTB España and certainly knew how to play the game. Only a couple of years before, he told me, he had been driving at some extraordinary speed on the road to Barcelona in his new car, a Porsche 911 Carrera, when he had been flagged down by the *Guardia Civil*.

'So this armed traffic cop told me to wind down my window,' he told me. "You were driving at 150 kph. The speed limit on this road is 90. I am administering a spot fine."

"There is one thing you should know', I replied with great civility. "I am the natural son of the Duke of Medina-Sidonia, a Grandee of Spain. Have the courtesy to use your radio and inform your chief that you are about to administer justice to a nobleman."

"¿El Duque de Medina-Sidonia? ¿Es verdad? En ese caso no hay problema. Por favor, siga su camino, señor. Ten un viaje seguro."[173]

'He actually saluted me as I drove off.'

Paco Compes, in his little story, had been merely hoping to amuse me. In fact, he had told me a lot about Spain.

I had already seen that travelling round Spain could be a time-consuming business. Although the national roads out of Madrid - numbered in Roman numerals from N I to N VI - were well surfaced, they were cluttered with huge, crawling pantechnicons. They had a particularly alarming feature: two left-hand indicators to the rear. The amber one was to indicate that they are pulling out or turning left, the green one with an arrow told the car behind that it was supposedly safe to overtake. It was your life in their hands and, when Sandro Ridomi had been at the wheel, it was of more use to say your prayers than to admire the view.

*

Davina Barclay was the 'country manager' of Singer and Friedlander, CTB's proprietary merchant bank. *La divina Davina* must have been at least thirty, was beyond gorgeous and was demonstrably a high flyer. Despite her senior rank, she might just let me take her to lunch? Who could know? Anyway, what had I to lose? I asked her and, to my delight and surprise, she agreed. She did impose a condition, however. She would choose the restaurant.

Her choice demonstrated what happens when a palace is mated with a railway station. Inside, even the tables wore underwear. Not one tablecloth but two, the first of some sort of calico and the second of that Egyptian cotton that Tutankhamen insisted upon for a

---

[173] 'The Duke of Medina-Sidonia? Is that so? In that case there is no problem. On your way, my lord. Have a safe journey.'

shroud. In the centre of the dining room stood a *careta*, a fixed one, apparently made of ivory. Its sloping sides held repositories for chocolates, sweetmeats and other delicacies, painstakingly made by brow-beaten captives in a secret and sweaty workshop, safely hidden somewhere within the Alhambra complex. The bread, brought in hand-beaten silver bowls to our table by a waiter who was in all likelihood thrashed every morning by his employers to ensure maximum humility, had been made according to four or five different recipes. Water arrived in a curious contraption that looked like a cross between a lamp from Aladdin's cave and a Montgolfier balloon, its basket below filled with cored olives from somewhere in Aragon. I knew instinctively that such olive groves would employ armed guards to keep a thieving peasantry out.

There is a ratio between the cost of dining in the cheapest and most expensive eateries in any country. In Madrid, at that time, it was reckoned to be around 40:1. I had lunched well at the *Casa Revuelta* the previous day, but when sitting in the opulence of the Michelin-starred *La Teraza del Casino*, that ratio was nearer 50:1.

I judged that Davina carried no surplus baggage but, my God, could she eat! The waiter had launched us on the road to some sort of gastronomic fantasy island by bringing us *boquerones in escabeche* as an *amuse bouche*. They had vanished even before my champagne flute was empty.

The *langosta Carlos V* was intriguing. Essentially it was a *thermidor* with a Spanish spin. In common with the classic French dish, the creamy mixture of lobster, egg yolks and brandy had been cooked and replaced in the lobster shell, but the Gruyère-mustard crust had been substituted with some sort of frothy *champenoise* and savoury meringue. There is such a thing.

Our waiters synchronised the swapping of our empty plates for new ones with a small portion of what transpired to be hake. The *merluza con pisto moruno* was a delight. Next, the waiters raised another pair of silver domes to reveal our main course. We saw our *filetes de ternera Carlomagno*, steaks surrounded with forest mushrooms, dressed with hollandaise, and our appetites rose to the occasion.

Quesas exóticas - rare cheeses - somehow found room in my masochistic stomach and still left enough space for the *fresas silvestres* - wild strawberries - that completed the feast. At last I understood why the Spanish customarily allow three hours for lunch.

Davina had chosen the wine and, fool that I am, I had submitted. It tasted great, nor that was not all. It's very label was a work of art. The dust on the bottle may have dated from days before Franco. Perhaps from before the *caudillo*'s parents even met (even if they married).

I took a deep breath. It was time to pay. I believe this was the second most expensive meal that I have ever eaten, from my first restaurant meal as a lad to the present day.[174] Fifty times the cheapest? Had I eaten fifty lunches in one go? What would CTB make of it?

Not that Davina was impressed. Clearly, her suitors took her to far more extravagant *endroits* all the time. She hadn't even been receptive company. If I had meant to impress her I had utterly failed. The restaurant had behaved immaculately - it had fêted us like grandees of Spain - but she took the twenty-four carat flummery in her stride. This may have been simple opportunism, perhaps, but it distanced her from reality. Her ambition to walk on water, even air, was only a short step from being realised. Hey ho, it was all research.

*

Some years before, I had met a very pretty Spanish girl in Rome. She was the daughter of the Spanish ambassador

---

[174] The most expensive will have been the one I shared with Tev in the Dorchester Hotel. *Vid supra.*

to the Holy See and she liked to visit her father at his official residence, the *Palazzo di Spagna*,[175] then a wholly appropriate thing for a student at Madrid's ancient Complutense University. Back then she was well *en route* to a first class degree in art history. On her return the university had snapped her up into its post-graduate hierarchy.

That afternoon, after my first successful siesta I rang her number. Ana Martínez de Alguilar suggested I come over to her parents' villa, near the *Puerta de Hierro*, on the Saturday, in the Moncloa district of the Spanish capital, near the *Monte de El Pardo*. They had a pool, she warned me, so I should bring my swimming togs. Her address translates as 'Iron Gate', near the University City and the Palace of Moncloa.[176] Built, not in metal but in carved stone, in the baroque style of the late eighteenth century. 'Iron' may have meant 'tough' in this context. Of course, it may once have had iron doors. Unlike Madrid's other monumental gates, those of *Alcala Toledo* and *San Vicente*, it does not protect the city centre but served as a ceremonial entrance to the Royal Park of El Pardo, a hunting area once reserved for the Spanish monarchy to hunt deer.

Ana's father, Gabriel Martínez de Mata,[177] had a fine modern house. All the *accoutrements* of material splendour surrounded him, including a personal bodyguard.

As I climbed out of the pool I saw the man whom I had last met in 1973 come into his garden. He walked unsteadily towards the pitcher of freshly-made lemonade that awaited him. His family and bodyguard fussed over him while his large eyes seemed strangely

---

[175] For details of my irregular visits to the Palazzo you will have to read *A Gap Year or Two*, by this author.

[176] The official residence of the President of the Government (i.e., the Prime Minister).

[177] In Spain, your father's name xxx is adjoined to your mother's maiden name yyy in the formula Paco xxx de yyy.

sad. When he finally sat, his staff spread a rug over his lap. That too was strange, at 35°.

Martínez, I would learn, needed a bodyguard, but not because some savage criminal had designs on his family or fortune. It was because the former ambassador had contracted a psychological ailment, some sort of acute melancholia, that made him liable to end it all. His minder was there to protect him from himself. I am flattered to say he remembered me from Rome. He almost cheerfully asked me if I would prefer Champagne to lemonade. I would have, truth be told, but instead I opted for the lemonade. It proved quite delicious; I had made a wise decision.

The family were soon to be joined by a military guest, a certain Lieutenant-Colonel Antonio Tejero. I was introduced.

'Coronel Tejero, le presento a usted un amigo de mi hija.'

'Es un honor para mí, Coronel,' I said, inclining my head. This gesture seemed to go down OK. The, with this elementary courtesy completed, Tejero and Martínez disappeared into the bowels of the house to discuss some more important issue.

'Colonel Tejero is Chief of the Planning Staff of Madrid's *Guardia Civil,*' Ana explained. 'He used to be the leader of the *Comandancia* in the Basque province of Guipúzcoa but, unfortunately, when he publicly opposed the raising of the Basque flag, the *Ikurriña*, he was informed he was 'no longer suited to such responsibilities'. He has since resigned. To regain a public role he needs to petition men like my father.'

Charles Cullum's exhortation, that I should learn how to read between the lines, was still my challenge. I knew there was something here below the surface but it was hard to discern quite what.

*

Understanding Spanish meant more than simply speaking their language. I adjusted my resolution to go to the cinema every afternoon to one where I would alternate my cinematic language lessons with a trip to a place of great importance in Spanish history. I thought I might begin with Toledo. The other reason was that Ana Martínez suggested it.

She told me a very moving story while we travelled by train the fifty miles from Madrid's Atocha Station. It had been in the Summer of 1936, early in their Civil War.

Toledo's then governor, a Colonel José Moscardó Ituarte, had about 1,300 monarchists ('Carlists') and nationalists ('Falangists') under his command. Most of these soldiers were lodged in Toledo's *alcázar*, a square stone fortress atop a hilly part of the outskirts of the old city. Soldiers on the ancient battlements could see, far across the River Tagus, the barracks of their ally General Franco.

Toledo's castle had started life as a semi-permanent Roman camp. After a few years it was rebuilt as the seat of the Roman Governor of Iberia. Later still, the Muslims built a keep there, which itself was beautified by Alfonso VI and converted by Alfonso X into a palace-fortress, an *alcázar*. It would serve the Kings of Spain as a royal residence until Ferdinand and Isabella moved the court to Madrid. Its weighty history made its defence a matter of honour for the monarchist-nationalist coalition.

Unfortunately, that was precisely why the Republican army, communist anti-clericals for the most part, had conflicting ambitions: to take it on or take it down. They began their siege with heavy artillery bombardment on July 21st and kept it up for two ghastly months.

Colonel Moscardó was holding the *alcázar*. He was both a Catholic and a Falangist. For Moscardó, losing it would have been unpardonable, even unthinkable. Despite several pleading telephone calls from Republican

Madrid - calls from two ministers and General Riquelme - Moscardó refused to quit his post. The siege had only just begun when Cándido Cabello, a Republican barrister in Toledo, telephoned Moscardó to say that if he did not abandon the Alcázar within the next ten minutes, he would personally shoot Luis Moscardó, the Colonel's 24-year-old son, whom he had captured that very morning.

'Para que Usted entiende que yo hablo la verdad, hable con su hijo,'[178] Cabello announced, passing the phone across.

'¿Que pasa, mi hijo?' asked the Colonel.[179]

'Dicen que se me fusilaron en seguida si el alcázar no se rindiese.'[180]

'Sea como sea, mi hijo. Que Dios te bendiga! Eres un hombre bravo. Encomienda a Dios tu alma y grite Viva España,' Moscardo replied. *'Adios mi hijo.'*[181]

'Eso puedo hacer,' answered Luis. *'Adios mi padre'.*[182]

When Cabello came back on to the telephone, Moscardó told him, 'The *alcázar* will never surrender,' and replaced the receiver. Time had run out. Cabelo took his revolver from its holster and fired a round into the boy's head, there and then. His bullet killed him instantly, spilling the lad's brains over the savonnerie rug.

When called upon to give his report for the day, Moscardó gave a reply that typifies *sang froid*, a quality long considered the private property of British heroes.

'Sin novedad,' he said. Nothing new.

Two desperate months would pass before General Franco could launch a large enough relief force to free the Alcázar. The Republican troops fell back in disorder and the siege ended with a victory for the

---

[178] He will tell you that I mean what I say.
[179] What is happening, my son?
[180] They say they will execute me if the alcázar does not surrender.
[181] If this is true then commend your soul to God, shout 'Viva España', and die like a hero. Good-bye, my son.'
[182] That I can do. Good-bye, Father.

monarchist-nationalist coalition. Sadly, in the process, the republicans badly damaged the *alcázar*.

As a postscript, well after the civil war, the fortress was rebuilt. That telephone, on which the conversation, between Colonel Moscardó and his son took place, is still on display. Tens of thousands come to see it every year and it symbolises that terrible conflict.

*

We had reached the Victorian but curiously Arabic railway station below the hilltop town by the time Ana had finished her sad story.

The historic city in *Castilla La Mancha*, sits proudly atop a promontory above the Tagus.

'*Hay una fecha para su primer ladrillo,*' Ana told me. 'We know when its first brick was laid: 192 BC. Then it was called *Toletum*. Traces of its circus are still visible outside the city walls.'

After the Romans left the town fell to the Visigoths, the Muslims and, finally, Ferdinand and Isabella's *reconquistadores*.

'*Toledo fuera la capital del imperio español, pero fue entonces cuando el Madrid se hizo cargo,*' Ana patiently explained. 'Toledo was our capital before Madrid took on the rôle.'

That will have relegated the town to merely a provincial capital, but explained how it had kept its centuries-old winding and cobbled streets unspoiled.

'*Me encanta esta ciudad vieja,*' Ana told me. '*Seriá un placer estar tu guía.*' I shall be your tour guide.

We started with the deceptively large cathedral, Toledo's centrepiece, atop its hill. Behind the main altar its wild baroque *transparente* was like nothing I had ever seen before. James Michener has suggested in his book 'Iberia' that the *transparente* was 'designed to allow light from the ambulatory behind the *reredos* to pass onto the

426

tabernacle. Otherwise it would have remained in constant shadow'.

Before I knew where I was going, or even what I was doing, we had climbed to the top of one of the spires of the *Iglesia de los Jesuitas*. I must admit the views of Toledo, the Tagus and the surrounding region were simply breathtaking. Rather like the stairs.

Ana did not let up. She still had a mosque up her sleeve. In no time we were on our way to the *Mezquita Cristo de la Luze*. A thousand years before it had been built as a little place of worship. Three hundred years after that it had been converted into a church, but an odd one. Its Mudéjar details were 'enhanced' with Christian frescos.

'Toledo has two mosques. Let's see the other one.' It seems the *Iglesia del Salvador* also started as a mosque and today combines the Mudéjar, Visigothic, and the Romanesque. I was saturated with beauty.

*

'Ana, let me offer you lunch. Now I need to attend to comparatively primitive needs, like lunch.' Enough rubber-necking. It was time to put up the white flag.

We were near a restaurant. One always is. This one was called *La Clandestina* and, as its name suggests, it was slightly off the beaten track. The stools that lined its bar and the tables inside were all already taken. Then I saw it had a quaint and rather cosy garden outside where, mercifully, it still had a table free for two.

We were offered a chilled *gazpacho con remolacha*. I had never had *gazpacho* with beetroot before and it was terrific. That followed with *croquetas* - small deep-fried and bread-crumbed oval food rolls containing ground veal, ham and cheese and mixed with a béchamel sauce. Bread, egg, spices, herbs may have been in the mix, even sautéd onions and mushrooms.

'These croquettes entrance my palate,' said Ana in her convoluted but wonderful English. I would have liked a second small glass of the chilled white wine but Ana touched only the water. I thought it best to hold back. She might have imitated me and gone horribly astray.

'Well that's that. Time to move on,' said Ana. 'I have another treat for you.'

In a few short minutes she was leading me into the Iglesia de San Tomé. There, once inside, I stood and gasped at one of El Greco's most celebrated works, *El Entierro del Conde de Orgaz*.[183]

'*¡Solo mira!*' Ana declared. 'This painting is considered by many to be his greatest. It took him two long years to paint. He worked every day, exploiting every hour of daylight to deliver this immense work.'

Immense is right. Four metres in height, three in width, it has two 'dimensions' - the hereafter above, the here-and-now below. They overlap to form a continuum, skilfully depicting the duality of what is metaphysical and what is physical. Arguably, it's the defining moment of late mannerism, its epitome, perhaps. It's also very daring as it wilfully traduces the Byzantine rubric, dragging it into the West. The artist was Doménikos Theotokópoulos much better known as *El Greco*, and his patron was the Count of Orgaz. Ana was kind enough to tell me the story behind the canvas.

'In 1312, a very old Don Gonzalo Ruiz, Lord of Orgaz, and a celebrated native of Toledo, finally died. He descended from a ruling dynasty in the Byzantine Empire, the noble Palaiologos family, and was a pious philanthropist. Among his many charitable acts was to impose a perpetual tithe on his own estate for the extension and adornment of his parish church. In

---

[183] The Burial of the Count of Orgaz.

428

'exchange' for his enormous generosity, the count besought the Church to let him be buried here.

'The Count of Orgaz clearly had admirers in heaven. Once his defunct body was carried to the church, Sts Stephen and Augustine came back to Earth and laid it in a glorious tomb.

'Two hundred and fifty years later, the Mayoralty of Orgaz decided to plunder the capital that Don Gonzalo had left to serve the spiritual needs of his community so long before. Andrés Núñez, the church's incumbent monsignor resisted, taking the town to court and, after protracted argument, he won.

'Once the legal battle was over, he redoubled his thanks to the church's great benefactor and had a strong idea of how to do it. Commissioning El Greco on March 18th, 1586, he instructed the artist to depict the local legend - that the count had been buried by saints - and their town's elite all attended the funeral. 'The work must 'engulf the space',' Núñez told him. 'You are to leave no part of the allotted wall untouched.' To make things even trickier, he only allowed El Greco nine months to complete the work and for a fixed fee of 1200 ducats.[184]

'El Greco, now at the peak of his fame and fortune, grudgingly accepted the deal. Núñez had played his trump card. He called on El Greco's pride; this was his home town after all and his work would be a celebration of another of Greek descent. Inevitably, therefore, El Greco gave way.'

Ana singled out a detail.

'In the centre, is Jesus, flanked by His cousin John the Baptist on the right, with His mother - our Lady - on the left. Above, and in the centre foreground, over her shoulder and in yellow robes, sits St Peter. Lazarus rises from his grave on the far right while on the far left are David, Moses and Noah. Below, on the freshly dug

---

[184] A gold ducat weighs roughly 3½ grams, or 0.11 troy ounces, 1200 ducats might therefore be £200,000 in today's money.

earth, St Stephen and St Augustine – both in cloth-of-gold finery – are lowering the late count in his armour to eternal rest in his lead-lined sepulchre. Up there, at the top, King Philip II and Pope Sixtus V make their grand entrée. The artist is thereby suggesting that the King of Spain and the Pope are together in heaven. It may seem a mere salute from the beyond,' said Ana, 'but few visitors today realise that in 1588 both men were still alive.'

What did this mean? Was perhaps El Greco saying that the king and the pope were in heaven and on earth at the same time? Every single surrounding mourner was of note. El Greco, a renowned portraitist, captured the likenesses of every one of the local luminaries. They are dressed in funerary black but sport extravagant white ruffs. Those with red crosses will have been members of the military-religious society, the Order of Santiago. Many of their names have been long lost but it is known that El Greco immortalised his old friend, the celebrated canonical scholar Antonio de Covarrubias. One of the two priestly figures to the right of the painting, either the one in the gold vestment reading from a book or the one looking upwards in a surplice, is believed to be Núñez himself. Do you see, just above the row of earthbound men, an angel in golden robes soaring heavenward. What do you think she has in her arms? A wispy human-like form that many believe El Greco used to describe the soul of Don Gonzalez de Ruiz on its final journey. In the line of mourners, a little to the left of centre, El Greco painted himself. He is looking straight at us, out of the painting. His young son Jorge Manuel is the one with one hand holding a long torch, while the other gestures toward the armoured count. A deliberate if somewhat cryptic clue allows us to identify the lad. On his square pocket is the year of his birth, 1578.

'This painting hangs exactly where the scene is set, right at the east end of the church, well behind the altar. On the Day of Judgement the sun will first shine above this monument. El Greco makes it seem that the saints are laying the count in his actual tomb. Above, Heaven's bright colours contrast with the darker colours below while stretched forms at the top haul the eye upwards from the realism of the earthly part of the canvas into the light and harmony of paradise.

'Only in one respect did El Greco fail to meet Núñez's deadline. He delivered his *magnum opus* a year late. Let's not be too censorious, however, since Núñez was a hard taskmaster. He paid for the nine months' work, as contracted, and that was that. Poor El Greco felt cheated and short-changed.'

> As surely as the rate of payment is inferior to the value of my sublime work, my name will go down to posterity as one of the greatest geniuses of Spanish painting.

El Greco may not have been naturally modest but he was right. He had deployed his wisdom, knowledge, expertise, composition and his unique expressive power. The *Burial* will forever define an extraordinary bold and fervent piece of mannerism, a living encyclopaedia without its ever ceasing to be a masterpiece.

From its unveiling it has drawn in the crowds. The inclusion of recognisable portraits of all those noteworthy subjects was a powerful draw for the Spanish court. Nor did it not take long for the incredible work to draw in the public. Almost from the outset the painting has been recognised as one of the most sublime artworks ever painted.

'Such acclaim was by no means inevitable,' continued Ana. 'In the eighteenth century, 'The Burial of the Count of Orgaz' was actually taken down. El Greco had fallen from fashion. Making matters worse, in the 19th century it was rolled up and abandoned somewhere in the church's vast crypt to wait until the early twentieth century before being 'rediscovered' and remounted. No one today, however, can doubt El Greco's mastery. The painting has become a tourist attraction and it guarantees El Greco's eternal place in the history of art.'

*

Contemplating this astonishing canvas, my brain, eyes and senses had slowly begun to reel.

Ana, I'm afraid, still had some treasures on her list. She had almost to drag me to see a former synagogue, now the church of *Santa María la Blanca*. Only three synagogues remain from before the expulsion of the Jews from Spain, and two of them are in Toledo.[185]

The other one is called *El Tránsito* and it houses the Sefardi Museum. It may well be wonderful. I was emotionally drained. Nevertheless I was still able to admire the stunning Monastery of *San Juan de los Reyes*. It is a sensational 16th century church in the old Jewish quarter, purpose-built to house the tombs of Ferdinand and Isabella. Unfortunately for Toledo and, following their 'reconquest' of Grenada, they elected to be buried in Seville instead.

Ana and I found our way to the station and home. I felt wiser than I had been before, if somehow slightly elongated.

*

Another week passed in the Madrid office, meeting a few clients, seeing many films, visiting countless museums and watching Spanish television. My Castillian was holding up but, every evening, the day done, I felt I had fought three rounds with Henry Cooper.

Just as my confidence was growing, it was time to go home to England.

*

---

[185] The third is in Córdoba.

I had learned, some years before, that it was possible to break my journey without incurring additional expenses, so I stopped over in Paris to see my sister. My mother Lisa and brother Giles happened to be staying with her that weekend, so it was something of a family reunion.

I had been away from England for some six weeks and I needed a separate case for my receipts. Settling my expenses would be high on my list of duties once I was back in CTB, and I had taken the time to get them into chronological order.

Kate found a number of large envelopes and at last that part of the task was done. My overall cost had not been that high, by City standards, even if Miss Barclay might need some explaining. All that could wait. Paris was fun for me but I bored everyone else with expansive accounts of Spain.

*

Now that I was back in CTB I had to deal with a brand new and unexpected problem. My envelopes, with six weeks' worth of receipts, were missing. We had searched Kate's Parisian flat, but to no avail. What would happen now? Six weeks' worth of expenses amounted to a lot of money.

I was going to have to bite the bullet. I knew exactly how much I had spent; it was on my credit card statement. The cash element I also knew, as I had only taken £200's worth of pesetas with me. I had had to obtain the Bank of England's permission and they had stamped my passport. There was nothing for it. I went to the department which had interviewed me a year or so before over that French matter and put my cards on the table.

'I have lost all my receipts.'

'That's not exactly clever.'

Stating the obvious makes repartee superfluous.

'Let's see, you were away for forty-four days. You spent this in total. That works out at, let me see, this much each day on average. You may be relieved to know you are not one of our big spenders. I'll have a word with your boss and I suspect all will turn out well. Just don't make a habit of it.'

*

My boss, Simon Galway, also chose to ignore my failings. He simply dismissed the issue, informing me that our Italian 'production broker', Sergio Corsi, wanted me and his chief executive Piero Petronio to visit the *Intesa Sanpaolo Assicura*, an insurance company in Turin. They had done a lot of direct business with Corsi, who thought we might sweet-talk them into giving us a treaty in return. I considered myself an expert on Turin. After all, I had seen *The Italian Job*. Twice. Once in English and once in Spanish.

I anticipated a whiff of Paris in its elegant tree-lined boulevards and echoes of Vienna in its stately *art nouveau* cafés. The city had once been a major European political centre. In 1563 it became the capital of the Duchy of Savoy. After that, it became the capital of the Kingdom of Sardinia and Piedmont, under the Royal House of Savoy. Its zenith was as the first capital of the Kingdom of Italy, from 1861 to 1865, before that role was ceded to Florence and thence to Rome. It is still an extraordinarily grand place, located on the western bank of the River Po and surrounded by hills. Many of its castles, gardens and town palaces, especially the glorious Palazzo Madama, were built during the 16th, 17th and 18th centuries.

Turin has some of Italy's best schools; universities, colleges, academies, lycea and gymnasia. It also houses fine museums, which, by all rights, should make it one of the world's major tourist destinations. However, it's only the tenth most visited city in Italy. By population, the city of

Turin is Italy's fourth-largest city. It is more inventive, industrious and is richer *per capita*, even than Milan. Some call Turin 'the cradle of Italian liberty' for having been the birthplace and home of some notable individuals who contributed to the *Risorgimento* - notably Count Cavour.

Not so many know that the world's first chocolate bars were made here. Well, you do now.

Even though most of its political significance had been lost well before the Second World War, Turin retained its status as a major European crossroad for industry, commerce and trade, a key apex on Italy's famous 'industrial triangle', a distinction it shares with Milan and Genoa. The city is also home to much of the Italian motor industry; Fiat, Lancia and Alfa Romeo are only a sample of its badges.

Above all, it houses the Shroud, a source of awe and euphoria. I was determined to see it. Historical and scientific discussions associated with the Shroud are compromised by the fact that the Church has never passed judgment on the Shroud's authenticity. Nevertheless it allows the Shroud to assist in devotions to the Holy Face of Christ, which guarantees that its cult will continue.

*

My airport bus let me out in the city's heart, in *Piazza Madama* at 4 o'clock that the afternoon, overnight bag in hand. It was raining when I arrived but I was forewarned to expect poor weather. Turin's autumn is famous for heavy rain and thunderstorms. Piero was still on his way from Milan and I would join him for a working supper and a planning session. That still left me a little time to soak up a snapshot of this magical city. Where better to start than the vast palace that was straight ahead. The palava of checking into my hotel could wait.

Palazzo Madama started life as a Roman gate and from there it evolved into a medieval castle. Rather later it became the home of *Madame Royale* (Marie-Christine of France) and Maria Giovanna Battista of Savoy-Nemours. With time, the politicians appropriated it. It came to house the *Camera Subalpino* in the *Risorgimento* (from 1848 to 1861) and, after the first phase of Unification, the Italian Senate from 1861 to 1864. Inside, the arrangement of the grand staircase would blow the socks off any Hollywood set dresser, even with an infinite budget. It has to be seen to be believed, for even a photograph would lose the scale of the vast sweep of solid marble that descends from the *piano nobile* to the ground.

Article 33 of the Albertine Statute established it as a 'House of Lords' whose senators were to be appointed by the king from members of the Savoyard nobility as a reward for the services rendered. In its last ever session, the lords nobly and voluntarily abandoned their own paramountcy.

Different horses, different courses. For Piero, Turin meant Juventus and Torino. Like Liverpool, Glasgow or Manchester, Turin has two football clubs, though they are not divided by sectarianism as in Britain.

When I delicately suggested that Piero might like to steal an hour from our crowded schedule to see the famous Shroud, he affected shock.

'We are here on business,' he told me sternly.

Over the next two days, our business went very well. That was good. Especially since it left me time to visit the Shroud.

*

The Shroud of Turin is a long, antique linen cloth, bearing the image of the man believed by most of the civilised world to be the Messiah. For centuries it has been revered as a holy object. Today, this delicate cloth is kept in a climate-controlled container in the depths of the Cathedral of Saint John the Baptist. It is not often

436

on view and I had to put up with a replica. A distinguished one, but a disappointment nonetheless.

Is it really the cloth that wrapped His crucified body? Could it be a medieval forgery, a hoax perpetrated by some heretical but clever artist? It's still difficult to say, despite its being the most intriguing artefact in the history of Man?

The Shroud first belonged to the Achaeans. It came to be housed and treasured in Hagia Sophia, where it would remain for centuries. In the end it was sold to the Venetians, weeks before Constantinople fell to the Turks. Those Venetians, in turn, took their time but eventually they sold it to the House of Savoy in 1578.[186]

We know from the Bible that Joseph of Arimathea wrapped the body of Jesus in a piece of linen and placed it in an open tomb. St Peter found multiple pieces of burial cloth there. The Gospel of the Hebrews, an unauthorised 2nd-century manuscript, reveals that the resurrected Christ gave the linen cloth to an acolyte. We do know that fragments of Jesus's supposed burial shroud are held by four churches in France and three in Italy but none has attracted as much veneration as the Shroud of Turin.

Many religions venerate the image on the cloth. Baptists, Lutherans, Methodists, Orthodox, Pentecostals, and Presbyterians all have replicas of the Shroud for didactic and sometimes even devotional purposes. No one can claim that some empirical analysis or scientific method will explain the image on the Shroud.

Was it produced miraculously at the moment of Resurrection?

The American scholar John Jackson has proposed that the image was formed by radiation 'beyond the understanding of current science'. There are some who hold by this.

---

[186] It wasn't until 1983 that the family gifted the Shroud to the Catholic Church.

In 1989, the physicist Thomas Phillips speculated that the Shroud image may have been formed by neutron radiation, following the miracle of the Resurrection. Personally, I have no opinion. The quasi-scientific explanations are all implausible, yet the metaphysical element is undeniable. The universe, the infinite, has always been and will always prove reluctant to submit to materialist explanation. As for me? Let me sit on the fence. It will forever remain a mystery.

*

In November, I had to be in Madrid a second time, this time to attempt to drum up a little more business for the London market. I unpacked in *The Europa* that evening, thinking I might watch the news in my hotel room. Get my ear in, so to speak. The very first item I watched was little short of apocalyptic.

It seemed that my passing acquaintance Colonel Tejero, together with a Major Ricardo Sánez de Ynestrillas, had attempted a *coup d'état*, known to the Press as *Operación Galaxia*. They had been joined and financed by a third whose name was withheld. Not even now has it been made public. The conspirators had chosen November 17th, 1978, for their attempt to subvert the Spanish transition to democracy. They chose a date when King Juan Carlos would be away in South America. When a Captain of the Police and a Commander of the Infantry managed to infiltrate their circle, their superiors were warned of the plot and their plan was exposed.

*

When I rang Ana that same evening, we agreed we would meet the next day for coffee in the *Bar Roma*.

She explained to me that the conspirators' codename derived from the *Cafetería Galaxia* where it seemed they liked to meet. I asked after her father.

438

'Thank you for asking. His strange ailment besets him still. Some time ago he was advised to retire from public life. He is in a psychiatric hospital and will stay there until it is safe for him to be released.'

Before I could stop myself I exclaimed 'you mean he's been committed?'

Ana's smile, however, was a knowing one.

'His 'hospital' is a charming villa in Cantabria. He is allowed to have visitors and his man Pedro is there with him. There are no other inmates. He'll be fine until we have him back.'

'Your mother must be beside herself with worry.'

'I think she's just relieved. Now, Jeremy, have you been to El Escorial? No? For anyone who wants to understand our Spanish soul, Philip II's Spartan palace-monastery will explain it all. It is a concept cast in stone. One that no other country could ever conceive. We shall go there on Saturday.'

*

It took Ana about an hour to drive the twenty-eight miles northwest of Madrid to the Royal Site of San Lorenzo del Escorial. The lanes were in terrible shape and the thin little tyres of Ana's tiny car screeched horribly as they skidded on the loose stones. Passing through the grandeur of the *Sierra de Madrid* was more like a terrifying funfair ride than a quiet road trip and her car looked all too likely to lose whatever sense of direction it may have had in the first place.

Deep in the *Sierra de Guadarrama*, at the foot of Mount Abantos, we found a stern and austere palace-monastery. Not the most obvious choice to site a royal palace. Nevertheless, it had been the choice of a resolute king, who built El Escorial out of locally quarried granite. Square and sparsely ornamented, it is forbidding in appearance - more fortress than royal residence. Each of the four corners has a square tower topped with a spire, while at the centre of the complex (and soaring above the rest) rise belfries and the dome of the basilica within.

Before we had even gone through the entrance gate, Ana had begun her promised personal tour.

'You're about to see the fusion of Royal Monastery, Residence and Pantheon. This breathtaking quadrangle has intersecting passageways, courtyards and chambers. They say that from space it would look like Laurence's gridiron.'

I was intrigued. 'Why here, not in Madrid? To what end?'

'In the 16th century the king had to deal with what looked like an irreversible march of Protestantism. Rebellion and discontent was stirring, even in the Spanish Netherlands. King Philip took it upon himself to oppose the trend. He dedicated much of his lengthy reign[187] and much of his seemingly inexhaustible supply of New World gold to stemming the tide. Philip meant El Escorial to be the campaign headquarters for planning and executing the Counter-Reformation and he furnished it accordingly.'

'Did he succeed?'

'The Counter-Reformation? He had a qualified success. De Salis and Ignatius Loyola were geniuses but even they faced setbacks. Philip's response to England's Queen Elizabeth's murderous execution of the Queen of Scots was his most urgent challenge. He believed, after the regicide, that he might bring England back to the faith by force of arms. As it turned out, his armada was rather less than invincible, but the march of Protestantism, at least, was halted. Today it is confined to a handful of countries in Northern Europe.'

And North America.

'Do you know what I think, Ana?'

---

[187] 1556–1598

'I do not,' she said immediately. Anyone who begins to opine with such a question is destined to make a fool of himself, but I pressed on. 'I think this building – in some ways like the imperial villas of Ancient Rome – shows how holistic the king was. He has brought every tenet of his ancient faith under one roof.'

'But why did he do that?' asked Ana with a politely amused smile, checking me in my presumption. I shut up. I could have been on the right track or wholly up the garden path. What was indisputable was that this enormous pile of a place had been designed to reflect the austere greatness of the Spanish Empire.

'This is one of the most important palaces in the world,' said Ana, with fervent pride. 'You'll find plenty inside to immerse yourself in, believe me. History, art and architecture. Its jewel of a Basilica, a Pantheon replete with the tombs of almost every King of Spain, including Philip's father, the Holy Roman Emperor Charles V. If that's not enough, there is an utterly dazzling Royal Library that celebrates its Arabic manuscripts. There are palatial suites of apartments, built or customised to accommodate the different reigning dynasties. You're in for a treat.'

Without more ado we went in, passing between two statues, just inside, one of King David, the other of King Solomon. I surmised that the statue of David represented the warrior-emperor Charles V and that the figure of Solomon was his son Philip II.

I was corrected immediately.

'These statues reflect King Philip's greatest ambition. Flavius Josephus's description of the Temple of Solomon in the heart of Jerusalem was for him canonical. Its portico would have to lead into a courtyard, open to the sky, and be followed by a second portico, a second courtyard, this time flanked by arcades

441

and enclosed passageways, which lead to the 'holy of holies'.

Philip's palace used this description as a blueprint.

'Our king was not alone in believing that those dimensions were handed down by God. Elements of it had been used in other buildings; the somewhat smaller Sistine Chapel in Rome, King's College Chapel in Cambridge, which dates from 1441. Another example is the old *Ospedale Maggiore*, Milan's first hospital.'

'And was that temple buildèd here, in Spanish scorched but pleasant land?' I asked.

'What Juan Bautista de Toledo, the 'architect royal', knew of that ancient Temple would have had to be extensively modified if it were to house the functions that Philip II intended his palace to serve. As well as a monastery, El Escorial is a pantheon, a basilica, a convent, a school, a library and a royal palace. It belongs to all of Spain, not just the king and his court, yet having all these roles caused the building to double in size. Philip's instructions were clear. He directed his architect to demonstrate 'simplicity in the construction, severity in the whole, nobility without arrogance, majesty without ostentation'.

A bit like himself.

I had been suitably impressed and we began with the monastery, as one should.

'This was a house for the Hieronymite monks,'[188] my guide continued with a sweep of her hand, 'but a little later gave way to the Order of Saint Augustine. Today the *Colegio Real de Alfonso XII*, a boarding school, makes good use of the Augustinian's over-provision of cells.'

Beginning to understand that El Escorial deliberately fuses two of the more elemental poles of the Spanish character, monarchy and Catholicism, it

---

[188] Followers of the Rule of St Jerome.

occurred to me that in every other Christian country an effort is made to keep them separate.

'King Philip II ruled Spain and its dependencies for more than forty years after the Spanish throne was detached from his father's Holy Roman Empire. In 1559, one of his earliest decisions was to employ the architect, Juan Bautista, as his principal collaborator in the palace's design. Bautista had spent the greater part of his career in Rome, working on St. Peter's. He had, therefore, the endorsement of the Almighty and it would have been a sin not to engage him. The king and his draftsman wanted El Escorial to reflect Spain's role as an earthly repository of divine purpose and to be sword arm of Christianity.'

'But why did he choose this unyielding place? It can hardly be described as an obvious location for a royal palace.'

'The king wanted El Escorial to be at the foot of a mountain. In consequence, the landscape would lead the eye upwards to God. Everything here turns on symbolism and allusion. Beneath Mount Abantos in the Sierra de Guadarrama, the palace celebrates the king's stern vision of the Garden of Eden, set like a jewel in an otherwise inhospitable valley. He also wanted to commemorate his August 10, 1557 victory over the King of France, Henri II, at the Battle of St Quentin in Picardy. St Lawrence's feast day is on that day. Poor Lawrence! The Romans roasted him to death on a grill. The floor plan of the complex was deliberately designed to look like a gridiron and it commemorates his horrific martyrdom in the third century. Death and its legacy mattered to Philip. He wanted his palace to serve as a quiet and remote necropolis for the mortal remains of his parents, Charles V and Isabella of Portugal, himself, his queen – Anne of Austria - and all his future descendants.'[189]

Poor Juan Bautista de Toledo never saw his project completed. With his death - in 1567 - his apprentice, Juan de Herrera, took over. The building was topped out in 1584, having taken twenty-one years from when the first cornerstone had been laid on April 23, 1563.

'In Spanish there is a telling phrase. *Una obra del Escorial* means a task that that takes a long time,' Ana added.

Today, the complex is an enormous storehouse, almost a warehouse of art. Its walls hide behind masterworks by El Greco, Velázquez, Jusepe de Ribera, Titian, Tintoretto, Paolo Veronese, Roger van der Weyden, countless others.

We went for the Spanish collection. To avoid having our senses dulled by over-indulgence, I insisted we should pause here and there. After an hour, Ana had shown me barely half-a-dozen. It was quite enough, however. Great art is terrifically demanding and it's all too easy to try and see too much. I was almost relieved when a grimy curator took me by the arm and asked me if I wanted to see his bearded woman. The question was so odd I actually laughed. Ana smiled at me in her most patrician manner.

'You'd be silly not to take a look. *La Mujer Barbuda* is probably by Jusepe de Ribera. There are several, so it may be a copy. The very sight of it is barred to women. Once you've seen it I want you to tell me all about it.'

The curator unlocked a door and ushered me into a small room. There, an easel bore a painting under a shroud. He shifted uneasily. I proffered a 100 peseta

---

[189] They are all here bar two. El Escorial has been the burial site for five centuries' worth of Spanish kings, Bourbons as well as Habsburgs, starting with the tomb of the Holy Roman Emperor, Charles V.

note and he accepted it greedily, stuffing it into his breast pocket. He then unveiled the source of Ana's intrigue.

The painting is certainly odd. A woman suckling a child and sporting a full beard? It was also extremely naturalistic. She is wearing a simple outfit, its folds and stitches carefully and skilfully executed, but what stopped me in my tracks was her creased and utterly masculine face. The tone of the image was grave but somehow empathetic. Wholly devoid of humour, it had a psychological depth that made it more than just an inconsequential curiosity. Dramatic tenebrism made the odd subject matter more sinister, even ominous. A strange moment indeed, and another insight. I was definitely earning my keep.

*

Before I could even think of tackling the Italians I needed a break. Ana suggested I should look at the library. How wise she was.

The library at El Escorial is a princely collection of priceless manuscripts, most of which predate the printing presses of Venice and Gutenberg. In its centre is a terrific fresco, celebrating Solomon's legendary wisdom.

That wise old king was Philip's rôle model, even his mentor. He hoped his subjects would remember him as well as they did that Old Testament king, and determined that the monumental temple of El Escorial would reflect a similarly thoughtful, logical character.

For me, however, it was the collection of Sultan Zidan Abu Maali, معالي أبو زيدان, the embattled ruler of Morocco from 1603 to 1627, that stole the show. Zidan had been facing chaos in his patch of North Africa. At the time he only held the southern half of his country. His brother had the northern half. All this while a Sanhaji rebel from Tafilalt was marching on Marrakesh, claiming to be the Mahdi. And, if that were not enough, the situation was exacerbated by a plague which, before it burned itself out, would leave a third of the country dead.

The conclusion of the Anglo-Spanish war saw the end of the Anglo-Dutch axis that Morocco had relied on as a means of protecting itself from Spain, ten miles away. When the Spanish resumed their lightning raids on the Moroccan coast, one of Zidan's provincial governors rebelled and established his own independent nation between Azemmour and Salé. Inevitably, Morocco descended into anarchy.

A ray of light on his benighted kingdom fell in the early seventeenth century when its sultan successfully re-established friendly relations with the Low Countries. Finally, James I of England could send a negotiator, John Harrison, to purchase the release of English hostages, but the situation remained unstable.

By 1612, Morocco was again embroiled in civil war. Maali Zidan told the French privateer Jehan Philippe de Castelane that he would pay him 3000 escudos to shift his household effects from Safi to Agadir, or Càdiz. Castelane waited six days. Still unpaid he unilaterally decided to sail north, the priceless cargo still aboard. A Spanish fleet of four ships intercepted his vessel and took it to Lisbon (then part of Spain). Every member of Castelane's crew was convicted of piracy and hanged, aside from the captain. No such courtesy for him. He was sentenced to be torn apart by wild dogs.

As for Maali Zidan's collection, it was taken to El Escorial, for 'safe-keeping', which is where it remains to this day. It is, of course, breathtaking.

*

It was time for a sandwich and, to my delight, Ana did not merely agree. She had a restaurant in mind. The Italians would have to wait.

'We shall go to *La Granjilla de la Fresneda,*' she pronounced. 'It is a royal hunting lodge and former monastic retreat, about five kilometres away in the foothills of the Sierra de Guadarrama.'

Who knows? It didn't exactly sound like a sandwich bar, but it did sound good. It turned out to be an architectural complex, laid out in the Renaissance, a muddle of different buildings surrounded by ornamental, ethnobotanical and spagyric gardens, artificial dams, waterways and a hunting reserve, elegantly contained within dry stone walls.

Friar Marcos de Cardona, a Hieronymite, was the designer and gardener while the Royal Lakes are owed to the Catholic Dutchman and hydraulic expert, Petre Janson.

There is not much the Dutch do not know about managing water. The highest and largest one draws its water from the River Aulencia to feed the three artificial lakes downstream. From there, Janson's inspired hydraulics power the whole marvel through a suite of dams, conduits and waterways.

Civil engineering on this scale was merely a small part of a vast network of environmental and infrastructural transformations, stretching from Madrid to the slopes of Abantos and mountain-tops of Santa María de la Alameda. It provides the starting point for *El Canal del Escorial,* which greedily shares the source of the River Alberche. *La Casa de Campo de Madrid, La Granjilla de La Fresneda del Escorial* and *El Canal del Escorial* (built to supply water to the Palace-Monastery) and *La Cacera de La Granjilla de La Fresneda* (the aqueduct to feed the ponds of *La Granjilla)* were designed by Juan Bautista de Toledo and his assistant, a young Juan de Herrera.

*

It was time to grab that hypothetical sandwich. Lunch would have to be modest as Ana still planned to show me the *Valle de los Caídos*, the Valley of the Fallen. It would have to be a sober affair if we had to climb up the steep Valle de Cuelgamuros, a few kilometres away. The plan was to see the monumental site from the great height of the Madrileñian mountains.

What Ana hadn't yet divulged was that she had long been invited to a wedding breakfast at the *Finca de la Granjilla de la Fresneda*, part of the royal retreat. The marriage itself had been in the Basilica below. The sumptuous feast was up here in the farmhouse, overlooking El Escorial and she had somehow wangled an invitation for me.

Instead of a *tapa* or two washed down with a glass of gassy water, we were treated to a fantastic cava-canapé combination, superb paella and some sort of fig cake, all in an enchanting place. Over the pudding we promised ourselves that we would one day return to El Escorial, but now it was time to visit the Valley of the Fallen.

Here, a colossal granite cross, at 150 metres and possibly the tallest in the world, surges from the rock of the *Sierra de Guadarrama*. An extraordinary monument, it controversially combines architecture, sculpture and engineering to honour the fallen Christians of Spain's Civil War.

The whole thing had been raised after the Civil War, while elsewhere the Second World War still raged. Spain was famously 'neutral' in that conflict. The Generalissimo commanded Pedro Muguruza and Diego Mendez to build an esplanade. It serves as a colossal platform for a basilica whose vaulted crypt had to have been bored into the mountain. It took the 1940s and '50s, two whole decades to build. Franco referred to it as 'a national act of atonement', a quasi-mythic space that would resonate with 'the grandeur of monuments that defy time and memory.' The idea was to neutralise the belligerent factions that had bedevilled Spain for too long and, in this, it more or less succeeded.

It is a vast monument to Franco's victory and security was tight. It is unashamedly divisive. Flag-waving Francoists and Catholic-authoritarian Falangists tended to be a little over-enthusiastic while paying their respects. Spain was still split between 'Fascists' and 'Republicans'. Plenty of Spaniards would pay good money to spit on the grave of General Francisco Franco. Yet there were just as many who would happily part with the 500 peseta admission fee to come and lay flowers on the plain stone that bears his name but not his rank inside the Basilica of the Holy Cross.[190] It was and I believe is still Spain's most sombre tourist attraction.

*

My Spanish adventure was over. It was time for me to head back to London for another 'renewal season', the time when all our annual contracts were renegotiated. I told Ana, sincerely, that I would be back in the New Year.

There is a cosmological, metaphysical question some like to ask.

Q. How can you make God laugh?

A. Tell Him your plans.

---

[190] Neither form of 'tribute' is now permitted in the church, where today the former military leader of Spain lies surrounded by the bones of followers and enemies alike.

CHAPTER SIX

A Gap in the Market

In which the author flies too close to the sun. To cure the blues he travels to Jamaica, his first time out of Europe, and meets a theatre producer, hoping perhaps to find a literary string to his battered bow. He resigns, with hindsight unnecessarily, from CTB.

In March, 1979, my immediate boss Simon Galway, asked to see me in his office.

'Jeremy,' he said, 'please sit down.'

I knew from his tone I was in trouble.

'Jeremy, I want you to find another job.'

'Have I done something wrong?'

'Dozens of things. To put it simply, you are not one of us. You're a psychological curiosity. I don't believe that even you know who you are. You are just too odd to be a member of my team. History, music and painting? Real brokers are interested in football, cars and television. You would do better to rethink your future.'

I had no idea who I was?

'Are you firing me?'

'No. Not yet, anyway, but the list of issues grows daily longer. There was the Montedison business. You almost blew up the whole company! Somehow you got away with it. On your trips overseas you appear to spend more time in art galleries and opera houses than in front of our customers. You also spend more of our money than your pay-grade warrants.'

'At least I get results. Four new treaties so far, combined with increased shares in existing ones. I even think I have become an established face in the market.'

'Jeremy, let us not bandy words. Your heart is not in the City, not in our dreary British ways. I don't know where you would fit in but, if I were you, I should, look elsewhere. Spain, perhaps?'

450

I had the stomach-churning feeling he was right. Maybe I did not fit in?

'You're suggesting I find a position in Spain?'

'Yes. I've had a word with Andy. You'd be more than welcome in our Madrid office, he says.'

'That would be as an assistant director?'

'No. That would have to be earned out there.'

'Well, thank you for telling me your thoughts.' What was I to say? 'I like candour. I'll reflect on everything you have said. Kind of you not to mince words.'

*

My mother, bless her, had emigrated. She had decided to move to Athens, for motives that I hadn't clearly understood. One factor may have been that her children had moved out and a four bedroom mansion flat in Kensington was far too big for a single person. Though by itself, that does not necessarily point to Athens.

I was awarded the task of packaging up her belongings and sending them to Greece. I did my best. Not that my arrangements were perfect. She would later complain that all her electrical bits and pieces were smashed by the time they arrived. Some dated back to the days of round pins, fragile Bakelite, and in some the live wire was brittle and had cracked with age. I think they were largely that way, long before I packed them.

It was not my fault, I remonstrated, though I'm not sure that I was ever believed. Still, I had recently been to Athens and I thought it not too a bad place to start over. My mother, her letter said, had somehow discovered a flat in *Plaka*, the nearest quarter of Athens to Bohemia; its Chelsea, if you will.

Her flat, she said, was light and airy – all good stuff for an artist - but it had a peculiarity. Its vast plate-glass windows overlooked a nondescript and scruffy little square below. Considering her flat was just beneath the

Parthenon, only one small window looked out over what may be the greatest building ever erected. It was the kitchen window, and it measured two foot by two.

*

I went to my then flame's house in Fulham where I was expected for dinner. Vesta Sumner, a pretty girl, was on a golden ladder at Citibank. My despondency was tangible. Like a gentleman, I decided to share it with her. No point in only one of us being unhappy.

'Why don't you invite him and his wife to dinner? That way he could learn exactly who you are.'

'That might make matters worse.'

'Don't be silly. We'd spoil him. And his wife, of course. Does he know how much you know about everything?'

'Yes. He repeatedly tells me that I know nothing.'

'How very Socratic. Well, why don't you tell one of those head-hunters who buy you drinks so regularly that you might be open to persuasion?'

'A company car might be good. So would £10,000 a year,' I mused.[191]

'There's some tasty food for thought. You need time to think. My brother has been posted to Jamaica. Why don't we go and stay with him for a week or two. He won't mind and you will love it.'

*

The journey was simple enough. We were wearing light but smart clothes, as we were likely to be met and, being well dressed, we thought we might be offered an upgrade. Sadly, the latter didn't happen. Not this time, anyway.

When we touched down at Kingston, the captain ordered his stewards to open the doors. Air flooded in,

---

[191] £10,000 (1979) maybe 3 x or 4 x the average wage of the time, might be more than £150,000 in 2022. The £7,000 I was actually paid was a reasonable income for an ambitious 29-year old.

hot enough to roast a turkey or, in our case, two. A semi-comatose set of passengers had to stand and clumsily retrieve their precious duty-frees from the overhead lockers before Vesta and I could step into a scene already familiar to me from an early scene in *Dr No*.

Vesta's elder brother Ignatius had sent a car for us, an ancient black limousine with a driver to match, but one whose smile might illuminate a whole village. Moses, for that was his name, smoked like the proverbial chimney. By the time Vesta and I reached the residence in New Kingston we smelled like the *fabricantes de cigarros* in Carmen's tobacco factory.

A minute or so later we were admitted by a Cerberus in charge of the barrier into the compound where Ignatius and his wife Blanca had their apartment. 'Gated communities', at that time, were wholly unknown in Britain. At least we were safe from the regiments of villainous *impis* that surely comprised the native population of the island.

Ignatius, better known as Natty, and Blanca made us very welcome.

It was midday, and Vesta and I had slept, after a fashion, on our way across the Atlantic. Some of the time in my case, most of it in hers.

Natty and Blanca's pad was modern and comfortable. Its furnishings were plain and simple, and obviously provided by their landlords. Vesta's brother and sister-in-law had added little save a couple of local paintings.

'You will need to freshen up the ex-pat way,' Natty told us. 'We have the finest coffee in the world on our island so, to compensate, we have the worst milk. Sugar was in the stores again this morning, so what would you say to a cappuccino?'

Seemed like a good way to start an adventure.

'I have to apologise for Kingston,' he continued. 'What you will have seen coming in is admittedly scruffy, I must agree. Once you've fully recovered from your journey we'll show you some of the better or more exciting bits; the old town, the docks.'

Not even an hour later we were, recaffeinated, unpacked, showered and ready for anything.

We were now heading for the city's waterfront and Natty drove us there himself, telling us as he drove that the city had world class museums and galleries. From the car's window I saw imposing buildings and great monuments. Occasional Glimpses of the Caribbean made it all the more attractive.

'The city centre underwent a lot of change in the '60s.' Natty had assumed the helpful role of *vademecum*. 'A terrible time for architecture, here as everywhere. While the rest of the world was entranced by reggae, the very places where those sounds were invented were being demolished and rebuilt. Ninety-five acres of downtown Kingston were bulldozed and identikit shops replaced haphazard market stalls. What had been colourful hovels had given way to concrete offices and a new financial centre. The Knutsford Racetrack was replaced with 'New Kingston', where we live. They called it 'progress', this abolition of the old, the familiar, the romantic. Modernists so hate local colour. You will have already been disappointed by the ugly concentration of multi-story buildings and over-wide boulevards. Saying that, the west of the city has been left as it always had been, a smelly squabbling stew of drug-dealers and building contractors, enlivened with sporadic bursts of gunfire.'

'Gunfire?'

'The political atmosphere here is tense. Manley's government looks fragile and our economy is in free fall. Mercifully, I am paid in US dollars. Recurring violence has been rewarded with a decline in tourism, our most important industry, which may go some way to explaining why we live in a compound and submit to what amounts to a voluntary curfew. We only hope they do not choose the Soviet set of solutions.'

Blanca wanted us to see the Craft Market. It was in the old covered market, close to the shoreline, and it was certainly bright. It was also fragranced with the sickly-sweet perfume of *cannabis sativa*. Reggae, everywhere, delivered a constant, unyielding, pitiless pandemonium into the ground bass of traffic. As for the goods on sale, the market's mainstays were straw and wooden souvenirs, dolls, Panama hats, and baseball caps emblazoned with images of Bob Marley. Heady stuff, the latter.

'Reggae aside,' said Natty, 'Jamaica's main attractions are architectural, historic, religious and cultural. The urban parks brim with monuments, statues of iconic figures, while the domino addicts sit in verbal silence under them, playing their noisy game. Especially in the National Heroes' and St William Grant's parks. Kingston boasts a large number of places of worship, including a Catholic Cathedral and the Shaare Shalom Synagogue. You will have freedom of choice at the weekend.'

'They're not here to spend their precious time on their knees,' Blanca accurately told her husband. 'They may want to see the National Gallery, however.' She turned to us. 'It's the largest gallery on this island and it's here in Kingston Mall. It's not just international collections, there's local stuff as well. It has some pieces that relate to the island's first European settlers in the 1500s.'

We were being offered a chance to look into the Jamaican mind and Natty pulled into the Nat Gal's carpark. It was exciting and fun. The old stuff was far more distinguished than I had dared hope.

The latest offerings, however, were not even up to the standard of a bog-standard English school's end-of-term exhibition. We spent an hour there, the last half feeling twice as long as the first.

'If you really want to deepen your acquaintance with Jamaican culture the Institute of Jamaica is where you should begin. It's that big red-brick building. It has galleries filled with weird insects, strange animals, seashells, fruit seeds, local crafts...' Natty was forced to draw breath. 'It's a truly venerable collection, started a century ago.'

Either Vesta or I will have yawned, as Natty looked at his watch. 'Good God, is that the time?'

It was five o'clock.

'It gets dark here very quickly, in around an hour. We still need to get to Devon House.'

'Devon House?'

'Yes. It's a huge eighteenth-century mansion. It regularly has music in the grounds. Do you like classical music?'

'I like some.'

'What d'you like best?'

'I don't know. After so much Reggae, Bach might be an antidote,' I said.

Natty actually gasped.

'Bach? How extraordinary! Well, you are in luck! That's what's on this evening!'

Devon Park was as billed, an amazing survivor of an elegant age, privately owned but open to the public, house and garden alike. We paid a small fee and walked through the state rooms, marvelling at the comforts its colonial builders had contrived to install. It was like a stately piece of Gloucestershire, spirited from home and forcibly mated with a plantation mansion. That said, much of Jamaica feels that way. Even the people.

We stepped back into the open air, just in time for the concert. Our places were numbered on canvas chairs in the garden, tidily arranged around a sheltered stage. Mercifully a breeze had softened the stupefying heat. Blanca handed us a programme. It listed just one work. J S Bach's Toccata and Fugue in D minor, BWV 565, to be played by the massed steel bands of the Commonwealth of Jamaica.

Forty musicians, all with hollow steel cans, came on stage. Their music was unalloyed magic. It was so good that Bach himself must have written the transcription.

'I'm sorry to be a party-pooper,' said Blanca, all too soon, 'but Natty and I must get back home before nine o'clock. In a troubled Jamaica it's wise to get home early.'

'Is there anything you particularly want to see tomorrow,' asked Natty. 'We have to work. I have arranged for Moses to be your driver.'

'What do you suggest?' asked Vespa.

'Why not visit *GoldenEye*?[192] Until his death in 1964 it's where Ian Fleming would sit at his little wooden desk, in a corner of the house that he designed for himself. He wrote all fourteen James Bond novels there. He lifted the name of his over-masculine hero from a local ornithologist, the author of *Birds of the West Indies*.'

'What is it? A shrine? A pleasure palace?'

'It's a small hilltop villa. It lets out its three bedrooms - a master suite, a queen-sized bedroom, and a bedroom with two twin beds - at huge cost to pilgrims, but visitors are encouraged to visit the villa's tropical garden. You'll be particularly pleased to learn it has a bar in the garden hut.'

'How perfect is that?'

---

[192] Ian Fleming briefly shared the house with Noel Coward. Fleming did the cooking, which Coward described as 'tasting of armpits'. Coward christened the house 'Goldeneye, nose and throat'. Today, Goldeneye is an exceptional, boutique-size resort hotel run by music-business legend and pioneering hotelier Chris Blackwell. He founded Island Records and made Bob Marley the first international reggae star. Marley bought Goldeneye from Ian Fleming's estate in the late 1970s, and sold it to Blackwell in 1981.

'Isn't it? The story began when an Anglo-American intelligence summit took Fleming to Jamaica in 1942. He stayed in what was then a B & B and swore that he'd return to the island after the war and make it his home. To create his muscular cynic, James Bond, he drew on his years as a journalist at Reuters and even earlier days of penning intelligence reports. His creation, a larger-than life version of himself, has a few better clothes and certainly more dramatic gadgets but Fleming could always rival his creation for one-liners and conquests.'

'Well, that was a great sales pitch. We're on our way.'

'Good. Moses has orders to bring you back here before 5 pm. We're going to a cocktail party in Port Royal in the evening. You will never have experienced anything like it, that I guarantee.'

Vesta and I were in good time. *GoldenEye* itself was almost unspoiled, though there were already twenty or more tourists there, bent on undoing its serenity.

We had a tour. It didn't take long as the 'bar', in reality a tool shed just outside the little house, was open. Vespa's *martini* was ready to be shaken not stirred but, disappointingly, Vesta preferred an orange juice to the cocktail named after her.

We sat with our glasses, pleased with life and ourselves, on the villa's delightful terrace, cleverly cantilevered over the hill.

'How charming it must have been here before the place became famous,'[193] she said.

Moses, however, was not playing. He stayed in the air-conditioned car, inhaling the sweet Jamaican air via a vile cheroot while we looked over Oracabessa Bay,

---

[193] It still has massive charm today but a whole number of lodges have been built around it. Something like forty people can now stay there, and the true memory of Fleming/Bond has been overlaid with post-facto invention and myth. Fame can be destructive.

A tiny hummingbird hovered beside us, extracting the nectar from the bougainvillea that lined the verandah. Its plumage was iridescent but it was so small it could hardly have startled a bumblebee. Absolutely stationary, its wings made this almost invisible feat a blur. I could have watched this aerodynamic marvel for ages but we had to return to the compound in good time for what our hosts had planned for us in Port Royal. Having been to a few cocktail parties in my thirty years, in London, Munich, Rome and Paris, as far as the institution was concerned, I was a veteran. Nothing, surely, could surprise me. We drove up a long drive to an ostentatious mansion, simultaneously rural and urban; *rus in urbe*, six hundred yards from the main road and three hundred from a similar pile to the right.

This was not a cocktail party in the sense that (1) we would have cocktails, or (2) we would go on somewhere better for dinner. Instead, it combined the two with a band, hot and cold running staff and unlimited Californian Champagne. From my insular perspective, the first thing that struck me was that the guest list was colour blind. Today, I would be ashamed of myself for even noticing. The better-dressed two thirds of the guests were not white.

All mixed easily, but I came from a country where coloured folk would seldom be included in such events. Not, I think, because of any entrenched racial prejudice but because we had all grown up so separately. We just didn't know each other.

In the US a different format prevailed. There the prejudice *was* entrenched, reinforced by the fact that those who gave cocktail parties had been to schools like Groton or Exeter where, realistically, the fees were at a level where our differently coloured cousins could not or cannot afford. That and the fact that their national story - the Confederacy, Lincoln, Martin Luther King, Rosa Parks, the Ku Klux Klan and their Civil War - was etched into their collective soul. None of that applied in Jamaica. Everyone looked terrific, especially the darker women. They had taken great care to compliment their hostess by wearing their finery, making their mark, at best in a blaze or at worst in a clash of colours. The atmosphere quite made my head spin. Expensive scents competed for supremacy.

'Most of these people,' Blanca told me quietly, 'have businesses in the tourist sector. Overall, these guys own Jamaica.'

'Who's that man over there, that tall fellow surrounded by adoring girls?'

'That's Chris Blackwell. He owns Island Records. He has made millions from Jamaican talent and, through him, so have his artistes. Bob Marley and the Wailers are on his label and he has just signed U2. They say he means to land Grace Jones.' I had not even heard of Grace Jones. Not then, anyway.

Vesta and her brother were in deepest chinwag with our hostess and, when I approached, Natty steered me towards a beautiful Jamaican girl. Have I already mentioned that she was a dramatic dark goddess with a perfect figure?

'This is Yolanda. She likes banter. Amuse her.'

With that he was gone. Moses side, Yolanda was the first true Jamaican I had ever met. Her charm and poise were utterly admirable. Nor was she a dullard. She was at university in the US, at Yale no less, and was reading an English major with a Drama minor. When she spoke, her glorious Jamaican lilt added something seductive, sensual, provocative and possibly primordial to her voice. What I heard in her lilt derived from Ireland, the West Country, and possibly West Africa, a composite we have come to call 'Caribbean'. Her English was a marvel. She needed no fillers like 'know what I mean' or 'let me see' to bulk out a point. She had what I fancied was more-or-less the language that Shakespeare would

460

have heard every day. It would certainly be closer to the Bard of Avon's than my own more modern drama. Sitting out in the grounds, Yolanda and I chatted about Miami (where she had cousins), the Ivy League, Oxbridge, and of course Shakespeare, Milton - even Chaucer. Yolanda knew them all.

Of course, it was a great party. No less than Chris Blackwell had organised the music. We went back in to hear the girl band perform for us. In my opinion it owed something to Detroit, with that inimitable 'ska' beat at the end of every bar. I saw at once that the singers were those I had idiotically mistaken for groupies.

Waiters moved among us, distributing small plates of 'finger food' - curried goat, ackee and saltfish, crayfish tails – while refuelling our glasses.

I danced with Vesta, Blanca, and - how good can life get? - with Yolanda. Possibly as a result of our little exploration of English drama, Yolanda asked me if I would allow her to introduce me to someone – another English guest – who was pivotal in Jamaica's collective thespian aspirations. Her name was Jillian Binns. Her touring company was called *The Shakespeare Players* and she had brought it to Jamaica at the invitation of Government House. In Mr Manley's opinion, Jamaica needed Shakespeare, and she had agreed. Yolanda had played Juliet in one of her productions.

Mrs Binns' house was in Port Antonio, overlooking the Blue Lagoon. 'Graham and I would love to meet your friends,' Jillian told me once introductions were effected. 'Not now of course. We have to go home.'

'Where do they live?' she asked me.

'In New Kingston.'

'Then bring them over. Wednesday would be good. 6 pm? Buy yourselves some coffee on the way. The road from Kingston will take you over the Blue Mountain.'

461

All too soon it was time to go home. Natty and Blanca were more than a little paranoid about staying out late.

*

The following day, after a wonderful night, Blanca wanted to play tennis with Vesta. I suspected they were both rather good.

'Why don't you let Moses take you somewhere? Natty is in his office all day. Vesta and I can enjoy a girlie moment or two together. Come back for lunch or let Moses show you where you can grab a simple bite and be home in time for drinks?'

'Great plan.'

Not that I had any choice. I don't play tennis. Sitting by the court, turning my head mechanically from left to right, is a bore. Even strawberries, after the first punnet or two, have never had that much appeal.

Blue Mountain was something else altogether. Its smarter houses on the lower slopes soon gave way to a jerry-built shanty town. Though the road deteriorated, Moses was unaffected. He took me onward, upward, if carefully.

Higher yet, we reached a humid and damp region with little in the way of housing. That was where we discovered the coffee plantations, high up the northern side of the mountain, cloaked in mist and fog.

'This is coffee heaven,' the taciturn Moses condescended to inform me. 'Though it's well hot, the morning mist slows up the ripening. The plants grow slow and mama's little beans are born in clusters, beautiful black babies full of flavour. When the time is right, each of them is picked and immediately readied for twenty-four hours in the vat. All this is done by hand. Over the several days that follow the beans are allowed to dry in the sun before being bundled into sacks for another three months. All this before they can walk.'

Roasting (for those who did not want to roast the beans themselves) took place in the plantation kitchen, in small batches, a process peculiar to Jamaica. It was said to account for the distinctive tang of Blue Mountain Coffee.

Ah hour or so later Moses let me down at Wallenford Farm. I had arrived in perfect time to join a guided tour of the mill. I was astonished to learn for just how long this wonderful coffee had been cultivated here. I wondered how could anyone in 1746 have known that the soil and climate could be so ideal?

It was the hey-day of empires and the European coffee house, that's how. Captain Matthew Wallen had sailed to Jamaica, back in the day, determined to farm the land where he had sown his coffee beans. Over the following three centuries he and his descendants would grow his precious crop and he became the largest producer of Blue Mountain and High Mountain coffee in the country.

Today, a producer, not a grower, manages the Wallenford 'empire', its former ambitions reduced to its mill. It processes the coffee grown by its many tenant farmers, paying them a 'living wage'. Not very much, in other words. Wallenford's does support, however, the infrastructure in the area - schools, drainage, buses and so on.

At the outlet I bought some beans from the *Old Tavern Coffee Estate*, advertised as the only remaining coffee estate on the Blue Mountain where coffee is grown, processed, roasted, packed and sold by just one family. The shop has a speciality. It exploits an unusual but natural occurrence. 'Peaberry beans' are large, as their cherries only produce a single bean, rather than two smaller ones. Their flavour is mellower, fuller. The estate carefully handpicks the berries and it has become the most sought-after coffee in the world. The price, however, can cause an investment banker to weep.[194]

*

It was time to eat something and we had already passed several stalls on the road. I told Moses to stop at the first to display the faintest hint of respectability. 'Jerky' had to be tasty and, after forty eight hours, Red Stripe beer was already an old favourite of mine.

Moses stopped at an undistinguished little roadside stall. The board outside had the all-important if poorly painted words 'Beef Jerky' on it. While Moses elected to remain in the car, despite my generous offer of a tinny and a morsel, I alighted. Half-a-dozen native Jamaicans stood around, a beer in every other hand, while two small tables accommodated the ubiquitous domino players. Thin strips of marinated air-dried beef hung from the stall's 'eaves'.

This was the legendary 'jerky'. When in Rome, etc, and I asked the enormous smiling Gentleman of the Stall if I might have a portion.

'Hey, sure you can. You tried it before? You're a lucky man, this is the best Jerky in Jamaica. Probably the world.'

'No, I haven't had it before. Sounds as though I'm in the right place.'

'Well, then, your first taste is on the house!'

I tore off a tiny strip and tasted it. An explosion filled my palate as far back as my ears. The onlooking Jamaicans gave me a little round of applause.

'Where are you all from, man?'

'From London.' They seemed puzzled, so I added, 'England.' Not Ontario, I thought.

I earned another burst of appreciation.

---

[194] Jackarta has a rival. There the indigestible raw berries are eaten by apes but, when excreted, the berries have mellowed like a vintage wine.

'That Jerky needs a beer to wash it down. Here's a Red Stripe, the best beer on earth. Say what you think. I bet you've never tasted anything quite so good.'

This initially unprepossessing bar was rocketing skyward in my estimation. I was watching a morning flower unfurl in the heat. One of the locals turned to me with a question.

'You never tried Appleton's?'

'Appleton's?'

'Daniel, give our English friend a shot.' He turned to me. 'It brings out the joy'.

Daniel poured a tot of a white rum and slid it over the bar.

'That has to go down in one,' he instructed.

I did as instructed. I hadn't believed I liked rum, or 'ron' as they pronounced it, but it was good. It actually worked well with the beef.

'You like that?'

'Yes I do.'

'That ron is for our picaninnies. Let the English gentleman have a shot of the overproof.'

Daniel shook his head to himself but did as he was told.

'Five dollars say you no can drink that in one go,' wagered my new friend.

Like most businessmen, I enjoy a challenge. When I put the empty glass back on the counter, all my new friends were looking at me curiously.

'My five bucks say he no drink none other,' said one.

'Hey, so do mine,' said another.

Appleton's Overproof Rum is produced by carefully distilling dynamite, but I thought I knew what was going on. American tourists drink Coca Cola and fall down after a couple of beers, while few Europeans would ever stop at a shebeen like this one.

These Jamaicans could not have known that we have somewhat harder heads for the demon drink than our transatlantic cousins. It might even be that I was the first white man ever to join these guys for a noggin. The first European, anyway.

Add to that, I was enjoying myself. When I got back in the car I was richer by thirty Jamaican dollars and by a wonderful experience. I was also more than a little tipsy. Going off by yourself can be a great adventure, though I cannot say this road-side version of Paradise was a tourist magnet.

*

'The biggest tourist trap in Jamaica is Montego Bay, or Mo' Bay as the locals would have it,' Natty told us that evening while feeding the barbecue. 'Would you like Moses to show you Jamaica's most energetic city tomorrow?'

'What is it like?'

'Well, bright blue skies, ice-white beaches and miles of colourful coral reefs, all bubbling with life all day and, regrettably, all night.'

I glanced at Vesta, who nodded.

'OK, bring it on!' proudly demonstrating the idiom I had learned at my school on the Blue Mountain.

Mo' Bay, on the other hand, had a different beach for every day of the week. The real celebrity spot, Moses told us, was 'Doctor's Cave'. Swimming was somewhat hazardous, he warned, due to the huge numbers of idiots on waterskis who skimmed the surface at breakneck speed. A pity, then, as I would have liked to have explored the coral reefs.

It's the nearest bay, Cornwall, was less crowded with sunbathers, but that may have been because it was already filled with children and stalls selling fried fish. The busiest beach, '*Walter Fletcher*', had a go-kart track, tennis court and an aquatic theme park. Great. As for the town itself, its high street, Gloucester Avenue, ran parallel to the ocean front. It had been rechristened Hip Strip, either by the tourists or by the promoters, possibly by both. By day, this two mile stretch of shops, restaurants and bars teemed with street vendors and sun-burned holidaymakers. It was Magalufe, or Torremolinas, but where the tones of Wolverhampton or Dagenham had been swapped for loud American voices. Either way they still drowned out the canned reggae.

A brochure advertising Montego Bay and its century-old bathing club caught our attention. Marine Park, just off the coast, provoked us to put on our snorkelling masks. We were wise. Nine square miles of luminous coral reefs and mangroves had been colonised by grouper fish, barracudas and stripey Sergeant Majors. I also thought I saw the notorious rainbow-coloured Widow Maker, a carnivorous barracuda, but I have lived to tell the tale.

*

Natty and Blanca had nobly planned to share a week or so of our vacation and accordingly hired a house-and-butler in Frenchman's Cove. The beach below the villa, a swathe of shelving sand, was bordered by lush greenery, a little capsule of heavenly design.

The ensemble overlooked the limpid waters of the Blue Lagoon. The sea must have been sprinkled with fairy dust as it changed colour throughout the day, depending on the way the sun shone through the surface. When we first arrived, it had looked turquoise but once in a glass-bottomed boat, it changed though sapphire to royal blue.

'Locals used to believe that the lagoon was fathomless,' Natty told us, 'but they have since learned that its depth is a mere two hundred feet. There is a legend that a dragon dwells here.' I knew this already. I had seen *Dr No*.

The 'Blue Hole' (as it is locally known) opens to the sea through a narrow funnel, fed by freshwater springs that come in about a hundred feet below the surface. That is why the water introduces every shade of jade and emerald during the day. Cold freshwater floats over the warmer seawater beneath.

'If you care to take a dip, you'll notice the alternating temperatures - the warmth of the Caribbean and the ice-cold waters from the underground streams. It's quite an experience.'

With that, Natty went over the gunnels.

'We're having lunch on the Rio Grande,' said Blanca, in answer to an unasked question.

'Is that near here?' asked Vesta.

'Not especially. It's on the river that runs through the centre of the island. Our destination, *Belinda's*, is on a quay. From there we can go punting. It's a rustic spot with a wheelbarrow load of awards and accolades.'

'Punting?' I asked. It seemed weird.

'Yes. I thought you might both like to go punting. You were at both at Oxbridge. It's just like the Isis or the Cam, but with added alligators.'

Now, having proved ourselves inedible to alligators and, having seen Ian Fleming's little place, Natty and Blanca thought it only fair, in the interest of a balanced overview, to take in Noël Coward's house, *Firefly*. Natty took pleasure in briefing us that Coward had adapted a simple single-bedroom house on the site of a pirate lookout on a hill overlooking the Spanish Main above his first Jamaican home, *Blue Harbour*.

Noël Coward's second mountaintop Jamaican hideaway had once been owned by the infamous pirate and one-time governor of Jamaica, Sir Henry Morgan.[195] He chose it for its commanding view over St Mary Harbour. To be on the safe side, Morgan had caused a secret escape tunnel to be dug from the house to Port Maria – in itself a considerable feat of engineering. *Firefly*

---

[195] 1635-1688

was to become Sir Noël's burial place and as a result, Michael Manley, the Prime Minister, had listed it as a National Heritage Site.

The house, only twenty-four years after its conversion to plausible dwelling, turned out to be surprisingly Spartan, especially considering just whom he entertained there.

His jet-setting and royal friends will have been as surprised as we were. Over many a warm evening, Sir Noël Coward had demonstrated his talent to amuse. His guests might occasionally include a pair of queens - the Queen Mother and Queen Elizabeth II. Lesser mortals also attended many a marvellous party there. They included Sir Winston Churchill, Sophia Loren, Elizabeth Taylor, Sir Alec Guinness, Peter O'Toole, Richard Burton, and his neighbours Errol Flynn[196] and, of course, Ian Fleming. These glitterati were accompanied by clusters if not clouds of luminous insects. Sir Winston was particularly annoyed by them.

'An Englishman has an inalienable right to live wherever he chooses', he said. 'He has a similar right not to be as mad as a hatter.'

Churchill used his time in Jamaica teaching Coward how to paint in oils. *Firefly*'s studio displayed a number of Coward's paintings. Two grand pianos were in the 'drawing room' as Coward called the room the guides insisted was a 'lounge', just as they had been when the Master was present.

On the pianos, in silver frames, were signed photographs of famous friends, including Sir Laurence Olivier and Marlene Dietrich. Of his time at *Firefly*, Coward wrote in his diary

---

[196] Errol Flynn lived in Port Antonio. During a storm in the 1940s his yacht was forced into Kingston and he decided to stay. Flynn said Port Antonio was more beautiful than any woman he had ever known. He bought a hotel and a ranch and, local legend has it, he won Navy Island in Port Antonio's harbour in a rum-fuelled card game.

> '*Firefly* has given me the most valuable
> benison of all: time to read and write and think
> and get my mind in order . . . I love this place,
> it deeply enchants me. Whatever happens to
> this silly world, nothing much is likely to
> happen here.'

Writing, he believed, came most easily when he was
here, since

> 'the sentences seemed to construct themselves,
> the right adjectives appeared discreetly at the
> right moment. Firefly has magic for me. . . .'

Coward would die of a myocardial infarction at *Firefly* on
March 26, 1973, the same age as the century. He was then
one year younger than the Queen Mother, but she
departed this world twenty-eight years after he did. Gin
and Dubonnet have to be the key to longevity.

As for the 'Master', he was interred in a marble
tomb in his own garden, at the spot where he had liked
to sit at dusk and watch the sun set, sipping a brandy and
ginger ale. He had converted the stone hut on the lawn,
Henry Morgan's former lookout, into a bar. It has been
preserved as a gift shop and restaurant.

Someone had painted his last poem on one of
Firefly's walls.

> When I have fears, as Keats had fears,
> Of the moment I'll cease to be,
> I console myself with vanished years,
> Remembered laughter, remembered tears,
> And the peace of the changing sea.

*

The beach at Negril is renowned for its breathtaking
seven-mile beach. Sober souls go there to appreciate
one of the best, least interrupted, most ravishing sea-
girt goings-down of the sun in the world.

We changed quickly and within moments we
found ourselves in incredibly warm water. For half a

mile out to sea it was barely waist-deep. Curiously, at least for us, the long beach was patrolled by Rastafarians, selling their wares. Or, rather, ware, the version of floral cannabis known as 'lambsbread'. I might have been tempted but Vesta would never have approved.

Rick's Café, however, is perhaps its most famous hot spot. It had been founded five years before. At the time, Negril had been without electricity, telephones, even tap water. Rick added another dimension to what was already paradise. His was the first bar and restaurant in the area to accompany that crepuscular drama with the finest planters' punch in the Caribbean.

Forewarned is forearmed and we arrived in unnecessarily good time, fully briefed, looking forward to yet another thirst-quenching adventure.

Rick's may be a bar and restaurant but many go there to jump off a thirty-five foot vertical cliff.[197] The cliff had originally been owned by a local doctor, Richard Hershman, the son of the first Governor-General of a newly independent Jamaica. I'm sure he never felt suicidal nor, I suspect, do the jumpers. They are merely intoxicated by the exuberance of the place. Some, of course, may be a trifle inebriated with the distillate of cane sugar.

I had already made the decision that I would spend my time there snorkelling but a new if crazy idea was forming in my mind. I too would jump off the cliff. The local lemmings were weaving and waving their weird wands at me. Overruling Vesta's remonstrations I joined the queue. Once in the collective jostle, the massing allowed of no reversal. Eventually I would have to jump.

Beneath the cliff there had to be a deep natural pool as the jumpers went well below the surface before rising in a mad, almost drunken celebration of their

---

[197] 10 metres

survival. My choice was Cromwellian - death or the west.

I jumped.

Once my foot had left the ground, at the edge of the cliff, time froze. I fell for what felt like half a minute. It was of course about a second but time flows differently in the void between life and death. I clearly remember thinking, why haven't I reached the water yet? Everything within me was rushing to my head; blood and fear in a terrible cocktail. Then, for some reason, I started to worry that I might be leaning forward too much and about to do the fiercest belly-flop in history. I started to flail and flap, but at last my feet touched the water and the roar of Jamaica's most fabulous beach resort fell silent.

I saw the Montedison refinery in flames and a thousand fingers pointing at me. I saw my mother in Athens, opening the case of her ancient electrical appliances and concluding that I had wilfully broken them all. I relived a horrible argument with Tev about money and the future. After seeing my entire life flash before my eyes, the evidence that I was still alive was concocted of ill-coordinated human legs at the surface, six or seven feet above, and shoals of tiny fish swimming leisurely around a submerged idiot.

Surfacing, I was relieved to discover that I was safe and more or less unharmed. I watched with mixed feelings as that potent blend of testosterone and Dutch courage persuaded the local lads, queuing on shore, to climb to the top of a tree and jump. It had to be an eighty feet drop. It made my effort look amateurish.

Vesta and I thought it time to sit on the sidelines and await the sunset. Natty and Bianca, with some difficulty, had secured a spot at the leading edge of the cliff. Everyone wanted to bag the best viewpoint. It was half past five and dusk approached. While the sky posted its dramatic red hues, an in-house band started to play *No*

Woman No Cry. It was the national composer. Not J S Bach, this time. As for celestial matters, the event was so awesome it made us feel we were on some other planet.

Time for supper. Rick's Cafe's menu included such gourmet delights as 'buffalo wings', chicken 'tenders', salsa and chips. Not exactly *haute cuisine*, though in any case the adrenalin rush had stolen my appetite. I would have been happy with a bag of crisps. Vesta seemed proud of me, if questioning my sanity. I felt very alive and put my arm around her, looking forward to the evening. She was in the same frame of mind.

*

Natty and Blanca told Vesta and me that in the early 1970s, Graham Binns had accepted a founding directorship in a new radio station, *Capital Radio*, the first (legal) radio station in England to be independent of the BBC.

The Binns' house in Port Antonio, as we discovered on Wednesday evening, was barely a stone's throw from ours in Frenchman's Cove. An Olympian stone's throw, that is. Not the sort I can deliver.

Now it had just turned 6 pm. Jillian and Graham seemed delighted to welcome us all into their lovely cliff-top house. They were wonderfully hospitable and Graham mixed a *planters punch* according, he claimed, to a secret family recipe. There was quite a lot of rum in it but then, I had acquired the taste.

They asked Vesta and me to tell them who we were. I think they may have mildly disapproved of Vesta, a corporate banker but they appeared thrilled to learn that I had worked a summer holiday with Radio Caroline. I was a little surprised, as the pirate radio station was such a conspicuously capitalist organisation and Graham dressed so painstakingly to the left but our host explained that in its early days Capital Radio was almost a public service broadcaster, with agony aunts on tap to help listeners, though as cash came to prevail over content he gently disengaged.

'Radio Caroline was Capital Radio's ethereal parent,' said Graham.

'Your one time boss, Ronan O'Rahilly,'[198] said Jillian, 'helped us acquire our theatre in London.'

'I think we can safely claim that were it not for us it would long ago have been demolished.' Graham gently corrected.

'Where in London' I asked.

'The Holloway Road. The Royal Theatre, in fact. It was once a music hall - vaudeville - of course. It has a fine proscenium arch and in its heyday could probably seat a thousand in comfort.'

'It belongs to you?'

---

[198] O'Rahilly's grandfather Michael, the O'Rahilly, had been a leader in the Easter Rising who died in Dublin in April 1916. His parents owned the private port of Greenore in Carlingford Lough, County Louth. O'Rahilly managed a number of pop stars, most notably Georgie Fame and Alexis Korner before launching *Radio Caroline*. When he took his Georgie Fame record to the BBC he discovered that the record industry was dominated by EMI and Decca. Trying to get it played on *Radio Luxembourg* he found that its shows were 'owned' by EMI, Decca, Pye and Philips. Radio programs were essentially 'payola', only broadcasting music from paying labels. 'I have recorded the guy. If I can't get it played, I shall start my own radio station.' He launched a pirate radio station, *Radio Caroline*, mostly financed by John Sheffield, the great uncle of Samantha Cameron, Carl Ross of the *Ross Fishery* frozen food business and Jocelyn Stevens. It broadcast off the Essex coast. O'Rahilly was executive producer of a number of films including Marianne Faithfull's film, *Girl on a Motorcycle*. *Two Virgins* featured John Lennon and Yoko Ono. O'Rahilly appeared in Lazenby's film *Universal Soldier* and managed the Australian model-turned-actor George Lazenby. During a production of the 1969 James Bond movie *On Her Majesty's Secret Service* O'Rahilly persuaded Lazenby to refuse a seven-movie Bond contract on grounds that the James Bond character was out of touch with the times. Roger Moore wrote in his autobiography, *My Word Is My Bond,* that 'George took some bad advice... I knew George then and have met him many times since. He readily admits he made a mistake'. In the 1970s O'Rahilly, noticing that people 'found it easier to talk about hate than love', developed the philosophy of 'loving awareness'. It has been heavily promoted on *Caroline* ever since. In 1976 an album of sympathetic songs was recorded by the *Loving Awareness Band*, a group assembled for the purpose. O'Rahilly was inducted as a Fellow of the Radio Academy and into the *Hall Of Fame* at the PPI Radio Awards, held at the Lyrath Hotel, Kilkenny, Ireland on 12 October 2012. In September 2013, O'Rahilly returned to live in County Louth, Ireland, in sight of the port of Greenore where *Radio Caroline* had been 'conceived' 50 years before. The last time I saw him was in the *Chelsea Arts Club* in 2005.

'Theatre belongs to no one,' said Jillian.

I had not really been expecting such an agit-prop reply. I might have argued the contrary. Some of my friends (well one, actually, Giacomo) really did.

Graham explained the situation a little less politically. 'We were able to persuade The Royal Holloway College, named after the theatre, before it became the less elegantly named *The North London Polytechnic*,[199] that it needed to teach drama. I volunteered my personal and corporate support and the college took on the abandoned music hall.'

'We treat it a prep school for the West End,' Jillian added. 'It has the lights and flats and rigging of a surviving great stage and all the dress and make-up challenges. The Poly picks up the tab.'

'Do you have a company?' I asked.

'Oh yes,' replied Jillian. '*The Shakespeare Players*. It's a traditional strolling company, words full of sound and fury, strutting its Shakespearean stuff upon an international stage. It will be here in three weeks, but you will not. Come and see us in Primrose Hill, when you're back.'

I just might, I thought to myself.

*

Jillian and Graham Binns really were a remarkable couple. Graham's waspish wit combined with her courage and sense of adventure to make them delightful. Between them, their huge personalities in the world of radio and theatre were particularly felt in Malta, Jamaica and Corfu, where they enjoyed a felicitous marriage of splendid residences and powerful friends.

Graham's grandfather had been a pattern maker, and one who fought his way through a skyscraper's worth of glass ceilings to become Lord Mayor of Manchester.

---

[199] Following yet another name change, it is now the University of North London.

His son had been an ICI engineer and, later, a Labour MP. Both father and grandfather had been fired by their enthusiasm for socialism. As a consequence, they were then fired with enthusiasm by their employers.

In 1919, Graham went to Bembridge, a school on the Isle of Wight that had been specifically founded to keep the spirit of John Ruskin alive. During the Second World War the whole school was evacuated to Brantwood, Ruskin's former home in the Lake District, where Graham would spend his teenage years browsing the art critic's diary in its original manuscript. A string of visiting and often unconventional aesthetes introduced Graham to the dons and admission tutor of one of Oxford's ancient colleges. In those days that, and being willing to pay the fees, was more or less the admissions process.

During the war he read English at Worcester. He co-directed *The Tempest* with Neville Coghill in an outdoor production by the College's lake. He followed Kenneth Tynan as theatre editor of Oxford's magazine *Isis*. His deferred military war service was in India.

Jillian Palmer, on the other hand, was from an industrialist Portsmouth family that manufactured the once ubiquitous *Victory* brushes, sturdy wooden implements, found in the better sort of English lavatories.[200] Graham and Jillian married in 1949 and spent their first year together as Fulbright scholars in the drama department at Syracuse University, upstate New York, and that's where they directed Christopher Fry's *A Phoenix Too Frequent* and *The Boy With A Cart*. Both she and her husband were big fans of Fry's poetic drama, having trained at the Webber Douglas School in Kensington. Jillian went on to work with Fry at the Oxford Playhouse.

She starred in a great many productions. In one, she played a notable Cordelia in a performance of

---

[200] Plastic made them redundant.

Nahum Tate's late-17th-century adaptation of *King Lear*. That's the infamous version with the happy ending.

Things were panning out well and the Binns had the confidence to start a family. The Fates, however, conspired to cast a spanner into their works.

Christopher Fry's neo-baroque style was superseded, in the '50s, by 'kitchen sink' drama in Chelsea's ground-breaking Royal Court. Neither Graham nor Jillian had much enthusiasm for it. Graham gave up, in 'despair' he said, to join the Arts Council. When, in 1956, Arts Council England shut down its regional activities to concentrate on metropolitan high art, Graham joined the BBC. They sent him to Malta to chair the committee that oversaw the restoration of the magnificent 18th-century *Manoel Theatre*.

Through his Arts Council connections he enticed a glittering array of performing and visual artists to the island in the run-up to independence. He had already taken over the management of Rediffusion's Radio Jamaica, turning it into a counter to the predictable, staid government-owned station set up on independence.

Jillian was travelling widely too. She set up and managed local theatre productions everywhere she went. In Jamaica she claimed she heard the unchanged tones of its 17th-century settlers, realising it would have been close to the voice the audience of the Globe in London would have heard. When she brought Shakespeare to Jamaica 'it was close to time travel'.

He and Jillian were in position to revitalise Jamaica's *Ward Theatre*, back in the sixties. 'A Colonel Charles Ward, then Custos of Kingston, had commissioned and then given the *Ward Theatre* to the City of Kingston, back in 1912,' Jillian explained. 'Its site in downtown Kingston has been in continuous use as a theatre since the 1770s. The first one was the *Kingston* and the second the *Theatre Royal*, which was lost in the 1907 earthquake.'

'So it was fifty years old when you brought it up-to-date?'

'Graham was and is a terrific fundraiser. We have seen the greatest personalities perform on its stage. Half of them actually live here, at least for some of the time. We tried to give the place an extra dimension, an association with Jamaica's indigenous theatre. It still holds a special place in our hearts.'

*

What a fortunate introduction this would prove to be. In 1979, Jillian was 54 years old,[201] apparently in her prime. Sadly, this was an illusion. In 1974, after surgery to remove her cancer, she had a terrible set back. A heavy-handed combination of chemotherapy and radium treatment had not been kind.

Retained by Reuters as a journalist, now in her forties, she had a chance to visit Cuba as it nervously re-opened to tourists. She cleverly evaded her government minder and even chanced to meet Fidel Castro.

They bought a house in Malta, but like me, she was in love with Jamaica. She bought in, resolving to return to their mountain-top retreat above Port Antonio whenever she could.

Graham, meanwhile, was appointed chairman of the *British Committee for the Restitution of the Parthenon Marbles*. During his chairmanship a more productive dialogue would develop between the British and Greek governments. The matter, however, was an emotional one and has still to be resolved. If the marbles were to be reattached to the Parthenon, I would be in favour, most probably, but a little museum in downtown Athens versus a great international one like the British Museum? Surely an easy decision? The answer is 'no'.

---

[201] She died on May 4th, 2003.

*

Blanca wanted us to see 'Crocodile Farm.' It was where giant reptiles were husbanded until it came to their time to metamorphose into handbags.

'Just give me a crocodile wallet and make it snappy', went the old joke. We turned off the main road at the sign that read 'Crocodile Farm. Trespassers will be eaten.' The farm had a role in *Live and Let Die* when Roger Moore evaded Ross Kananga's clutches by stepping or jumping onto the backs of the creatures until he reached solid ground.

We entered via the shop, which was filled with unctuous shop assistants, impressive luggage and dangerous price tags. That crocodile wallet was ready to fight me off. Inside a small enclosure, something of a nursery, inch-long hatchlings could safely manage the journey between embryo and something the size of a Manolo Blahnik high-heeled shoe. From there they could be taken outside and let loose in the highly contained groves and swamps.

The croc farm had become an attraction for locals and visitors alike who came to take in the daily shows that featured the owner, the aforementioned Kananga, playing with his crocodiles, caymans and alligators or teasing his leopards and lions. Scouts for Bond's *Live and Let Die* decided to have the farm double as the fictional San Monique.[202] Shooting began in November 1973.

Ross Kananga himself suggested the now legendary croc-jumping escape and the directors urged him to perform the dangerous stunt. It took five takes to complete and Kananga suffered a number of injuries.

Sadly, he was struck down by apoplexy a few months after the shooting had moved elsewhere. He did recover, however, and his extraordinary courage earned him a role as a stuntman in *Papillon*.

---

[202] I know. It ought to be Santa Monica, but nonetheless that is what Cubby Broccoli called it.

We had time for one last outing before our return. It had to be the Dunns River Falls, one of Jamaica's most precious treasures. There can be few places where the *Arawak*[203] word *Xayamaca* - land of rivers and springs – is more apt. The Spaniards had named the area *Las Chorreras* - the waterfalls. It is truly one of the very most attractive spots on the island, barely a stone's throw from Ocho Rios. It regenerates itself from deposits of travertine rock, a result of the precipitation of chalk from the river as it flows over the falls. Since it constantly grows, it is only slightly fanciful to describe the falls as a living phenomenon. Its domed cataracts are more often associated with thermal springs in limestone caves. Here, however, they are in the open air. This, combined with its closeness to the sea, gives Dunn's River the distinction of being the only one of its kind in the Caribbean, if not the world. This geological adventure has been going on for a million years. Within the chalk are the fossilised remains of ammonites and trilobites. Where the stream no longer passes they are easy to prise from their final resting places with a penknife. I was not merely travelling between continents, I was travelling through time.

We began to climb the slippery falls. They were unfenced (I would put money on this being no longer the case) but I am not sure whether the word 'falls' refers to water or to tourists. It was exciting stuff, especially when the cascade tried to brush us aside but we outfoxed it by going barefoot. Our simian forefathers had bequeathed us with toes and the grip we need to withstand the torrent.

---

[203] One of the handful of languages I do not speak fluently.

On the flight home we evaluated the experience. We had had a truly wonderful break from the tensions and stress of 'real life'.

I was about to turn thirty. I felt ready to take any risk. After all, my faculties were as sharp as they ever had been, and if Simon Galway didn't want to hear me whistle, some other outfit would just have to develop a musical ear. I was back in London, rested, tanned and happy in my skin.

Andy called me into his 'office', *The Ship* in Hart Lane.

'It's beginning to look as though you may have more friends in Madrid than you have in London. I've had a word with our Spanish friends. They are minded to offer you sanctuary. Are you sure your Spanish is good enough?'

'It could be. Practice makes perfect, they say.'

'So, do we have a deal? You'll move to Spain?

'Provided I gain my assistant directorship. Otherwise it's not a step forward but a step to the left. I'm almost thirty. Careers can get lost when you get as old as that.'

'I see. Well, I'll have a word with Simon. We'll speak soon.'

What was certainly the case is that things were complicated at home and a move abroad had its appeal. Money was a worry. Foreign parts cost a lot. Not that a loaf of bread was substantially more or less expensive, here or anywhere else, it was just that one did not know which shops to patronise. Renting a half-way decent flat especially needed local knowledge. Even worse, there might have to be a period of celibacy while one became accustomed to, shall we say, local customs.

In the meantime, Piero wanted me in Rome to coax the *Assitalia* into putting some business our way, and I hadn't been to the eternal city for what seemed like ages.

Rome will always draw you back. She is a seductress; there is no use in resisting - her lures are utterly irresistible. It is not merely her Corinthian antiquity, nor the twists and turns of her Baroque architecture, nor yet her princely collections of art. Nor is it the food, while it's brilliant. Nor even the wines. Frankly, the wines from Frascati are really as good as the Romans claim.

No, the clue is in the word 'eternal', its magnet is made of pure immortal bonhomie. This most marvellous of capitals exudes it by the cartload. Everyone, over the centuries, has wanted a part of it, including some of the Goths, most of the Huns, a smattering of Franks and a few crowned grandees, including Charlemagne and Charles V.

Of course, there are exceptions to every rule. One such was H G Wells, who thought we should bomb it.

There was a friendship, too, that I wanted to rekindle, that of Violante Sersale. I gave her a call.

Could I take her to dinner? I was in Rome on business.

No, but lunch would be welcome. She knew a pizzeria in Trastevere. It had recently opened and its pizzas were the best in the ancient world.

Don't get the wrong idea. I should have been happy if she had wanted her husband to come too. Nevertheless, that it was just the two of us was not exactly a disappointment.

I arrived, as was my wont, in good time for my evening briefing with Piero. I had also made a number of appointments of my own, as I had vague hopes of finding a job in Rome, now that Simon had resolved to escort me to the escape hatch.

In London, news of the difficulty I was having with Simon had trickled down to the accounts department, as these things will.

'That man is a complete Sir Anthony,' said a cheerful Cockney accounts clerk. He may have been referring to Sir Anthony Blunt who had just been accused of espionage.

*

Violante was exactly on time. Happily, I had arrived two or three minutes early at my café table in the picturesque Piazza Santa Maria. Violante looked just as lovely as she had at her wedding but I thought I heard stress in her tone. Still, even if I were right, no such sinister thread would weave its way into our conversation. She declined the offer of a glass or even a coffee.

'It's lunchtime,' she said briskly. 'You have stuff to do and so do I. Let's not waste time. Let's find our table in the pizzeria and swap our news and gossip.'

Her writing was going very well, she assured me. She was already fêted among the Italian literati – her just deserts, I volunteered - and she was finding the weight of her laurel leaves easier to bear as every day passed.

'I have had a royalty cheque,' she told me, over her margherita.[204] 'Quite a considerable one. Why don't you abandon this 'career' of yours? I don't believe your heart is in it. You have what it takes to earn a living from your pen.'

I admit I was heartened by her approach.

'You have already published some bits and pieces. They were good.'

'Violante, what delightful tosh you talk. You are a marchioness, with houses in Paris, Munich, Rome and Venice. I live in a small terraced house in London with a girlfriend. In any case, whatever talent I may or may not have would pale into insignificance beside yours.'

---

[204] The pizza, not the cocktail.

'You have not been tested. Two bits of unsolicited advice. Find the time to write and drink less. I sincerely believe you can do it. Or both.'

'Well, if I ever do write something that sells, you must come to the launch.'

'It's a deal. New York, London, Paris, Berlin, you name it, I'll be there. Just don't make it in some dreary classroom in some forgettable corner of your windswept countryside.' Lunch was done but the launch not begun. Violante reached into her bag and retrieved her American Express card. I remonstrated.

'No, no,' she insisted. 'My treat. Next time, in London, it will be yours. You'll be married soon, I expect. Choose the girl well. You are the best, so don't waste yourself on the also ran.'

I had not been expecting a pep talk.

'You are so sweet,' I said, not knowing quite what to say. Of course another matter was on my mind. Should I broach it?

'Should I move to Madrid?' I asked her, out of the blue. If she was startled, she answered straight away.

'What? Of course not. Not without a terrific offer, anyway. Make your fortune in London and grow into your own skin. Become what you are, what your father is already, a writer. He is a playwright, I remember you saying. Write a play yourself. It will be an exercise in self-discovery, of that I am quite certain.'

*

Back again in London, Andy recalled me to his office in Hart Lane. 'Find an excuse to go to Madrid. The people there want to see you and confirm their willingness to be your fast-track elevator. You have impressed them, I strongly suspect.'

While I was in two minds, a position in Spain would be marvellous. I had made a few mistakes in London, but surely they would not dog me all the way to Madrid? I had committed some sins, of course, but the Lord our God is long-suffering, of infinite mercy and He forgives iniquity and transgression.[205] Yes, I had had a good Catholic education, yet Spain still prevaricated.

And so did I. Financially, London was the centre of the universe. Despite their ambitious claims, Singapore, Frankfurt, Hong Kong and even Wall Street ran a distant second equal.[206]

While I was riding high, London had to be my haven. It was just that, and very sadly, it could not be with CTB.

*

In May, with the tacit connivance of our Madrid office, I arranged a business trip and won't deny I was looking forward to it. On Monday, May 6th, 1979, I was reinstalled in the *Europa*.

My meetings with our Madrid office's clients were paying off. They reported back that my Spanish was up to the demands the job put on it. There were restrictions the authorities still placed on their insurance companies – national legislation discouraged them from reinsuring their portfolios with foreign companies through proportional treaties – but that still left room for non-proportional ones and I was asked to meet as many of our Spanish customers as I could. The good news was that our Spanish office appeared to be seriously toying with the prospect of my pitching my tent on their turf.

Every night I renewed my efforts to polish my Spanish by watching the TV in my hotel room. On the Wednesday, by some weird coincidence, I found myself watching the news, where two principal suspects of the intended coup of the previous November, Tejero and

---

[205] By no means does He clear the guilty. Indeed, to the contrary, he visits the iniquity of the fathers upon the sons unto the third and fourth generation.
[206] London does not merely do Banking. Think Insurance, Commodities, Futures and Options, Accountancies, Auditors, Shipping, Metals and Bullion.

Sánez de Ynestrillas, were being taken to their court-martial. I watched the crowds cheer the 'black maria' on its way, waving their nationalist flags, while others jeered noisily, operatically underlining the dramatic rift that still split Spain.

The judge found them both guilty. The attorney general asked for six years for Tejero, and five for Sánez, but the judge sentenced the former to seven months and a day, and the latter to six months and a day.

The minimum sentence, in other words. You could get more for picking a pocket or two. Nor did either of them lose their military rank. Sánez was even promoted to Commander. The 'third man' was never identified. He was not even on trial. He must have been holed up somewhere safe.

*

My head-hunter rang to tell me he had just the perfect job for me. 'You've heard of Edmund Hoyle Vestey, of course,' he told me. 'His family business owns cattle ranches in Brazil, Venezuela and Australia with meat processing factories in Argentina, Uruguay, and New Zealand. To ship the meat back to the UK the Vesteys long ago created their own shipping company, the *Blue Star Line*, a great fleet of refrigerated ships. You've seen Dewhursts, the high street butchers? That's theirs. So is Oxo. They own the Oxo Tower.'

'Yes, I've heard of them. They're rather rich.'

'Did anyone ever tell you that you're a master of understatement? Sam - Lord Vestey to you - is the current head of the family and Chairman of the Group. He owns Stowell Park, six thousand acres of sylvan Gloucestershire,[207] as well as a villa near Nice and a townhouse in Belgravia.'

'Lucky man.'

_____

[207] 24 km²

486

'Edmund has something similar. His spread straddles Essex and Suffolk. He has bought a reinsurance broker and it needs a senior bloke. Could it be you?'

'What's it called?'

'Robert Barrow.'

'I've never even heard of it.'

'You speak Spanish. Many other languages. You work for a huge concern. I believe CTB employs around twenty thousand people. You can rise to the top much faster in a smaller outfit. Vestey is offering £10,800 a year. That's close on £1000 a month.[208] A fortune for you, a tip for the cloakroom girl for him.'

'Well, I don't know...'

'You've got all the contacts you need already...'

'I'll go to an interview. If I like the look of what I see I'll think about it.'

'That's all I needed to know. I'll be in touch.'

*

Simon Galway came into my office but chose not to acknowledge me. Instead he had an inconsequential word with one of my colleagues and left.

I knew he was off to Japan, one of a number of territories he had chosen to retain personally. After all, it was a very profitable account. His absence from London would give me the time I needed to go unobserved to an interview. There was also the unimportant little matter that Madrid had not yet deigned to confirm an offer.

The following week was cluttered with 'events', the nemesis of planning. I was about to take an underwriter to Myttons for a half-way decent lunch when I was caught in the act by Anthony Robertson, one of Galway's fellow directors.

'Have you heard about Simon?' he asked.

---

[208] Actually £900 before tax. Perhaps £600 after all deductions.

'What?'

I had not. I was all ears to say the least. In fact, auricle gristle that instant became my chief constituent.

'He has had an accident. He has broken or dislocated a hip. I shouldn't count on seeing him for a month or two.'

'How on earth? Has he been playing hopscotch? Spending too much time on the dodgems?'

'Strangest thing. It seems he was on the direct flight home from Narita Airport. He had squeezed in one last appointment before his flight, hoping or gambling he would be lucky with the traffic. Narita is thirty-seven miles from Tokyo and Japanese food does not agree with him. The traffic didn't move and his stomach had begun to revolve like a milk churn. While he endured the airport's labyrinthine bureaucracy he barely managed to contain himself as far as check in. Desperate, he took his seat, horribly uncomfortable, only to suffer an interminable delay while the plane readied itself for takeoff. As soon as the safety belt sign was turned off he struggled awkwardly to the lavatory. Just in time, he told me.'

'My God! I actually feel for him.'

'No sooner had he sat down in the privacy of the little cubicle did the chief steward's voice come over the PA system to inform the passengers that they expected to hit severe turbulence over the East China Sea. Passengers were 'to resume their seats and buckle themselves in'.'

'Poor chap. He was busy elsewhere.'

'He certainly was but he managed to bring matters to a hurried if temporary conclusion. At last he could open the door and begin to head back to his seat. Unfortunately, that was when the 747 hit an empty air pocket and went into free fall. Simon flew the length of the cabin to hit the screen by the cockpit, some thirty feet distant. He had to lie there, just where he fell, folded like a rag doll, until the air stewards were allowed to help him to his seat.'

'They didn't turn the plane around?'

'It was not obvious yet that he had done himself a serious mischief. Only when he had sat down did his hip begin to swell. A doctor on the flight had some painkillers but they had no perceptible effect and his agony only developed as the long haul got truly underway.'

'Torture might have been more comfortable.'

'You're telling me. Well, you had better run Italy, Greece and Yugoslavia until he's back. And, of course, Spain. Make sure nothing is outstanding on his return. Do a superlative job and watch what happens. It could be a lucky break for you, if you'll excuse the pun.'

*

Yet another week sped by without any news from Madrid, but I did get a call from my head-hunter.

'Can you come and meet Edmund Vestey? He wants to have met everyone in his company paid more than £10,000 a year.'

'I suppose so. When and where?'

'He has suggested his shipping office, Thursday next. At ten past ten for ten minutes.' I took down the address. I might as well have a look. There's no harm in taking a peek is there?

Well, the Victorian offices I saw were wholly devoid of glamour or comfort. They were peopled with stressed, middle-aged men, scribbling away in rolled up sleeves, held in place with elasticised metal armbands. Their worried faces were obscured beneath peaked green-plastic eye-shades and thick spectacles. They all drew disproportionate pleasure from smoking evil Patagonian cheroots.

They certainly were busy. Everything told me their frenzied work-ethic was less about the inextinguishable flame of loyalty. It was more akin to the survival ethic of the one-time slaves of the former Confederate States.

I suspected that very few of them would be paid as much as £10,000 a year. More likely, an eighth of that.

I did know the Vesteys were big in beef. 'The boss is a liveryman of the Worshipful Company of Butchers,' the head-hunter had helpfully told me. 'He also hunts with some Suffolk pack of hounds.'

'Though not for beef,' I thought.

Looking at the wall charts I immediately realised that they owned Fray Bentos[209] and what were probably the world's largest food canning factories. Grateful veterans of the World Wars still recalled opening their cans of corned beef.

> Try a tin of Bully Beef,
> As good as good can be.
> First it killed the enemy,
> Now it's killing me.

To tell the truth, it didn't really look like my sort of place. I must admit to a weakness for creature comforts; mostly insignificant ones like relationship building over lunch in the Square Mile.

I was issued into Mr Vestey's presence by a grovelling lackey. The boss's expression showed every sign of tedium. An acceptable price, no doubt, to pay for a billion pound fortune. Edmund Vestey was a short man, twenty or thirty years older than me, very trim and filled his exquisite suit to perfection. I knew instinctively that he was a huntsman, as had his tailor. He did not trouble to smile in greeting. His eyes were weapons and he looked as though his only joy lay in chasing small mammals to the brink of extinction.

'You will not be based in this office,' he told me. 'This is our shipping business. You'll be at the broking

---

[209] Portuguese for 'Friar Benedict'.

office. There is a vacancy and you might fill it. It is our intention to replace the boss, and in that we want you to help us. Through talent or whatever it takes. Let me have your decision before lunch on Tuesday.'

Rather like his American longhorn cattle on their final, fatal journey to Chicago, I was being railroaded. Up with this I would not put.

'I have to be in Madrid next week,' I told him. 'I have to give three months' notice. I would still like to meet my future colleagues before I make my final decision. I'll speak to the head-hunter on my return.'

*

That Sunday, after church, I joined my father for lunch in his Kensington house (which, idiosyncratically, he insisted was in Chelsea, which it wasn't).

'I think I may have been offered a job by the Vestey brothers,' I told him. 'They want an experienced non-marine broker to handle that side of their business. Do you know anything about them?'

'Oh my God! I thought we'd left that name behind. Of course I've heard of them. During the war we had to endure their powdered eggs.'

'What I remember,' said my stepmother Wendy, 'is that they installed plate glass windows in their shops. Before them butchers had shutters that opened onto the street.'

'They've been in the news recently. They've just sold their East Anglian supermarket chain to FineFare,' said my father.

'Really? How many shops?' my stepmother asked.

'Downsway had about a hundred,' I replied. 'I suspect the Vesteys came out of it very well.'

*

Back in the office on Monday morning I had no choice but to put in a call to Paco Compes.

'We can't just poach you, Jeremy,' he said, sadly I thought. 'It's just not that simple. Simon Galway has to authorise your transfer. There will have to be a legal process in which you become a resident, even if a temporary one. There may also be an issue with military service. We know it can be done. We had to do all of that for Davina, but there is a cost to it: legal fees, stamp duties, taxes and the like. Simon has still to agree to pay for it.'

'You are aware that Simon has had an accident?'

'No! Is he OK?'

'He has a dislocated hip. He is in traction.'

'Then I suppose matters will have to wait for him to return to work.'

*

My banker friend Adrian Stroude had taken a shine to another old friend, Caroline Smythe. It might have been vice-versa, of course. They had thought it nice to splice. Though I encouraged them, I was wrong. Their marriage was ill-advised.

Stroude had left *Kleinworts* for *Manny Hanny*,[210] some months before, mildly disgruntled with his old employer, even though his friendship with its ruling family had left him secure. Adrian was an old-fashioned relationship banker, no technocrat, but at his new bank he was battered (and it should be admitted, bettered) by more narrowly-focussed wide-boys from the Bronx and the East-End. His battle seemed vaguely similar to the one I was now fighting, so I called on him for advice. Should I go or should I stay? Of course, if I said no to the Vesteys there could well be another offer in 'the fullness...'

But when? Violante's words were also reverberating in my head. Perhaps I could write? I had written a little light-hearted nonsense. Let's take a foot

---

[210] Manufacturers' Hannover, the investment bank.

forward, so to speak. I was not scared of putting one word in front of another.

With hindsight, Adrian's was not really the best counsel to heed. He was already deeply regretting his own move. Not only that. He smelled strongly of cider. Was he was seeking to drown his depression in a tankard of the fruity potion?

Sadly my affair with Vesta was not working out. She was bright and affectionate but expected permanence. She was not the girl I wanted to bear my children or push my bath chair when the time came. I made the executive if difficult decision to move out of Fulham to a room in a Glebe Place mansion, well within my ancestral turf of Chelsea. If again unattached, I felt a great weight had been lifted from my halter.

I had had a letter from *Robert Barrow Reinsurance* inviting me to an interview with their MD in an office off Leadenhall Street. I seemed to be changing address, setting myself free from an unsatisfactory relationship, and was coming to the conclusion that a change of employer might complete the hat trick.

As it turned out, the company had part of a floor in a modern office block. The door from the corridor had the words *Robert Barrow, Reinsurance Brokers*, painted on the frosted glass. It housed two male staff, one all purpose female, all sharing a general office and a meeting room. Walls of expanded polystyrene, bare save for fading post-it notes and a scattering of drawing pins that long ago had secured urgent pressing matters.

'Come in,' said the Boss as I hesitated in the door frame. 'Come in, Chap.'

I had heard 'Dear Chap' or 'Old Chap' many times, but the simple noun, stripped of its preamble, seemed forlorn and unloved. Just like me.

At the other end of the office to the Boss's very large wooden desk was a far smaller metal one, at which sat a swarthy bloke with long sideburns and greased back hair. He may even have auditioned for *The Fonz* in *Happy Days* but, sadly for him, it was Henry Winkler who got the part. His hair was obviously unruly as his metal comb was on the blotter, just where the dessert spoon in a B&B is traditionally placed.

The Boss was standing, his hand outstretched, so I crossed the office and took it. 'Barbara,' he said to his shapely factotum, 'two cups of tea. D'you take sugar, Jeremy?'

'Thank you. Just one,' I replied.

'Well, then today we'll spoil you. Give him two, Barbara. Jeremy come on through. We'll have a chat in there.'

We were now in the meeting room where a sofa, a coffee table and two armchairs floated like icebergs in a hessian sea. True, in City meeting rooms there is often a bookcase, filled with untouched reference books, but in this one there was not even that much erudition. We were in that seaside B&B again. In fairness - if not my longsuit - I should concede that the offices were rented so the Boss's taste was not really up for debate.

'I've had reports about you. You made a good impression on Mr Edmund.'

I was only surprised I had made any sort of impression. I remembered ten fraught minutes in his presence and had no recollection of either of us saying anything of any importance.

'So are there any questions you want to ask me?'

Two men and a secretary? There is more to a brokerage than its executives.

'Where are the technical accounts and the policy wordings devised?'

'In the shipping office. You've been there, Chap?'

'Yes.' I needed to think.

'So why do you want to work for us at Robert Barrow?' I heard him ask through the whirring of my brain.

Of course, if I had prepared an answer I might have replied more intelligently.

"Mr Edmund' promised me a fine salary and a chance to travel.'

'Ha! Has he, Chap? Well, don't imagine you'll be on the next plane to Paraguay.'

'No? Hasn't 'Mr Edmund' extensive interests there?'

'You'll begin in England. Next will come Europe, as and when I judge you ready. The rest of the world after that. Let's not rush our fences, Chap.'

'Your non-marine account? Do you have a lot of business?'

'Very little, as it happens. Most of our existing business relates to *Blue Star*. Alonso, who you saw outside, is our marine broker. You will be our non-marine production broker.'

Barbara came in with the tea and a smile – the latter not for me but the Boss.

'Barbara, be a helpful sexpot and send Alonso in.'

To my surprise Barbara did not flinch at his affectionate banter. She even waggled her hips for him as she left.

Alonso brought his highly trained quiff into the little parlour. It would be over-promoting the room to call it an office.

'Here I am, Boss.'

'Alonso, this is Jeremy. Mr Edmund is giving him our non-marine business.'

'Very droll, Boss. We don't have any.' He had an accent. Spanish, perhaps?

'That's what Jeremy is for. He currently works for Bowring's but we're about to put that right.'

Now that Alonso had sat down I noticed his bracelet. It was made of heavy gold links. He wore a Rolex on the same wrist. He will have swung to the left when he walked. Perhaps he dressed to the right to even it up?

'I do hulls and cargo. I also do the Baltic,' he said proudly. 'Are you a member of Lloyd's?'

'I am an associate of George Bowring.'

This was a technical answer. I expected, if hired, to be made an associate of Mr Robert Barrow, whoever he was, if not 'Mr Edmund'.

'Thank you, Alonso. You may go.'

Before Alonso had even returned to his desk, the Boss had resumed. 'Alonso is Maltese. A fine nautical vein runs through his blood.'

This was not the moment to point out that veins, even in Malta, do not run through anyone's blood.

'So,' the Boss continued, 'let me understand, how you would set about developing our non-marine account?'

'I would meet my contacts here and abroad and ask for a share of their reinsurance business. Where possible I would design treaties to reduce the impact of a poor year or a catastrophe.[211] I would explain that smaller outfits work harder than larger ones, because we have to.'

'Well, Chap, that was well said. I shall faithfully report your response to Mr Edmund. I think that concludes this meeting.'

I put my undrinkable cup of tea back in its saucer, neither shaken not stirred.

'Thank you very much for taking the trouble to see me.'

'My pleasure. We'll meet again. Soon, I fancy.'

*

---

[211] In reinsurance, a catastrophe is where a single event causes two or more losses.

Our newspapers were valiantly making a collective effort to prove that we were in a silly season in an uneventful year.

True, some of the matters that kept our journalists in work were indeed trivial. Summer brought some bonuses: the dry and sunny summer had filled the city parks with semi-naked women. I heartily approved. In Brighton, Britain's first official nudist beach had been declared open for business but, being the shy fellow I am, I was not so sure that I was in favour of the Full Monty.

It had been a cold winter, that was true. Gurus, pundits, tabloid editors and 'climate scientists'[212] claimed was the coldest winter 'since records began'.

Whatever they might claim it was not. In the late nineteenth century, there was a year when every lake and river in the kingdom had frozen and ice-skate manufacturers thought they had died and gone directly to heaven.

Then, in the mid twentieth, there had been an even colder freeze. During the winter of 1962-63, Arctic north-easterlies had brought blizzards and freezing winds to everywhere in Britain. February and March left the country buried in deep snow. Predictably, that year (and every year since) the London County Council lacked snow ploughs and ran out of grit. The capital ground to a halt.

February 15th, 1963, had been one of those rare days (in my lifetime at least) when the temperature had remained below zero from dawn to dusk. The weather forecasters repeated their dismal mantra, 'since records began', which they still bring out every second Tuesday with an 'R' in it. The BBC and its bizarre meteorologists were predicting 'global cooling' and a new ice age. As always, they were pretending to the gullible and Professor Dawkins that they were privy to God's plans.

---

[212] Weather forecasters prefer to be called this. Don't listen to them. They can't even say what the weather will be like at the weekend.

This time round, warm pubs had filled with drinkers of chilled lager. Old fashioned bitter had fallen out of favour, at least with the young. The brewers had been lured by cunning new incentives to get the people of Burton-upon-Trent to drink more (and thereby pay more tax) and had copied the European versions of beer with signicantly poor results.[213]

The admen and government formed an unholy alliance. Between them they meant to take the shirt from your back, replace it with a cheaper one. Many spendthrift idiots failed to notice. Publicans were busy replacing their skittles, pocket billiards tables and mechanical one-armed bandits with computerised Space Invader, fruit machines and electronic quiz games.

On May 3rd, 1979, the Conservative Party, led by Margaret Thatcher, ousted the incumbent Labour government of James Callaghan with a parliamentary majority of forty-three. The Labour party was destined to stay out of power for the next eighteen years.

Elsewhere, John Wayne proved, to the world's great astonishment and greater sadness, that he hadn't licked cancer after all.

For the first time, pedestrians - hitherto thought sane - were falling under buses. They were listening to Bob Marley on their brand new Sony Walkmans and failing to hear the traffic.

Sid Vicious, the rebel, was summonsed to Creation's highest court. He had been found dead in an apartment in New York. In more earthly charts, the Village People found their *YMCA* had reached the top. Art Garfunkel would follow them up to the top with *Bright Eyes*.

---

[213] Burton is still a significant beer town, but through numerous consolidations, closures, and changes in ownership, just two big breweries remain today. The combined sites of Bass, Ind Coope, and Allsopp are now owned by Molson Coors Beverage Company, while down the road is Marston's, now part of Carlsberg.

Airey Neave and Lord Mountbatten were assassinated by the IRA, while Blair Peach was assassinated by the police.

The Hitchhiker's Guide to the Galaxy, a 'five volume trilogy', was published to well-deserved acclaim.

Telly-addicts watched the *Antiques Roadshow* for the first time.

Someone somewhere paid £1 million for a footballer. That little? We can do rather better these days.

Mother Teresa deservedly won the Nobel Peace Prize, to objections from atheists, Protestants and Professor Dawkins.

The Shah of Persia was (at last) forced into exile, allowing the Ayatollah Khomeini to take the Peacock Throne and declare his renamed country, Iran, to be an Islamic Republic.

Greenland was awarded Home Rule by Denmark, but few noticed. Deng Xiaoping began his economic reforms in China, and everyone noticed. In politics, like everything else, size matters.

The Soviets invaded Afghanistan. Apparently the Great Game wasn't yet over. The current score was Britain Nil, Afghanistan Two. The Ruskies thought it was their turn. If they failed perhaps the Yanks would have a go. We might even need a league table.

A pope with a tongue-twister for a surname, John Paul II, had been elected. He paid a visit to Poland and single-handedly overthrew communism. Who needs battalions, Mr Stalin?

All quiet, then, on every front.

*

My stepbrother Kevin, the son of an actor and the stepson of a playwright, had pledged to uphold the family tradition. The roar of the greasepaint was in his ears, the smell of the crowd in his nostrils. He had won

499

a place at North London's Poly, no less, to study drama in its full-scale 19th-century theatre. It liked to put shows on stage every year. He told me all this enthusiastically but then, I already knew.

'They normally keep to plays with small casts but they have a trump card up their sleeves. Every so often they are assisted by Jillian Binns, the distinguished director.'

'In this,' I said solemnly, 'you and the whole Polytechnic have fallen on your collective feet.'

I shared with Kevin that I had met Jillian in Jamaica and he was mightily impressed. He suggested I should watch him in one of Jillian's shows at the NLP. When I went I was bowled over by the production. Kevin's acting was impressive, too.

The production was eye-opening, brilliant, and the young student ladies, who made up the greater part of the cast, had their own attractions. What stood out, however, was Jillian's intelligent and subtle direction, her skilful husbandry of very limited resources and a generic skill born of great vision and long experience.

In one play that we went to see, Kevin particularly excelled. After the show we joined him and Jillian back stage. She shyly suggested I might join a production of Shakespeare's *Pericles* and I was predictably flattered. I brought my old friends Richard Turner and Felix Pryor along to an early rehearsal. Richard and Jillian immediately hit it off and he too was offered a part. She was, I hope, amused when Richard insisted on calling her 'Billion Gins'. She was about to take her *Players* to Valletta for a production in its venerable *Teatru Manoel,* the oldest and one of the most impressive proscenium arches in Europe. The Binns were that theatre's angels. She and Graham had enabled the stately four tier theatre to be restored and, in the process, had secured a venue for her company.

I invited her and her apprentice thespians over to my digs in Glebe Place. She came but once, though the rest of the company came quite frequently. These gatherings were certainly unpretentious. They were defined by a lot of noise and much cheap plonk. The younger members of our company were barely twenty, but the age range spanned the spectrum. Richard Turner and I were a little older. We would soon turn thirty, while Richard Bealing, an aspiring director, was perhaps thirty-five. Jillian was our patron saint, her age not mattering a jot.

The stress of the rehearsals, and the release when they ended, was like a drug and a good one, too, and I became an enthusiast. If to a far lesser extent than the rest of the company, acting was also in my veins. Five years before, back in 1974, John Molony had cast me as Algernon, arguably the leading role in *The Importance of Being Earnest*. As a result I knew I could learn my lines.

*

The Boss at Robert Barrow had sent me a letter. The gist was that I should defecate or get off the pot.

There was still no sign of Simon Galway. Was he still on the rack in the *Wellington Humana* or somewhere? I would soon know. When, in due course, I paid Andy of *Bowrings Overseas* a visit, he told me that the Madrid 'offer' had reached an impasse. It would need Galway to sign it off. Even if he did, it might easily take a year, even two, for *Bowrings* to make me an equally valuable deal.

Just like that infernal dance, limbo was giving me a pain. I could not see a future at *CTB*. Should I really accept *Robert Barrow*'s kind offer? Yes, I somehow knew it would mean becoming a serf in 'Mr Edmond's' сословие, his 'soslovie'. I was contractually restricted by a three month notice period. If I resigned, would *CTB* agree to 'gardening leave'?

It was immediately granted, and rather too readily. I was told that Simon was on his way back to work and that I would not need to attend the office from the day that Simon reclaimed his desk. Charles Cullum, my CEO, had the grace to wish me good luck. He knew, I felt, how much I would need it.

Though disoriented, I was vigorously struggling to identify some embryonic plan that might yet to mutate into a stategy. As soon as I had donned my new harness I would ask every reinsurance underwriter I knew and even the ones I didn't if I could have the tail end of their treaties. After some months of banging on doors, someone, surely, would say 'yes'? It was a strategy said to work for sex-starved men at cocktail parties.

I did my remaining duties at CTB as well as I was able but my heart wasn't in it. I felt unloved. Making matters worse, however, I was beginning to suspect that I had been a fool to accept an underspecified position at *Robert Barrow*. What that company really needed, I concluded, was someone far senior to me, someone with connections, loyalties so tentacular that they would effortlessly build a non-marine account.

*

Eventually, as it had to, my 'gardening leave' began. I suggested to Richard Turner that he and I should meet. He was reluctant to travel from Highgate, where he lived, to Chelsea, so the mountain (me) had to travel to Mohammed. Richard was of independent means. He had no reason to seek paid employment.

I might as well have been in a parallel universe. Having little better to do, we liked to invent and play literary games. Our first we called *Aunt Ethel*. That was succeeded by *Blenkinstop*.[214] Both these games meant

---

[214] Aunt Ethel has to travel from A to B but can never arrive. The narrative must include buses, taxis, tea rooms, even arrests and the associated exasperation will pick off the competitors one by one as they resign in a huff. As for the legendary

writing alternative paragraphs with no pre-conceived outcome. These two games would coalesce into *The Novel Game*, based on the same discipline, or lack of it. The first paragraph would need some sort of pointer within it, and the second had to follow the given theme but add a twist. At last, after something like five hundred words, the original writer had to bring it all to a conclusion. It was a great game, and I looked forward to these sessions.

Richard Turner was also a bridge freak, a game I also liked. There were evenings when we would repair to *Boodles* in St James and play for terrifying stakes though my heart was never in gambling. I will only claim to have played a passable hand.

It was *The Novel Game*, however, that turned my head towards creative writing.

*

My new life, if that was what it was, began at *Robert Barrow* in the Autumn. I'm afraid the Boss and I, predictably – I hear you say - never got on. For him, I represented everything he disliked. First, I had been appointed by Mr Edmund, not by him. Secondly, I was some sort of weird aesthete and, in all probability, I could hear him think, a friend of Dorothy's.

Alonso was a considerably more accommodating. He was a competent linguist himself. His first language, he explained, had been 'Malti', a very obscure dialect. It had only become formalised in the latter half of the 19th century, when its grammar was finally written down.

'Malti is the only Semitic language written in Latin characters', he told me over a beer after work. 'We think it derives from the language of the Phoenicians. They arrived in Malta in 750 BC.'

Colonel Blenkinstop, he was a prolific letter write, whose epistolary efforts were directed to various people in power. In other words, Henry Root, *avant la lettre*.

'If that is true', I mused. 'then after Greek it must be the oldest surviving European language?'

'Spoken, yes, but it took the Knights of Malta to reletter it in Latin. In 1485, one of their number, Pietro Caxaro, left us a ballad.' He quoted it from memory, but all I could discern was its rhythm. I revised my impression of Alonso, however. It seemed that hidden behind his noisy façade was an unsung scholar.

His English and Italian were not bad either.

Alonso and I may have made an odd couple but I made an effort to show him my haunts and meet my friends. Not altogether happily; I will admit that making favourable impressions was not his long suit.

As for the Boss, he was a self-disciplined man who never, ever, took lunch if it were not with the Vestey brothers (which in any case would be a frugal affair). At weekends, lunch would amount to a hot dog in the stands of Southend United, the football team he supported. He had no compunction as to satirising me wherever and with whomever he could. My accent - as he saw it - was the voice of the landowning classes of the United Kingdom by whom, of course, he was employed. It teased a strange Jacobinism out of him. He would have gladly have watched me ascend the scaffold in the Place Louis XIV at the height of the Reign of Terror, and he would not have bothered with the *tricotage*.

I had no stipulated expense account. Any expenses I might incur had to be agreed in advance with the Boss so my attempts to seduce a market were hamstrung from the outset. I know, this was my fault; never presume. Perhaps I should have stayed put, but without Simon Galway's support I had no career prospects at all. Most ill-thought strategic errors are, in the end, the consequence of haste. Three weeks of thumb-twiddling passed before my associate membership of Lloyd's was confirmed. I celebrated with a wary tour of the market.

'*Robert Barrow?* Never heard of them,' was the greeting I most frequently received.

'We have some good new business,' I lied.

'Then show me.'

'I have still to put the stats together. I'll be back.'

*

The year, 1979, already on life-support, saw me handsomely paid but doing very little.

My requests to visit my contacts on the continent were routinely declined by the Boss. Alonso never understood my despondency. He was riding high and thought it inevitable that I would too.

'Look at me,' he declared over a coffee. 'I was a humble Maltese taxi driver before I found this job. Now I am an international reinsurance broker. You could be up here with me. The Boss, he's not too bad. Give him some space.'

Was that what I was failing to do? Respect that oafish, chippy bully? I was becoming all too aware that I had made a decision even poorer than average. I even wondered whether *CTB* might ever take me back.

The Boss asked me if he might have a few words and, of course, I was at his desk like a shot.

'You have contacts in Spain, Chap?'

'Yes, I do.'

'The Vesteys have many friends in the Hispanic world. Go and press your luck. Mr Edmund thinks you should visit Madrid. Have Barbara book you in for a week at a modestly priced hotel.'

I remember lighting up.

'Will my expenses cover an occasional lunch?'

'Or discotheque, or nightclub? I'm not sending you to *Club Méditerranée*, Chap. Go, speak to the relevant people, bring home some business, and in that order.'

'Does Mr Edmund have any friends of his own he would like me to see?'

'Don't get above yourself, Chap. Mr Edmund is a friend of the king. D'you actually think he needs a galley-slave to mix in his circles?'

I almost warmed to the Boss for his classical allusion.

*

It was not quite true that we had no non-marine business of any sort. We had to cover a dozen or so canning factories in South and Central America. These were single policies, not treaties, of course; what were known in the market as facultative risks.

It occurred to me they could be amalgamated into a treaty or two. I rewrote the stats, which was easy as they had few losses. I consolidated the risk into what the market calls a 'quota share' and a 'surplus treaty', setting out into the Lloyd's market to find a keen price. Well, it would keep me out of trouble, I reasoned.

I was quite wrong.

At around four o'clock I was back in my office, feeling rather pleased with myself. I had halved the cost of insuring the Vestey non-marine interests in Latin America. When back in my office, however, the Boss greeted me with a smile he had borrowed from a crocodile.

'Where have you been?'

I explained.

'Who asked you to do that?'

'I acted on my own initiative, Boss.'

'Well, don't. I placed those risks myself last November. Let me see those slips. I thought so. You've designed two treaties. I don't hold with treaties. I doubt if anyone fully understands them. When the time comes I want these renewed as before. Do you understand me?'

So far, not so very good.

*

I wrote to the *Maltese High Commission*, off Oxford Street. I had absolutely no idea how many insurance companies there might be in that gallant little island, but I began to plan a visit. The Vesteys flew the Maltese eight-pointed star on their ships, so the natives should be reasonably familiar with the corporate name.

I had never been to Malta, but I knew a little of its famous Knights, St Paul's brief visit and the Crusader tombs in Valletta's cathedral. It would also be wonderful to coincide a business trip with one of Jillian's productions at the *Manoel*.

Had I still been at *CTB*, I would have put in a request for a production trip and, in all likelihood, it would have been granted.

Only a few days later I had a reply from their officials. I was able to build an itinerary. I sent a telex to half-a-dozen local companies asking for a meeting. Their agreement came by return. I put my plan together and took it to the Boss.

*

'Are you quite mad, Chap?' he asked me. 'That is Alonso's turf.'

'I'm not pitching for marine business, I am your non-marine broker. I was looking for property, financial and fiduciary risk.'

'Alonso does Malta. That's that.'

'Has he tried for a non-marine account?'

'Of course not. He is a marine broker.'

It was occurring to me that the Boss was slightly more obtuse than the late Czar of Russia. Or was there another explanation? I had frequently seen the shapely Barbara fussing over her employer. There is a fellowship among secretaries. Had Mr Edmund's secretary told Barbara that Mr Edmund wanted me to replace the Boss? Had she let on? Was that why he already trying to engineer my demise?

*

That night, in the boisterous company of apprentice thespians in my house in Glebe Place, I was unable to share the general gaiety. The odour of some black dog had overpowered me. Despondent doesn't even begin to describe it.

Everyone seemed to think I was doing famously, earning a fortune, able (at last) to buy a round, as my more cynical acquaintances liked to quip. I had finally impressed my 'friends'.

Then the front door bell rang. Raising my sorry arse to my feet I went to open the door. A very beautiful girl was standing there looking puzzled, even lost.

'Jeremy! It is you! Your former girlfriend Vesta gave me your address.'

I am sorry to say I had not recognised her, but her accent was familiar. While it was the purest Jamaican, she only looked vaguely familiar.

'You'll have to remind me where we met?'

'We met at a cocktail party in Port Royal. You said I should ring you if I ever came to London.'

I remembered a dark sensation called Yolanda, but this girl was white.

'You're not Yolanda? Is it really possible?'

'Of course I am. Aren't you going to ask me in?'

'My God! I'm so sorry to be unwelcoming. You must come in, and right now.'

The party was in full swing but despite the racket I worked it out. Yolanda had been a white Jamaican all along. She had simply been darkly tanned.

She had been at Yale, probably still was. What asinine assumptions we can all make. I introduced her to various members of the *Shakespeare Players* and she was a complete delight. No one (at the time) fully realised that I was a common or garden idiot. I went on to overplay what little I had in the way of charm by way of apology.

Yolanda seemed not to notice. When I offered her a glass of wine she at first declined but, when she saw that everyone else had a glass in hand, she demurred.

'How long are you here for?' I asked.

'Two whole months. I've been seconded to the London School of Economics for one of my modules.'

'Do you know England? London? Would you let me show you some of my favourite places?'

'I would be so grateful.'

'And I would be proud to do so.'

*

I was facing my first renewal season in my new company and I had almost no business to renew. The lack of urgency gave me a chance to see my family and go to some Christmas parties. At one of which, given by an acquaintance, Jilly Dulapp, an old friend, Michael Evans, introduced me to a lady he (and I) liked the look of, Helen Kelsey by name. I took her telephone number.

The holidays gave me a much needed chance to reconsider my future. It was all too clear I had to play my cards very carefully. I rang my head-hunter and picked a bone with him. Robert Barrow?

'I told you I needed to be hired by a major international organisation, underwriter or broker,' I told him forcibly. 'I do not need to be in a rat's nest of an office, infested with plague-nits. You have sent me into a tedious idiot's lair where I need tuition in how to cater to so great an ego that he has no idea that his own chief wants him replaced!'

'You have chosen a poor season to complain. Take a closer look at the economy. You are expensive and no one is hiring.'

Should I be looking even further afield? Abroad?

*

I was doing my very best to spoil Yolanda. I suggested she might come with me to Spain. To my surprise and delight she agreed. She declared herself ready to explore the Prado while I went to a few meetings.

What I couldn't explain was why was a London broker be trying to develop business in their Hispanic kingdom with few established contacts or, especially, without the support of his business's owners? My Spanish counterparts were as baffled as I was. At least they had heard of the Vesteys.

'We know your Lord Vestey from our society pages,' said Señor Marías, chief underwriter at *Mapfre Aseguro*. 'He's the world's greatest cattle dealer. We Spanish like beef and his ranches are in our old dominions in South America.'

'They tell me he is a friend of the king?'

'Yes, that's true. I recall a photograph of him and Juan-Carlos in *¡Hola!* My wife showed it to me.' He seemed a little absent for a moment. 'Or was it my hairdresser?' He mulled the matter over. 'Unfortunately, we have nothing to offer you at, ah, *Robert Barrow*.'

'Perhaps you might let me survey your reinsurance overall? There might even be something we could contribute?'

I was feeling guilty. Not as much about my own performance as I deserved. Yolanda was on my mind and I had left her in the Prado so long she may well have become the world's greatest expert on Spanish old masters.

'I'll be here at eight tomorrow morning, if you will allow me,' I pressed on. 'I will go through your entire reinsurance program. I may be able to make a useful suggestion.'

'Well, in the circumstances that's very good of you. When you arrive, ask for me. I will have found you somewhere to sit down and go through the books. Until tomorrow, then. *¡Hasta Mañana!*'

I decided to make my own way to the Prado and soon discovered Yolanda in front of, and hypnotised by, Picasso's huge *Guernica*, a picture that had long fascinated me.

'It says here that this was painted during the Nazi bombardment of the Basque country before World War Two,' she said. 'The figures at the bottom are presumably victims of the raids. What can these bulls and cartoon-like animals signify?'

'I think that Picasso meant this painting to reveal the devastation and chaos of war.'

I was flattered to have the role of mentor forced on me.

'He finished it in 1937, a time of terrible political unrest, everywhere, not just for Spain. He has depicted victims of the bombing, ordinary men and women, innocent civilians, some still alive, most of them dead. Look at that figure in the foreground. That's a corpse, I'm certain. The survivors are victims too. They are not rejoicing. Look, at them, their heads thrown back, they wail in agony. That mother on the left is clutching a baby, killed in an air raid.'

'Is this 'cubist'?'

'Yes. You see how he has overlaid humans and animals onto a melange of disconnected hard-edged geometric shapes. The texture of the horse - newspaper print - may be a throwback to Picasso's early *Journal*, which almost defined the movement. This is cubist for sure.'

'I still don't quite get it. Why, for instance, is it free of colour? It's almost monochrome.'

'Perhaps it's because Picasso so clearly believed the issue was, morally at least, black and white? As for the form, he has drawn on Goya, who often painted war. He has added bullfighting, which he saw as a peculiarly Spanish metaphor.'

'Bullfighting plays a part in this painting?'

'It's a 'war painting'. Picasso has used every symbol at his disposal. A bull, a horse, a man with a sword, they're all part of Spain's particular tradition. The bull is effectively the national symbol of Spain. Picasso wants us to see the destruction of Guernica as a national tragedy, not a local one.'

'It seems to me,' said a thoughtful Yolanda, 'that Pablo Picasso wants us to *experience* the brutality, the reduction of men women and children in war. That's why he makes so much of the animalistic reaction that all living things, animal or human, have to fear from death.'

'A reflection of the bullfight, perhaps?'

Yolanda and I went back our hotel. I love museums, especially such marvels as the Prado, but they are taxing.

'We should lie down, take a siesta, get a little sleep, as the natives do. We'll be out late and I have to be in a meeting first thing after lunch.'

'I see! What do you expect me to do while you're busy doing your thing?'

'You could go shopping? The Madrileños are great with leather.'

We lay down on our huge bed a little circumspectly, with the purest intentions. Well, perhaps hers were. Or maybe not. Anyway, I had no intention of sleeping. An hour or so later, a rather tired version of my generally chirpy self had an insurance company to visit.

*

At last, it was time for supper. We headed for the *Corral de la Morería*, a restaurant where they serenade the guests with flamenco. The *Corral's* shows are so famous that politicians, actors and artists come from all over the world. It has to be one of the thousand places to see before you die.[215] Each set lasted an hour or so, in which two male dancers appear to fight over a coquettish *femme fatale*. All this was accompanied by a female singer, three male singers and two guitars.

We were brought tapas - roast tomatoes, stuffed with a black risotto of baby cuttlefish, and 'pizzas' of *idiazabal* cheese with onion, aubergine, green and red peppers. All this was followed by chicken in a Parmentier sauce. Yolanda was as impressed by the five-chocolate cake as I was by the Rioja. All too soon it was 2 am and high time to have a second attempt at sleep.

This time, Morpheus should have had his way.

*

Considering my exertions, I was buoyant and alert when I reached my meeting. A small, airless meeting room, smelling strongly of tobacco, had been readied for me. Some twenty box files were on the floor, challenging me to discover how they might be managed better.

I picked up the first one.

It was a correspondence file. Inside were several hundred handwritten letters, each stapled to a carbon-copied and formulaic reply. Every nation has its own handwriting, I thought, and the blasted Spanish one is especially illegible. As I struggled to decipher them my gloom deepened.

Ten minutes in and I had deciphered just one, a non-specific enquiry about vehicle insurance. The reply informed the most dear and honourable petitioner that it had enclosed an application form. Aside from the baroque gallantry, it really didn't say much else.

---

[215] Which is how the New York Times described it. A favourite haunt of politicians and celebrities, including George Bush Snr, Richard Nixon, John F. Kennedy, Nicole Kidman, Harrison Ford, Sandra Bullock, Hugh Grant, Adrian Brody, Natalie Portman, Richard Gere, Pablo Picasso and Salvador Dalí are there in framed and signed photographs.

The write-off value of a motorcar, with many exceptions, is more-or-less the same to insurers; 80% of cars are worth around a quarter of what they cost when new, and the popular ones conform to a surprisingly narrow price range.

Every piece of correspondence in the file concerned the same class of business, some reporting losses, others more generic. One wanted to insure a road-worthy go-cart, no doubt with go-faster stripes. Could I really have stumbled on some valuable prospective business so readily? Still, car insurance could be the starting point for a treaty. A motor quota, I thought. I scribbled the idea on a blank sheet of paper.

I ploughed on. It's 'third party' that can take an insurance company by surprise. 'Catastrophe' can also cost an insurer dearly, as it had done the previous year. That was when a particularly ferocious hailstorm in Mantua had wiped out a football stadium's carpark's worth of Fiat *Cinquecentos*.

On opening the next box I learned that the company offered householders' comprehensive policies. The first letter queried whether a dog and a cockatoo would be included in the policy. They were both adorable, apparently, provided you were neither a postman, travelling salesman or a priest.

Domestic property insurance is and was very different to insuring your car. All cars are worth much the same, to an insurance company that is. A country cottage, on the other hand, is worth around a tenth of a house in the capital, and a mansion in Puerta Hierro was worth ten times that. To reinsure a property portfolio needs a very different approach.

The more I perused the papers I had been shown, I discovered that the company offered insurance on almost everything.

Small aeroplanes, garden tools, veterinary risk, cinematic hazard[216] and pleasure steamers (which was odd as Madrid does not have a river let alone a coast).[217] All of these categories were at least in principle amenable to reinsurance.

By midday my sheet of paper had twenty headings, two thirds of which were 'non-marine'.

Señor Marías came in at the twelfth stroke of noon.

'Have you spotted an opportunity to make us all a little richer?' he asked with a smile.

'I have identified fourteen classes of insurance where the London market might be able to hedge your bets.'

I pushed my scrap of paper towards him. Property, Motor, Vetinerary, Catastrophe, Aviation... Still, car insurance could be the starting point for a treaty. Perhaps a motor quota, I thought. Or maybe a catastrophe? The previous year a singularly ferocious hailstorm in Mantua had wiped out a football stadium's worth of Fiat Cinquecentos.

'I see. Yes, we do have significant portfolios in all those areas. We also have existing reinsurance in all of them, excepting vetinerary. There the premiums are so high we have few customers but we make so handsome a return for so little risk we wouldn't want to pay any away.'

'You also have a sizeable share of Spain's construction industry's business. It's an area where the unexpected happens predictably,' I volunteered, thinking I was being amusing. Raised eyebrows suggested that I was not. Marías obviously thought me absurd.

'The Munich Re covers us in that sector.'

'Would you allow me to quote in competition?'

---

[216] Bruised starlet's legs are a speciality but photographs will be needed risk.
[217] It does have a fine boating lake, *el Embalse del Pardo*.

515

'All right, why not. Let's start here. Which is your hotel? Really?' He glanced at my card. 'I'll have someone bring over all the papers you will need. Can you send me rival terms this evening? Or let's say tomorrow? But be aware; we are nearing the end of the year. If you cannot improve on Munich's terms, our current arrangements will carry over.'

'Nothing could be fairer. Thank you, Señor Marías. I'll be in touch as soon as I have something to report.'

*

I was feeling faintly more secure in early December 1979. I had not actually developed any new business, but I was sure I had made myself useful. The Boss, however, was unimpressed.

'We pay you an inordinate salary. So far, all we have had from you are expenses. Are we about to see you conjure up some business, either from Mapfre or from LUFE?'[218]

'It will be hard to undercut the Munich Re, but I shall try.'

'You're not giving up?'

'Certainly not. I'm far too busy knocking at doors to consider lying doggo. In Spain, what we need is a little momentum but we have to start from scratch. According to Newton, a body at rest continues to be at rest unless acted upon by an exterior force. That is my challenge.'

'Eh? Is that more of your highfalutin' Cambridge claptrap? Stop showing off, Chap. It sounds to me like an excuse not to give the envelope a push of any sort. Newton? This is not a maths class, we are a reinsurance broker.'

Nor did the market help. I was unable to better the Munich Re's price on the Mapfre construction

---

[218] *La Unión y el Fénix Español.*

treaties. Nor did the Boss let me merge his facultative covers into a treaty for Vestey's canning factories. Our existing business, such as it was, renewed well enough, but I had landed no new business before Christmas.

*

The call from Mr Edmund did not come until February.

'Thank you for coming by. You have not lived up to my expectations and so I will let you go. How much notice do I have to give you?'

'The contract says three months. I also have three weeks of holiday still untaken.'

'I see. Well that takes us to the end of May. I don't believe either you or your boss will want to work together in the circumstances. We shall pay what we owe. Collect your stuff and go home today. Oh, and on your way, ask him to come and see me.'

With that my brilliant career at Robert Barrow was over. My only consolation was that the Boss's, most probably, was too.

*

I rang my head-hunter but he opined that little was happening in the reinsurance market, just at present.

'My advice? Take a holiday. The latest boom is coming to an end. They are cyclical, you know. The government's clumsy attempts to boost growth have merely created a wave of inflation. Unemployment is surging. South Africa is lovely this time of year. Have you ever been? Jo'burg is screaming for talent. You might consider doing a little hunting down there, on your own.'

It was not entirely a bad idea, but it would have to go on hold. I would have to sell it at home. I also had plans in London, if not of a business kind.

I had decided to develop my acquaintance with Graham and Jillian Binns. Among other things, they effectively owned the old *Theatre Royal*[219] in London's

---

[219] Otherwise known as the *Royal Holloway*.

517

Holloway. I had enjoyed my sessions with Richard Turner, endlessly playing *The Novel Game*. They must have amounted to some sort of unidentifiable training for something?

My father was a playwright. Some of his stuff had been produced by Gielgud, no less, and he might help.

I decided to write a stage play. It would be a classic comedy, farcical perhaps, but with a bathetic undertone. Sheridan, whom an ancestor of mine had defended on a charge of duelling, always kept his plays to five acts. I would follow his example. But what could it be about? Well, what about a reinsurance broker who thinks he has wings? Or who actually has wings? What would happen?

I sharpened my pencil. It would have five acts. (1) Let's begin with a hero who discovers he's not like everyone else. (2) He tries to get his wings removed before they grow too big. (3) Yet they do grow and he tries the church. (4) Desperate, he applies to the circus? (5) Gets shot down. Let's make it over Mr Edmund's sporting estate.

This was going to be fun. Now all I had to do was write it.

*

My new friendship with Helen Kelsey was looking up. I suspect she still thought me something of an ass, but I thought I might impress her by taking her to the opera, though I soon discovered she already knew the opera house well.

'I was at its ballet school,' she told me, 'before my legs grew too short.

'Would you like to come and see *Boris Godunov*?'

'What is it about?'

'It's about Russia,' I told her. 'Pushkin based his story on a true one and then Mussorgsky fashioned it into something universal; a blend of the grandiose and the tragic. He ignored the conventions of grand opera -

he introduced peals of church bells, for example. The music walks a tightrope between extraordinary flights of fancy and riotous choruses. Contrasting themes give the piece enormous strength. Mussorgsky has written a pitiable portrait of Boris, the usurping Tsar, eaten up by self-destructive omnipotence. The Tsar collides with a musical portrayal of the Russian people, the opera's real hero. They appear in the very first scenes, regularly returning to comment on the state of Russia, always wanting change.'

'All right, I'm on,' Helen conceded, smiling at my improvised prospectus.

*

My literary *alter ego* was busying himself in the doctor's surgery where my hero was attempting to discover whatever it was that was causing those bumps on his shoulder blades.

I was so pleasantly distracted I failed to notice the leaves on the calendar flicking over.

Mercifully, I think, I had a telephone call from my old and platonic friend Caroline Swan, whom I knew from my gap years. 'Are we still on for Boris G?' she asked.

My God! I had completely forgotten! Now I had two guests and only two tickets! Where were we going to sit? Could I even go? I rang the booking office. Was there even a microscopic chance - the proverbial snowball's chance in hell - of a ticket for tomorrow night?

'Let me have a look. Yes, we have had a return. You're in luck; it's in the fifth row of the stalls.'

That was a far better place to sit than the tickets I already had bought. To hell with the stratospheric cost, I told myself. God had decreed that you must pay the highest prices if you want Boris Christoff to sing the eponymous lead.

'I'll be there in around an hour. Put the ticket to one side. Please.'

*

'I have written a play,' I told Jillian on the telephone, fully expecting to her say 'so what?' I pressed on. 'It's called *A Flight of Fancy*'.

'Any fool can write a play,' she told me truthfully, if somewhat unnecessarily. She was, after all, talking to the fool in question. She also left unsaid that it takes a genius to get one on stage. But no, that's not what she said.

'Bring it to our theatre on Tuesday. I'll have the *Players* read it through.'

A ray of sunlight had found its way into an otherwise gloomy season.

*

Helen arrived at Glebe Place. When she saw me in my dinner jacket she was a little flustered. She was in a pretty day dress. When she saw Caroline, however, she was clearly cross. I was embarrassed, mostly because I hadn't mentioned the latter to the former. What's more, it was about to get worse. If the three seats had been in a row it might have been easier.

'I'm afraid I couldn't get three seats together,' I owned up. 'We have two good ones at the back and one terrific one in the front. Who wants to sit where?'

Helen, my new friend, nobly decided she would have the better seat. Of course, she had no idea that her rival and I were merely old friends. Caroline was in fact walking out with Robert Booth.

The interval heralded problems and I had little to offer in self-defence. Champagne in the Crush Bar might rescue the evening in the interval. It often has that power. The ladies were of course aware of my *faux pas*. There was little I could say; I would only have dug my hole a little deeper.

Nevertheless, Helen's *sang froid* impressed me. She was proving to be a determined and courageous lass. While not classically educated, she did not lack Poirot's little grey cells.

She was also deeply interested in theatre, in all its forms. She worked in cinema as a film editor and had already built her own company, *Kelsey Kuts OK*. It rented a cutting room in Wardour Street, at the very beating heart of the British film industry. She had been in the business since she left school, barely sixteen. Her talent and energy had been obvious to the whole of her industry from the outset.

She also had a wonderful, irreverent sense of humour, dangerously counterbalanced with a villainous temper.

Perhaps I should also add that she was the most lissom beauty within the four corners of Europe. Of course she was ill at ease. She was marginally underdressed, in the company of two who were clearly familiar with grand opera, but she crossly (and correctly) asserted her right to be included without a belittling commentary.

After the curtain finally fell, we enjoyed a decent dinner at Delmonico's. The cocktail of Boris and Champagne was good enough and the girls could return safely, I hope happily, to their own homes.

*

Over lunch on Sunday, my father handed me back the draft of *Flight of Fancy* I had given to him to read.

'It's very good,' he told me, 'if sometimes a bit predictable. I loved your satire on the Church of England but it should be more mordent. Aside from the nurse and the victim's wife you have no female roles. Make your nurse a male and the doctor female. Camp up the priests in Act III. When's your first reading?'

'Tuesday,' I replied. 'Tuesday the 13th.'

'At least it's not a Friday. Break a leg.'

*

Very early, that Tuesday, just as dawn let daylight take me by the shoulders and shake me back to life, I was at *Rymans* with my hastily revised manuscript. A quarter of an hour later, I owned a dozen expensive photocopies of my stageplay.

Over a coffee in one of the *Kahdomah Cafés*, this one a marvellous place with a distinctly Central-European flavour, quirkily designed by Sir Misha Black,[220] I looked at one of my poorly laid out typescripts. It had an over-liberal sprinkling of typos. Oh well, they would just have to be corrected later.

*

Jillian, bless her little cotton socks, and ten members of her *players,* brought my characters to life.

'You will not read, Jeremy,' she said sternly, before we began. 'Stay quiet. Just listen. You will hear your own words.'

She then relaxed a little.

'When you get home you may make your words sadder or funnier as needs be.'

I expected long pauses and much ribbing, but the cast was in tears of laughter, paroxysms of mirth, even before we had turned the first page. I half expected a bout of thigh-slapping.

'Don't be too encouraged,' Jillian said, after the reading. 'We laughed a lot, but it's only because we know you. Your audience will not. Your script walks a fine line between comedy and tragedy. It may puzzle the less than literate. Saying that, *The Shakespeare Players* will put it on. The first performance of an unknown writer's first play will be in our *Theatre Royal* in Holloway

---

[220] Black designed many memorable posters for London Transport and became the chief consultant on their Design Committee.

but, from here on in, you are no longer a playwright. Henceforward your task is to persuade your friends to come to the opening night. We need a full house. That's three hundred. At least it's many fewer than the thousand the theatre seated in its heyday. The second task will be to find the sponsorship we will need for advertising, the programmes, the ticket office and so on. It's not all bad news; most of the actual costs of the hire, the props, the lighting, the costumes and the set can be left to us. Graham and I will invite *The Guardian*, *The Times* and *The Telegraph* to the première. They may even come. Who knows?'

'How much money do I need to raise? Do you need the folding stuff or will pledges do?'

Jillian Binns mentioned an enormous sum. I may have gone white.

'Don't panic!' she said. 'There is masses of time. Maybe six weeks. We might stretch it to eight – I shall have to check with the Poly. Sell advertising in the programme, that's a fast and reliable way of doing it. Oh yes, I shall need some copy about yourself, what inspired your play, a synopsis, anything else you can think of to bulk it out. We shall dress it up as a souvenir edition, put a ribbon in it, that sort of thing, and charge for it. I trust you're looking forward to your opening night as much as I am?'

*

I began what amounted to a telethon. I rang every friend I had who was a director of his or her company. The first half dozen calls were disheartening, but the seventh was not.

'OK, Jeremy, we'll take a half page, internal, and will send you what you need. Add a message to the logo and background saying something useful. Here's my suggestion.

Gaul, Sheppard and Company

wish
The Shakespeare Players
the best of luck
on this, the first night of a new play

'Once you've laid it out, bring it over so we can OK it and give you the money. No, no need for thanks, it's been a pleasure.'

I was suitably emboldened. I asked Helen who her current contract was with. It was a company called MediCine. Since my play started in a surgery, I emphasised the medical nature of the drama. She took my proposal to her principals and the filmmakers graciously coughed up a few bob. I ploughed on.

'Why have you not yet tapped Graham Binns directly?' asked Helen, astute as always. 'It's always a mistake to treat husband and wife as a single item.'

I duly made an appointment to visit him at Capital Radio. It was an interesting experience in its own right, and not only did he find some money to put our way but he decided to advertise the play on his radio station. Soon I had a twelve page programme and so much money I could almost have rebuilt the long lost *Globe*.[221]

*

Jillian called me in with a little problem. One of her cast, Emma Hamilton-Brown, had taken sick. She had been cast as a secretary. 'Did I know anyone who had the ability and willingness to play a hussy in a hurry?'

Of course I didn't. I had few friends in the arts and hardly knew how the theatre worked. Robert Booth was already in the bag.

---

[221] Here I must confess to wild exaggeration. It took Sam Wannamaker to overcome the pedestrian and leftist objections of Lambeth Council and rebuild the original *Shakespeare Players'* 'great O', in the 1980s. I had the great privilege of meeting him before the first performance there and thanking him for his astonishing efforts on behalf not just of London but of the whole world.

After Bedales and Cambridge he had joined LAMDA, the London Academy of Music and Dramatic Art. It is the oldest drama school in the UK.[222]

*

When I shared my anxieties with Helen she thought for a moment. 'I could play the secretary.'

I was expected to make some grateful observation.

'Listen,' Helen continued. 'Your money is fast running out. In the fullness of time even that will sort itself out, but in the meantime, you might consider sharing my flat in Wimpole Street. And yes, I would learn my lines. I've read the script. I only have to appear in acts II and V. It's not too steep a hill to climb.'

'Brilliant! Jillian is in charge, of course, but I'll ask her. You're absolutely certain?'

*

Jillian was a little diffident. She didn't really take to Helen from the off but, once she saw her act, she relented.

'Helen is a natural', she reluctantly admitted. It was true. She hardly needed direction and she knew how and where to move instinctively. From the first rehearsal she had her lines quite faultlessly.

Jillian awarded my stepbrother, Kevin, a small part as the terrified curate and my father and stepmother loyally bought tickets for the first night.

That scary night approached like an express train hurtling towards a stalled motorist on a level crossing. Posters were going up everywhere, outside the theatre, all over North London. Former colleagues rang me up, claiming that they did not know how to buy a decent ticket (while actually hoping to get one free). Elegant friends, most of whom I had not heard from since

---

[222] It was announced, on 16 January 2018, that Benedict Cumberbatch would succeed Timothy West as LAMDA's President.

those distant days when I had seemed to live in a dinner jacket, remade contact.

It would appear that I was the most brilliant man that ever walked the Earth, but that was before anyone had actually seen the play.

Richard Turner had thought to write an inclusion in the programme over a pseudonym, of the *Littlehampton Mercury*. This is what 'Felix Wake' wrote:

THE PREMIERE OF

Flight of Fancy

A NEW WORK BY
JEREMY MACDONOGH

DIRECTED BY JILLIAN BINNS
PERFORMED BY
THE SHAKESPEARE PLAYERS

HOLLOWAY'S
THEATRE ROYAL
A PART OF THE NORTH LONDON POLYTECHNIC'S FACULTY OF DRAMATIC ARTS

While Jeremy lives in what amounts to a 'consulting room in Harley Street', and was himself an insurance broker for many years, he assures me that his play is not autobiographical.

Not one of his characters is based on anyone he knows or has even heard of, except as they say, purely coincidentally.

He tells me the idea came to him while he was staying with friends in Rome, and that he was reminded of it by conversations touching on the Year of the Disabled.

This I believe, for surely this light comedy does provoke disquieting reflexions on the plight of a man who becomes disabled during a rising career. That his protagonist is unable to deal successfully with his problem perhaps emphasises how terrible the lack of understanding and compassion of a busy society can be, and how we, the healthy, must remember to do all in our power to make sure such people are offered the same opportunities and friendship as their more fortunate counterparts receive without hesitation.

It was well-meant, if a little earnest, I thought. I would have a go, posing as an irascible don at my former university.

I can claim credit for most of the original ideas in this play, if indeed there be any. Mr McDonough enjoyed the privilege of being supervised by me at Cambridge, where he was lucky enough to hear me pronounce wittily and intelligently on almost every subject, and on at least two occasions I observed him taking notes. That he consistently missed the point is, I maintain, due to the total inadequacy of the present educational system, and the fact that so many young students today can boast little more than a dismal and inaccurate acquaintance of Tolstoy or Zola in poor Oxonian translations. I would have been greatly honoured to have attended the 'Gala Première', as he ambitiously calls it, but more pressing business in Soho will sadly keep me away.

Dr Loewentahl, Senior Fellow of St Francis College, Cambridge, has recently published his collected works, *A Study of Wagner, Zola and 'Machine-Gun' Kelly, Founders of Western Civilisation*, in forty-two volumes.

Richard was never going to put up with this. Yet another 'review' was handed to the programme's publisher for inclusion in the programme.

It was in 1949 that I first met Jeremy McDonagh. The memory of a gaunt, overcoated figure, blinking in the early morning sunshine just outside Pentonville Prison, will always be with me. Our later encounters, elusive but ever illuminating, found us as far afield as Vladivostok and on ground as familiar as the snug bar of the 'Cardinal's Hat', Westminster.

I have often wondered why the world has had to wait so long for his first literary offerings - perhaps it has something to do with the shape of his head? Certainly his wasted years, spent under the unsteady hand of that charlatan Loewentahl in Cambridge, may be said to have retarded, but never to have quenched, McDonagh's pristine genius. Most sincerely do I wish him and his play every success.

Dr Philboeuf is Egregious Professor of Mid-Nineteenth Century Writings in Translation at the University of Oxford.

The first night itself went wonderfully. Jillian's organisation proved flawless from the off. Friends arrived, hundreds of them. Some were mine and, of those, some I had even met.

So did a theatre critic. Very happily for me, the crowd roared like greasepaint and smelled far worse, just as it should.

*

In the national press the following day, Charles Spencer of *The Times* applied nib to paper.

It has long been a pleasure to see Jillian Binns' efforts come to life. Last night was no exception. Alongside RADA and LAMBDA, her theatre school - in its unlikely location in Holloway, North London - is a teeming womb of international stars. Aspiring thespians from Malta, Jamaica, Corfu and, perhaps improbably, Holloway, breathe life into Shakespeare or Sheridan, or any of our hallowed greats. It was therefore a complete surprise to see a drama that trod a fine line between comedy and tragedy with such verve. 'Flight of Fancy', a five-act stageplay by Jeremy Macdonogh, brought the house down. Miss Binns herself played the role of a doctor who is besought to amputate the wings of an otherwise tedious businessman whom God, in His infinite wisdom, has decided to reincarnate as an angel, while still alive! All great fun and, who knows, it might even make the established repertoire, one day.

Nick Monson had been persuaded to write some advertising copy for *Club 18 – 30*, the singles holiday company. The deal was good. Some pocket money and a free week in a villa in Kos but Nick felt reluctant to accept. He told the business owner he would do it, but he would need two weeks to catch the mood of the place and would need a friend 'of his own age and style' to make it bearable.

Amazingly, his conditions were agreed. He rang me up to see if I were game for a laugh.

In the meantime, Helen had been offered a contract in Johannesburg as a film editor. The offer included a flat.

She wanted to accept. She had never been to South Africa. it would certainly be an adventure but what would I do? 'I'll join you in South Africa,' I told her decisively, 'directly after my trip to Kos.'

It was agreed that our belongings - furniture, linen, clothes, crockery, paintings, rugs, sound systems, all the paraphernalia of a London flat - would be stored for the duration of the posting by one of her friends who had volunteered an unused garage. How long would that be? A year? Two? Indefinitely? It would be a laugh, one way or another.

What would I do down there? Well, there was reinsurance. There might also be a chance as a writer. One way or another I'd be all right. I saw Helen off as she set out for Jan Smuts International Airport,[223] before changing terminals to fly to Kos with my old friend Monson.

---

[223] Now renamed Tambo International.

The rest of the world was looking the other way. The wedding of Prince Charles and Lady Diana Spencer would shortly take place - on Wednesday 29 July 1981 - in St Paul's Cathedral. No surprise there. The groom was the heir to the British throne, while the bride's family - the Spencers - had, if anything, an even older pedigree.

No wonder that Nick had been allotted two places over this particular fortnight. Everyone else in the world would be glued to their TVs.

On arrival we discovered we had been allotted single rooms, which sounded promising, but the tourists were beginning their second week. All their alliances and cabin friendships were already written in, well, sand. The 'singles' had successfully metamorphosed into 'pairs'.

Nick and I were interlopers, and suspect ones at that. If anyone misbehaved, Nick might write it all down. Heaven forefend, that would not do. As a direct result, they became secretive and withdrawn, trying to avoid us wherever possible.

'We have been ostracised,' I told Nick.

He was unconcerned and laughed.

'I'd make it all up anyway,' he said.

We did the stuff you must do in Kos. We burned our fair skins until they hurt, ate defrosted moussaka until we could stand it no longer and, in my case at least, looked more and more ridiculous while vainly trying to rise from the water on my skis.

We went to see Hippocrates' tree where, in its shade, the doctor had taught his pupils. We mused about his Oath and how it had been revered and thought sacred for the two thousand years prior to 1965. Since then we have been told that it's rubbish. Cosmetic surgery? The Oath says firmly that no surgery should ever be performed except when it is necessary.

For most of history this was against the rule. Abortion? Not a problem, not any more. Half the fortunes of Harley Street are due to breaking or ignoring the Oath. Thank goodness our generation knows so much more that the thousand generations that preceded it.

Then a flight full of 'innocent' boys and girls, the contents of our villa, took off for Barnsley, Birmingham or Burnley, only to be replaced by a new complement of pleasure seekers.

I must say, the new lot were rather more game for a laugh than their predecessors. This bunch were all single, footloose and fancy-free. It was the beginning of the '80s but they made it feel like the mid-'60s. This time there was no *froideur*. Nick and I joined them for paragliding, when we were not too busy enjoying the warm and close friendships they had so readily on offer.

Some things should not be written down. What happens in Kos stays in Kos, but an intense saturnalia served as a farewell to silliness. I was about to press the restart button on my life, having resolved that I would remount the slippery treadmill I had fallen off so spectacularly. Kos was an enjoyable intermezzo, an interval from my time as a reinsurance broker. Yet, if you fall from a horse, the best advice is you should get back in the saddle as fast as you can.

Helen would have settled into a flat by now and I needed to find out what my new home looked like.

It was time to close the gap in the market.

CHAPTER SEVEN

Growing Up (at last)
1980 - 1981

In which the author flies to South Africa to move in with his new girlfriend. He becomes a journalist and an underwriter. He and Helen go to a wedding in Kenya, are in a plane crash in the Okavango Delta in Botswana, and conclude this first phase of their lives as a married couple.

Helen and I had agreed to join up in South Africa. The hint that it might be to my advantage helped me embrace the idea.

I would need a wardrobe for the Dark Continent and I wandered along Chelsea's King's Road, peering into its infinite parade of plate glass windows. I spotted a wonderful suede blouson. Its cut resembled James Bond's safari jacket and it oozed sophisticated explorer magic.[224]

I went in. John Michael, whoever he may have been, liked to embroider his initials on everything he sold. Since his initials were the same as mine, it doubled my smugness to have the monogram JM emblazoned over my heart. While I preened myself in the wildly expensive boutique's cheval glass, an unnecessarily camp sales assistant came up and shared my enthusiasm.

'May I venture to remark how svelte Sir looks in our little number?' he sussurated.

If its design was by Yves St Laurent, its price tag was by Croesus. Of course, I bought it.

*

Now I would have to ease back on the cost of my plane ticket to Johannesburg. I approached a travel agent, in desperate need of a deal.

---

[224] Roger Moore, in *The Man With The Golden Gun*

The cheapest way to Johannesburg was by sea, but I wanted to keep my clothes on and I'm not a great swimmer. The travel agent wisely advised me to fly BA to Brussels, transfer to Sabena, travel on a Royal Belgian subsidy as far as Kinshasa in the Belgian Congo[225] and complete the onward journey to Johannesburg via Swiss Air.

Complicated, certainly, but you cannot argue with numbers. It was far and away the most economical route.

The travel agent, saying 'travel well', almost rubbed my hand as she shook it. Her eyes seemed moist. Three tickets in as many minutes? It will have been a record. I judged she had achieved the executive quota that month and earned the chance to join other top achievers on a corporate week in Benidorm.

Second prize will have been two weeks.

*

In a more devout, more metaphysical world, that jacket - or my pride in it - would have sentenced me to walk barefoot to Santiago de Compostela or some other hallowed place of pilgrimage.

I had however saved a considerable sum over the regular flight and, almost before I knew it, I was checking in at Gatwick, looking a million dollars in my magnificent coat. Never mind that it had depleted my funds to somewhere worryingly close to extinction.

A few hours later I was in Brussels. I thought I would have a couple of hours in the duty-free shop or in the bar, but then I saw the size of the crowd swarming around the check-in desk for the Kinshasa leg. Dozens of bad-tempered Congolese ladies, all lavishly clad, accompanied by their silent beaux, squabbled with the

---

[225] For a while the Democratic Republic of Zaire. It is now the Democratic Republic of Congo. Kinshasa's maiden name was Léopoldville. It is the largest French-speaking city in the world, dwarfing Paris, and is the third largest city in Africa, coming in after Cairo and Lagos.

officials. The gist of it all was that Sabena had seats for forty of them and the other forty would have to remain behind. Somehow I forged a path to the desk and showed my reservation. To my overwhelming relief my ticket was endorsed, stamped and countersigned. I had a safe seat.

No one had cursed me with that famous Chinese imprecation, that you have an exciting journey. The flight to the Congo was uneventful. My trouble was that it too much so. As the in-flight cinema screen flickered into life, it turned out that we were about to be treated to *The Wild Geese*, an adventure set in Africa and starring, well, everyone. I had been meaning to watch it for some time, so I was in luck. I searched for the headphones in the pouch in front of me.

There were none, so I reached up to call for a stewardess. Time races by when you're having fun but I wasn't.

Without the faintest hint of urgency, a Congolese air hostess eventually condescended to come to my seat.

'How can I help?' she asked - in French, of course.

'I seem not to have any headphones,' I protested.

'No one has. We haven't any.'

'Oh well, there it is. While you're here, can I have a gin and tonic?'

'Sorry. No drinks on this flight.'

It promised to be a long journey and it was. Three hours after take-off we had crossed the Mediterranean and the Atlas Mountains.

The immensity of the Sahara unfolded beneath us. We were in a colourscape devoid of detail, a vast *shisha* tent whose orange carpet merged into an azure canopy. There was no horizon; no way could one know how high we were nor, if miles below, there might be Bedouins driving overladen camels towards an oasis. We were flying into a colour palette, the drama of which forbore description.

At last, after an age, we were in Congolese airspace. We should have been on our final approach but, we slowly discovered, we were destined to circle the terminal interminably like lost souls.

A syrupy disembodied voice came over the PA system.

'Ici votre capitaine. Avant qu'on puisse atterrer, chers citoyens, je regrette de vous tous informer que nous sommes obligés de circuler au-dessus le capitale. On se permet de vous suggérer que la vue sur Afrique Centrale dès nos fenêtres vaut la peine.'

The rust-coloured traveller beside me, whose French may have been equally rusty, asked me what had just been said.

'We're going to be stuck up here for a bit,' I told him. 'Let's just hope the fuel doesn't run out.'

The recommended view was in fact alarming. A squadron of fighter planes, tooled-up with underwing missiles, was escorting a Boeing 747. They obviously meant to brook no opposition. The Jumbo Jet in question was lavishly and picturesquely decorated, and my knowledgeable Afrikaner neighbour usefully told me that the colours were those of the Chad flag.

'His Excellency the President must be paying a visit,' my companion declared, visibly pleased with himself. Even Sherlock Holmes could not have done better.

We idly circled Kinshasa airport for the best part of an hour, nervously watching while Mugabe's Mirages refused to quit the airport's skies. Nor would they until their very important person was safely in the arms of the President of Zaire.

Finally we glided onto the runway to be marshalled towards a waiting room by machinegun-toting soldiers. Meanwhile, the crew busied themselves emptying the plane of alcohol and headphones. My brilliant Watsonian skills let me deduce they had some value on the black market. Sherlock, however, would have known exactly whom they would be sold to.

'*On regrette de vous informer que vous venez de rater l'avion pour Johannesburg,*' said a lightly-armed policeman, who compensated for his gentle appearance with medals, épaulettes and a lanyard. '*Vous devrez attendre le prochain vol. Ça aura lieu demain.*'

'What's that he's saying?' asked my arm-tugging fellow-traveller.

'He says the next flight is tomorrow.'

'Ask him what on earth we're supposed to do overnight.'

I did as I was told.

'*Montez cet escalier-là, citoyens*' came the reply. '*Vous y trouverez un bar et quelques chaises. Vous pouvez dormir en haut. Il n'y aura pas d'autre vol ici jusqu'à ce que le vôtre.*'

I relayed this somewhat disappointing message - that there was a bar where we could sleep - to the dozen or so of us who were also onward bound, and we trudged up the rickety staircase with our bags, most of which were very heavy. At least there really was a bar, equipped with a barman, which in the circumstances was already something of a result. There was of course no telephone. Helen was due to meet me at Johannesburg's Jan Smuts airport and I had no means of contacting her. Perhaps she would telephone the airport before she set out? There was a small chance that she would hear our news.

In the bar, the bland uniformity over our heads was interrupted by long semi-transparent strips of frosted glass. Above each one we saw housed pairs of fluorescent tubes.

Beneath the lamps some local creatures scampered over the glass. Their large bodies could not be seen, yet their feet could. Great clawed things, like some avian predator, and there seemed to be hundreds of them. Rats. We had achieved common purpose: we all needed a glass.

I asked the barman for a *Leffe*, one of my favourite Belgian beers.

'*Dix-neuf*', he said.

Nineteen? Was this some form of code?

'*Dix-neuf? Dix-neuf quoi ?*'

'*Qu'est-ce que vous avez comme monnaie?*'

'*Quelques francs belgiques.*'

'*Alors, dix-neuf francs belgiques, s'il vous plaît.*'

There were sixty francs to the pound, so that beer was going to break no-one's bank. My South African friend, however, demanded a tin of *Castle*.

'Nineteen,' said the barman, in heavily accented English, having recognised his customer's language. 'Nineteen Rand.' There were four Rand to the Pound. That made his glass extremely expensive.

An Englishman, clad in blue Lycra onesie complete with medallion, declined to pay £19 for a beer. A wise fellow if a curious system. This strange arrangement was interrupted by the policeman who had scared us with his Kalashnikov on the runway.

'*Citoyens, nous avons effectué un transfert à l'Hôtel Léopold.*[226] *Il y a un autobus à l'extérieur qui vous mènera en ville.*'

He smiled graciously. He then aimed his weapon at me.

'*Vous. Le mec en veste safari. Vous vous débrouillez en français assez bien. Expliquez à vos copains ce que je viens de dire.*'

'Ladies and gentlemen,' I obliged, 'the airline has arranged for us to stay at the Leopold Hotel. It might even have a bar. We should get our cases back down.'

One of my aerial companions came up to me.

'It seems you can speak French. The rest of us have had a chat. We would like you to be our

---

[226] Now the Park Hotel.

spokesman, interpreter, what have you, while we are in this mess.'

'Of course. It would be an honour.' It's always amazing what a safari jacket can do. James Bond did well with his.

The *Hôtel Léopold* is a fine if faded colonial outpost with an outdoor swimming pool. True, it was empty of water but some kind souls had filled the gap with discarded beer cans. As I peered into this unenticing pit, I also saw some cartridge cases. God alone knows what sad tales they could tell.

Still, not all was so bleak. The bar was open. We oddly matched travellers sat around that melancholy pool, the twelve of us, and chewed the cud. Minded to conform to local tradition, we tossed our own empties into the shallow end.

To our collective relief, our rooms were clean, serviceable, charged to *Sabena*, and we woke to a decent breakfast. An airport bus returned us to the Swiss Air shuttle to Johannesburg. The Swiss meant us to know what a flight could be, or should be, a prime example of creature comfort.

Once on board we breathed the air that Zurich's top hospitals still have, the odour of Calvinist sanctity blended with the smell of ready money. The service was therefore somewhere between the faintly disapproving and the mildly cordial. The Swiss are an odd lot. Rather formally clad (and probably gay) cabin staff kept my glass fuelled if always with the faint admonition that is owed to the great unwashed – i.e., anyone not Swiss.

The pilot effected a perfect landing, as might be predicted. As I came through passport control, I was met by the indefatigable Helen, as gorgeous as ever. After my epic journey I almost dropped to my knees in thanks, mostly to my Maker but not a little to Helen.

*

Helen's taxi took us and my bags to a district of Jo'burg called Hillbrow. It was where her company had rented her a flat.

Hillbrow proved to be a crowded, lively suburb near the heart of the city. Like most of downtown Johannesburg was reserved for whites but, rather like its inhabitants, it had seen better days. It was notorious for muggings and 'white-trash' poverty. Its alleys, designed for use as 'sanitary lanes', ran behind the houses where horse carts had once collected 'night soil' - a euphemism for human excrement - in the mornings.

Helen's neighbourhood was the kind where people chained their steering wheels to the driving seat. Next door to Helen's high-rise was an ominously busy gun-shop.

Opposite was a slots arcade ironically, or possibly wittily, called 'amusements'. Restaurants selling pizzas or kebabs punctuated this unappealing townscape. The flat that Helen had been allocated was small and on the sixth floor of a tower block. It had some features that merited a tick – a lobby, a doorman and a lift, even if all three smelled faintly of urine – but once inside, the flat's entrance hall had a metal table, presumably for dining, attached with bolts to the floor. I placed on it the bottle of KWV pinotage that I had bought in the grocer below and opened a packet of ostrich biltong, placing it decorously in the centre. Style is always important, and a celebratory dinner was totally in order.

The beautiful and generous Helen, however, had already thought about supper. I was in store for a feast and the very best kind of cuddly good night's kip.

*

The change in clock-time between London and Johannesburg was only an hour, but the tiring journey in a cocktail of thin air and engine noise forced me to sleep late. By the time I surfaced, Helen had already left for her studio and I went out into the street to explore and find a coffee.

While I had resolved to find my way back into reinsurance, a nearby newsstand caught my eye. I bought a copy of every newspaper, wondering if one might employ an arts correspondent. I would be more than happy to be paid to go to the theatre. Once back in Helen's flat I rang the *Daily Citizen*. I was put through to the arts editor.

'I'm just over from England,' I told him, 'and I'm looking for work as a 'stringer': festivals, theatre, restaurants, galleries, that sort of thing.'

After an exploratory conversation, the fact that I had had a play on the London stage seemed to impress.

'All right,' came the reply. 'There is an *eisteddfod* in Braamfontein on Saturday. Take a train to Zoo Lake. There's a lot to do out there on Saturdays - paddle boat rides, *braai* areas, picnics under the oaks. I'll have a messenger get two tickets to the admissions clerk. Take a friend, enjoy the show. Copy has to be tasted before midnight and if it's any good you'll be in the Sunday edition.'

As it turned out, the *eisteddfod* was wonderful. It had nothing to do with Welsh gatherings of the same name: this was to be a showcase of Zulu talent and, for thirty miles around, everyone had made their way to watch the spectacle with the solitary exception of Michael Caine. He had already seen quite enough of that sort of thing.

There must have been fifty near-naked Zulu warriors there and they were going to sing and play for us. Some of them must have been selected for their ability to sing so profound a bass that not even Paul Robeson could have followed them down.

During the first few minutes these men, more used to the mines in the Transvaal than a whites-only park, sang *a capella*. The vocal dimension was greatly augmented when the performers stomped their feet on the dry earth. It created a thrilling, martial sound.

But how to write it up? Everyone reading the *Daily Citizen* would have seen many dozens of such shows. The only approach I could take, therefore, would be to relate the wonder of seeing it for the first time. I bought a pseudo-scholarly programme and Helen and I were lucky enough to sit next to a helpful lady who, on observing two innocents abroad, took pity and filled us in with what was happening.

*

Back in Hillbrow, later that evening, and while Helen rustled up something delicious in the pathetic kitchen area, I confessed in writing to being a stranger in South Africa, keen to relate my first impressions. Of course, thanks to that useful programme and my *aficionada* of the dance, I was almost able to pose as an expert. I reproduce here, in full, my very first ever contribution to the world of journalism.

> For centuries, dance has lent the Zulus a sense of solidarity during their recurring seasons of stress, joy or change. In their most traditional dances, musical instruments are not used, but at Zoo Lake last night we were exposed to that nation's entire gamut of terpsichorean talent.
>
> Your correspondent had a coruscating evening. He and his partner were serenaded by a peaceable *impi* of fifty fit, half-naked tribesmen.
>
> Following Mr Samuel Goldwyn's excellent advice, we began with an earthquake and worked our way towards a climax.
>
> In the African light the performers darkly gleamed. A sequence of soloists accompanied themselves on a *Ugubhus,* a string between two ends of a wooden bow, to which a gourd is attached. The musicians move the gourd up and

down the bow to strike it with a thin stick and create different tones.

Your correspondent was almost overcome by the *IziGubhu* - Zulu drums - made out of metal containers and covered with taught animal skins. The very sound of these drums, the Zulus believe, coerce the cowardly to run fearlessly into battle. European armies can also vouch for the martial effect of the drumbeat.

When all fifty warriors presented themselves to us at once the audience drew its collective breath.

Everywhere in the world there is a need for a ceremony, the kind lady sitting next to me explained, when a boy or girl reaches puberty. The first dance the Zulus performed equated to the Bar or Bat Mitzvah elsewhere, my vademecum explained. The Zulu nation sings and dances. At weddings, the stories of the betrothed are narrated by means of dance. One might say that Dance is coded into their DNA. For the huntsmen, dancing was a ritual to be performed before setting out. It leant them agility and courage. At Zoo Lake they used sticks in place of more lethal *assegais*. Health and Safety at it again?

The most spectacular dance we saw last night was when the King of the Zulu's soldiers, in their full regimentals of feathered 'kilts', showed their readiness for battle. We might easily have been at the king's palace, just after the *Feast of the First Fruits*.

We were treated to a 'bull dance', a dance whose origins lay somewhere in the mines. Either that or in Spain. The dancer imitates a bull with his arms aloft, leaping and bringing his legs down to earth with a terrifying thump.

> Proud warriors then showed us their rhythmic *Dance of the Small Shield*, usually reserved for royal occasions.
>
> The *umQhogoyo* came next - an extraordinary and athletic shaking of the upper body.
>
> Next, the *umBhekuzo* reflected the ebb and flow of the tides. The dancers advanced, retreated, while those at the end on the tide lifted their aprons to expose their buttocks. It brought out a little shocked laughter, mostly from those who had never been to the *Folies Bergère*.
>
> The *iliKhoba* was a particularly graceful dance. Rhythmic movements of the upper body were made yet more dramatic by the swinging of a beautifully carved stick. Then the warriors showed us the *umGhebulo,* and the scene became more fantastical. The dancers tried to pull down the sky or even climb an imaginary ladder into it.
>
> Your correspondent had never seen such things before and his opinion of the Zulus' heroic mastering of the dance soared, with them, into the skies.

My five hundred words of 'copy' was in the hands of some luckless subeditor at *The Citizen*'s offices off Main Street, just after ten o'clock that night. Yet it clearly worked; a redaction was in the next day's edition. The sub had reduced it to two hundred words. Not in the least upset, if slightly irritated by the by-line, which read 'from our own correspondent'. I had in fact signed it with my middle name, Felix. If they published anything else it would be over that name, I resolved. This is what the newspaper actually published.

> For centuries, dance has lent the Zulus a sense of solidarity during their recurring seasons of stress, joy or change. Your correspondent and his partner

were serenaded by a peaceable impi of fifty fit, half-naked tribesmen.

When all fifty warriors presented themselves to us at once the audience drew its breath and, in the African light, the performers darkly gleamed. Your correspondent was almost overwhelmed by the Zulu drums, designed to coerce a cowardly kinsman to run fearlessly into battle. The Zulu nation sings and dances at weddings and when hunting. At Zoo Lake they use sticks in place of their assegais.

The most spectacular dance we saw last night was when the King of the Zulu's soldiers, in their full regimentals of feathered 'kilts', showed their readiness for battle. Warriors then showed us a rhythmic dance, usually reserved for royal occasions. The dancers advanced, retreated, while those at the end on the tide lifted their aprons to expose their buttocks. The scene became ever more fantastical. Your correspondent had never seen such things before. Dancers tried to pull down the sky, or even climb an imaginary ladder into it. Their dance soared into the skies.

On Monday I made a call to my useless head-hunter in London, but was surprised and encouraged to learn he had persuaded someone called Max at the *Swiss Re*, the global professional and international reinsurer headquartered in Zurich, to give me an interview in its Jo'burg subsidiary. I rang said Max and he duly agreed to see me that same afternoon.

It was a short taxi ride away. I put on my best suit. It was also my only suit. That's what comes of travelling light. My shirt had experienced a little trauma in the journey to the Southern Hemisphere but my skills with an iron made some modest reparation.

*

It went well.

'I'll have to have a word with Mr Keel. He's the boss but I think I can safely predict you'll be joining the team. Before we settle the deal I will need to have an idea of how much you want to be paid?'

I should have prepared myself for this but of course I hadn't. I also knew that I could not prevaricate for very long.

'What are your other underwriters paid?' Pawn to king's four.

'I think we could manage forty thousand rand a year.' Knight to bishop's three.

I was unemployed with no connections, and in a country I didn't know. It was a terrific offer, more than forty thousand glasses of *Castle* a year, an undrinkable amount. Only just, my inner voice corrected me.

Yet it was vital for me to negotiate if, for no better reason, to demonstrate that I could.

'I was thinking of sixty thousand.'

'Well, we might stretch to fifty. Oh yes, throw in a car.'

I stood up and reached over his desk to shake his hand. We had lift-off. In that instant I had again become a businessman. It was as a journalist, however, that I could take Helen to the theatre from time to time, courtesy of *The Daily Citizen* who picked up my tab. All in all I was doing well. After all, I had been in South Africa for less than a week.

*

The following Monday, the first of June, I began my term as an employee in the Swiss Re in downtown Johannesburg.

I had become Mister Non-Marine Treaty. I was introduced to Carlos, the Motor Treaty man. Carlos was from Mozambique. His Portuguese ancestry showed in his face and his manner.

545

Another member of our team was of pure Afrikaner stock. Mendes had the famous easy-going sense of humour associated with his race. Both he and Carlos were married, both had 2.4 children, and both were courtesy incarnate.

'So you're new to SA,' said Mendes. 'We do things differently here to England. Have you ever attended a hanging?'

For an errant second I thought he was thinking of the galleries where my mother exhibited. Then I realised he was not.

'What? Of course not!'

'No, you won't have. I understand. You don't hang your murderers in England any more, do you? You put them up in hotels at the taxpayers' expense for a few years before releasing them to repeat their old tricks.'

'Well...'

'I have two tickets for the next hanging in Pretoria's gaol. It's on Friday. My wife can't make it – she has a whist drive that afternoon. Would you care to take her place? It will be a good one. To make the world a better place they're dispatching four kaffirs. Come along and we'll go for a bite after the show.'

By now I had collected my wits.

'Thanks, Mendes, but I'm afraid I promised my girlfriend Helen I would take her to dinner on Friday. No one refuses Helen anything and lives. Particularly me.'

'That's all right. I understand. Happily, these opportunities come along quite frequently. Next time, eh?'

'Of course,' I said, shrinking into my paperwork.

*

The Swiss Re asked me if I was happy where I lived, in Hillbrow. I was not, but I was not going to whinge to my employers.

'Yes,' I said, therefore.

'That's a pity. The company owns a block of apartments in Rosebank,' said my boss. 'One of the flats has just been vacated and I thought you might like it. It has a dining room, a lounge and two bedrooms.' In other words it was twice the size of Helen's place in Hillbrow.

'Rosebank?' I queried.

'Yes. It's one of our northern suburbs. The locals refer to it as being in the 'mink and manure' belt. It will have parking for your new car.' It seemed we were to be rehoused in a leafy suburb. Things were looking up.

*

Ah yes, the car.

I had been retained by the Swiss re for less than a week before someone from the garage rang me to say my *chevette* was ready for me to collect. The company had four subterranean levels of parking that, I guess, had once been cleared of rock and earth by desperate Europeans and captive local labour in a painful search for gold or diamonds.

My new car was on the lowest level, and when I saw it my heart sank. My brain, which pretends to control my heart, immediately concluded that I had only been retained because my head-hunter had promised my sister in marriage or had issued a personal guarantee that the money that I'd ask for would be trivial. I also had, he will have said, the one quality that would be appreciated in South Africa - I was white. He must have added that I couldn't care less about cars.

The Swiss Re certainly appreciated this last point. The Chevrolet *chevette* had four doors. That was it. No radio, no casual fripperies like a heater. This car was barely a notch up from a cart. In the motoring press, I would soon discover, it had already been derided for its terrible performance. *Time Magazine* listed it as 'one of the fifty worst cars of all time. The engine puts out 28 hp of shame', it wrote. 'The *chevette* sucks its pitiful rivulet of horsepower through the straw of a torque-sapping three-speed automatic transmission'.

I had an even greater problem than a lack of oomph. I didn't drive. I had occasionally had a go and most of my kindly car-owning friends had grey hair in consequence. That wretched fleet manager studiously watched me walk around it. 'Here are the keys,' he said at last.

'Thank you. I'll take it home at the end of the day. Thank you so much.'

He was still looking at me suspiciously as I returned to the lift and back to my desk.

I rang Helen in her office to tell her the good news - that we had a car - and the bad - it was four stories underground and to reach the road outside I would have to drive it up a circular ramp that resembled a corkscrew. Helen was unfazed. She had been driving since her seventeenth birthday.

'I'll be there at six. The coast should be clear by then. See if you can't smuggle me into your car park and I'll drive it out.'

Clever, but not clever enough since that is not how it turned out. Bern was at my desk at exactly 5 pm.

'Come on, I need to go home. I lock up the garage at half past. Park your new car on the road. The coons will have gone back to their townships by then and she will be perfectly safe.'

What could I do? I took the lift fifty feet into the earth's crust where Bern made me sign some sort of transfer and indemnity documents, all written in Afrikaans and therefore incomprehensible.

548

Bern then filed them in his briefcase but, alas, he did not leave. He just stood there. He clearly felt there was something in my make up that smelled of rat.

Getting in, closing the door, fastening the safety belt – all the time the bastard was still there, smiling in his revolting way. I turned the ignition. The engine started and immediately stalled. Bern knocked on the window.

'She's in drive. Put her in park.'

He was still smiling. What was the matter with him? Had he never seen a white man drive a newish car into a wall before? I did as I was told.

This time the engine wheezed a little but it did turn over. Now that it was running in neutral, it was time to put my foot on the brake and the car into 'drive'. I gingerly eased off the hand-brake.

I felt it trying to pull itself forward, against the will of either the driver or the engineers who had designed it. I turned the wheel a little, meaning to direct the car towards the ramp that led to the street. It was a steep ramp. From where I was it looked like the north face of the Eiger. The car needed full power to climb it. I was over-revving the bloody thing. I was also oversteering so I turned the wheel back a little. That felt better. Bern was not merely still there but was walking behind the car.

Not really a problem as my new car was moving at two mph. Somehow, miraculously, I managed to guide the damned thing up all four stories.

When I reached street level, the gate onto the outside world was closed. Now what was I to do? Bern, standing by the wing mirror, shouted 'open the gate, man!' but how did one do that?

There was a pole with a box on top, just out of reach. It boasted what looked like a button. I would have to reverse and drive back more closely. This was becoming a nightmare.

Then a miracle occurred. Bern pressed the button himself, the chancel rolled up and the outside world was finally exposed to an idiot in a *chevette*.

Back in 'drive', I gingerly edged forward. There was a place to park just in front. I managed to reach it without hitting anything, put the car back into park, turn off the motor and step out of it. I smiled at Bern in an attempt to pass myself off as a seasoned motorist who I did this sort of thing every day. I also knew was that Helen would be here any minute and I would, thenceforward, be safe and sound.

'The *Esso* sign means happy motoring,' sang Bern, an accommodating tone in his voice. 'She's an automatic. You probably don't have those in England, yet. You'll get used to her.'

In fact, Helen had witnessed the last bit of the debacle from a safe distance and was laughing like a drain. 'You'd better give me the keys,' she said as she came up to me. 'Come on, get in the passenger side. By the look of you, you need a drink. Let's go and celebrate your new wheels in *The Radium Beerhall.*'

*

By now *The Daily Citizen* had published two or three of my film reviews and I sensed danger. Carlos actually read the populist tabloid. My own contributions aside, naturally, it was only fit for wrapping one's fish and chips. He might easily have realised that 'Felix' was my middle name, while the eccentric turn of phrase and the impiety of my judgements all bore my autograph.

The editor and I were getting on famously, however, and he knew I enjoyed my work. Now that I had controlled my 'urge to use long words', he told me he intended to reward me with my full name and a photograph.

'You have a career in journalism if you want it,' he told me. Of course I was flattered, but words, as Byron memorably said, 'cannot sustain you lest sometimes you eat them'.

I didn't even need his money, though I was all too aware that the Swiss Re might direct me towards the escape hatch. They considered they had the right to consider all twenty-four hours of the day at their exclusive disposal.

*

One morning that week I was the first to arrive in my office. Helen had dropped me off before taking the *chevette* out to the suburbs and her studio. She would pick me up at close of play.

Carlos arrived a few minutes later. He had the newspaper open at the page I was on and was, I thought, studying me attentively. He seemed to be on the point of asking me something. At that very moment, thank goodness, Mendes came in, looking darkly furious.

'What's up, Mendes?' I asked him, relieved.

'Bloody Coons,' he said. 'One tried to overtake me on the road into town.'

Mendes drove a 7-series BMW. No one overtook Mendes du Toit and lived.

'He passed me at Sandton, in a lorry! In the fast lane!'

Lorries were specifically banned from the overtaking lane and the police were only too happy to apply the law.

'Perhaps he was in a hurry?' said Carlos.

'He had no right.'

'Will you do anything about it?' I asked him. 'Report him to the police?'

I imagined the driver, losing his job, cast into the outer darkness. Of course, being a black South African, he had been in trouble from birth.

'No. It would take too long, too much paperwork. I gave him the lesson he needed there and then. I took my automatic from the glove box and put four rounds in his bonnet. Wherever he was going, he'll need a change of trousers.'

*

Helen's and my new residence was in the upmarket, green and lush suburb of Rosebank, a few yards from a Catholic Church. Fr Kelly, its incumbent, was a priest from the old school. He drank too much, delivered holy mass on autopilot and, at eleven o'clock every Sunday morning, headed for the golf course.

After the service we would make for the Rosebank Hotel for a glass of something. Licensing laws in SA were severely limited. The hotel let us help ourselves to drinks and had an 'honesty bar' into which we were encouraged to contribute. An interesting testament to honesty which clearly worked.

The hotel also boasted a pleasant garden and a fine restaurant. Not that we cared. We were in the bar, overlooking the outdoor pool in which little children noisily splashed.

Our flat was in walking distance of the popular Rosebank Mall, which offered a half-way decent choice of boutiques and shops. On Sundays there was even a rooftop market. It sold, for the most part, ghastly tat.

As both of us were working we decided to employ a maid. This was neither sybaritic nor ambitious - everyone did. When we asked a neighbour in the block of flats how much we should pay, we were a little shocked by just how little.

Helen thought we should pay her a little more than that derisory going rate but thank goodness we had the wisdom to consult before offering any unilateral generosity. We were informed, in terms both bald and unkind, that if we did so we would have to live elsewhere. Our mad and spendthrift plan would force every other occupant, who appeared to manage their domestics in an informal cartel, to increase what they paid their own staff. We would single-handedly cause an inflationary wage spiral, effectively fining every other employer in the block.

We made the obvious decision. Our maid, in any case, accepted the meagre wages and corrected the underpayment with eggs and other surplus comestibles she clearly felt we had bought for her benefit.

*

We had started to make a few friends. Sunday lunch in our little place was always a treat. Helen was and is a stickler for tradition in such vital matters and our new cat, Shiva - named after the Hindu goddess of destruction - sat beneath our table, longing for a morsel to fall on her like manna from heaven.

My editor at *The Daily Citizen* wanted me to review an *avant garde* production at the *Market Theatre* and sent over a pair of tickets. The *Market* was an interesting institution. It was an oasis in the very heart of Johannesburg where by common consent, no attention whatsoever was paid to apartheid. The three official colours south of the Equator – Black, White and Coloured – all sat next to each other in the audience, if they so chose. Those appearing on stage were from the same palette, and all three 'colours' manned the ticket office, the backstage and the bar.

It was at that bar that Helen and I discovered its barman was fluent in all seven South African languages; the five native ones plus Afrikaans and English. He spoke them flawlessly. He even had a smattering of French.

'That's impressive,' Helen told him. 'So why do you work as a barman?'

'It's not too bad a job. I don't even have to stand as long as barkeeps have to in more regular places.'

'Yet with all those languages, could you not manage a more senior career?' persisted Helen.

'Not in the Republic of South Africa, I'm afraid. The Brotherhood has decided not.'

It seemed there was no way that one could evade the vicelike grip of the *broderbund*, the sinister force that successfully saw off all attempts to bring South Africa into line with the rest of the world.

Of course, I loved Jo'burg's old-fashioned *Alhambra*, with its proscenium arch and its comfortable seats but, like a bigamist, I also loved the informal theatre-in-the-round where more radical theatre-goers hung out.

The play we saw, and which I wrote up for my paper, was a wonderful version of *A Street Car Called Desire*, Tennessee William's closely observed drama. The editor himself took the trouble to ring me and congratulate me on my turn of phrase. That made a change. I put it down to avoiding the word 'coruscating'. He said my simplified piece was 'hi-faluting', which I took it as a compliment. English may not have been his first language.

*

My old friend Nicholas Monson had made great strides with his lady friend Hilary. He had bowled her over to such a degree that she had consented to become his bride.

Helen and I received an invitation to the wedding. It was to be in Mombasa, a Kenyan town on the shores of the Indian Ocean, blessed with the world's most beautiful beach.

Getting to Mombasa from Johannesburg was something of a challenge. We had to fly to Nairobi, the capital. From there, we would need a twelve-hour train journey past Mount Kilimanjaro to the coast. That was the most desirable route. Failing that, we could take a local flight. After some 'debate' we decided we hadn't time for the 6 am train. We would take a plane the next morning at 10 am. We would still be in good time for the splicing.

We booked ourselves into Nairobi's *Panafric Hotel* in the centre of Nairobi, scarcely ten miles from Jomo Kenyatta International Airport, but insanely pitted roads made the journey from the airport last an hour longer than it should. People grow old in such traffic.

At last we were deposited in our recently decorated six-storey hotel where I told Helen to stay in the cab while I changed some money to pay the driver. I didn't have to. The concierge paid him and charged the fare to our room. There was clearly some local scam going on but I had no idea what it might be.

Our double room was air-conditioned and had every feature, including a minibar. The bed was comfortable and I planned to make good use of it. I met no opposition.

*

Nicholas had been raised by his Anglican father and Protestant mother. Lady Monson was no shy retiring Calvinist – she was chair of the British Huguenot Society.

Hilary, *per contra*, was a Roman Catholic. Two priests, therefore, had been engaged to concelebrate the rite, before Nicholas remembered his manners. A local tribe provided most of the labour that kept Diani Beach so pristine. He decided they should employ a shaman of some kind - a witch doctor in other words - and give the nuptials a third dimension. Both fair and shrewd, the two priests, one Catholic, one Protestant, supposedly antagonistic, were united in disapproval by Nick's gesture since they both hated pagans and now outnumbered the interloper two to one.

*

Meanwhile, Helen and I had dined and arrived in the bar for a night cap. A serviceable band was playing the *American Song Book*.

I would pay the bill on my shiny new Diners Club credit card, but it would be helpful to have a few Kenyan Shillings for tips and the like. I went downstairs to the hotel foyer and tried to exchange a few Rand for the local currency. Like the most well made plans it went immediately asunder. I was brusquely informed that South African money was not welcome in Kenya.

It might help to explain what happened next if I report that Helen was (and is) a striking beauty, a petite, green-eyed redhead. She was the very picture of an ideal colleen, straight from a painting by Jack Yates, if with shoes. At the bar she directed my attention to a number of Indian traders at a table in the bar playing poker. In front of one of them was a bottle of Johnny Walker Black Label, corralled by tumblers.

'If anyone can change your money they can,' she said brightly. I went over to ask and they smiled graciously.

'We can do it,' said one. 'How much do you need?'

They offered me what will have been an appalling exchange rate, but it would do. The deal was struck, our purses recharged. The downside was that they wanted me to join in their game. I looked at these turbaned businessmen. These were the sort of men who could persuade a chicken to pluck itself and leap in the oven.

I played my cards as well as I could but these men were far more skilled than I. Nevertheless, they filled my glass with enthusiasm and great frequency. By the time we finally left the bar, at something like three in the morning, I had deduced that my future was neither as a gambler nor a foreign exchange dealer. With far too much whisky inside us, especially me, we fell into what proved to be a platonic bed and were in the Land of Nod before our heads had touched the pillow.

At 8 am the alarm rang. Helen told me later she had reached out to turn the damned thing off and had immediately gone back to sleep. Since I was enfolded in the arms of Morpheus I didn't even hear it.

A few more hours passed before we finally surfaced and, when we did, we were in a muddle. The airline had a second flight to Mombasa, but it was that afternoon and, one way or another, we had missed the service. That really was a shame. We had been looking forward to the oddest of concelebrations.

The concierge booked us onto the later flight and we took a taxi along those frightful roads to the airport, hoping all would end well. If we were still too late, this time it was a stroke of luck. We watched from the departure lounge, aghast, as the Dakota's starboard turboprop caught fire and fifty disgruntled passengers had to slide down the shutes onto the runway, leaving their luggage on board.

Helen had a word with the airport staff. We had to get to a wedding, she told them. That 'fact' was relayed onwards and upwards. For some reason, possibly Helen's hat and my suit, it was assumed that *we* were to be married in Mombasa. The airport people would do everything in their power to get us there.

A charter flight was about to depart. It was not quite full. There would be room on board for us. An airport bus took us and our bags out onto the runway to clamber aboard a Fokker *Friendship*, bound for the coast. There was no time to store the bags in what passed for a hold.

An indignant stewardess insisted they should stay behind but old-fashioned belligerence prevailed. Finally, and at long last, the plane, ourselves and our bags taxied towards the runway. I'll admit to looking forward to the flight.

The overhead wings meant the views would be unobstructed. We were in for some sightseeing, as the little plane would fly low over the plains and their herds of wildebeest, only to reach for the sky over snowy peak of Kilimanjaro.

By the time we reached Mombasa we had indeed missed the wedding but, as our taxi deposited us on Diani Beach, the reception was only just beginning.

We immediately saw that Diani, tucked away as it was on the East Coast of Africa, between the ocean to the east and the open plains of the Shimba Hills National Reserve to the west, was the world's most perfect strand. Over countless centuries, the ebb and flow of the tides had created a talcum beach that stretched a quarter-mile between land and sea, running north/south for twenty miles along the coast. Lush green forests provided a backdrop to the serenity that most of us call paradise, while the pearl-white sand tucked itself gently into the deep turquoise of the Indian Ocean. Light fails in Kenya at six on the dot. That barely left an hour or two to admire the beach and its fishing boats, apparently weightless in the clearest of all waters while enormous crayfish heard us paddling and promptly buried themselves in the powdery silica.

Hilary's mother's resort had a considerable number of fully inclusive canvas 'villas', along with a spectacular Presidential Villa, all staffed with personal chefs, butlers and maids.

Our beachside tent was of quite extraordinary comfort. Air-conditioned, hung with local art, it had an *en suite* bathroom. Our double bed was protected from flesh-eating insects with a net. Mercifully it was also arguably secure against flesh-eating leopards, snakes, dwarf mongooses, ostriches, hippopotamuses, termites, elephants and disgruntled natives.

When dusk fell, like the fire curtain in a theatre, the stars made an heroic effort to compensate. They hung in the firmament like Arabian lamps, barely out of reach.

When the band finally struck up, the party hit the dance floor. The singer did his best, if almost drowned out by the groans from the nearby trestle tables, volubly protesting their mouth-watering burden of lobster, *githeri* (beans and corn) and coconut rice. How we partied! Hilary's mother had somehow imported real Champagne into Kenya (despite a prohibitive tariff) and, when you're having fun, that classic wine only enhances your stamina.

Sadly, all good things must come to an end. At three in the morning we were exhausted. Helen and I decided to retire to our tent.

Not *too* exhausted this time, I'm pleased to relate.

The downside was that, again, we overslept. Tired, still a little drunk and deprived of most of our quota of eight hours sleep, we got a lift to the local hotel from where we planned to get a taxi to Mombasa's airport. This proved a poor idea. The reception told us it would take at least twenty minutes to arrive, so we headed to the bar, just to pass the time, you understand.

That's where we met Johnny Hunter. I already knew Johnny from CTB. He was a broker in their marine division. He was not in Kenya on a corporate ticket, however. Nor was he here for The Wedding. Johnny was a member of a club, or association, that made the Dangerous Sports Club look like a walk in the proverbial park. Its members called themselves The Pisstwits.

It turned out that a chapter of Pisstwits, or whatever the collective noun may be, were in Kenya to play polo. Not the version played at Hurlingham, or at Cowdray Park, nor yet the version played in Afghanistan. The Pisstwits play it on motorbikes on the shores of Lake Amboseli. The polo mallet is replaced with a croquet mallet, and the ball is the mangrove crab, a large and vicious crustacean that has a propensity to bite tourists.

'That's why the authorities turn a blind eye,' said Johnny.

'So you come to Kenya to mallet the local crabs into the great beyond?' asked Helen incredulously. 'Isn't that cruel?'

'None of us has ever heard one complain,' he easily replied.

'We have to get to the airport, Johnny,' I said. 'If we don't get a taxi soon we'll miss our flight.'

'No need to panic. There are very few taxis minded to come out this way. I'll get you there. Waiter, another bottle of Champagne and two more glasses.'

Champagne is expensive, close to unobtainable in Kenya but then, Johnny had inherited a Malayan plantation. We were there for another hour

Helen became more and more nervous, a condition which people who don't know her could easily mistake for anger. That said, Johnny was wholly impervious.

'We really must go, and now,' I declared decisively.

'Oh, very well,' said our white knight, but it was fully another twenty minutes before Johnny actually rose to his feet.

'Come on,' he then said. 'I don't want you to blame me for missing your flight.'

It was rather further to the airport that I had guessed, and we took the wrong turning more than once. Johnny's hire car seemed to have a mind of its own. I'm not entirely convinced, however, that Johnny did. Nevertheless, we did eventually get there, retrieved our cases from the car and waved a thankyou to Johnny as he sped off into the sunset. Unfortunately, our adventure was not yet over.

Though our plane was on the runway, no amount of coaxing would persuade those at the departure gates let us on board. All they would do was swap our boarding passes for the next flight. That was twenty four hours later. We had arrived eight minutes too late and, eight minutes after that, the airport was deserted.

*

Mombasa airport is an unusual place. It serves tourists who use light aircraft for the most part. The handful of airlines that it serves lock down their nests after the last bird has flown. What remains is basically a vast hanger with closed-off bits.

A kindly policeman confirmed that the next flight to Nairobi would be the following day. Bugger. What to do? We asked this fellow that very question.

'It's too late to do anything. You can't sleep here. People have tried. Thieves kill them or they end up as a big cat's dinner. You have no choice. You must come back to ours. My wife will look after you and I'll get you back here in time for tomorrow's flight.'

It was a lifeline and you don't debate with one of those. Our new Kenyan friend drove us to his concrete box of a house, not so very far away, where he presented us to his wife. He said a few words to her in Swahili and she curtseyed, no less, telling us in English that her home was our home.

This magical couple, who will have long since assumed their well-earned place in heaven, issued us into a windowless room, previously owned by their children. They would now sleep with their parents. They were not exactly overjoyed but they were obedient.

We slept in our clothes and their beds, only slightly concerned by the strange scratching noises coming from the skylight. Something very large and very determined was trying to get in. In the morning an instant coffee set us up for a lift back to the airport and, after a change of planes in Nairobi, we were back in Jo'burg.

*

We were barely at the outset of feeling the layout of the land we now lived in but it was time to give our adventure a little wellie. We decided we'd start in the eastern Transvaal.

We set out in my petulant motorcar with the best of intentions but, sillily, without a map. Our journey was consequently mysterious, enigmatic and wrapped in a conundrum. We were looking for what had been described us as one of the wonders of the world, God's Window.

The wretched *chevette* took a wrong turning and fetched up in a long abandoned mining village, now maintained as a museum. The miners had sheltered across the road, there to dig for coal, the world's most valuable natural commodity in the Industrial Age. The country was still mining, and more intensely than ever. With an international embargo on petroleum, they were making their own from coal, and very successfully.

To either side of a road that divided the races were many crosses. They spelled out graphically how dangerous mining was and is. If anyone needs to see just how hard the lives of these determined men had been, let them visit this graveyard and remember all those long defunct souls who had unearthed the vast wealth of their nation with shovels. They enabled the former Union of South Africa to compete with the rest of the world and this village bore a silent witness to their heroic labours.

One ancient hut bore a red cross over the door. It was a clue as to its purpose before we even went in. Inside, a row of waist high beds showed us where injured miners were taken. In the nineteenth century, medical skills were few and far between. Surgical skills ran only as far as amputation.

Bored or injured miners used their 'leisure' to carve the brown coal they unearthed into figurines. A number had been gathered into a glass cabinet. Some were decoratively clad ladies, carrying urns on their heads. Others were altogether less modest. The ruder ones were at the front, to emphasise that the subject peoples were primitive, even primordial, perhaps? One thing is certain: their sculptors were truly talented if pagan artists.

One of the huts was furnished, after a fashion. For a few rand, we were able to secure it for the night. That too was quite an experience. Outside it, Helen came across some sort of butterfly or moth. It was fully eight inches across - the size of a tea plate.

*

When dawn came it was time to see God's Window. This time, equipped with reliable directions, we were there in no time.

At the heart of the Eastern Transvaal is a plateau, framed and contained by a mountain range. The road leads gently uphill until one arrives at the eponymous restaurant, promising the dirt-encrusted traveller every earthly delight.

God's Window
Braai and Pizza
Cold Beers
Your Host: Herb

The 'window' itself is a gap in the curtain walls that enclose the plateau. It opened onto the plains a thousand feet below and, as we stood at the edge, we looked out over unspoiled country, as far as the eye could see. We saw eagles, circling effortlessly beneath us, no doubt exploiting the impressive thermals. We guessed they were searching for a small impala for their offsprings' supper.

It was yet another of the burgeoning list of the most amazing sights I had ever seen.

*

Back in Johannesburg, Helen and I agreed that the *chevette* the Swiss Re had given me was arguably the most irritating car ever built. I was driving it some of

563

the time, quite illegally, but only for short distances and, so far, more or less uneventfully.[227]

Helen and I had to formalise our work permits at the Department of Home Affairs at New Canada Point at the western edge of Johannesburg. The office was open on Saturday mornings, as were most shops and smaller offices. It really didn't take too long to do, except that we had to listen to the official's opinion that the two of us should marry.

Having done our business we treated ourselves to lunch. The nearest restaurant was on a steep hill which gave us an uninterrupted view over the terminus that served Soweto.[228]

Helen was driving but even she could not get the wretched *chevette* up the hill. Every time she tried, it refused, rather like the horses I have occasionally ridden. The only way to get the thing up there was to do it in reverse.

We were rewarded with an amused or maybe bemused doorman's smile as we drove backwards up to his restaurant. We were allotted a window seat to eat the caviar and drink the champagne that let us celebrate that we were at last quite legally in the country.

From it we watched the extraordinary sight, far below, of a million native South Africans, swarming like ants, scurrying into the station to return to their township, laden with huge parcels and rucksacks, clambering onto the roofs of the trains or hanging on for dear life to the outside doors and windows.

*

---

[227] One morning I caught the passenger door handle in a bus. The door came off. Mendes would have blamed the bus driver and, when I did, no one paused for thought.

[228] These days. Johannesburg has a good metro system. Back then, however, the luckless denizens of Soweto had to shop in Johannesburg and carry their purchases out of town to the terminus to take the train home.

At huge personal expense I had had a local company install a state-of-the-art cassette player in the *chevette* and Helen bought me the wonderful *Deutsche Grammophon* recordings of *Don Giovanni* and *The Magic Flute* to play on it.

This while the *chevette* preferred to remain stationary, whenever it could, we listened to the operas in the car while I pretended that we would soon be in Swaziland or Lesotho. Vroom vroom. Pathetic, I know, but in the car we felt like a prince and princess in a royal box. Since we hadn't a system at home, we would park the *chevette* in picturesque locations, and let the machine serenade us like young lovers. Which, of course, we were.

That stereo filled a hole in my life, the big one called great music. True, Jo'burg had a concert hall in the centre of town but the concerts we had attended had been worthy but uninspiring.

The car's cassette player was a good one. Mozart's take on Bach as he let Tamino and Papageno march into their Masonic initiation was amplified by Dietrich Fischer-Dieskau's wonderful baritone. He seduced us while Birgit Nilsson's *Donna Elvira* was a revelation.

Even so, I was aware that I would need a domestic system of some quality if I was to reproduce the swish of Karl Böhm's baton as it cut through the air. I wasn't there yet.

*

We had been given an invitation to stay for a couple of nights before Christmas near Kimberley in the Orange Free State at a colleague of Helen's, before some other friends would congregate at a villa a few hundred yards from *The Nelson Hotel*, better known as *The Nellie*, on Capetown's oceanfront.

We began our Christmas break - our summer holiday - with a safari. I wore my monogrammed safari jacket, constructed from the finest antelope suede. Its bone buttons confirmed its provenance and it was my intention to look a million dollars and I almost did.

An open Landrover took us for a drive around Kimberley's impressive opencast diamond mine - the largest manmade hole in the world - startling kudu and gnus as we went along. We arrived at Elspeth's comfortable spread in the late afternoon to be rather formally introduced to her brother, her parents and her mastiffs.

There was still plenty of light - though even in summer the sun sets pretty punctually at around seven - and we were conducted to the pool for a dip and, should we want one, a sundowner. Then, at seven o'clock, their man told our hostess that dinner was ready and we traipsed back inside.

This would be the first time I ate *bobotie*, spiced beef mince under an egg-based topping. Almonds and raisins are added to the mix to sweeten the dish.

'We hope you like it,' said Elspeth's mother. 'It's a favourite of the Cape Coloureds. They call it 'curry', which of course it is not.'

'It's very good,' said Helen.

We had Malva Pudding for, well, pudding. It was a spongy cake containing apricot jam and it tasted of caramel. Elspeth's mother poured a cream sauce over it.

'It's terrific,' said Helen nobly.

If you like that sort of thing, I thought. Then, after a swim and with the sun going down, it quickly grew cold.

'You'll excuse me for a moment,' I asked our hostess. 'I left my jacket outside.'

'Of course,' said Elspeth's mother.

It was, after all, my favourite jacket. I had only managed to buy it because of the money I had been able to save on my ticket to Jo'burg, and the discomfort of that journey made me like it more. Unfortunately I was not the only being in that household to take to antelope

566

suede. When I got outside I discovered that those nice bull mastiffs had eaten it.

Napoleon famously described Talleyrand as 'a shit in a silk stocking'. Well, somewhere in the Orange Free State lie my initials, embroidered in blue silk, on or in an enormous dog turd.

*

It was time to move on. Our next stop was near Stellenbosch. Emma French's sister Charlene lived with her husband Charles Milner outside South Africa's wine capital. We motored south-east from Kimberley to pull up outside their thatched 'Cape Dutch' farmhouse, a long eighteenth century building, gabled at either end and with a characteristic pillastered gable in the centre to house the front door. The house was surrounded by horses. They looked like racehorses to my undereducated eye.

Despite our parked car spoiling the exterior aspect of their mansion, the Milners were the very epitome of hospitality. Aside from the wine from their own estate that flowed from decanter to glass like Rome's Trevi Fountain, their home-produced *biltong* was a taste explosion.[229]

The original settlers of the Cape Colony were the Dutch, and they had loyally built their larger houses in the style they remembered from their homeland. The Milners' furniture, too, was in the shape and style their forebears would have known, except that in Holland they imported mahogany from Batavia. In the eighteenth century the African settlers had a choice of local woods to choose from, among which Iroko, Padauk, Merbau and Afrormosia were the most favoured. I was also shown and duly admired some 'patrician' pieces from the seventeenth century, and some 'pioneer' pieces made after the Great Trek, the

---

[229] Wind-dried beef, similar to jerky.

Afrikaner exodus from the Cape after the English took over. The presence of so many antiques made the house smell pleasantly of beeswax.

*

Charlene liked to spend every other Christmas in England, to see her sisters who would gather at her mother's place at Stow Bedon in Norfolk.

We talked a lot about Emma, and about her father, the third Earl of Ypres, whose fortune had evanesced and finally evaporated. He was now the concierge of a block of flats in London's Chelsea. This was when I realised that the French family had a long standing association with South Africa. It was spelled out in the four large military scenes, great paintings hanging on the walls. Lieutenant-General French, later the first earl, served in the South African War.[230]

Commanding the Cavalry, he won the Battle of Elandslaagte in 1899, relieved Kimberley in 1900, stemmed the invasion of the Cape Colony and played a leading role in Lord Robert's advance from the Orange River, as the canvases graphically revealed.

*

The *chevette* now carried us into Cape Town, where we would stop and join our party for Christmas Day.

First, we would have to bag a place to sleep in the sea-side house we and our friends had rented. When we had unpacked we waded into the confluence of the Indian and the Atlantic Oceans. The way the two seas contested each other for pre-eminence reminded me of Gibraltar and we peered out unsuccessfully for whales or dolphins. We did see a Portuguese man-o'-war, a dangerous jellyfish, so we staged a tactical retreat.

As we explored we were rewarded with the sight of giant monitor lizards clambering over the rocks.

---

[230] More generally called the (first) Boer War.

568

They looked liked dinosaurs and must have weighed as much as a sumo wrestler.

Behind us soared the mass of Table Mountain. We took the cable car up to the top where, a thin layer of cloud looked for all the world like a tablecloth. Some families were appropriately picnicking. 'How very suitable,' said Helen.

Looking over an infinite seascape towards Antarctica, we felt we were on the roof of the world. The views there, predictably, spectacular. Table Mountain is the perfect place from which those unafraid of heights can survey the twelve 'Apostles' - Table Mountain's closest courtiers.

Below us we could easily see the Capetown waterfront, whose shops, restaurants and bars were reverberating to the sound of African beat. We could even make out the inviting harbour and beaches of Bloubergstrand. We could also see Mitchell's Plain and the Cape Flats, a large area of barren, sandy land. As non-whites had been forcefully rehoused there it was cruelly referred to as 'apartheid's dumping ground'. The republic's less fortunate denizens were allowed to rebuild their troubled lives on this unpromising turf.

The way down looked more vertiginous, steeper, more perilous than it actually was. It whispered to us in the windswept silence that we were in mortal danger. Were it not for the reassurance of the sure-footed baboons, clambering easily over the rocks, we might even have panicked. We also knew that no matter how badly we fell, we would not fetch up in Robben Island, beneath us and not that far from the shore.

Like the Chateau d'If near Marseilles, or Alcatraz near San Francisco, the island had become one of the world's most secure prisons. Its most distinguished occupant was the lawyer Nelson Mandela. Unlike Hess in Spandau, he was not alone. He had a cohort of fellow members of the African National Congress inside with him, to keep him company. The Bureau of State Security, BoSS, had been after Mandela for many years, ever since they had accused him of plotting to blow up a train.

One thing was sure. Mandela, probably born political, had joined the ANC in 1944. When young he will have seen those black-and-white Second World War films in which some brave partisan in occupied France attempts to add his little nail to the Third Reich's coffin. In fact, even though still in his teens, Nelson Rolihlahla Mandela had already helped to form a Youth League.

1944 was also the year he married for the first time. He began to rise through the organisation's ranks, slowly using his growing influence to persuade the ANC to adopt a progressively radical position. In 1952 he was elected National Volunteer-in-Chief of the 'Defiance Campaign'.

He and Maulvi Cachalia mounted a campaign of civil disobedience against the six laws they felt the most unjust but BoSS somehow penetrated their organisation. Mandela, with nineteen others, was arrested and charged, under the Suppression of Communism Act, for his part in the campaign. All were sentenced to nine months hard labour, suspended for two years.

That August, he and Oliver Tambo established South Africa's first black law firm - *Mandela & Tambo* - but at the end of the year he was 'banned', declared a 'restricted person' and could only watch in secret as the ANC's Freedom Charter was adopted in Kliptown on June 26, 1955.

The *Broderbund* and BoSS felt they needed to contain all organised dissent. In December, 1956, they again ordered his (and his friends') arrest. A countrywide round-up led to a marathon trial for treason. During the long trial Mandela had time to marry a second time, this time to a social worker named Winnie Madikizela. Only days before the end of the Treason Trial, Mandela travelled to Pietermaritzburg to speak at the All-in-Africa Conference. It resolved that he should write to Prime Minister and request a national convention on a non-racial constitution. The trial only ended in March, 1961, when the last twenty-eight accused, including Mandela, were acquitted.

He was not 'unarmed'; he would warn Verwoerd that if he failed to agree to repeal the 'six acts' that underwrote apartheid there would be a national strike. Henrik Werwoerd reacted to this message by mobilising the military machine of state security. Mandela was forced to call off the strike in favour of a more radical approach.

In June Mandela accepted the role of leader in the armed struggle. The risk was great, but he established *Umkhonto weSizwe*, the 'Spear of the Nation'. Its dramatic launch, in December that year, was heralded with a fanfare of explosions.[231] Then, the following January, 1962, under the pseudonym of David Motsamayi, he left South Africa. He travelled around the dark continent on an Ethiopian passport, raising support wherever he went.

For some of this time he had military training from sympathisers in Morocco and Ethiopia. When he finally returned to South Africa, in July 1962, he was arrested at a police roadblock outside *KwaZulu*, Natal, where he had been debriefing ANC President Chief Albert Luthuli about his trip.

---

[231] Verwoerd's National Party won the 1966 general election and continued to foster the development of a military industrial complex that successfully pioneered developments in aircraft, small arms, armoured vehicles, and even nuclear and biological weapons. He had held talks with the Prime Minister of Lesotho, Chief Leabua Jonathan, at the Union Buildings in Pretoria, from where a joint communiqué was issued with special emphasis on 'co-operation without interference in each others' internal affairs'. On September 6, 1966, a uniformed parliamentary messenger named Dimitri Tsafendas stabbed Verwoerd in the neck and chest four times, shortly after Verwoerd entered the Cape Town House of Assembly. Verwoerd was rushed to Groote Schuur Hospital, but was pronounced dead upon arrival. The assassin escaped the death penalty on grounds of insanity, but was imprisoned indefinitely at the 'State President's pleasure'. He died aged 81 while still in detention.

BoSS charged him on two counts - leaving the country without a valid authority and inciting workers to strike. He was sentenced to five years' imprisonment and sent to Robben Island. From there he was repeatedly brought to Pretoria for interrogation. Within a month, the police had raided Liliesleaf, the ANC's and the Communists' secret hideout in Rivonia, an attractive suburb of Johannesburg. Mandela's comrades-in-arms were now themselves arrested.

What became known as the Rivonia Trial began in October 1963. Mandela joined ten others in the dock, charged with sabotage. Of course, he knew he would be sentenced to death. On April 20, 1964, he made an impassioned speech from the dock.

> I have fought against white domination, and I have fought against black domination. I have cherished the ideal of a democratic and free society in which all persons live together in harmony and with equal opportunities. It is an ideal which I hope to live for and to achieve. But, if needs be, it is an ideal for which I am prepared to die.

In June that year, Mandela and seven others were convicted. They were sentenced, not to death - the government was not overkeen to create martyrs - but to life imprisonment. Goldberg was sent to Pretoria Prison because he was white. The others went to Robben Island.

As Helen and I queasily looked at it, Mandela and his co-conspirators were all inside.

Back in Jo'burg one of my colleagues had thought I might benefit from a debate at the University of the Witwatersrand.

The motion before the house concerned the future of Namibia, or 'South West Africa' as the Afrikaners stubbornly insisted. Everyone had their own perspective. The only nation not involved was its former colonial power, Germany.

It was divided between the half that was propped up by delusion and propaganda, and the other that thought the world could see plainly that theirs was the only viable road ahead. That's of course is Germany's eternal lot.

In 1945, after the defeat of the third German Empire, or 'Third Reich' in the more familiar hybrid phrase, South Africa had replaced South West Africa's *quondam* colonial overlord and effectively ruled Windhoek from Pretoria.

For some reason, the Wits had invited an American senator to address the House. He made an anodyne speech along classic lines, his larynx possessed by the shade of Lincoln. Neither he nor the students were embarrassed that his was the only other nation on Earth to have enacted racial division into law. He used his speech to make an anti-apartheid appeal by proxy, carefully deflecting his assault away from his host nation and on to Namibia with a diplomat's blend of skill and courtesy.

As the senator droned on, I reflected on apartheid, a system condemned by every other country in the world. Did it really differ that much from 'multiculturalism', a 'philosophy' extolled in Britain and most everywhere else?

Multiculturalism itself has its own right and left wings. One of them wanted to distribute migrants and refugees into the wider community, believing that those varied cultures should share the same space and learn from each other. The best cases of this were when the newcomers were found lodgings in prosperous and established parts of major cities. Buildings like the Trellick and Grenfell Towers were springing up in the prosperous Royal Borough of Kensington and Chelsea. There, local shops and pubs were still British and integration apparently worked.

The other wing of multiculturalism prefers to let these pioneering peoples have their own districts. Unfortunately they soon become ghettoes, some even adopting Sharia courts. Given enough time and money the inmates build and segregate their own schools, allowing their elders to insist on divisive dress codes. Isolated in such single cultures, suburbs like Toxteth, or even whole cities like Bradford or Leicester, they gradually endorse cruel and alien practices such as female genital mutilation, slaughterhouses that insist on the vile practice of hallal, and encourage arranged marriages in which romantic love is overruled by parents and even whole communities.

Our British version keeps the races apart, in 'estates', suburbs, even whole towns, and the French do much the same.

Our governments simply did not need to mimic apartheid, relying on the ghettos to do this for themselves. The result might as well have been called 'reservations'. The only difference was the statute law, the law of the land but, in reality, the glass (or concrete) ceiling stays in place. Apartheid was the latter type of multiculturalism, i.e., the one preferred by English socialists, but against which they rail so ironically. If that sounds counter-intuitive, I should remind the reader that, in 1980, the UK had no coloured MPs, no 'ethnic' university professors, no senior black businessmen, no black bishops. There was one black Lloyd's broker, a peerless fellow of distant African origin, a most charming man and a friend. He had been educated at Bryanston.

When the debate opened to the floor I stood and gave the house my two cents worth. The gist of my little contribution was that countries grow strong if they are founded on their own traditions. If they try to impose a new body politic onto a reluctant majority, governments

574

become unpopular, peoples rebellious. Citizens then long for the *status ante*.

How many times do we need to have it demonstrated that the *imposition* of a 'vision' leads inexorably to tragedy? We saw it in France in the sixteenth century, in England in the seventeenth, in France (again) in the eighteenth, in Ireland in the nineteenth (well, forever, really), and in Cambodia, Russia and China in the twentieth. Essentially, I concluded all politicians - radical ones especially - are a damn nuisance. I did earn a little applause for my peroration.

*

Helen's occupational treat was to sail with her boss on the Witwatersrand reservoir where he had a racing dinghy.

Howard Rennie was a film director, mostly making commercials for SATV. He still enjoyed female company, though he was as gay as the proverbial hussar. I had nothing to fret over. One day I joined them on Howard's little yacht and the sailing thing was kept to a polite minimum. Essentially we talked film and TV while quaffing some excellent Stellenbosch pinotage on a ripple-free nirvana. Around us, young people on little yachts struggled to race in the light wind. A waterborne idyll.

*

Back in the real world, one of my colleagues at the Swiss Re, Egidio Rossi, had been called back to Zurich.

There was almost a year left on his lease. Would Helen and I take it up? It was a detached dwelling in Rivonia; four bedrooms, a swimming pool and a landscaped garden. The deal also included a maid and a gardener, attached contractually, which in South Africa almost meant physically. Of course we agreed.

The house was pleasantly airy, a large modernist bungalow with sliding doors that open its rooms onto walled and manicured lawns. The pool was utterly charming; even the fence that SA law obliges all pools to have was discreet. At one end was a waterfall, made out of artificial rocks, kept damp by filtered water that flowed on a hedonistic journey into the aquatic bliss it shared with us. It was the sort of pool to tempt one to swim a couple of lengths before setting out for the office.

Helen and I found ourselves in a corner of paradise; no mink, no manure, but space and creature comfort in spades. One day we decided to give a dinner party for a few of our new friends and Helen worked her customary magic in the kitchen. Over our dining table the conversation turned to the crime wave that every newspaper occasionally reported. In fact, *The Daily Citizen* printed little else. Our guests liberally handed out the blame. It was the police – they were far too lazy. No, it was Pretoria, the punishments were far too lenient. No, it was the green-eyed monster. These useless kaffirs were too thick and clumsy to get a decent job and so they took what they wanted by force. Had we heard of car-jacking? If you stop at traffic lights in downtown Jo'burg some coon will open the car door, point a gun at your head, and the next thing you know you are looking for a taxi while the kaffir is driving off in your car.

There was a moment's silence. Then Mendes added, 'well, not in yours, obviously. Not even a coon will want to be seen in a *chevette.*'

'Aren't the Africans scared of the consequences?' asked Helen. A good question, I thought.

'They ought to be,' said Aneke, 'most of us have guns.'

'What, on you?'

Six handguns were suddenly on our dining table. Three of them butch and ugly, three rather daintier with enamelled handles.

South Africa still had surprises up its sleeve or in its handbag.

*

The Daily Citizen's editor was a gracious and amusing Afrikaner who would occasionally ornament our dining table in Rivonia. Though I was unpaid he covered my expenses and supplied us with tickets to many great events. Helen and I saw countless films at his suggestion while writing them up was never too onerous.

One day he suggested we go and see a stage play at the *Alhambra Theatre*.

'It's a new drama by Peter Schaffer. It's called *Amadeus*. It turns on Mozart's supposed rivalry with Salieri', he told us. I had never even heard of Salieri.

A small orchestra, crammed into the pit, played extracts from Mozart's sublime corpus, punctuating the arresting dialogue in a solemn or humorous way, as the script required. Between them the play and its concomitant stagecraft forged a masterpiece.

Since then I have seen the film and a London production with David Suchet, but the Jo'burg one remains the version I have most enjoyed.

*

When *The Daily Citizen* asked me to interview Arianna Stasinopoulos[232] I readily agreed. We had been pals at Cambridge, after all. She was in Johannesburg to promote her latest œuvre.

Back then, Arianna had been President of the Cambridge Union,[233] no less, and had subsequently enjoyed an over-publicised affair with Bernard Levin of *The Times*.

---

[232] After Cambridge, she settled in California and married, in 1986, the Republican politician Michael Huffington. They divorced in 1997. In the meantime Arianna Stasinopoulos Huffington had founded and established the influential on-line publisher, *The Huffington Post*.

[233] Its debating society.

I had already read her debut work, *The Female Woman*, which she had published in 1974. Her second was a very readable biography of Maria Callas. By the time I put it down I felt I knew Maria Callas better than Aristotle Onassis.

Now my editor had sent me her latest. It was a biography of Pablo Picasso. I put my back into it. It was no hardship. By around four in the morning I had read her great tome and, by the time I fell asleep, I realised how little I had known before. I had not even known Picasso's real name. His father was Don Jose Ruiz y Blasco. It was his mother whose name was Picasso.

Who would have guessed that he had begun to visit brothels, with his father, at the age of thirteen? That's where he first met the *Demoiselles d'Avignon*.[234]

He can only have been encouraged by what he saw as over the course of his long life he had two wives, six mistresses and hundreds of affairs. He also lost, to suicide no less, one wife, one mistress, one son and one grandson. I had also learned that Picasso, who in his stockings was five feet four inches tall, would not even talk to a female who was taller than him. A second marriage took place when he was 79 years old. What Oscar Wilde called a triumph of hope over experience?

*

When I met Arianna at the Carlton she appeared delighted. She indicated a seat beside her at a fragile table. An annoying pack of paparazzi immediately encircled us but none of their snapshots had me in the frame, I would relievedly discover. The last thing I

---

[234] *Les Demoiselles d'Avignon* (1907) was Picasso's first step towards Cubism. He would become the leader of Paris's avant-garde. In preparation for it, Picasso did hundreds of drawings and other preparatory studies, including the charcoal drawing *Nu aux bras levés* (1907), and *Head of a Sleeping Woman* (1907). It is also worth noting that it was painted at the end of his 'negro' period, when he was heavily influenced by primitive carvings, notably the African sculpture on show at the time at the Ethnographic Museum in Paris. As a result, his 'negro' paintings feature some disturbing anthropomorphic features and imagery.

needed was to have my ugly mug in *The Daily Citizen* and have Carlos say 'I told you so'.

'So you've moved out here?' said Arianna. 'I will say I would not have predicted it. And you've become a journalist? I thought you were some sort of financier?'

'I have something of a cub-reporter's role at *The Daily Citizen*, Arianna. It's my first job as a journalist. Having an interview with you will give my fledgling career a flying start.'

'OK, then shoot. Ask away.'

'Well, Miss Stasinopoulos, what sort of family do you come from?'

'Jeremy, you know all this already. All right, for the record, my father Konstantinos owns a newspaper and my mother, Elli, works for the Red Cross.'

'Where in Athens did you live?'

'A leafy suburb in northern Athens. Kifisia. My father built a house there in the sixties.'

'I believe the Stasinopoulos family is still an influential one in Greece?'

'My uncle Nikolaos is an energetic captain of industry, if few have heard of him. He's a very private man, but he's one of the handful of businessmen who developed the post-war industrial sector.'

'What is his company called?'

'There are dozens of them, I can never keep track. The one that matters is *Viohalko Holding*. Nikolaos is interested in metals. Greeks always have been. Bronze was invented in Greece. Helen was not a princess, she was a metaphor for a metallurgical process that hardened copper, itself discovered in Cyprus. Nor is Vergil's *Aeneid* a history, it is a tempered allegory, describing this military invention. It is a gripping story of industrial espionage. It is at the heart of the story of Troy and it was bronze rams in the bows of our triremes that sank those thousand ships. We learned how to extract gold dust from mountain streams by using oiled sheepskins to attract the flecks. Hence the 'golden fleece'. One of my uncle's companies, *ELVAL* builds aluminium stuff. *ETEM, Halkor, Sidenor* and *Fitco* involve themselves in copper, steel and plastic, and have essayed successfully into the international marketplace. In fact, six percent of Greece's total exports come from his string of companies.'[235]

'What do you put his vast reserve of energy down to?'

'I would say his principal characteristics are caution and discretion; he avoids every display of wealth and tries to keep out of the press.'

'Moving on, you came to school in England when you were quite young, I think?'

'I moved to England when I was sixteen, to a sweet little boarding school near Ascot. I went on to Cambridge where you and I met. I read economics while you, if I recall correctly, read history and philosophy?'

'I believe you were the first ever foreign-born student to serve as president of the debating society, the Cambridge Union?'

'That's what they tell me.'

'When last we met you were living in South Kensington. You left us for pastures new?'

'Just like you, it seems. I relocated to the USA last summer. I liked New York, but California, where I now live, has a closer climate to the perfect one we all carry with us from our childhoods.'

'But you are an author? A biographer?'

'Yes, and I love it. I love words, I love truth.'

'Your words are marvellous, *The Female Woman, Callas, Picasso,* all wonderful reads.'

'That's very kind.'

---

[235] According to Fortune Magazine, the Stasinopoulos fortune stands at around $1.2 billion, though its sheer number and diversity of interests makes it difficult to estimate with precision.

'I mean it. From tomorrow, droves of readers of *The Daily Citizen* will, I guarantee, luxuriate in them.'

'Thank you, Jeremy.'

*

The chance of a great adventure had arisen. An acquaintance had an aeroplane and every year he had to put in a number of hours to maintain his pilot's licence. He suggested that we might fly as his passengers to Botswana and have an adventure. I was up for it and so was Helen, despite her having some reservations about little aircraft.

I looked up Botswana. The Tswana tribe lives there. Its principal river, the Okavango, may be the only river in the world to flow away from the sea. Rising in Angola it is known by its Portuguese name Rio Cubango. To enter Botswana the river drops four metres in an almost unknown series of rapids known as the Popa Falls, visible only when the river is low. It goes on to flow into the desert[236] which absorbs it as blotting paper does ink.

Every animal or human that lives there, in that desert or delta, has evolved slightly differently to their cousins in the rest of the world. Botswana's giraffes, for example, have hooves like plates, the better to support them on the soggy sand. Crocodiles, dangerous everywhere, are especially alert (and dangerous) in the very shallow flood water. Leopards, Africa's deadliest fauna, lazily wait for their prey to pass beneath the branches of the trees they rest in. The native tribesmen and women are used to not having ready access to water for half the year. Over countless generations they have evolved protruding, water-bearing buttocks which store the precious liquid for days. It is the clue to their survival.

Botswana boasts every conceivable enticement to the tourist. We took off from Lanseria Aerodrome with

---

[236] Also known as the Moremi Game Reserve.

581

cameras, our wallets stuffed with *pula*, the Botswana currency. We had been advised to buy it in Jo'burg at an advantageous rate of exchange.

We squeezed on board the little plane. Including the pilot there were six of us. We buckled up. Helen was nervous; she had remembered she didn't much care for small planes.

Klaus, our pilot, tried to calm her by explaining that he had been trained for engine failure over the Indian Ocean under the watchful eye of a Natalian instructor. It can be catastrophic, he said lightly. We passengers sat back, resigned to our destiny.

Before long, we were in the air, heading due north. Klaus kept the plane low, at around a thousand feet, which may sound like a great height but, believe me, it's not. Nevertheless, thanks to the overhead wings, we had a terrific view of the unravelling countryside below. Klaus obligingly banked to the left or to the right to let me snap away at an unspoiled Africa below.

We landed at 'Crocodile Camp', a tourist enclave at Maun on the banks of the Thamalakane River. Klaus had booked us in for the night. It had a attractive supply of creature comforts. The camp had a couple of dozen individually decorated huts, a restaurant, a dining room, and the Croc Rock Bar - an elevated space on the banks of the river with a great view over the reptile-infested waters which, we were not very reassuringly informed, could and did flood from time to time.

No need to dip our toes, the bar would keep us busy until it handed us over to the dining room.

*

The next day we traipsed into Maun to admire its tidy rondavels. We all agreed that Botswanan ladies dressed very well. Their traditional costume was a complicated fusion of Western, Victorian and Tswana. Animal skins were in the mix. A century ago, apparently, the people wore clothes exclusively made from hides and furs but a hundred years of missionary admonishment had refined their pagan dress code. Now the women of Maun wore an apron in front, a *khiba*, a skirt beneath called a *mosese*, all surmounted with a *kaross*. Their costume once extremely modest, almost Puritan at least in town, now permitted jewellery - necklaces, bracelets, rings, earrings - and other things for which I will never know the name. The young mothers among them carried their babies on their backs in a baboose; a *thari*.

When we returned to the camp for our lunch – a barbecue beside the pool - Helen discovered an East African tiger snake in the hall. These little critters are extremely venomous, their bite invariably fatal. Mercifully, this one had already died. Maybe it had overdosed on its own poison? Wouldn't it be marvellous if political agitators could do the same?

*

Klaus wanted to show us the Okavango delta from the air on our way home and, once the last morsel of seared Red Lechwe was inside us, we were back in his plane's little cabin.

We flew over the weird Okavango Delta, spellbound, and saw where the great river seeps into the sand. Klaus kept his plane as low as he dared. Beneath us, the river was fading to an end in a million tributaries. In the shallows, pigmy elephants, huge reptiles, gazelles, kudus, hippos and porcupines debated supremacy with each other, while above us, eagles and carrion crows circled in their search for a feed a hundred feet below.

We were spellbound, at least for a while. A crack as loud as a gunshot shattered our reverie. A great chunk of the starboard wing was on its way to earth, along with the vulture that had collided with it. Klaus was a great pilot, but even he could not stop the plane from turning over. Our possessions tumbled around us like clothes in a washing machine.

I remember saying to Helen that she should take my camera. Of course, if we died the suggestion would have been both ludicrous and redundant. All I was thinking was that some sort of distraction was vital.

Klaus managed to level the plane - hard without the starboard aileron - and was saying 'mayday' repeatedly into a microphone I had not previously noticed. He also was struggling with the undercarriage. He needed to slow the plane as we descended. It was not possible to lower the wheels automatically as we were flying too fast. He had to resort to some sort of hand-pump and was working it for all it was worth.

God, perhaps, chose this moment to intervene. Ahead of us was a landing strip. We were flying at around 150 mph and the little plane was supposed to touch down under 90. Even so, Klaus clearly thought he might yet save our lives. Another problem, as if we needed one, was that the strip had not been cleared and was bestrewn with fallen branches and termite nests. Not that we had any choice. Klaus put us down at a speed that might easily have snapped off the wheels and forced the plane into a cartwheel, killing or maiming us all.

We all assumed a foetal position, curled up into the nearest we could manage to a ball, but we came through. We halted around six feet from a fallen tree as big as our aircraft. Clambering out of the damaged craft, Helen burst into tears. Were they tears of relief? We boys however were apparently unaffected. For a while, that is. We had a few beers in the hold. They had earned the right to work their magic.

Our only hope, here in the middle of nowhere, was to be rescued and there were two chances of that, one flat and the other slim.

Klaus had an idea.

'You will wait here, under the shade of the wing. I'll go and find help.'

'Yes? And where will you find it?'

'I'll find it.'

And off he went, on foot, straight into the crocodile-infested river. Soon he was in it up to his knees. On the far side he pushed his way through the reeds. Then he was out of sight.

We, on the other hand, had the beers and were still alive. We sat down, congratulating ourselves on not being a reptilian lunch. We thought ourselves the luckiest people on the planet and, in the circumstances, we probably were.

Some of us were happy to sit there patiently in the shade of the wing. Others wanted to explore the clearing. I wandered up to the river where a termite colony had built a nest fully ten feet tall, and climbed it. As I looked over a branch of the great Okavango, two oddly shaped pieces of mud slowly became the nostrils and then the entire head of a hippopotamus. As the creature hauled itself out of the delta, I saw it was the size of a small bus. One that was coming my way, and at 30 mph.

I had read that hippos are even more dangerous than leopards. They are deeply territorial and do not care for idiots who trespass onto their patch. This one had me in its sights.

'Jeremy, get back here, now!' I heard Helen shout.

I did not need further instructions. I leapt off my termite hill and ran for the plane. The hippo was satisfied. It turned around and sauntered back to its watery lair.

Suddenly we had a different sort of company. A tribe of river Bushmen was coming our way in Indian file. Mostly females carrying parcels and other baggage, they were being guided by four males, one in front, one behind walking backwards and one to either side.

585

These shy nomads were not as small as pure-blood Bushmen. Their complexions were duskier and their deeply wrinkled faces made them look vaguely oriental. Two of the Tswanas wore a loin-skin, a *tshega*, under a rug or blanket made out of animal skins, a *kaross*. They supplemented this outfit with leather caps and sandals. The one with a belt of tails was clearly their chief. The other two wore little save for a small flap of skin in front, copper wire necklaces, some strings of beads and armlets.

The girls, the youngest of whom were gracefully turning into women, wore a fringe of strings, nylon petticoats and an awesome amount of ornaments. The old ones, in their thirties perhaps, were dressed in *mosese* and *khiba*.

Flies festooned their bodies like festive ornaments. At least their smiles suggested they were pleased to see us. They sat down in the shade of the undamaged wing of our plane. Their speech was peppered with the clicking consonants of their diminutive Xhosa forebears.

Another hour passed. Klaus was back, hugely pleased with himself. He had found a place with a landing strip and a radio.

'A plane will come for us tomorrow. There is a landing strip nearby, Dinaka. Now we have to aim for a nearby camp; Khugana it's called. We'll be able to freshen up and sleep there. It's not far. Shouldn't be too expensive for just one night.'

Somehow he had communicated with the river Bushmen. Two of them looked after their females and he had bribed the other two males to carry our belongings. Not that we were in a position to argue. Even though it would soon to turn dark, within an few minutes we were on our way, fording the shallows of the Okavango river, brushing aside the bamboos fronds of the reeds that grew so prolifically in the swamp,

586

searching for *terra firma* while swatting away some very large insects that had more than a genealogist's interest in our blood.

We walked in a single column. While our guides surveyed the overhanging branches with their torches, they chose to ignore the sinister splashes as the great reptiles in the river studied the menu and paused to debate whom they should have as a first course. Out here, the true gourmets were the leopards, sleeping hungrily in the trees, hoping for a plate of rare human flesh to pass by below, rather like Japanese diners in a sushi bar.

The bearers, our luggage on their heads, were plainly scared. Not a good omen. Nevertheless, on we went. The swamp writhed with crocodiles, while the branches above our heads swayed as stealthy cats considered eviscerating us. Not that we had any choice.

Then we came upon a jetty, lit with fairy lights. There was a large rowing boat waiting for us, an oarsman at the ready to hand over the tiller. Once our cases were loaded on board, the river Bushmen could return in safety to their party.

Ten minutes later we were in Camp Khugana, alighting on a floodlit pier, where we were welcomed by a beautiful woman, wholly clad by Yves St Laurent, bidding us to come up a few more stairs.

'Welcome to my little hideaway,' she said. 'You are so very lucky. We do not open for business for another two weeks, so you will have the place to yourselves. Please, come on in and make yourselves at home.'

It did not take us long to realise that Khugana was no backpackers' retreat. At most a second. The baroness who owned the place had her staff ply us with champagne, which certainly made me feel better.

Helen's and my double tent had in its *en suite* bathroom a sample of every one of those priceless necessities that Dior, Chanel and the others have foisted on us all for so many years.

Glasses still in hand, Helen and I came back out of our new lodgings to admire the Okavango's natural phosphorescence. Helen had already experienced and recovered from the shock of our terrifying landing, and we men had thought, well, that's women for you. But now it was the boys' turn. Essentially, our collective knees gave way. If alcohol helped, chairs did more so.

Ursula, the baroness who owned the place, showed us into the dining room where her staff had soon prepared a sumptuous meal for us. Of course, we were too shocked and disorientated to have much of an appetite. The only one of us who did the table any justice was Helen, who was now on top of the situation.

'Come on, you chaps, eat up. This has been an adventure you will bore your children with and tomorrow we will all be back in Jo'burg, thanks to Klaus and Karen Blixen here.'[237] With that she necked the fabulous wine and poured herself a second glass.

*

I'm not sure if I slept that night, in that extraordinary location, designed to cater to those North and South Americans who were willing to spend a thousand dollars a shell to take a pot shot at an elephant.

Yet the next day, Klaus's conversations with the airport at Lanseria proved their weight in gold. A telephone call alerted us that rescue was at hand, at Dinaka's little landing strip, where we had escaped the unwelcome attentions of leeches and water snakes.

A hour later we were on our way home, through a severe windstorm, but what did we care? We were alive and had never before felt quite so pleased with the fact.

*

---

[237] Baroness Blixen was the Swedish author of, inter alia, *Babette's Feast* and *Out of Africa*.

Montserrat Caballé appeared on the front of every newspaper, the next day, except of course on my philistine *Daily Citizen*. She was coming to pay the Republic of South Africa a visit. The subequatorial whitemen of the African continent had decided, despite the international veto on supporting South Africa's apartheid, in any way, that a star as bright as her might loosen the first brick in the *cordon sanitaire* the rest of the world had built around the Boer republic.

She would be a guest of President Vervoerd himself.

Verdi's *La Forza del Destino*'s Leonora was a role she had already made famous at *La Scala* and at *Covent Garden*.[238]

---

[238] The Marquis of Calatrava bids his daughter, Leonora, the leading soprano, an affectionate goodnight, not knowing that she intends to elope with her lover Don Alvaro, a Peruvian of noble Inca stock. He opposes the union.

Meanwhile Curra, Leonora's confidential maid, readies her mistress for here elopement, while Alvaro climbs in through the window. Just as they are about to depart, her father enters and challenges Alvaro to a duel.

Alvaro throws down his weapon but it goes off. The marquis, mortally wounded, curses his daughter while her lover flees. Months later, at the inn at Hornachuelos, muleteers, mostly deserting soldiers with their women and other riff-raff are making merry. Supper announced, a 'student' (in reality Don Carlo di Vargas, Leonora's brother) says grace. Leonora and Alvaro both think the other dead but Carlo knows they are both alive and wants to restore his family's honour. Leonora enters, clad as a young man and immediately recognises her brother.

Preziosilla, the gypsy, tells their fortunes. Carlo, she says, will have 'a miserable future'. Leonora prays for divine mercy and the pilgrims depart. Carlo's fellow traveller is Pereda, helping to track down his sister and her lover. Leonora realises that Alvaro is still alive and feels abandoned. She seeks sanctuary (and atonement) in a monastery.

Melitone, a friar, answers the door. Leonora reveals her identity to his Superior. She rejects the veil but wants the life of a hermit. She is directed to a cave where food will be brought. She is allowed a bell but it's only to be used in great danger. The Superior tells his friars that no one must disturb the 'hermit' in the holy cave.

Don Alvaro, meanwhile, has enlisted in the Spanish army under the name of Captain Don Herreros. His enemy attacks and is defeated. Alvaro/Herreros is badly wounded but Carlo saves him and promises him the Order of Calatrava.

Alvaro, reacting to the name, gives his new friend a packet of letters. If Alvaro dies, the letters are to be burnt. Nevertheless, Carlo suspects him of being his sister's lover. His conscience prevents him from opening the letters with them is a locket containing a portrait of Leonora.

589

The editor asked me to take Helen and review the show. How could I resist? Not only does its music portend that of *The Godfather*, the opera tells a gripping story of monasteries, South America and war.

I had heard the Opera House in Pretoria wittily if unfairly described as South Africa's 'Gross National Product'. Nevertheless, we were disappointed to learn that La Caballé had cancelled at the last moment.

Mimi Coertse was famous in her own right and knew the part already. She was readily able to step into the diva's shoes. It was just that I had never heard of her. I was disappointed, of course but, as it turned out, we were sublimely lucky. Besides, we had free tickets and one should never say nay to a gift horse, especially one that can sing. In 1981, La Coertse was forty-nine years old. Her reputation had been earned in Vienna but, in 1973, on a whim and at the height of her international career, she had decided to return to what amounted to the cultural wilderness of the Republic of South Africa.

The surgeon pronounces that Alvaro will live. Carlo is overjoyed as he is now free to wreak vengeance. He addresses Alvaro by his true name and reveals his own identity, while Alvaro tries to persuade him that he is innocent of the marquis' death. Carlo challenges him, Alvaro refuses, but Carlo insists. The two fight but are separated by a passing patrol which drags Carlo away.

Alvaro resolves to spend his remaining days in the cloister.

The camp now refills with riff-raff. Preziosilla plies her trade as a fortune-teller, cheering the conscripts. When Melitone appears, Preziosilla chides them for their behaviour but they chase the friar away. Preziosilla sings of victory.

Five years later we return to the monastery to discover Melitone spooning soup to the needy. Alvaro has become a monk and has taken the name of Father Raffaele. Carlo still wants a duel but Alvaro offers peace. An angry Carlo calls him a half-breed, so an affronted Alvaro accepts the challenge and the two rush off-stage.

Leonora declares her love for Alvaro. She begs God for the solace of death. The two men duel on the crags near Leonora's cave. Alvaro wounds Carlos and invades the hermit's sanctuary, asking for the last rites for the dying man.

That's when Leonora and Alvaro recognise each other. Alvaro tells her what has happened. She embraces her dying brother but, as he expires, Carlo stabs her.

The Superior, who has come in answer to Leonora's alarm bell, orders Alvaro to stop cursing fate and to humble himself before God. Leonora, dying, joins him in this plea, and Alvaro proclaims that he is now redeemed.

All very Italian.

She made her decision irreversible by marrying and setting up home in Pretoria, close to the opera house. Her husband affectionately gave her two children, Mia and Werner.

Hers was a fairy tale come true. She had arrived in Vienna in 1954 as a humble Afrikaans, a naive *boeremeisie*, armed with nothing but a beautiful voice. She stunned the Viennese public at the *staatsoper* as Mozart's *Queen of the Night*, one of the most testing roles in grand opera. Not yet steeped in our European ways, she was to admit she knew little or nothing about the legacy of the late classicists or the early romantics. Nevertheless, she was about to become one of the greatest exponents of their music.

She was the youngest singer in history to join the permanent ensemble. Nor did it take the Austrian Government long to recognise her with the title *Kammersangerin*, their equivalent of our 'dame'. She is still remembered in Vienna as a Mozartian.

In South Africa, her climb was both gradual and painful. Reprising the roles that had brought her fame and fortune in Europe, she was on the way to becoming South Africa's first primadonna.

Nor was it only her own career that did well. She would open the door for many other South Africans. The ground they stepped onto was fertile. Cecilia Wessels followed in her tracks. She would sing in many concerts and operas in England. Emma Renzi, Joyce Barker, Wendy Fine, Marita Napier and Elizabeth Connell - who all followed her lead with fine careers. Some would even achieve the 'grand slam' the *Staatsoper* in Vienna, *La Scala* in Milan, *Covent Garden* in London and the *Metropolitan* in New York, but none would do what Mimi Coertse had done in her seventeen glorious years in Vienna, under the baton of Herbert von Karajan, Karl Böhm, Lorin Maazel and Dmitri Mitropoulos.

Helen and I thought the opera a terrific success. From its wistful overture, through an act with an astonishing caravanserai on a revolving stage, Helen and I were ravished. I lavished praise in my copy that night for all those opera lovers that read *The Daily Citizen*. Both of them. Helen and me.

*

I still enjoyed an occasional game of Bridge. Lenz Keel, the regional CEO of the Swiss Re and the son–in–law of the local chairman was an *aficionado*. The Swiss Re's engineering underwriter, Lawrence Lee, was also keen. He brought his wife Nicky along to keep Helen company. If playing for modest stakes, let that not deceive you. Our game was about winning. South Africans are not greedy, but neither are they Olympians.

My boss had made sure I would enjoy a glass or two as I played and, as I sat at their card table, a huge tumbler of very fine scotch was poured for me.

I was a good bridge player, though I say so myself, but as the evening wore on, for some reason, my standard began to slip. Every time my glass was refilled, whatever skill I might have had, slipped another notch.

Inevitably, when we left to go home, I paid my dues to a very happy boss and a weary girlfriend.

Since those days, in truth, I rarely play. I find it easier to resist the sepulchral atmosphere that true dedicatees want to accompany their game.

*

In downtown Jo'burg, the Main Street Hotel dated from the city's gold rush days. It had a ballroom, long disused but peopled with the ghosts of white-tied or gowned dancers. The elegant chamber was filled with stacks of spindly gilded chairs, a pretty if plangent reminder of grander days. Many South African journalists liked to gather there at its bar to swap stories, rumours and small talk well after their papers had gone to press.

After a drink or two had loosened their tongues they were garrulous and humorous, crude and rude. The whole thing was brilliant. It was how I imagined the ideal cocktail party, minus the starlets.

In this company there was no subject off limits, BoSS[239] and apartheid could be slandered or impugned with fearless abandon. For me, the time I spent there was like the best sort of tutorial.

*

Helen had decided we should enter a dance contest. I asked her to explain what might be involved.

'We are going,' she stated baldly.

This was clearly not a matter for debate.

'We'll dance rock-'n-roll. If we're good enough, we will win.'

'Well, I'm not sure…'

'Come on. It'll be a laugh.'

Of course, I gave way.

*

There was a bar in Commissioner Street, one which I confess to frequently frequenting. I met there a proud old Jewish tailor who had once won a coveted gold medal, the one that Savile Row tailors award one another.

I needed a dinner jacket and this great fellow agreed to build me one. Around a month later I put in for my final fitting. I saw a character in his cheval glass.

It was that same fellow who normally stood so lopsidedly, suddenly looked like James Bond. It was me! He charged me less than 10% of what Savile Row would have charged. Even more interesting, over another beer, he told me of how his old firm, *Huntsman,* had built a

---

[239] The Bureau of State Security was a greatly feared institution.

593

suit for a pilot in 1944, as a reward for saving the life of an airman whose plane had ditched into the channel.

I had heard a version of the same story from my father, only a few months before. His plane had been shot down just off the Sussex coast. He had managed to climb out of the cockpit and was swimming as fast as he could towards a British MTB when he remembered his navigator. Looking back he saw that he was not being followed. No choice but to turn around and swam back. His navigator had been trapped by his harness. He was struggling to extricate himself before the crate sank and he drowned. My father helped him free himself and the two of them could now be lifted from the water to safety. He would earn the DFC for this act of selfless heroism.

The navigator was a young Jewish fellow who, before the war, had worked as a cutter for his father, one of *Huntsman's* top tailors. In 1945, when returning servicemen were donning their demob suits, my father was trying on the suit that a grateful Savile Row tailor had built for him. It might even be that my dinner jacket and my father's pinstripe were cut by the same man.

*

My company had made sure that Helen and I were included in a grand event in one of Johannesburg's grander hotels, the Carlton, a dinner-dance.

There would be a charity auction and a speech from a guest of honour, a Rhodesian general who had commanded the Selous Scouts, a commando unit that at the time I had never even heard of. Wearing my new dinner jacket for the first time I was proud of Helen, amazing in her fabulous formal frock. We made a great couple.

The general began his speech with a smile and the words, 'we are not the Grenadier Guards. I'm afraid that ancient regiment has sacrificed its brains by over-enthusiastically stomping its Prussian heels at Aldershot'.

He earned a round of applause and some laughter but he and I were no longer destined to become the best of mates.

'You already know us as the most feared counter-insurgency force on the African continent. I am particularly proud of our record. During the Chimurenga War that began in 1966 and only ended last March - when to their shame we were disbanded by Verwoerd and his commie friends - we can claim responsibility or credit for the death of two thirds of all the terrorists in Rhodesia, losing only forty scouts in the process.

'Those of us who fight insurgents need to be very special. Not only do we have to hunt or stalk an elusive enemy in forbidding terrains that few of you will ever experience, we have to be self-reliant. That means very little solids, a small amount of water, and big hairy balls. Excuse my soldierly brashness, madam. I'll put it another way. We must be fit, resourceful and capable of working under conditions that push us to the limits of human endurance.

'It is not our practise to drink champagne by candlelight in the luxurious officers' mess of the Wellington Barracks. We are soldiers, hardened by hostile harshness. Our successes reflect the quality and quantity of our strenuous training.

'The British Grenadiers are unfamiliar with the terrain in which we have been raised. They like to avoid what they call 'theatrical trials of strength and stomach'. Well, my Grenadier friends, our training has paid dividends in the field. You have no need to whinge about our 'special' treatment and casual dress. If we are alive, our enemies are not. We may eat and drink tonight in a grand hotel that white men like us have built. And some of you want to accuse us of gun-running and poaching? Grow up is my answer.

'On one occasion, my men and I surprised a campful of terrorists, twenty of us, two hundred of them. I remember it as if it was yesterday. We had infiltrated - completely unseen - an enemy camp. As we opened fire I remember seeing their black arses diving over their clay walls while my scouts gave them an extra arsehole.

'We neither invite nor desire your approbation. We are merely the muscular means by which our politicians realise your dreams. Every one of you, in this great room, owes us the privileged way of life that we in this great country all enjoy tonight.'

I recall concluding, through the tumultuous applause, that South Africa was truly a strange place.

*

It was at last the day of the Rock-'n-Roll Championship. Helen wore a delightful dress – very fifties, very appropriate – while I was again able to show off my amazing dinner jacket.

That, however, was my only talent. For her part, Helen as a schoolgirl had danced at the Royal Ballet's school in Covent Garden.

I was reasonably confident. In the days leading up to the contest she had led, and I had followed, as she turned me around our floor at home. At last I had vaguely got the hang of it. Helen is a great dancer, a great teacher, and we won first prize.

*

My life as a bachelor was almost over. I felt it instinctively, while Helen suggested that I should feel it practically and decisively.

Her wish, from that time forward, has been my command. Fr Kelly married us at St Mary's Rosebank, and Marjorie Hughes was Helen's maid of honour. Laurence Lee was my best man, while Robbie Hinds, Helen's boss, gave the bride away. Ten of us celebrated the wedding breakfast at *The Brazen Head* in Sandton, while the reception was at Robbie's lovely house in Sunninghill and Helen was as pretty as a picture in her strapless cream silk gown.

Photographs of our wedding, today on every surface of our house in Suffolk, continue to remind us both of a great start to the Next Phase of Our Lives, one in which we would raise our children, if we were fortunate enough to have any, to benefit from all we had seen and done; one in which our careers would liberate us from drudgery and banality, and one where our affectionate natures would reward us with a steadfast circle of friends.

FINIS

Ingram Content Group UK Ltd.
Milton Keynes UK
UKHW010800270323
419227UK00001B/2